Hyperinflation

Since 1970s when the world was experiencing an "age of inflation," a great volume of academic research about hyperinflation has been conducted. However, it is also true that parrot-like superficial talks abound, without questioning the economic, political and social foundations existing underneath the economic phenomenon.

Based on research results of contemporary economists, media reports and historical works, this book will be the most comprehensive narrative of all major events of hyperinflation worldwide from the turn of the first millennium to the mid-2010s. Firstly, it gives a brief illustration of the basic concepts of hyperinflation, starting with the definitions and price measurement. Then it traces and analyzes all major episodes of hyperinflation that occurred over the past two thousand years or so, from the earliest incidence to the four tidal waves in the twentieth century, and to the three latest episodes in the twenty-first century. Using basic concepts in modern finance such as indexation and dollarization, this book explains why hyperinflation in some countries could explode into astronomical levels, while rhythms of hyperinflation in the twentieth century world are in resonance of megatrends in world economy and politics. Finally, this book underscores the importance of policy making, institutional building and international relations in the process of hyperinflation and stabilization.

Scholars and students studying money and finance, economic history, international finance and economics will be attracted by this book.

Liping He is Professor at the School of Business and Economics, Beijing Normal University. His research interests include international finance and economics.

China Perspectives

The *China Perspectives* series focuses on translating and publishing works by leading Chinese scholars, writing about both global topics and China-related themes. It covers Humanities and Social Sciences, Education, Media and Psychology, as well as many interdisciplinary themes.

This is the first time any of these books have been published in English for international readers. The series aims to put forward a Chinese perspective, give insights into cutting-edge academic thinking in China, and inspire researchers globally.

For more information, please visit www.routledge.com/series/CPH

Existing titles in economics:

Internet Finance in China
Introduction and Practical Approaches
Ping Xie, Chuanwei Zou, Haier Liu

Regulating China's Shadow Banks
Qingmin Yan, Jianhua Li

Internationalization of the RMB
Establishment and Development of RMB Offshore Markets
International Monetary Institute of the RUC

The Road Leading to the Market
Weiying Zhang

Peer-to-Peer Lending with Chinese Characteristics
Development, Regulation and Outlook
P2P Research Group Shanghai Finance Institute

Forthcoming titles in economics:

Tax Reform and Policy in China
Gao Peiyong

China Economic Transition Research
Zhao Renwei

Hyperinflation
A World History

Liping He

Routledge
Taylor & Francis Group

LONDON AND NEW YORK

First published 2018
by Routledge

2 Park Square, Milton Park, Abingdon, Oxfordshire OX14 4RN
52 Vanderbilt Avenue, New York, NY 10017

Routledge is an imprint of the Taylor & Francis Group, an informa business

First issued in paperback 2020

British Library Cataloguing-in-Publication Data
A catalogue record for this book is available from the British Library

Library of Congress Cataloging-in-Publication Data
Names: He, Liping, 1958– author.
Title: Hyperinflation : a world history / Liping He.
Description: Abingdon, Oxon ; New York, NY : Routledge, 2018. | Series:
    China perspectives | Includes bibliographical references and index.
Identifiers: LCCN 2017029011 | ISBN 9781138560086 (hardcover) |
    ISBN 9780203712061 (ebook)
Subjects: LCSH: Inflation (Finance)—History.
Classification: LCC HG229 .H42 2018 | DDC 332.4/109—dc23
LC record available at https://lccn.loc.gov/2017029011

ISBN: 978-1-138-56008-6 (hbk)
ISBN: 978-0-367-52920-8 (pbk)

Typeset in Times New Roman
by Apex CoVantage, LLC

To

Ziyu

who has been studying the world

in China, Britain, Spain, and America

Contents

List of figures	xi
List of tables	xiii
Foreword by Prof. Dr. Steve H. Hanke	xiv
Preface	xvi
Acknowledgements	xx

1 Introduction: basic concepts of hyperinflation 1

What is hyperinflation? 1
   Three quantitative criteria of hyperinflation 1
   Measurement of inflation and hyperinflation 2
   A qualitative definition of hyperinflation 4
What causes hyperinflation? 5
What are the impacts of hyperinflation? 8
   Gresham's Law vs. Thiers' Law 9
   The Olivera–Tanzi effect and Laffer curve of seigniorage 10
How to end hyperinflation? 10

2 Monetary adventures before the twentieth century 13

Money and inflation in the ancient world 13
Wang Mang: a most bizarre adventure in coinage 16
The Roman Empire: unstoppable debasement 19
Sung, Jurchen, and Mongol rule: the world's first paper
   currency hyperinflation 22
   Hui-zi and hyperinflation in the Southern Sung 23
   Hyperinflation in the Jurchen 24
   Paper currency under Mongol rule 25
   Ch'ao in Persia 26
King Henry VIII: great debasement in Renaissance England 27
The Ming and Ching: aborted paper currencies amidst
   the menace of hyperinflation 30
   Emperor Hsien-feng's monetary adventure 31

Paper currency and the American Revolution 33
Assignats *and hyperinflation during the French Revolution 36*
  John Law and his paper currency experiment in France 37
  The French Revolution and assignats 38
  *A footnote: French and British experiences in financing the
    Napoleonic wars 40*
Contrary experiences of inflation during America's Civil War 42
  The Southern extreme of inflation 45

**3   The first wave of hyperinflation in the twentieth century:
      Germany, Russia, and CEE countries in the 1920s   51**

Five basic facts of hyperinflation during the 1920s 53
  Fact I: real money balance was declining 53
  Fact II: deposits tended to shrink in the money supply 55
  *Fact III: exchange rates depreciated faster than domestic
    prices rose 56*
  Fact IV: real interest rates became negative 57
  Fact V: real wages tended to fall 59
The gold standard and the rise of the banking industry 60
Alarm bells for hyperinflation: Lenin vs. *Keynes 63*
The Treaty of Versailles, reparations, and Germany's reaction 67
  *The first period: from the Treaty of Versailles to the
    London Schedule, 1920–May 1921 68*
  The second period: May 1921–January 1923 69
  The third period: 1923 70
  Currency reform: October 1923 72
Soviet Russia: hyperinflation under "New Economic Policy" 72
*The political economy of hyperinflation: Austria, Hungary,
  and Poland 78*
  Austria: devaluation preceded inflation 78
  Hungary: inflation-led devaluation 81
  Poland: inflation and devaluation in parallel 83
  *Czechoslovakia: a silver lining to the cloud of hyperinflation
    during the 1920s 85*
The League of Nations: an emerging role of multilateralism 86
Hyperinflation and the rise of the Nazi Regime 89

**4   The Second World War and the upsurge of hyperinflation
      in the 1940s   96**

Greece: wars and long stabilization 97
Italy: rising inflation in the last stage of the war 102
Hungary: the world record hyperinflation 107

Japan: surge in inflation after the war 113
The Philippines and South Korea: hyperinflations before
*   and after 117*
Germany: bitter escape from hyperinflation 119
*   Appendix note on Austria: earlier currency reform and*
*   higher inflation 124*

5   War finance and its aftermath: China in the 1940s   129

War finance and high inflation in the first half of the 1940s 129
*   China split into multiple currency areas 129*
*   Deficit financing by low-yield bonds 133*
*   Rising inflation and declining seigniorage 136*
*   Ineffective price controls 140*
Internal war and hyperinflation waves during the late 1940s 142
*   Temporary cooling-down 143*
*   Battles to contain inflation, 1946–47 146*
*   Weird banking industry and its role in hyperinflation 149*
*   1948: Gold yuan program and hyperinflation 152*
*   Economic and political impacts of hyperinflation, 1946–49 155*
Ending hyperinflation in China mainland and Taiwan 157
*   Ending hyperinflation in China mainland 157*
*   Ending hyperinflation in Taiwan 160*
Appendix note: Friedman's view on FDR, silver, and China 162

6   Hyperinflation in an "age of inflation"   167

The collapse of the Bretton-Woods System and the advent of an
*   "age of inflation" 168*
Bolivia: the first peacetime hyperinflation in the world 171
Brazil and Argentina: hyperinflation in parallel 174
Israel and Turkey: contrasting experiences of high inflation 182
Chile, Nicaragua, and Peru: hyperinflation in unsettled
*   societies 186*
*   Chile in 1973: hyperinflation in a coup 186*
*   Nicaragua in the late 1980s: hyperinflation with a falling*
*   administration 187*
*   Peru at the turn of the 1990s: hyperinflation in an uneasy*
*   society 188*
Zaïre (Congo) and Angola: hyperinflations in failing states 189
*   Zaïre (Congo) in the 1990s: hyperinflations amidst power*
*   struggle 190*
*   Angola in the 1990s: hyperinflations in civil wars after the end*
*   of the Cold War 191*

7   A wave of hyperinflation in transition economies   196

Repressed inflation in planned economies 197
Hyperinflations in Russia and other USSR successor states 200
  Eruption of inflation in the Baltic States 200
  Russia's economic woes and a surge of hyperinflation 203
  The dismantling of the ruble zone: a currency war in a
    currency zone? 205
  Stabilization and reform: divergent routes and results 208
  "Better a hundred friends than a hundred rubles":
    some long-standing effects 211
Twice the hyperinflation in Yugoslavia 213
  Hyperinflation in the socialist Federal Republic
    of Yugoslavia 213
  Much higher hyperinflation in the Federal Republic
    of Yugoslavia 214
Inflation and hyperinflation in Eastern European countries 218
Fighting high inflations: China and Vietnam in East Asia 223

8   World trend outliers: Zimbabwe and Venezuela in the
     twenty-first century   231

The world trend: a "Great Moderation" in the twenty-first
    century 231
Zimbabwe: a hyperinflation that ends its own currency 233
  Events leading to hyperinflation 234
  Hyperinflation and the end of a national currency 236
  De jure dollarization and its impacts 238
Venezuela: heading to hyperinflation and crisis 240
North Korea: "Unrepressed" hyperinflation in a Hermit Kingdom 244
Appendix note: did China help? 248

9   Conclusion   253

"How high can hyperinflation be?" 255
"How long can hyperinflation last?" 256
"How disastrous can hyperinflation become?" 256

References   258
Index   273

Figures

3.1 Monthly price movements in Austria, Germany, Hungary, Poland, and Russia, 1918–25 53

3.2 Real money balance, Germany, Austria, and Hungary, January 1921–December 1923 54

3.3 Deposits as a proportion of money supply, Germany, Austria, and Hungary, January 1921–December 1923 55

3.4 Domestic inflation relative to exchange rate change in Germany, Austria, Hungary, and Poland, January 1921–December 1923 56

3.5 Reichsbank discount rate, daily money rate, and "forward" inflation rate, January 1920–December 1921 58

3.6 Money wages, cost of living, and real wages in Frankfurt and surrounding districts, January 1920–June 1923 59

3.7 Monthly changes in wholesale prices and exchange rate (marks per U.S. dollar), percentage, Germany, February 1920–July 1923 68

3.8 Monthly rises in general prices, percentage, Russia, 1921–23 74

3.9 Monthly changes in retail prices and exchange rate (Austrian crowns per U.S. dollar on the New York market), percentage, Austria, February 1921–December 1922 80

3.10 Monthly changes in retail prices and exchange rate (Hungarian *krones* per U.S. dollar on the New York market), percentage, Hungary, August 1920–March 1924 82

3.11 Monthly changes in wholesale prices and exchange rate (Polish marka per U.S. dollar), percentage, Poland, February 1921–April 1924 84

4.1 Monthly changes in drachma price of gold sovereign and real money balance, percentage, Greece, January 1941–June 1946 98

4.2 Real wage indexes, percentage, Greece, 1940–January 1946 100

4.3 Annual changes in wholesale and consumer prices, percentage, Greece, 1947–61 101

4.4 Annual changes in consumer and wholesale prices, percentage, Italy, 1939–48 104

4.5 Indexes of wholesale prices, money stock, and real money balance, log scale, Italy, 1939–44 105

4.6   Cost of living index and exchange rate of the pengő with
      the U.S. dollar, log scale, Hungary, August 1938 and
      April 1945–July 1946   108
4.7   Government fiscal and debt positions in constant prices, millions
      of pengő, Hungary, July 1945–July 1946   112
4.8   Annual changes in retail and wholesale prices, percentage,
      Japan, 1939–50   113
4.9   Indexes of retail prices, money stock, and real money balance,
      log scale, Japan, 1939–47   115
4.10 Cash as a percentage of narrow money stock and quasi-money
      as a percentage of broad money stock, Japan, 1939–47   115
4.11 Annual changes in WPI and CPI, percentage, log scale,
      South Korea, 1944–54   119
5.1   Fiscal deficit and domestic borrowing, Nationalist China, 1937–45   135
5.2   Annual increases in currency issues and wholesale price index,
      percentage, Nationalist China, 1938–45   137
5.3   Fiscal expenditures, nominal and in 1939 prices, C$ million,
      log scale, Nationalist China, 1939–45   139
5.4   Annual growth in money supply and bank deposits as a
      percentage of money supply, Nationalist China, 1937–45   139
5.5   Monthly changes in wholesale prices, percentage, log scale,
      for all of China and Shanghai, February 1946–April 1949   146
5.6   Growth in money stock and real money balance, China, 1945–48   151
6.1   CPI and official and black-market exchange rates of peso/dollar,
      log scale, Bolivia, selected months in 1981–85   172
6.2   CPI inflation rate, percentage, log scale, Brazil and Argentina,
      1970–97   176
6.3   CPI inflation rate, percentage, Israel and Turkey, 1970–2007   182
6.4   Index of CPI, 1980 = 1, log scale, Israel and Turkey, 1980–2007   183
6.5   CPI inflation rate, percentage, log scale, Chile, Nicaragua, and
      Peru, 1970–2000   187
6.6   CPI inflation rate, percentage, log scale, Zaïre (Congo) and
      Angola, 1970–2000   190
7.1   CPI inflation in Poland, Bulgaria, Romania and Albania,
      percentage, 1980–99   219
7.2   CPI inflation in China, Vietnam, and Mongolia, percentage,
      1980–99   224
8.1   Monthly and annual inflation, percentage, log scale, Zimbabwe,
      March 2007–mid-November 2008   236
8.2   Change in annual average CPI in Venezuela and Latin America
      and the Caribbean countries, percentage, 1980–2016   240
8.3   Weekly or bi-weekly exchange rates and rice prices in Pyongyang
      markets, new won, North Korea, August 2009–December 2015   247

Tables

3.1 Hyperinflations in Germany, Russia, and CEE countries during
the 1920s   52
3.2 Consumer price index in four belligerent countries, 1913–18   63
5.1 Currency regimes and levels of inflation in "Greater China,"
1941–45   131
7.1 CPI inflation in Russia and other USSR successor republics   201
7.2 Annual CPI inflation in the Baltic Three and the rest of
the USSR successor republics, percentage, 1989–93   202
7.3 Timeline of introduction of new currency in USSR successor
republics   206
7.4 CPI inflation in former Yugoslav states since 1991   215

Foreword

Professor Liping He has produced a most comprehensive and useful scholarly treatment of world hyperinflation. This is a welcomed addition to the literature. Indeed, *Hyperinflation: A World History* is destined to become a standard reference on the topic.

My basis for this judgement rests on my own experience in grappling with the literature and data on hyperinflation. The Hanke-Krus *World Hyperinflation Table* first appeared in the authoritative *The Routledge Handbook of Major Events in Economic History* (2013). What was the genesis of the Hanke-Krus *World Hyperinflation Table*?

In 2010, I was invited to write the survey article on hyperinflation for *The Routledge Handbook of Major Events in Economic History*. I accepted the invitation, thinking it would require routine work on my part and that I could complete the task in short order. I had already surveyed the literature on hyperinflation and accurately estimated the inflation rates in several countries. These included two relatively recent, dramatic hyperinflations – Yugoslavia (1994) and Zimbabwe (2008). In addition, I had designed and implemented currency reforms that had stopped hyperinflations, notably Bulgaria's in 1997.

While reflecting on the hyperinflation literature, I was struck by its lack of uniformity and clarity. The literature was widely scattered in time and space; it had been written by many different researchers, and those researchers had used diverse methods to estimate and analyze the inflation episodes studied.

So, I concluded that the best way to "clean up" the subject of hyperinflation was to create a "World Hyperinflation Table." In my mind, this table would include all of the world's hyperinflations. The data would be presented in a uniform and clear manner, so that all hyperinflations could be compared. But, what criteria would be used for an episode of inflation to qualify as a hyperinflation? I specified the following three criteria:

1   Following Phillip Cagan's classic article on hyperinflation, the economics profession adopted the following criterion: to qualify as a hyperinflation, the inflation rate had to be at least 50 percent per month. I adopted this convention.
2   In addition, I specified that the 50 percent rate had to persist for at least 30 consecutive days.

3   Lastly, I concluded that the inflation episode had to be fully documented and that inflation estimates had to be replicable.

It turned out that the third criterion was the most difficult one. Fortunately, my chief research assistant at the time, Nicholas Krus, was capable of, and interested in, taking on this research task. Krus and I spent the better part of two years constructing what has come to be known as the Hanke-Krus *World Hyperinflation Table*. We documented and recalculated the inflation rates for all alleged hyperinflations in history. The project required the gathering of primary data for each potential case of hyperinflation. This proved to be very difficult and time consuming. For example, primary data for the French hyperinflation of 1795 to 1796 – the first verified hyperinflation – had to be obtained and analyzed. But, that was not the most difficult set of data to obtain. That "prize" was awarded to the Republika Srpska, which experienced a hyperinflation in the 1992–1994 period. Fortunately, I was able to use my extensive contacts in the former Yugoslavia to eventually obtain high-quality inflation data.

After a long and onerous research effort, the Hanke-Krus *World Hyperinflation Table* was published. It is contained in "World Hyperinflations," a chapter in *The Routledge Handbook of Major Economic Events in History* (2013), which I co-authored with Nicholas Krus.

I recount these reflections because I thought there would not be too much to say about hyperinflation after the publication of the Hanke-Krus *World Hyperinflation Table*. However, Prof. Liping He has proven me wrong.

Dr. Steve H. Hanke
The Johns Hopkins University
Baltimore, Maryland
August 2017

Preface

This book came about as a result of my teaching a course, *International Finance and China*, at the Beijing Normal University. The course is part of the curriculum of the University's World Economy and China Program for international students, which was instituted in 2011. Each year since then, a dozen or so senior undergraduates and junior postgraduates from all over the world – Africa, Asia (ex China), Australasia, Europe, North America, and South America – who are students of the broad discipline of economics have enrolled in the course. Somewhat to my surprise, they have all shown keen interest in the subject of hyperinflation, choosing to study it over many other areas that I believe are equally stimulating.

The intensive interaction that I have had with these students has left an enduring impression on me; namely, there is a significant gap in the general knowledge of even the brightest students on the subject. Since the 1970s – an era in which the world was experiencing an "age of inflation" – a great volume of academic research about money, finance, and inflation, including high inflation and hyperinflation, has been produced and published by scholars from many different countries. This literature has been written from both an historical/realistic vantage and also from various theoretical perspectives. The field has apparently become one in which even a great deal more intellectual input would result in only a small amount of new insight, if any. Scholarly consensus has been widely established at this point with regard to questions about (for example) the causes and effects of inflation and hyperinflation, conditions required for a successful macroeconomic stabilization program after an incidence of hyperinflation, and so on.

However, it is also true that parrot-like superficial talks on inflation or hyperinflation continue to abound, inside and outside the classroom. Various causes are lifted as being to blame for the incidence (or the imaginary incidence) of hyperinflation, including a paper currency system, an expansionary monetary policy, or a government budget deficit. Such opinions are often espoused without much questioning of the economic, political, and social foundations existing underneath the economic phenomenon. Time and again, the causes and effects of inflation and hyperinflation have been oversimplified to the point that they do not capture the real-world circumstances that framed the economic situation in question. If monetary policy alone were the main reason for hyperinflation, why did this extreme economic condition keep coming back in certain Latin American countries during the 1980s and early 1990s, when central banks in those countries already employed many professionals and experts? If government budget deficits alone were the cause instead, then again, how could a country fall into hyperinflation when its budget deficit was as low as 3 or 4 percent of GDP (for example, Argentina in the early 1990s)? Answering these questions clearly requires a robust understanding of the complexity of the appropriate real-time application of theoretical concepts.

Incorrect perceptions or misinterpretations about hyperinflation have circulated in part because many of those who are interested in this topic do not have access to advanced academic research results. However, the more significant reason for the prevalence of misconceptions about hyperinflation is that it is often very easy to lose track of the links between theoretical thinking and the object of its reflection when contemplating a real issue, which affected real people in extreme ways, such as hyperinflation.

Building a theoretical framework with all its beauty of logical consistency, and looking unflinchingly at the details of a hard-biting reality, are two important ways to study anything in the world. Yet, as cited by a well-known economic historian, "It is a close matter whether it is worse to be lost in the woods (without a theory) than in one's theory, pursuing its internal consistence to the point where contact with reality is lost."[1]

To avoid losing contact with reality or clutching at the apparent links between theory and reality, we must bring our concepts and hypotheses down to the ground and into the actual history of the world. To use a metaphor, the world of money and finance from past to present is the forest, and episodes of hyperinflation are some of the "tallest trees" in that forest. To properly understand the economic concepts behind an event as unusual and devastating as hyperinflation, we must see both forest and trees.

The mid-2010s seems a perfect time to study hyperinflation, as we are now able to see the rise and fall of hyperinflation in the world in a full cycle lasting about a century. Wars and revolutions are factors that people once believed to be the most important causes of hyperinflation. No one who lived in the first half of the twentieth century would have doubted this view. Yet, in the later decades of the century in particular, when war and revolution "fell out of fashion" as it were, hyperinflation continued to erupt in many countries. "Only when the tide goes out do you discover who's been swimming naked." These somewhat saucy words of wisdom that have been attributed to Warren Buffett, an American investment guru, may shed light on the study of hyperinflation from a world historical perspective.

This book begins with a short introductory chapter on the basic concepts of hyperinflation, which may be found in any intermediate textbook of macroeconomics. With no exception, hyperinflation has happened only in certain monetary and/or financial systems, no matter where or when in the world it occurred. Chapter 1 illustrates all the factors that have been identified as causes of hyperinflation and discusses the economic conditions in which hyperinflation most severely affects the economy and finances of a country in a given period. All the important elements of a stabilization program are highlighted, which are often combined in various ways to form the recipes of measures nations adopt to end hyperinflation, with greater or lesser degrees of success.

Chapter 2 traces all major episodes of high inflation or hyperinflation that occurred in the world before the twentieth century, starting with Wang Mang's monetary adventure at the dawn of the first millennium and ending with the contrasting experiences of inflation in the North and the South during America's Civil War in the 1860s. Modern hyperinflation has ancient precursors, precisely because rulers in the past, just as those in the present, were able to take advantage of benefits made possible by the course of monetary evolution. When such benefits were abused, disasters generally followed, which has been the pattern from the earliest times up to the twentieth century.

Chapter 3 sets the first modern wave of hyperinflation, which occurred in the twentieth century, into a broad historical and intellectual background; it examines Germany and Soviet Russia, with special reference to factors related to international relations and ideology. The large scale of the incidence of hyperinflation in the early 1920s in Central and Eastern Europe clearly demonstrates how global political and economic systems had been shifting and struggling to navigate the heyday of capitalism and industrialization. The Treaty of Versailles and its resultant League of Nations were symbols of both progress and frustration during the period between the two World Wars. Their principles and actions had huge impacts on both the occurrence and the cessation of hyperinflation at the time.

Chapter 4 looks at individual episodes of hyperinflation or high inflation that occurred in different locations in Europe and Asia at different stages of World War II. Unlike those affected by the first wave of hyperinflation, the countries hit by hyperinflation during the WWII era had little commonality in terms of their economic and political systems, except perhaps that some had a paper currency regime. The effects of war, the weakened function of the governments, and in some cases, the emerging role played by the perhaps initially somewhat inexperienced Americans, who were on the way to lead the postwar world reconstruction, are shown to be starkly apparent in many of the episodes discussed. In a seeming "political vacuum," the world record of hyperinflation was created in Hungary in 1946, as the laws of economics inexorably unfolded.

China in the 1940s is singled out as the object of Chapter 5, because China's experience differed from that of so many others during the period, for many reasons. Disastrous experiences of an earlier adoption of a paper currency system mired China in a primitive monetary setting for centuries; it has lasted almost up until the modern time. The Nationalists seized a golden opportunity to modernize China's monetary system; yet, their efforts and power ended in catastrophe, largely because they overplayed their monetary policy. At times Nationalist politicians resorted to price controls and ideological means to suppress inflation, but ultimately they had to admit the laws of economics.

To the surprise of the world, hyperinflation looked like an epidemic disease from the 1970s. It raged in many Latin American and African countries in the decade, and to some extent, in several Asian countries as well. With wars becoming less relevant and less virulent, the reemerging incidence of severe hyperinflation in the world underscores the importance of understanding the economics involved in the process of rising inflation. The stories of Bolivia, Brazil, Argentina, Israel, and Turkey discussed in Chapter 6 all show how a poorly structured economy, an unsound economic institution, or mismanagement in macroeconomic policy could trap an economy in hyperinflation or chronic high inflation if public inflation expectations could not be stabilized.

Chapter 7 provides an analytical narrative of the wave of inflation and hyperinflation in transitional economies in the 1980s. Seeds of rising inflation and hyperinflation were already planted in the very structure of the central planning system of these countries, including a form of repressed inflation. In Russia and the surrounding areas, poor handling of the Ruble Zone was the main culprit for the wave of hyperinflation that struck all of the USSR successor countries. In Yugoslavia – the smaller entity left after the breakup of the Socialist Federal Republic of Yugoslavia in 1991 – the hijacking of certain policies ignited the flame of inflation, which was further fueled by the *de facto* dollarization that was already pervasive in the country. The specter of inflation haunted every transitional economy in this region in this era. After bouts of high inflation, China and Vietnam in East Asia managed to escape from it, largely by quickly joining the new tide of globalization that began to bloom in the 1990s.

With the rise of globalization at the turn of the twenty-first century, the incidence of hyperinflation in the world declined considerably. Chapter 8 finds only three cases to scrutinize: Zimbabwe in 2008, North Korea in 2009, and Venezuela from 2015. These were obvious outliers in terms of the prevailing world trend in the new century. A common lesson that can be drawn from the experiences of these three countries is that if the laws of economics are ignored, capital controls cannot always save an economy from knockout of hyperinflation; rather, they more often become an accelerating factor in the process of rising inflation and emerging crisis.

The rhythm of hyperinflation from the early 1920s through the mid-2010s – the subject studied in Chapters 3 through 8 – appears to have coincided closely with certain megatrends in world politics and economics. Reflecting on this wide background, the last chapter focuses on three things that are critical for the study of hyperinflation in the contemporary world: policy, institutions, and international relations. Use of these broad concepts is intended to emphasize the interaction among price movements and social environments, and the profound implications these relationships have for the continuing development of economic and political processes in an increasingly globalized world.

It is the hope of the author – one perhaps shared by any reader of this book – that hyperinflation has largely become a "dead issue" in our contemporary world. Yet, no one may dispute that our present world is far from perfect, and that improvements in policy, institutions, and international relations are as necessary now as ever before. Seen in this light, the history of hyperinflation around the world that is narrated in this book may serve as a reminder of our progress and our lingering imperfections after a century of struggle and search for economic progress and stability.

Note

1 Kindleberger (1984, p. 310).

Acknowledgements

The list of intellectual liabilities I accrued in writing the book is a long one, and I must keep this section short by expressing my principal thanks here only to those who directly helped.

The CPI and PPI curves in Figure 4.11 are based on the statistical information provided in the *Sixtieth Anniversary of Korean Recovery in Statistics*, edited by the Bank of Korea, Seoul, 2003, which was provided by, and translated into Chinese, thanks to the courtesy of Park Jae Hyun, a Korean friend who once studied at the Chinese Academy of Social Sciences.

The section on Japan in Chapter 4 relies on the publications of some Japanese scholars that have been translated into Chinese. Professor Zhang Jifeng at the Institute of Japanese Studies of the Chinese Academy of Social Sciences helped me translate several Japanese (Chinese) names into English.

Table 5.1 (currency regimes and levels of inflation in "Greater China," 1941–45) uses statistical or quantitative information about several "regions" that have not been covered in mainstream studies on Chinese inflation during the first half of the 1940s. For West China (Xinjiang) and Tibet, I benefited from Professor Pan Jiao at the China Central University of Nationalities (now more often called the Minzu University of China in English); for Taiwan, from Ms. Ching-Tzu Liu in Taiwan; and for Macau, from Professor Fung Kwan at the University of Macau.

Conversations with Professor Jiang Shixue at the Institute of Latin American Studies of the Chinese Academy of Social Sciences gave me a knowledge of economics and finance in Latin American countries, especially those that were at play in Bolivia during the 1980s.

Professor Wing Thye Woo at the University of California, Davis, offered insightful knowledge on the comparative development of transitional Russia and China, and I benefited greatly from his knowledge, both by reading his publications and by having many conversations with him.

Two of my friends, Mr. Wu Xiaodu and Ms. Su Ling, both research fellows at the Institute of Foreign Literature of the Chinese Academy of Social Sciences, happened to be in Moscow when the "Pavlov Reform" and the Yeltsin Economic Program were announced. Talking with them was invaluable, and felt as if I had read first-hand journalists' reports.

Walter Molano at BCP Securities, in Connecticut in the United States, has regularly commented on Latin America's economic movements through the digital newsletter of his *Emerging Market Advisor*. I learned a great deal about Venezuela from this invaluable source.

Two international students who attended my course, *International Finance and China*, at the School of Business and Economics, Beijing Normal University, helped me in collecting information related to different countries. They are Pouneh Soleimaninejadian from Iran and Teodora Ilic from Serbia.

I was fortunate to have had a number of research students at the Beijing Normal University who offered great assistance in various ways in locating numerous publications. Without their help, this book would have taken several more years to complete. They are Chen Chen, Chen Su, Li Na, Ma Wei, Wang Jia, and Yu Hang.

I also had two copy-editing professionals, Chris Surtees in Beijing (originally from London) and Rebecca Vollmer in California, who helped to improve the English of the book. In some cases, their help went far beyond just a language service.

I received tremendous encouragement and professionalism from Ms. Sun Lian, my book's editor at Routledge, who made it possible for the book to appear as it does.

Needless to say, any remaining errors or imperfections in the book are entirely mine.

Liping He
Beijing Normal University
May, 2017

1 Introduction

Basic concepts of hyperinflation

"*Natura non facit saltum.*" (Nature does nothing in jumps)
An axiom cited by Alfred Marshall in his
Principles of Economics, 1890

"Nature abhors a vacuum."

Aristotle

Inflation as an economic and monetary phenomenon usually refers to a rising trend in general prices in a country over a period of time. Hyperinflation is an unusual type of inflation wherein general price rises reach such unusually high levels that the currency tends to become no longer able to perform its normal functions in part or wholly. Monetary conditions in the economy have therefore rapidly become enormously aberrant. The causes of hyperinflation may be easily confused with those of inflation, but they are distinctively different. As a type of financial crisis, hyperinflation can lead to economic collapse, and a stabilization program is necessary following an outbreak of hyperinflation. Correcting policy, building institutions in sensible ways, and having access to international resources are the most important elements of a successful stabilization program.

What is hyperinflation?

Inflation has been common worldwide from past to present, but hyperinflation has not. Over the course of history, the known incidence of hyperinflation is not high. From the late eighteenth century to the 2000s, 56 episodes of hyperinflation involving nearly 40 countries or political regimes have been recorded, based on a "monthly" definition of hyperinflation,[1] and 16 countries have witnessed at least one hyperinflationary incidence between 1800 and 2008,[2] according to an "annual" definition of hyperinflation.

Three quantitative criteria of hyperinflation

The first quantitative definition of hyperinflation is that a general price level increases 50 percent or more from one month to the next. And, the second is that a general price level climbs at least 500 percent year on year. The two definitions of hyperinflation are not directly comparable; there is no way to say which is greater. Of course, in a year when the monthly inflation rate is 50 percent every month, the annual inflation rate will be nearly 13,000 percent – corresponding to an almost 130-fold increase in prices – far greater than the annual criterion of 500 percent. In reality, however, hardly any country would see such an inflation rate sustained over a long period. In other words, an economy experiencing a monthly rate of 50 percent for one month or a few months may end up with an annual rate below 500 percent for the year. Or, an annual rate of 500 percent may be accompanied by a monthly rate of at least 50 percent for one or more months during that year.

The monthly definition was first suggested by American economist Phillip Cagan in a research paper published in 1956 on hyperinflations in five countries during the interwar period: Austria, Germany, Hungary, Poland, and Russia.[3] In light of his systematic analysis, the term "hyperinflation" became popular in academia. Before then, many phrases were used to describe high inflation – including "very high inflation," "severe inflation," "rapid inflation," "acute inflation," "gallop inflation," "runaway inflation," "explosive inflation," and "extreme inflation" – and some are still in use to a certain extent. A concise, mathematically rigorous definition facilitates accurate analysis and also discards many other "unimpressive" cases of inflation, both past and present.

In the history of hyperinflation, Hungary holds the all-time world records, measured on both monthly and annual bases. In 1946, her consumer prices rose 4.19×10^{16} percent month on month in July and climbed at an annual rate of 9.63×10^{26} percent that year.[4]

Some economists suggest a much lower criterion for hyperinflation or "very high inflation": an annual rise of 100 percent in general prices.[5] This does not mean, however, that economists disagree on the criterion of hyperinflation. Rather, different quantitative thresholds serve as a reminder that other circumstances may be used to determine whether a country has encountered hyperinflation. For instance, in today's world, when single-digit inflation is the norm, any country that has double-digit inflation would be regarded as having "very high inflation." In ancient times, when people's incomes were considerably low by contemporary standards, and their daily necessities relied on market supplies, a 10 percent monthly rise or 50 percent annual rise in prices would harm people's living standards tremendously, often leading to malnutrition and even starvation. Such situations should be taken into account when studying high inflation or hyperinflation.

Measurement of inflation and hyperinflation

The study of hyperinflation requires appropriate price indicators, a number of which are widely used nowadays in routine macroeconomic research.

Consumer price index (*CPI*): a general price index consisting of a basket of consumer goods and services.

Producer price index (*PPI*): a general price index consisting of a basket of producer goods, mainly industrial products, as they are delivered to others.

Retail price index (**RPI**): like CPI, a measurement of prices of a basket of consumer goods and services, with the information collected from a large number of retailers. In earlier times, RPI mainly covered goods.

Wholesale price index (**WPI**): a measurement of prices of a basket of merchandise that is frequently traded in a country's wholesale markets.

All these price indexes are compiled with similar statistical methodologies and can be fairly used for historical comparison purposes.

Influenced by the rise of labor movements during the first half of the twentieth century, many countries started to compile and publish a cost of living index (**CLI**). While CPI and CLI are basically the same, the two may differ in the weights they assign to individual categories or items in the basket of consumer goods and services.

In recent decades, many countries have also published price indexes such as **Core CPI** and **GDP deflator**. Core CPI excludes food and fuels, which conventional CPI[6] includes, mainly because prices of food and fuels tend to be more vulnerable than others to short-term shocks. Without these two, Core CPI may show relatively stable movement over time or mostly reflect the effects of economic activity within a country. GDP deflator – an implicit price deflator for gross domestic product – is a comprehensive measure of price changes in both the production and consumption sectors of an economy. Its scope is much wider than those of CPI, PPI, RPI, or WPI. Usually the information of GDP deflator is published on quarterly base, so that it has a lower frequency than many other price indexes.

Sometimes, when no price index information is available, other indicators may serve equally well for gauging inflation or possible hyperinflation. *Interest rates* and *exchange rates* are such indicators. In theory, interest rates and exchange rates change quickly and accordingly when price inflation is happening, because participants in credit markets or foreign exchange markets should be able to properly adjust their use of money based upon observed and anticipated price changes. Even if price index information is available, interest rates or exchange rates can be used either to confirm the occurrence of hyperinflation or to reveal its impacts in the economy.

Usually when hyperinflation takes place, the domestic credit and foreign exchange markets of the country concerned are in chaos. Consequently, black markets for credit and foreign exchange typically emerge, and people tend to rely on interest rate and exchange rate information derived from these unofficial markets as it reflects actual market transactions.

In absence of all of the above-mentioned price indexes and interest and exchange rates, inflation or hyperinflation may be gauged by reference to the prices of single commodities. In Asia, price information about rice provides a good example in this regard.

Collecting price information is time-consuming and costly. As a result, compiling and publishing price information on a regular basis and in a transparent way is a public service provided by government. Yet, in reality, governments from time to time attempt to distort price information for short-term political gain. *The*

Economist, the weekly periodical based in London, once suspended the inclusion of the Argentine CPI in its regular tabulation of the latest international macro-economic data on suspicion of the Argentine government's manipulation of the information.[7] Scrutiny is always needed with regard to the reliability of price information.

A qualitative definition of hyperinflation

From past to present, money performs three basic functions in an economy:

- *A unit of account* – values of any commodity in a society are expressed and measured in a unit of currency, therefore transactions and trade can take place in accordance with the principle of equal exchange.
- *A medium of exchange* – money is used as a means of payment for anything else in a society, and it saves the cost of transactions which use non-monetary means of exchange, such as in the case of barter.
- *A store of value* – money can be saved by its holders for future use, as long as its value (purchasing power) does not fall over time. The purchasing power of money is the total quantity or quantities of goods and services that a fixed amount of money can buy. As such, the purchasing power of money depends on given prices of goods and services and their changes over time. How much money people save – to what extent money is used as a store of value – is thus affected by price inflation as well as by other factors including income, wealth, and degree of uncertainty about the future.
- By law, a form of money can become *legal tender* in a country, to be used in settlement of debts and obligations between members of the society. If the money is sound, its role as legal tender should have no problems. But if the money becomes unsound, even the law cannot stop people from discarding it.

A practical definition of sound money is money that can perform all of its three basic functions at the same time. Correspondingly, unsound money is money that can no longer properly fulfill some of its functions, primarily because of serious inflation. During periods of inflation, the purchasing power of money tends to decline. When no possibility exists in the domestic monetary system for money holders to offset the diminishing effect of rising inflation on purchasing power, they tend to seek alternative ways of saving, whether foreign currency, commodities, or something else.

A qualitative definition of hyperinflation, therefore, is loss of the function of money as a store of value. When this happens and domestic money holders begin to seek alternative assets or forms of money, *asset substitution* or *currency substitution* occurs. In these circumstances, domestic money may continue to perform its functions as a unit of account and a medium of exchange. But, hyperinflation can lead to an outcome where people even abandon the use of national currency in domestic transactions, i.e., the money loses its other two functions as well. Economists nowadays refer to this situation as "*dollarization*" – the widespread use of foreign money in domestic transactions. When the situation is not recognized by the government concerned, it is *de facto* dollarization. And when a government formally endorses a foreign currency as legal tender in its jurisdiction, it is *de jure* dollarization. *Partial* dollarization means that domestic and foreign currencies coexist in domestic transactions, and this most probably suggests that the domestic money has lost its function as a store of value.

What causes hyperinflation?

The causes of hyperinflation are easily confused with those of inflation. With regard to the latter, the following are often regarded as necessary candidate factors:

- *Shortages*: Excess demand caused by either a demand or supply shock such as a sudden drop in output due to a natural disaster;
- *Balance of payments shocks*: For example, a sudden rise in international oil prices (terms of trade shock); overvaluation of domestic currency leading to deterioration of the currency account balance; or unsustainable accumulation of foreign debt;
- *Government budget deficit*: Such as a sudden loss of revenue or an irresistible increase in fiscal spending;
- *Expansionary monetary policy*: Monetary authorities in a country adopt a policy of continually increasing money supply and pushing down interest rates in real terms;
- *Paper currency system*: Governments with paper money systems are constantly tempted to resort to an inflationary policy to finance budgetary needs as and when necessary or desirable.

Modern periods of inflation have been closely related to these factors. When inflation occurs in a country over a period of time, people can often identify at least one of the five factors. Clearly, though, these factors are not sufficient conditions for inflation, not to mention hyperinflation. In a paper currency system, for instance, deflation can occur as much as inflation. In the 2010s, many governments around the world run budget deficits, yet their national economies barely see any significant inflation. For hyperinflation to arise, something else must be in effect. Often before a period of hyperinflation, an economy has already experienced substantial inflation, which the government has already attempted to contain through certain policy measures. Hyperinflation very rarely occurs all of a sudden, without any early warning signs. Rather, hyperinflation usually results from previous inflation that has eventually escalated to an astronomical level.

Therefore, hyperinflation has its own causes, distinctively different from those of "ordinary" inflation, the following three of which are the most relevant:

- Policy failure in an inflation stabilization process;
- Institutional deficiency that causes the public to lose trust in the government and confidence in a stabilization process; and
- International isolation.

Understanding these three points requires a little knowledge of the framework of modern finance, in which governments play the role of money creator. Milton Friedman's popular statement that "substantial inflation is always and everywhere a monetary phenomenon"[8] captures the essence of the quantity theory of money, which says the relation between money supply and price level in an economy at any point in time is constant under given economic conditions. In plain words, this relation implies that price inflation cannot rise beyond the maximum level the money supply could possibly accommodate. As a unit of account and a medium of exchange, money sets the limit for how far price inflation can go. However, the quantity theory of money itself does not suggest any cause-and-effect relationship between money and inflation. Since ancient times, money has been under government control, in the form of coinage or paper currency. In the modern era, central banks act on behalf of governments to implement monetary policy, which greatly influences money supply (money stock) and interest rates. Just as in a commodity money environment – when gold or silver is used as currency – central banks can gain the benefit of *seigniorage* through managing the money supply. Literally, seigniorage is the difference between the increase in the money supply and the cost this increase incurs, providing price levels in the economy do not change during the money creation process. It is usually calculated as the product of the increase in money supply and *real money balance* – an index of the nominal money stock relative to a given price index over time.

As central banks are part of government systems, seigniorage can be a source of government revenue. When this is the case, seigniorage is also known as "*inflation tax*," and this tax is implicit to its payers – those who hold money. Whether a government is willing to collect seigniorage is a matter of policy, and how much the government can raise seigniorage in real terms depends on the momentum of inflation and public reaction to the policy.

Under normal conditions, when a government has a budget deficit and is unable to raise ordinary taxation to meet its expenditure obligations, it can borrow either in domestic financial markets or from overseas. Budget deficit is a prerequisite for neither inflation nor hyperinflation. As long as the government pays reasonable interest on its borrowings – often in the form of market-based government securities – the value of money will seem sufficiently stable, and domestic money holders will be willing to subscribe for government securities and thereby contribute to financing the budget deficit. In such circumstances, a budget deficit need not be followed by an inflationary deficit-financing policy. Underdevelopment of domestic financial markets and incorrect policy on interest rates on government securities can cause problems with securities-based deficit financing. When a government has already become highly indebted, it would be tempted in some cases to reduce the cost of servicing the debt, or even to eliminate the mountainous debt, by adopting an inflationary policy fit for the purpose. As an undesirable consequence, however, rises in inflation would ultimately reduce the real value of ordinary government revenues and, thereby, cause the budget deficit to deteriorate further.

In theory, a government can also borrow from abroad. Yet, international borrowing requires certain conditions such as policy credibility, institutional reputation, and (in some cases) the government's foreign policy approach. It is likely that when a government finds itself unable to borrow either domestically or abroad, for various reasons, an inflationary deficit-financing policy will be set in motion and thus orient the economy on a pathway to hyperinflation.

To reiterate this point regarding the possible causes of hyperinflation, as long as a government has the ability to borrow either domestically or internationally at reasonable cost, a budget deficit – no matter how large it is – should not necessarily lead to hyperinflation or even result in significant inflation. It is a government's inability to borrow that leads to adoption of inflationary policy and eventually causes hyperinflation amidst policy and institutional failures during anti-inflation programs. Governments may sometimes welcome a "moderate" inflation, but hardly any national administration would like to have a hyperinflation. In the process that leads from inflation to hyperinflation, certain other factors would come into play. If the response to the government's inflationary policy were only passive, the actual level of inflation would not escalate into the territory of hyperinflation. But once the government's inflationary policy becomes public knowledge, active responses such as price and wage hikes ensue. Speculation and hoarding also emerge and inevitably intensify over the course of an accelerating inflation. People are guided by their inflation expectations, which largely result from government policy moves under certain institutional constraints. While inflation is rising fast, simply announcing a new policy to check inflation does not suffice. And, any failed policy attempt to control inflation gives rise to a new round in the inflationary spiral, vicious circle connecting government policy failures with unsettled public inflation expectations and unremitting speculative and hoarding behavior.

An ancient Chinese proverb says, "The government has strategies. The people have counterstrategies."[9] In our world of money and finance, if a government's strategies are perceived by the public to be best making use of inflation, the people's best counterstrategies would necessarily be to drive prices higher than what the government could better use. Needless to say, such an interaction can ultimately lead to nothing but hyperinflation.

"Nature abhors a vacuum." When the deficit-reducing effect of an inflationary policy is threatened by faster price inflation, a government has to further expand its money creation, which in turn necessarily leads to even higher inflation. Policy measures, whether for anti-inflation purposes or not, have been wrong in many ways: artificially too low interest rates on government securities; prolonged overvaluation of the domestic currency; improper indexation linking the return on certain financial assets with price inflation, which can accelerate the money creation process and undermine the role of the domestic currency as a store of value; almost unlimited supply of cheap credit to public-sector enterprises; hasty default on public debt; drastic and desperate resort to capital controls and deposit freezing; introduction of price and wage controls without sufficient institutional backup; inadvertent use of precious financial resources – gold or foreign exchange reserves – that are publicly known to be rapidly diminishing; and so forth.

Institutional deficiencies include lax discipline in budget systems and fiscal policy; absence of debt ceilings for the public sector; weak central bank independence; low transparency in the policy-making process; and low account-ability in policy implementation. In short, the nation's governance lacks checks and balances, and the government has not established policy credibility on the basis of its past record.

Needless to say, if a country has become an unwelcome member of the inter-national community for some reason, it will be unable to borrow from abroad, through either official or private channels.

An economy need not have all elements of the above-mentioned policy and institutional failures to incur hyperinflation. In some cases, just a few failures will suffice.

What are the impacts of hyperinflation?

"Nature does nothing in jumps." A market economy is a system in which people's decision-making on consumption, saving, and investment is based on price sig-nals that they have received from the market, and economic progress takes place on the basis of people's correct decisions. Economic growth is essentially an evo-lutionary process that cannot jump for any reason. Hyperinflation is nevertheless a process of price jumps. Prices continue to perform the role of signal, but the signals may be distorted for various reasons. As in the case of ordinary inflation, the impacts of hyperinflation on an economy depend on a number of contingent conditions.

First, the extent to which the inflation or hyperinflation is anticipated. If every-one in a society could form correct inflation expectations and make adjustments in nominal variables such as prices, wages, and interest rates, inflation or hyper-inflation would not affect real variables such as output, employment, and income distribution, though it could still impose adjustment costs on members of the soci-ety. On the other hand, unanticipated inflation can exert great impacts on real variables. One difference between ordinary inflation and hyperinflation is that, in many ways, hyperinflation is anticipated, although people may miscalculate its exact pace and rhythm. Therefore, the adjustment costs of hyperinflation should be much higher than those of ordinary inflation.

Second, how available is credit? As the costs of credit – interest rates – tend to lag behind price rises in an inflationary economy, at least in the short run, demand for credit necessarily grows rapidly as inflation rises. But access to credit, especially to cheap credit, differs considerably among a society's members or between sectors of an economy. Hyperinflation thus has an uneven impact on economic activity.

Third, how accessible are foreign exchange and foreign assets? As hyperinflation continues to diminish the value of the domestic currency, demand tends to grow rapidly for foreign exchange and foreign assets, different degrees of access to which result in divergent outcomes for people's money holdings and financial investments.

Compared to ordinary inflation, hyperinflation involves a higher frequency of price changes, the making of shorter term contracts, and a stronger willingness to default on earlier contracts and financial obligations when they are linked to non-inflationary monetary units. Consequently, transaction costs tend to increase, price transparency tends to decrease, and new uncertainties arise. All this not only increases frictions in trade and commerce, but also reduces people's incentive to save in conventional ways. Increased uncertainty and lowered price transparency typically motivate more people to engage in speculation and hoarding, which in turn further aggravate the inflationary spiral.

With regard to money-holding behavior, an indisputable effect of hyperinflation is that people hold less and less money relative to the rising price levels. In the jargon of economics, this is the tendency for the real money balance to diminish and the velocity of money in circulation to accelerate.

A rapid tendency of this effect in an inflationary economy has profound implications for the monetary system and government finance.

Gresham's Law vs. Thiers' Law

As we have seen, hyperinflation means that domestic money loses its function as a store of value. Thus, people tend to seek alternative means of saving, and foreign money typically appears in the domestic economy. Further worsening of hyperinflation may induce the use of foreign money – or specie money – in domestic transactions. As a result, two different currencies would circulate concurrently in the domestic economy. This situation of parallel currencies has occurred in many episodes of hyperinflation.

This brings up the issue of how the two monies would relate to one another. According to an old view, when two monies exist in an economy, the tendency is that "bad money drives out good." This is known as Gresham's Law, after medieval English financier Sir Thomas Gresham (1519–79), who once commented on co-circulation of mixed coinage in the Tudor dynasty. Many economists believe that Gresham's Law has the prerequisites that the two monies' exchange rate (conversion ratio) is fixed, while their time values may differ moderately. In this situation, people have an incentive to use the inferior one in the first instance and save the superior one for future use, provided the two are equally acceptable in the market, in terms of purchasing power, at the time of offering. For this reason, "good" money is saved and therefore disappears from circulation.

A phenomenon opposite to Gresham's Law was observed, however, during the French Revolution in the late eighteenth century. When the new regime issued *assignats* – interest-bearing notes – to replace all other monies, the French people actually tried to avoid using the new currency. Although *assignats* were apparently a "bad" money, they did not drive out the "good" money. Rather, in this instance, the reverse occurred: good supplanted bad.

Louis Adolphe Thiers (1797–1877), a French statesman and historian, described the *assignats'* development in his *History of the French Revolution*. Economists hold that what Thiers demonstrated is effectively a reverse of Gresham's Law: The falling exchange rate (conversion ratio) of a bad money inexorably results in loss of its use in domestic transactions in the absence of enforceable legal tender laws. No one would be willing to accept a money that has been rapidly losing its value over time. Money that is to be accepted by people voluntarily must have a stable value.[10] This reverse of Gresham's Law, known as Thiers' Law, is most likely to occur in the later stages of hyperinflation.[11]

An implication of Thiers' Law is that a parallel currency environment enables people to get rid of the inferior domestic currency at a faster pace than would otherwise be possible. Consequently, the pace of inflation further accelerates, and the tendency for the real money balance to diminish is further strengthened. An interpretation of Thiers' Law is that hyperinflation may ultimately destroy the very foundations of a monetary system in which an inflationary policy has been implemented.

The Olivera–Tanzi effect and Laffer curve of seigniorage

A commonplace in economics is that inflation tends to increase government tax revenue. In a progressive income tax system, inflation increases the number of workers obliged to pay income tax or to pay at a higher rate, as nominal incomes grow. Taxation imposed on nominal incomes necessarily results in "inflation-induced tax distortions" when inflation exists.[12] In this case, people are actually discouraged from saving, and the government may find its borrowing base in the domestic financial markets dwindling. Another side effect of rising inflation on taxation is that people may be more tempted than before to engage in tax dodging.

A more serious problem is tax revenue's diminishing purchasing power as inflation accelerates. When prices are rising fast, the time lag between collecting tax revenue and disbursing the collected funds becomes significant. The real value of the tax revenue, which is usually calculated on past nominal incomes, diminishes significantly between the times of calculation and disbursement. Tax revenue's loss of real value due to rising inflation, which is known as the *Olivera-Tanzi- effect*,[13] is obviously positively proportional to the pace of hyperinflation.

Seigniorage may increase initially, as money supply expands more quickly than price inflation. Eventually, though, the relative speed of money supply and price inflation is bound to reverse – the pace of inflation overtaking that of money supply – and ultimately, seigniorage tends to decline in real terms. The pattern of change over time – seigniorage first rises and later falls over the course of rising inflation – is known as a Laffer curve of inflation tax. From a long-term perspective, then, seigniorage or inflation tax can never be a stable or reliable source of revenue.

In short, hyperinflation threatens to destroy not only the foundations of the monetary system, but also revenue bases which, in order to benefit from, the government should have cherished and protected. World history shows that, faced with revenue exhaustion during hyperinflation, all governments turn to a stabilization program sooner or later, no matter how potentially high the costs of reform.[14]

How to end hyperinflation?

At a certain stage of its evolvement, hyperinflation creates a dilemma for the government. On the one hand, its revenue bases are rapidly diminishing, as the economy heads to collapse; on the other hand, it may lack sufficient financial resources to undertake the bold moves required in a stabilization process, which may finally result in an output decline and higher unemployment. Besides, no panacea for curing hyperinflation straightway apparently exists. History shows that many governments have taken the chance to embark on a stabilization program, occasionally with timing that more or less coincided with the arrival of international assistance.

Just as each hyperinflation has its own "nationality," stabilization programs also differ from country to country. At least several major episodes of hyperinflation and stabilization, however, have shared the following eight elements in common:

- *Currency reform*: either a simple redenomination or a thorough change in currency unit, the latter of which may force out certain amounts of older, "unused" currency notes and help the government establish a new reputation.
- *Interest rate hikes*: a necessary move to establish positive real interest rates, thereby restore the work of the domestic banking industry and financial markets, and thus further improve conditions for the government to borrow at home.
- *Restoring currency convertibility and exchange rate stability*: an important move to establish a stable anchor for, and strengthen public confidence in, the currency, sometimes a new one. Convertibility, earlier often made to gold or silver, has been made to foreign exchange since the mid-twentieth century. The government may need substantial financial resources to maintain currency convertibility.
- *Fiscal austerity according to a budget balance*: a key factor believed necessary by many for success of the stabilization program and termination of expansionary monetary policy, which, however, may cause short-term setbacks to output and employment. Strong social resistance to fiscal austerity invariably appears. Insufficient financial resources may cause fiscal austerity to fail.
- *Establishing central bank independence*: an institutional reform that should considerably increase public trust of government policy and substantially reduce inflation expectations. A move whose positive effects are greater in the long run than over the short term.
- *International assistance*: an important factor in enhancing the stabilization program's chance of success. Often, new financial resources arrive with conditions that the recipient country may not fully welcome.
- *Price controls*: often a controversial policy measure that has varied in its range of coverage, length of application, and method of enforcement from country to country. Liberals see them as a temporal expedient which tends to have distortional effects, and authoritarians turn them into an opportunity to permanently shift toward a planned economic system.
- *Structural reforms*: a sometimes vague term that involves a great variety of institutional change – from taxation overhaul to liberalization and privatization – which may be complementary or supplementary to fiscal austerity and central

bank independence. Primarily with long-term effects on the economy, they may not have immediate or direct impacts on stabilization.

From past to present, many countries have adopted different approaches to stabilization programs. Some stabilization programs have succeeded without currency reform, and many currency reforms have been implemented without a successful stabilization. Price controls have invariably been absent in liberal stabilization programs, but have occasionally been put into effect by basically liberal governments to check climbing inflation. In economics textbooks, price controls are called income policies, and are part of a *heterodox approach*. Without such policies or controls, stabilization programs are regarded as following an *orthodox approach*.[15]

Whichever approach is followed, a stabilization program's chances of success essentially depend on the circumstances in the individual country at the time of hyperinflation. As shall be seen in this book, in a few episodes, governments have even had no chance to succeed in stabilization before being overthrown, or they had to finally abandon stabilization attempts by switching to *de jure* dollarization. In some extreme cases, whether or not a stabilization program has succeeded cannot be properly judged, as the economy has shifted into an obscure mode of operation.

Notes

1 Hanke and Krus, pp. 372–3.
2 Reinhart and Rogoff, Tables 12.1 to 12.3.
3 Cagan (1956).
4 Hungary's monthly and annual rates come from Hanke and Krus, p. 372, and Reinhart and Rogoff, Table 12.3, respectively.
5 Capie (1986, p. 147) suggests an annual rate of at least 100 percent for "very rapid inflation," which is shared by Sachs and Larrain, Chapter 23. Notably, Dornbusch, Sturzenegger, and Wolf (p. 2) prefer a threshold of 1,000 percent.
6 Due to the popularity of Core CPI, conventional CPI is sometimes called "headline CPI."
7 *The Economist* (2012); also Reinhart and Rogoff, footnote on p. 148.
8 Friedman and Friedman (1979, p. 265).
9 Cited in Sargent (2013, p. 1), where it introduces a formal analysis on the interaction between government policy and public reaction in macroeconomic modelling.
10 Robert Mundell (1998) noted that Gresham's Law could be more accurately rendered, taking care of the reverse, if it were expressed as, "Bad money drives out good *if they exchange for the same price*."
11 Bernholz (1989, pp. 98–9, 2003, pp.115 and 132). Thiers' view was earlier noted by Bresciani-Turroni (1937, pp. 120, 157).
12 Mankiw, pp. 356–8.
13 Blanchard, p. 437; also known as the "Olivera-Tanzi effect," see Sachs and Larrain, pp. 348–9.
14 Dornbusch, Sturzenegger, and Wolf have noted that "higher inflation leads to larger [budget] deficits and greater money creation unless governments actively intervene to change the fiscal structure. Moreover, even if they do act, the pace at which inflation can destroy the fiscal system may well overrun the government's attempt to reform the system." (p. 9)
15 Blanchard, p. 440; Sachs and Larrain, p. 754; Dornbusch, Sturzenegger, and Wolf, pp. 50–4.

2 Monetary adventures before the twentieth century

"What has been is what will be, and what has been done is what will be done, and there is nothing new under the sun."

Ecclesiastes, 1:4–11

"To know nothing of what happened before you were born is to remain ever a child."

Cicero, Roman philosopher, *Speeches*, 120

"Rather to his surprise the author discovered how many of the world's apparently modern problems have their precedents in the past."

John F. Choun, *A History of Money*, Introduction, 1994

Hyperinflation is largely a twentieth-century phenomenon, but it has had a plethora of ancestors in the past. China, the Roman Empire, Persia, England, France, and America, all had high inflations before the twentieth century, several episodes of which occurred even before the advent of paper currency systems.

Unlike ones caused by natural factors such as bad weather or discovery of gold fields, these episodes of high inflation were all results of monetary policy exerted by governments who were pursuing either economic or political gains for their own sake, be they kingdoms, empires, or republics. In the remote past, when technology of metal manufacturing was underdeveloped, ancient rulers could still play with coinage. With the advent of the technologies of paper making and the printing press, they quickly took advantage of the new technology and sought to play monetary games on a much larger scale than ever before.

In all cases, monetary adventures consequently generated high inflation and chaotic economic conditions that are surely comparable to their followers in modern times.

Money and inflation in the ancient world

Money is believed to have been put into use when civilization emerged. Barter can function for exchange and trade on a small scale and locally. As trade expands over long distances and credit-giving activities spread in a society, a more efficient means of payment and debt settlement is needed, and thus the use of money has to be called upon.

Genesis, the first book of the Hebrew Bible and also regarded as the Christian Old Testament, narrates that, "Then there passed by Midianites, merchant men, and they drew and lifted up Joseph out of the pit, and sold Joseph to the Ishmaelites for twenty pieces of silver, and they brought Joseph into Egypt."[1] Silver, as mentioned here, was apparently used as a form of money, though it was possibly by weight of bullion, not exactly as a hand-made coin.

The book is believed to have been written during the fifth and sixth centuries BC, and the time of events it narrates may date back as early as five hundred years before that. *Exodus*, the second book of the Hebrew Bible and part of the Christian Old Testament, which is largely a narrative about the Israelites' escape from slavery in Egypt and crossing of the Red Sea,[2] repeatedly referred to the term *shekels* when describing how much people gave as tributes to temples or as part of goods exchanges between them. This is another indication that efforts to find a unit of accounting and medium of exchange had already begun by that era.

In fact, the term *shekels* had been used much earlier than in *Exodus*, and it unambiguously referred to a monetary unit. Today, the State of Israel calls its currency *shekel* – actually the new *shekel* from 1985.

The geographical coverage of the two old books is the Middle East, a large region stretching from Egypt to Iraq via the southeastern bank of the Mediterranean Sea. The region is also known as the Fertile Crescent, where the world's earliest civilizations originated along the Nile river valley and in Mesopotamia – the land between the Tigris and Euphrates rivers.

Mesopotamia witnessed numerous rises and falls of ancient kingdoms and empires during the second and first millenniums BC. New rulers tended to proclaim "law codes" for social and economic conduct and put the texts into stone inscriptions, which have thus been preserved until today. A text of law codes discovered in the city of Eshnunna, northern Mesopotamia, is believed to have been formed at the beginning of the second millennium BC, during the rule of the Third Dynasty of Ur, also known as the Neo-Sumerian Empire. It states that the fine for biting a man's nose was 1 *mina* of silver (about half a kilo), whilst that for a slap in the face was 10 *shekels* – probably a sixth of the former.[3] Fines were obviously measured in weights of money, or more accurately, commodity money.

The law codes of Eshnunna are a predecessor of the more famous *Code of Hammurabi*, in southern Mesopotamia, of about two centuries later. Hammurabi, the sixth and last king of the First Babylonian Dynasty (1792 – 1750 BC), enacted the code, which consists of 282 laws covering a plethora of civil and commercial deeds. In particular, it stipulates interest rate ceilings on loans reckoned in silver, e.g., 20 percent for loans in silver (pure monetary lending) and 33.3 percent for loans in grain.[4] These codes reflect that financial dealings among members of society had become common by the time the codes were written.

Moreover, scholars have been able to decipher occurrences of price inflation out of hundreds of thousands of words and text fragments from that period. One study has found that as the relative price of silver to gold changed between 1894 BC and 1595 BC, prices of major commodities and wages also changed. Wages were paid sometimes in barley (a staple then) and at other times in slaves. At one time – possibly at the turn of the eighteenth century BC – the price level simply averaged over slaves, oil, barley, oxen, cattle, land, and house rental rose more than ten times in less than ten years.[5] Scholars have not yet found out what exactly caused the sharp price changes, but their findings have already shed light on several points relevant to our interest.

First, the ancient Babylonian people recognized the importance of prices. In principle, they wrote on clay or stones only for what was extremely important to them. They must have felt great impacts of prices and price changes on their lives, otherwise there would not have been such large amounts of this type of information written down. It is also an indication that exchange and trade prevailed in the region during that remote time.

Second, inflation – defined as a rising tendency in the price of a staple or in the average price of multiple items – occurred for some reason. The most probable causes were natural factors – either supplies of staples being cut short by floods or drought, or demand suddenly rising due to major victories in military campaigns.

Third, although silver and gold had been used as money to varying extents, they probably had not been manipulated by rulers back then. In other words, the value of silver or gold was like that of other commodities; it changed as a result of natural causes alone. Ancient rulers were not able to embark on monetary adventures until the advent of coinage.

Nevertheless, the fact that prices of commodities changed drastically at times led many rulers to resort to price controls to minimize the effects of inflation or deflation on their economy and society. Ancient Egypt, Sumeria, and Old Babylon all adopted numerous price control measures. Egyptian pharaohs adopted harsh measures to control grain prices in the Nile valley, and they built many large-scale warehouses aimed at stabilizing food supplies and grain prices. In Sumeria, there was once a king who lifted restrictions on prices and wages because he believed that government intervention in the economy had been too much. The *Code of Hammurabi* refers to many cases where a fixed price or rate in terms of barley or silver must be obeyed by the party concerned.[6]

It is the arrival of coinage that provided governments with new opportunities and new means to intervene in the economy for many purposes: fiscal, political, and social. Many records have shown the invention of coinage was related to a form of government.

Herodotus, "Father of History" in the west, who lived in the fifth century BC and travelled extensively around the eastern and southern parts of the Mediterranean, reported in his book "*Histories*" that gold coins were first made in a kingdom called Lydia in Asia Minor, today's Turkey. The area had a rich reserve of gold, and technological progress there in metallurgy had allowed gold to be separated from other metals and made into certain shapes of fixed weights.[7] The time when the actual events took place was probably the eighth century BC.[8] A few centuries later, as city-states rose in ancient Greece, coinage became a trend.

Money is a better means of exchange than barter, and so are coins compared with gold bullion or electrum, the natural alloy of gold and silver. Coins are standardized in weight and shape and, increasingly, also in other aspects such as purity and design. The value of coins is relatively easy to identify for ordinary people. In China before the late nineteenth century, all coins were made with a square hole in the center, believed to be for the sake of convenience in carrying. As a form of money, coins have been widely used in virtually all civilized societies since the technology became available.

When the use of coins became widespread in society, many ancient rulers also found opportunities to exploit to gain benefit for themselves. They deliberately reduced the purity of their constituent precious metals – gold or silver – cut their weights, adulterated them with base metals, or even falsely talked up their face values.

Dionysius of Syracuse in Greece, who lived during the fourth century BC, is said to have doubled the face value of *drachma*, the silver coin that was widely circulated then.[9] This is perhaps the earliest known incidence of large debasement in the ancient world. In China, debasement became one of the frequent pursuits of emperors during the First Han Dynasty (206 BC–AD 9), only two decades after the coinage system was first unified in the country during the Ch'in (Qin) Dynasty (221–206 BC). Apparently, ancient rulers long ago found the "Midas Touch" of monetary policy. They tended to first monopolize coinage and then to debase coins at their discretion. Sometimes, they even pursued monetary policy to its extreme. It was their debasement – the standard monetary policy before modern times – that became another source of inflation, especially high inflation.[10]

Moreover, from what we shall see in this chapter, high inflation does not necessarily require a paper currency system. Debasement in a coinage system can cause great inflation, with its disastrous effects more or less equally comparable to those in a paper currency system. The story of Wang Mang, which happened at the dawn of the first millennium, shows how a witty emperor set sail on a monetary adventure and plunged into an unruly fate.

Wang Mang: a most bizarre adventure in coinage

Wang Mang was probably the first Machiavellian Chinese who successfully enthroned himself in a centralized regime and fought hard against numerous political enemies in and outside of the court. He is remembered largely for his incessant monetary adventures during a brief reign lasting merely 15 years.

He rose from a moderate background and was lucky enough to be brought into the court by virtue of his blood ties with an Emperor's wife when the Former Han Dynasty (206 BC–AD 9) was on the descent in terms of economy and social order. He became a key cabinet minister for a young Emperor, who died a few years later. When the new, baby emperor was crowned, Wang was the regent. Two years later, he proclaimed himself Emperor, effectively ending the Liu Dynasty.

From AD 7–14, Wang Mang forcibly conducted four regime changes in China's monetary standards, once every two years on average. Most of the changes were about standards of weight, denomination, shape, and design of coinage, which was made mainly of bronze. Accompanying the standard changes, there were several policy Big Bangs:

First, gold demonetization and nationalization. Gold had not been used as money for ordinary transactions and trade in China, but it had been functioning as a store of value and was occasionally used for transfer of wealth. Use of gold was forbidden by Wang Mang in his first monetary reform, and all gold holders were required to exchange it for new coinage. The measure was relaxed in later years,[11] and huge amounts of gold were found in the court's vault when Wang Mang was overthrown by rebellious forces.

Second, great debasement. The weight of the new coins was deliberately reduced with regard to their actual market value, and exchange rates between the new coins and gold (and also old coins) were enforced against the latter. The first currency reform pressed down the value of some new coins by possibly 48 percent, in terms of gold, and the third reform further debased the new coins issued by the new regime. It was his fourth and last reform that attempted to stop debasement because of rising inflation and massive social unrest, but it arrived too late to save the regime, which collapsed in the midst of a rapid upheaval.

Third, coinage monopolization. Wang Mang outlawed all private coinage which prevailed at the time of his reign. Anyone found transacting in unauthorized coinage would be put into prison and his family members forced into public servitude. When the fourth reform was announced, anyone who was aware of private coinage but did not report it to the authorities would also be subject to similar punishment, as would their relatives. The number of coinage offenders sent into concentration camps in the capital city of the day once reached 100,000.[12]

Fourth, implementation of a grading system in coinage. In his third reform, a complex system of coinage was introduced consisting of 28 grades, each with a distinctive name, weight, and denomination. In today's world, the euro has the most denominations (15) among all popular currencies: seven in notes, from €500 to €5, and eight in coins, from €2 to €0.01. Wang Mang's system of 28 denominations was obviously unnecessary in economic terms, especially at a time when Arabic numerals were not in use and need for large denominations was not common. Perhaps Wang Mang had his own reason: to use the system for social management. People travelling in and out of cities were required to carry certain coins as a passport, otherwise lodges and security officers could refuse them entry or passage. Wang Mang also used large denominations to reward those whom he believed to be loyal or who had served his reign well. One trick in Wang Mang's currency reforms, especially the third one, was to cast larger denomination coins with increasingly lesser amounts of bronze. Smaller coins were more or less fully valued, but larger ones were substantially undervalued. This was undoubtedly a method of deceit. In reality, the circulation of the larger coins was scarce.

History books written by Wang's contemporaries mentioned little of the fiscal situation facing him. It is likely that having seized imperial power, Wang Mang was not actually in any significant budgetary difficulty. His abuse of monetary reform was most probably motivated by political calculations. At the center of the self-proclaimed "celestial dynasty," he was surrounded by a great number of marquises and other nobles, many of whom had been knighted and enriched by Han emperors before him. He perhaps foresaw threats from the established elite groups and so tried every means to weaken and marginalize them.

Monetary reforms were actually part of his broader political, social, and economic pursuits. He ordered a reorganization of government – introducing new ranking and knighting systems at the central and provincial levels. The buying and selling of private slaves was prohibited. Land was redistributed on an egalitarian principle, and sale of land was banned. Trade in liquor, salt, and iron was state monopolized. Concomitant with the monetary reforms, the well-being of formerly privileged groups was greatly reduced. On the basis of these rather radical measures, one modern commentator has even concluded that Wang Mang was a "socialist emperor" of 2,000 years ago.[13]

Were these measures really radical? Land and wealth redistribution were common from China's early history onward, and Wang Mang was definitely not the first Chinese ruler to implement them. In the monetary realm, there had been a tendency for new rulers to change the coinage when they took power. It is believed that coins made of base metals were circulating during the Spring and Autumn period (770–476 BC), a time when various regional lords gained *de facto* independence. Later, during the Warring States period (475–221 BC), many of the regional powers cast coins for use in their own territories. Ch'in (Qin), the first unified dynasty in China (221–206 BC), attempted to standardize many social and economic measurements including coinage. A grading system in denomination was introduced during this brief time, which consisted of yellow gold and bronze (the latter was known as "Half Ounce").

Mainstream scholars in the Former Han period all favored state monopoly in coinage, obviously to please the emperors. An emperor in the second century BC engaged in wars with mighty northern tribal forces, and his military campaigns exhausted budget resources at one point. He then started a debasement in coinage and was saved from financial bankruptcy.

What makes Wang Mang distinctive in the history of monetary policy pursuit is not that he reinforced the state monopoly in coinage, nor that he conducted a great debasement in currency. The uniqueness of his policy was the quest to push monetary policy to its maximum limits and to use it as an instrument in *realpolitik*. He may have gained by weakening his rivals and potential contenders financially, but later on, his reign also suffered from a depressed economy and lack of commerce. This irritated the masses, which in turn, caused the foundations of his rule to collapse.

Records of prices for the period of Wang Mang's reign are scarce. Two unrelated documents have been quoted as indicating that the price of rice rose four times in a year.[14] If that is true, the inflation was close to hyperinflation, according to the criterion of an annual price increase rate of 500 percent. What has been widely documented is that people then abandoned the use of state-issued coins and resorted to either gold or old coins in daily transactions.[15] It is unclear, however, whether the hikes in rice prices were due to supply shortages or excessive issue of debased coins. Wang Mang had debased coins considerably, but he may not have done so to excess. The fact that he instigated price controls on essential goods in his later years might also have helped deter the rising momentum of price inflation to some extent.

Nevertheless, as the economy and commerce had suffered greatly by some of his radical monetary and economic policy moves, adverse weather conditions dealt huge shocks to food supplies. And, this must be another important cause of the reported soaring of rice prices toward the end of Wang Mang's reign.

The fact that massive rebellions occurred in the second decade of the first millennium AD suggests that Wang Mang's rule had become increasingly unpopular. Several rebel leaders, remotely related to earlier Han emperors, gathered rebellious forces and ultimately killed Wang Mang. A new Han Dynasty was established, known as the Later Han or Eastern Han, which restored the earlier coinage system and adopted a rather liberal policy toward private coin casting.

Yet, Wang Mang's extremist maneuvering on monetary standards became a model example in China's history that was followed intermittently by many subsequent rulers, be they kings, emperors, or rebel leaders.[16]

The Roman Empire: unstoppable debasement

Originating in the Italian peninsula, the Roman Empire and its immediate precursor, the Roman Republic, rose rapidly in Europe and North Africa between the second century BC and the first century AD. At its zenith in the early second century AD, the Roman Empire's territories encircled the entire rim of the Mediterranean Sea. Its northern borders stretched into the Rhine and Danube river valleys. On its southeastern frontiers, Roman forces exchanged fire with soldiers of Persia and India and perhaps even marched into western parts of China.

The economy in the Empire's early time was booming. During the Republic period, agriculture, the textile industry, mining, and metallurgy were already moderately developed. Local farming output could not keep pace with population growth and the expansion of need brought by military campaigns, but trade and imperial tribute systems had been developed to meet the ever-growing demand in the economy.

Apart from the traditional agrarian sector, commerce had become an essential part of economic life for Roman citizens living in cities. Rome, the capital city of the Empire, had a population of as many as one million during the first century and early second century, undoubtedly the largest of any city in the world at the time. The people of Rome relied on supplies brought from various sources far away. North Africa – mostly Egypt – was a main source of grain (wheat and corn) supply for the Empire.

The first emperor, Augustus Octavian, who reigned between 27 BC and AD 14, restructured government finance, resulting in a system that remained basically unchanged for later centuries. There were three categories of taxation: a property tax of 1 percent on the value of land and real estate; a general sales tax of 1 percent on the value of transactions; and a succession duty (known as the "poll tax") paid by Roman citizens at a flat rate of 5 percent. The Roman fiscal system is believed to have been "very rigid," and the amount of revenue tended not to change greatly from year to year.[17] Occasionally, Roman army legions acquired huge amounts of confiscated property and looted assets, including precious metals. But, most of the booty would be given as rewards to generals and soldiers, instead of being paid into government coffers.

On the expenditure side, most notable is the Empire's constant need to support its army, which consisted of a garrison in Rome and legions stationed in numerous provinces, and navy. To preserve the *Pax Romana*, the military forces consumed a large fraction of, if not entirely exhausted, the Empire's financial and material resources. Influenced by democratic Greece's earlier example, the Romans not surprisingly established a social welfare scheme under which food and other necessities were provided free of charge to qualifying citizens in many Roman cities.[18] The government also operated merchandise houses to purchase goods even when prices were high and sell them to citizens at below-market prices. The welfare system's payments and subsidies have been regarded as the Achilles' heel of Roman government finance.[19] Needless to say, the Empire had a large administration system in operation whose cost would not have been small.

There was an active credit market, where private firms could take deposits and lend to others for a profit. They were like banks in modern times. But the government did not use the financial market to issue securities and borrow. At times when emperors were in need of additional finance to make up for budget deficits, they sought it through means other than taxation or borrowing.

Debasement of coins thus became one of the candidate methods for financing the Empire. Territories subsumed by the Empire already had silver and gold coins in circulation before the Romans took over, and the new rulers followed the examples of Greek city-states and Alexander the Great by minting coins symbolizing their own sovereignty. Augustus conducted significant minting of coins: the standard silver coin, the *denarius*, was struck at 84 to the pound, and the standard gold coin, the *aureus*, at 40–42 to the pound, with one *aureus* worth 25 *denarii*.[20] Issued at full value, these coins effectively served as a benchmark in terms of value for all later coinages.

It is known that Emperor Nero (AD 54–68) was the first Roman ruler to debase coins. He reduced the weights of silver and gold coins proportionally and increased their base metal content to about 10 percent.[21] This means that both *denarii* and *aurei* became lighter, and *denarii* contained more metal of less value. In the absence of price changes, Nero would have been able to buy larger quantities of goods and services with the same amounts of silver and gold.

Decades later, Emperor Trajan (98–117) debased the *denarius* by reducing its silver content from 90 percent to 85 percent. The practice was soon followed by one of his successors, Hadrian (117–138). This was the time when the Roman Empire was enjoying indisputable hegemony in the whole of Europe as well as in North Africa and West Asia.

While subsequent emperors tended to follow suit in debasing silver coins, some had insufficient time to engage in debasement under their reign because they were either assassinated or overthrown in political conflicts and civil wars. Several notable dates mark developments in the process of debasement.

By the time of Antoninianus (138–161), less than 5 percent of the *denarius* was silver, and the coin's weight had also substantially reduced.[22] A hundred years later, at the time of Gallienus (253–268), silver accounted for only about 4 percent of the *denarius*, and even the copper coins were also debased. By the end of Gallienus's reign, the silver content of the *denarius* was merely one five-thousandth of that contained in the coin minted by Augustus.[23] By then, banking firms had to refuse "grossly inferior coinage," many of which went out of circulation.[24]

During the reign of Aurelian (270–275), price inflation rocketed. He nevertheless invented a new way of debasement: increasing the face value of new coins by 2.5 times – more than some twentieth-century regimes did when issuing new notes of super-large denominations – an immediate effect of which would have been to more than double the existing money supply.

In fact, since the second century, the money supply may have been upset by gradual withdrawal of gold coins from circulation. Knowing the rising trend in their value, rich people tended to hoard gold coins instead of spending them. This is an effect of Gresham's Law: bad money (debased silver coins) drives out good money (non-debased, or less debased, gold coins). As long as debased *denarii* continued to flood into the market, prices would keep rising, and more hoarding would occur.[25]

The price of wheat in Egypt rose 32 times from the first century to the third, 44 times from the third century to the year 334, and a further 7.7 times between 334 and 344.[26] During this last ten years, the price of wheat soared at an average annual rate of 24.1 percent, a very high level even if viewed from a modern perspective.

Many history books have talked about the "Crisis of the Third Century" in the Roman Empire, which involved social, political, and economic upheavals intertwined with currency debasement and rampant inflation. If the Empire was to continue, drastic countermeasures had to be implemented.

Indeed this was reflected in actions undertaken by Emperor Diocletian (284–305), who issued the *Edict of Prices* in 301. It was a very comprehensive document which laid down official prices or price maximums for altogether 900 commodities, 130 different grades of labor, and a considerable number of freight rates.[27] Price ceilings had been tried earlier by rulers during the Republic period, but the *Edict* was on a much more prodigious scale. It required producing an annual budget based on a complete demographic census of the Empire and also directed that government payments and receipts be made in kind, rather than in money, wherever appropriate and possible. Finally, the *Edict* called for overhaul of the administration system.[28]

Diocletian attempted to address the issue of debasement and tried to normalize the coinage, especially the *denarius*. In essence, the *Edict* was an overambitious drive to restore monetary and economic order in the Roman Empire, which by that time had already been decaying for many years. But Diocletian and his government obviously lacked sufficient resources to implement the new laws. In the end, all their efforts were in vain. As it happened, silver *denarii* had become so thin and small, with such little silver content, that further debasement of them was not possible at the beginning of the fourth century. Diocletian had to agree to switch to minting copper coins, which was in effect a debasement from silver *denarii*.

An economic historian specializing in the Roman Empire has noted: "The great inflation of the third century had a permanent effect in reducing the real wages and salaries of all employees of the State."[29] Soldiers were increasingly paid in kind – food and clothes, among many other things. The value of cash payments to them, mostly in *denarii*, must have declined considerably in real terms.

Constantine I (306–337) did many things to save the Roman Empire, especially its eastern part, early in the fourth century. One of them was to implement the minting of a solid gold coin, the *solidus*, to replace the older, undervalued *aureus*. Diocletian had already had the idea, but he did not have the time and resources to do it before his abdication in 305. From 312, the *solidus* began to spread widely, and it remained in circulation in the subsequent Byzantine Empire – the Eastern Roman Empire, which existed for many centuries after the fall of the Western Roman Empire.

Sung, Jurchen, and Mongol rule: the world's first paper currency hyperinflation

After a thousand years had elapsed, China once again witnessed episodes of monetary adventure and high inflation in the early second millennium BC. But unlike previous occasions, paper money had arrived, and it helped worsen the situation.

Techniques of durable paper making were invented in the early second century (Later Han Dynasty). Around that time, the Chinese learned the methodology of seal making from Persia. During the middle of the eleventh century, a printing press was created in the capital city of the Northern Sung Dynasty (960–1127). Given the availability of these technologies, their combined application to make paper money was just a matter of time.

Earlier, in the middle of the Tang Dynasty (618–907) – a period when China was prosperous and commercially developed, an invention known as "Flying Money" was created. It was essentially bills of exchange, which a business person or government treasury official could use to send money from one city to another without physically transporting the funds. These bills were actually documents of certification printed and hallmarked on pieces of textile cloth. The invention may have inspired people in later times, when improvements in monetary arrangements were needed.

Such a situation occurred in Chengdu, Sichuan, in the early years of the second millennium.[30] Before that time, heavy iron coins had been struck by the court, and they caused inconvenience in circulation. Coincidently, when the city was once besieged during a peasant uprising, local business people thought of using paper-printed certificates as a means of payment between them. A small circle of 16 business people was formed for the circulation of the new invention.[31] They called it *Jiao-zi* (*Chiao-tzu*), which in Chinese means certificate of delivery or exchange.

The idea of paper money, which had originated in the private sector, was later adopted by the bureaucracy, who in the first instance exercised self-restraint by conducting the experiment on a regional scale. A special government agency was set up for the issuing and recalling of a new version of *Jiao-zi*, and the issue was both restrained in amount and subject to periodic review. At the time when the official *Jiao-zi* was first launched in 1023, it was convertible to coins. Sometimes, its value was higher than that of coins of the same denomination. Apparently, the paper money made trade and commerce more convenient.

Decades later, in the 1070s, Northern Sung emperors waged wars against rising neighboring forces. Issues of *Jiao-zi* began to expand. By 1107, the total amount of *Jiao-zi* issued was 20 times the initial level in 1023. *Jiao-zi* had rapidly devalued against coins, and price surges were widely reported. The dynasty had to abandon the notorious paper notes and replace them with new ones. The new notes were also made convertible to coins, but their issue was safeguarded by a reserve scheme under which 40 percent of any new issue had to be accompanied by additional coin reserves.

Hui-zi and hyperinflation in the Southern Sung

The Northern Sung regime lost its battles against the Jurchen (Nu-chen Tartars), from the north, and had to retreat to southern China. In 1127, it moved its capital to Hangzhou and started to rule just over half of China, mainly the Yangtze River valley and neighboring regions. This was the Southern Sung Dynasty, which lasted about 150 years. During its later years, the regime aligned with the Mongols and again fought the Jurchen. Yet soon afterward, it came under massive attack from the Mongols and ultimately collapsed.

Economy and commerce during the Southern Sung were better than before. Many new areas in the Yangtze valley were cultivated and became fertile. Trade with India and the Arabic world started along maritime routes and flourished. Except in areas at war, total output and income tended to grow, along with population. The Southern Sung Dynasty could expect rather stable revenue for most of its years, until tensions and hostilities with the Mongols broke out in the early 1240s.

Hui-zi (*Hui-tzu*), which in Chinese means certificate of meeting, was a nationally standardized *Jiao-zi* under the auspices of the bureaucracy from 1161 onward. In its first few decades, the court kept a close eye on the issue of the paper currency and, indeed, avoided inflationary expansion. Under an early arrangement, the paper notes were recalled, i.e., redeemed for copper coins, every three years. The period of three years was a term. At the start of a new term, new *Hui-zi* was issued to the public. The practice was kept basically unchanged until the last decade of the twelfth century, when budget needs for military spending ballooned, and emperors decided to lift the cap on issuance of the paper notes and let them inflate.

Based on court records of *Hui-zi* issues and raw rice price data, modern scholars have been able to compile indexes of money supply and price levels. One estimate shows that between 1161 and 1240, the total amount of *Hui-zi* issued increased 48.5 times, at an annual average rate of 5 percent. Meanwhile, price levels rose 39.3 times, averaging 4.7 percent annually.[32] The two rates were neither constant nor steady during the period. For instance, in the decade of the 1230s, the issue of *Hui-zi* increased about 80 percent, whilst price levels rose 1,002 percent, at an average annual rate of 28 percent. It is possible that in certain years during this period, or in some months during one of the years, price levels rose more than 500 percent annually or 50 percent monthly.

For most of the time, the *Hui-zi* was apparently not backed by any reserve or commodity money. The government required pecuniary taxation to be contributed in *Hui-zi* and occasionally sold its gold and silver to retire the paper currency.[33] In general, it was not convertible to metal coins. The banking system at that time remained in a primitive state, and the government did not rely on any financial institution to operate the paper currency. Moreover, at least six provinces issued their own paper currencies. They often pledged to maintain convertibility between the paper currencies and metal coins or silver, yet invariably failed to do so.

Hyperinflation in the Jurchen

High inflation certainly damaged the economy and commerce in the last decades of the Sung regime. Several years before the final fall of the Sung Dynasty in 1279, a key cabinet minister submitted a testimony to an emperor, saying that the Jurchen – a regime in northern China from 1115–1234 – had been destroyed by the Mongols as well as by its over-issuance of paper money and the consequent high inflation. He urged the court to change the course of its monetary management.[34]

The Jurchen people arose along China's northeastern borders. Not long before, they had been mostly nomads living on grasslands, primarily by hunting and grazing. From frequent contact and confrontation with the Sung, they soon became able to capitalize on weaknesses of China's corrupt regime, including its disorganized manpower. Upon occupying northern China, they also quickly learned from the Chinese how to apply social and economic management methodologies in the territory, including the issue of coinage and paper currency. For a time, the Jurchen were between the rising Mongols in the north and the falling Sung in the south. The Jurchen and the Sung were sometimes in alliance against the threat of invading Mongols. But the Jurchen were the force that had previously driven the Sung into the south. The Jurchen-Sung coalition did not last long for this and other reasons. The Jurchen found that they had to fight the mighty Mongols alone from 1211 onward, but obviously lacked sufficient resources.

The Jurchen first printed paper notes, called *Jiao-chao*, in 1154. *Chao* thus became the Chinese word for paper currency notes, used through to today. The *Jiao-chao* was convertible to copper coins for most of the period up to 1215. During the *Jiao-chao's* first five decades, the exchange rate between it and copper coins remained basically stable, and government agencies could impose surcharges for conversion between the two.

When war with the Mongols broke out in 1211, the Jurchen began to print large-denominated *Jiao-chao* and continuously ran their printing presses to issue more of them. At one time, supplies of paper were exhausted, and printing had to be suspended. Four years later, in 1215, circulation of copper coinage was outlawed in order to make more room for the *Jiao-chao*, which that year was worth 1,000 times less than it had been in 1211. The court started to impose price controls, especially in the capital city and its surrounding areas.

By the end of the Jurchen regime in 1234, the combined face value of its issued notes had exploded by over 20 billion times, with most of the increase occurring in a period of around a decade.[35] There are few records of comparative price data in Chinese historical documents, and what has been narrated mostly concerns the rapid devaluation of *Jiao-chao* against copper coins or silver. This may suggest that during the late Jurchen regime, people were hardly using *Jiao-chao* in their daily transactions. Nevertheless, if they were, the prices of commodities that they traded in *Jiao-chao* must have experienced hyperinflation comparable to any modern episode of the phenomenon by contemporary criteria.

When the Jurchen regime crashed, Mongol forces began to overwhelm the land of the Southern Sung, and China became part of the Mongolian Empire.

Paper currency under Mongol rule

While the Mongols set about conquering the whole of China, their regional forces started to issue and use paper money in their own right. Once a centralized regime was established, Mongol rulers began to consolidate the currency systems. Aware of the experiences of the Jurchen and the Sung, they appeared for a while to be determined to do it better than their predecessors, and there is evidence suggesting that they did so in the first few decades.

First, when a national paper currency was initially issued in 1260 during the reign of Khubilai Khan (1260–94), Mongol authorities guaranteed its convertibility into silver and maintained the exchange rate between the two. For this, the Mongol rulers in China – known as the Yuan Dynasty (1206–1368) – established a special agency to manage monetary reserves. The practice certainly helped win the confidence and trust of the public.

Second, when the Mongols decided to suspend the convertibility in 1285, they also started to prohibit the use of silver, gold, and copper coins in exchange and trade. This in effect created a monopoly for the paper currency they issued and circulated. The Sung, by contrast, did not make metal coins illegal when paper currency was in operation.

Third, the design and manufacture of paper notes had improved considerably. Simple text printed on the notes was bilingual in Mongolian and Chinese.[36] This would have made the currency welcome by both Mongol and Chinese people.

Fourth, Khubilai Khan appointed a Muslim as his financial chief to take charge of all monetary and budgetary affairs. In particular, upon his advice, a country-wide network of monetary reserves and exchange bureaus was established in provinces, and all regional agencies followed a common practice.

During its heyday in the middle of the thirteenth century, the Mongol Empire ruled more than half of the Eurasia landmass. Partly thanks to its liberal and pro-Islam policies, trade routes between East Asia and Europe – on land via Central Asia and by sea to the Middle East and on to the Mediterranean – were reopened. Flows of merchandise, together with dissemination of technology and cultural ideas, flourished between East and West.

Marco Polo, the traveler from Venice, Italy who lived in China for some years in the latter half of the thirteenth century, wrote in his book enthusiastically about the paper notes he saw during the Yuan Dynasty.[37] Muhammad ibn-Batuta, another international traveler, from Morocco, who arrived in China in 1345, also remarked positively on the currency system and business environment in the country.[38] Before these two, a Christian missionary and explorer named William of Rubruck (in today's Belgium) took a trip from Constantinople to China in 1253 and found currency notes printed on cotton cloth.[39]

Under *Pax Mongolica*, not only did transcontinental trade increase, the idea of paper currency also spread afar. Among others, Korea, Vietnam, and Persia are known cases where paper currency was adopted, at least for a while, undoubtedly due to Mongol influence.

Ch'ao in Persia

A notable episode occurred in Persia in the autumn of 1294, when the country was still under Mongol reign. A paper currency called *Ch'ao* was suddenly issued to the public, who were apparently unprepared for it. The government threatened the people with the death penalty if they refused to accept the notes. But even this could not prevent the issue from becoming a total failure. Soon, marketplaces were deserted, and commerce halted. In a little more than two months, the project was aborted – first, by allowing gold to be used in purchasing food, and then, by completely suppressing the issued note. It is also known that this incident took place mainly in Tabriz, Persia's capital city at the time.

The short-lived Ch'ao in Persia was documented in "*History of the World,*" a large book written by Rashid al Din, a Persian statesman and historian.[40]

In China, from the 1280s onward, signs of discontinuity and instability in imperial monetary policy surfaced. At times, silver and gold were allowed to circulate, while at other times, the court even ordered the reminting of copper coins. Later, earlier policies were cancelled or suspended all of a sudden. Policymakers betrayed principles they had earlier followed and often made new decisions haphazardly, apparently following an *ad hoc* or opportunistic approach.

Changing and pressing budgetary needs were reasons for inconsistency in monetary policy. The Mongols never really stopped their territorial expansionism until the end of the thirteenth century. During the first half of the fourteenth century, internal conflicts in mainland China erupted, either revolts by ethnic Chinese or political splits within the ruling class. Toward the end of Mongol rule in mainland China – the 1350s and 1360s – note issues had apparently become the only significant means of raising revenue. The Jurchen's experience of hyperinflation seems to have been duplicated during the last days of the Yuan.

King Henry VIII: great debasement in Renaissance England

In later medieval Europe, there were several historical events that caused inflation. Most notable was the Black Death, which devastated almost the whole of Europe during 1346–53. Price inflation was particularly severe from 1349–51, when according to one measurement, it equaled 33.6 percent annually on average and peaked at 56.3 percent on the same basis.[41] From the early sixteenth century, with the discovery of the New World and floods of new silver supplied from the Americas, Spain experienced triple-digit inflation. Moreover, many kingdoms and principalities in continental Europe conducted coinage debasement in various ways and during different periods through to the end of the eighteenth century. In some countries, the silver content in standard coins was reduced by as much as over 90 percent in less than 50 years. Emerging powers such as Russia and the Ottoman Empire all carried out debasement.[42] As such, inflation was quite common in Europe during this period. Among all the medieval European episodes, that which occurred in England under Henry VIII stands out as one that has been subject to the scrutiny of economic history.

Henry VIII was the second king of the Tudor Monarchy, who reigned in England between 1509 and 1547. He was succeeded, in sequence, by King Edward VI (1547–53), Queen Mary I (1553–58), and Queen Elizabeth I (1558–1603), each of whom was to born to Henry VIII and a different one of his six wives.

Under the House of Tudor, Wales became joined in union with England, with the relevant law taking effect from 1535. From this time, Henry VIII was also declared to be King of Ireland by statute of the Parliament of Ireland. Partly because of his marital and extramarital affairs, he was increasingly in dispute with the Roman Catholic Church and the Holy Roman Empire, and consequentially he helped the Church of England to become independent. The Protestant Reformation movement started to spread into the British Isles. English nationality was awakening, and the Renaissance had crossed the English Channel.

During the later years of his reign, Henry VIII encountered tensions and conflicts with major powers on the European continent, especially France and Spain. He was constantly preparing for military confrontation and occasionally engaged on the battlefield.

Henry VIII was impetuous in decision-making, extravagant in lifestyle, and highly ambitious in the international arena. All of this cost him dearly. Though he inherited colossal wealth and was further enriched by seizing the property of the Catholic Church in England, his royal finances became half exhausted in his last years.

Against this backdrop, Henry VIII started to debase coins beginning in the 1530s. Before his time, gold and silver coins were already widely circulated in England, very much in the same way as in many other European kingdoms and principalities. The first known coin debasement under the Tudors took place in Ireland in 1536, when silver coins were minted and issued which had 90 percent of the precious metal similar earlier ones had contained. Users of the coins appeared to be unaware of the change, and the "experimental" issue went on to succeed. This encouraged further debasement moves in both Ireland and England starting in the 1540s.[43]

Altogether, between 1524 and 1560, there were six mints of silver penny and gold coins under Henry VIII, six under Edward VI, two under Mary I, and two under Elizabeth I.[44] Except the first one and last two, all of these issues were debased. This "Great Debasement" mainly occurred between 1544 and 1551, overlapping the last years of Henry VIII's reign and the reign of Edward VI.

Debasement was achieved by one of three methods: using a lesser weight of precious metal to mint coins of unchanged face value; increasing the weight of cheaper metals such as nickel or copper used to adulterate gold or silver coins; minting coins of higher face value whilst not increasing the content or purity of gold or silver accordingly. All of these methods were ostensibly employed under Henry VIII and Edward VI.[45]

During the period, the true value of silver coins decreased much more than did that of gold coins. The value of a debased silver penny was broadly equivalent to one-fourth of that of earlier non-debased ones. Gold coins, meanwhile, lost merely 17 percent, or maintained 83 percent, of their former value.[46] Such levels of debasement were considerably lower than those instigated in the Roman Empire, yet they still had economic significance.

An estimate indicates that the net profits from royal mints, which expanded from one site to seven sites (including Crown-chartered ones), during the period 1544–51 rose remarkably and even exceeded both the taxation yielded to the court and the net proceeds from the disposal of monastic properties.[47] Without this prime source of revenue, whether it is called "hidden tax" or seigniorage, the reigns of Henry VIII and Edward VI could hardly have been sustained, at least financially.

In theory, the currency debasement, like monetary expansion in modern times, could serve either for avoidance of deflation in a case of population and output growth or for making of inflation. Data compiled by contemporary economists suggest that inflation indeed occurred during the period. Grain prices in England had already risen in the 1510s and 1520s by 28.6 percent compared with the two previous decades. Price rises gained a little acceleration in the 1530s and 1540s; reaching 28.9 percent compared with the two previous decades. And, inflation then escalated in the 1550s and 1560s to stand at 90.8 percent over the same comparative period. Meanwhile, prices of manufactured goods rose most quickly during the 1550s and 1560s: by 69.7 percent compared with the two previous decades.[48] These figures appear to be quite moderate by modern standards. Grain prices rose merely 3.3 percent per annum and those of manufactured goods climbed 2.7 percent during the two decades from 1550–69. Yet, we should be reminded that many English people then were living at the subsistence level, and for them, a small change in the value of money earned or held would probably have had a huge impact on their living standards.

Data indeed show that nominal wages increased much slower than grain prices or those of manufactured goods: 48.2 percent during 1550–69 over the preceding two decades.[49] As silver coins were mainly used in domestic commerce and daily retail transactions, and their devaluation was more than that of gold coins, people must have been severely affected by the "Great Debasement."

When Henry VIII first conducted a mint of debased coins, he ordered price control measures and forbade people from hiking prices in the name of the new currency. Though the effort was in vain,[50] it nevertheless showed that the inflationary effects of debasement were well acknowledged.

It is known that during the early years of the sixteenth century, annual interest rates on loans in England averaged about 10 percent. It is also known that Edward VI took a loan with an interest rate of 14 percent in 1547, Mary I paid interest at the rate of 12 percent in 1558, and Elizabeth I did so at 10 percent in 1561.[51] Apparently, there was a rise in interest rates in the first half of the century, and the magnitude of the rise was not small. Price inflation then was by all measures considerably lower than interest rates, as we have seen. Coin debasement and the related price inflation could not by themselves fully explain the large rise in interest rates.

With regard to the later fall in interest rates during the reign of Mary I and the early years of Elizabeth I, underlying inflation again may not be a sufficient explanation. Some historians have attributed the fall in interest rates to developments in England's credit markets as well as the start of English use of the Netherlands' financial market – for the latter, the merchant and financier Thomas Gresham was once dispatched to Antwerp by Elizabeth I to handle financial dealings on behalf of the English monarchy.[52] Documents show, in fact, that Antwerp's lending to the English had already started in 1544, when Henry VIII was still active.[53]

A more plausible explanation of the changes in interest rates in England during that period has something to do with Gresham's Law – in a bimetallistic monetary environment, when people are able to identify bad money and good money, the former drives out the latter. Presumably, during the 1540s and 1550s, when debased coins were in circulation and increasingly became known as such, non-debased ones ("good money") were accordingly kept out of the market. The total money supply in England may thus have decreased. If this was the case, it would be no surprise to see interest rates rise faster than price inflation, or to see interest rates fall in later years while inflation tended to remain.

Elizabeth I's return to a policy of non-debasement[54] should be therefore seen as conducive to stabilization of England's growing money market and falls in interest rates therein. Among the many factors that contributed to the rise of England under the reign of Elizabeth I, in Europe as well as in the world, the departure from debasement and falls in interest rates may have been a small, yet not unimportant, help.

The Ming and Ching: aborted paper currencies amidst the menace of hyperinflation

In its reign of 277 years (1368–1644) in China, the Ming Dynasty had paper currency in operation only for 61 years (1375–1435). It was in this brief period that Ming rulers encountered serious problems of inflation and ultimately decided to abandon their paper currency system.

The first Emperor of the Ming, Chu Yuan-chang, was a leader of rebel forces against the Mongol Empire. He must have witnessed the economic chaos resulting from the excessive paper note issues in the late Yuan. Before his final success in taking over the entire country, he ordered in 1361 the casting of copper coins, apparently with the aim of providing a new national currency. It was 14 years later, in 1375, that he made the switch to paper currency. An explanation is that the new regime lacked sufficient copper supplies, and the costs of coin making had become too high.[55]

But circulation of metal commodity money – old coins and silver – was not forbidden until 20 years later. The attempt to eliminate metal money was met with great difficulties, and it was the third Emperor – Yung Lo (meaning "Everlasting Pleasure" in Chinese), who was a son of the first Emperor and who overthrew the legitimate second Emperor by force – who reinforced the measure in order to take advantage of the paper currency system to finance his military campaigns. A few years later, when his power was consolidated, the restrictive policy on the use of coins and silver was largely relaxed.

During the later years of Chu Yuan-chang and earlier years of Yung Lo, when paper currency was in circulation exclusively, rice prices galloped ahead in terms of the currency unit. Estimates based on loosely defined figures suggest that in the former case, rice prices in the new currency rose 6.6 percent annually for 50 years (a 25-fold increase altogether); and in the latter case, they rose 11.2 percent annually for 32 years (a 30-fold increase altogether).[56] Other estimates show that large rises in prices – in terms of gold, silver, copper coins, and grain – occurred between 1375 and 1402 and again between 1407 and 1426.[57] From a modern point of view, these episodes are like periods of chronic inflation. Yet, it is unlikely that the inflation occurred in a steady manner. Most probably, inflation jumped in some of the years and, thus, was more like hyperinflation.

On the other hand, deflation – falling prices in terms of old coins or silver – would also have happened. When the government made their circulation illegal, their effective supply must have diminished. As a logical result, prices in terms of them would have fallen. Had this been significant, farmers who sought to maintain their purchasing power in markets could have suffered.

Problems of instability in the early Ming monetary system are believed to have prompted later emperors to change course by allowing the circulation of silver and gradually shifting away from paper currency. Ming authorities resumed the minting of copper coins from the 1430s and maintained the practice throughout the remaining years of the dynasty. Nevertheless, silver gained increasing strength in circulation. Land tax, a major contribution to government revenue, was allowed to be paid, partially or wholly, in silver from the mid-1450s onward. In the subsequent sixteenth century and first half of the seventeenth century, Ming trade with the outside world grew in both total volume and net surplus, the latter of which was paid mostly in silver. Worldwide silver supplies had increased considerably beginning in the second half of the sixteenth century, due to the advent of the Age of Discovery and European colonization of the Americas. Monetary developments in China benefited hugely from external trade and changes occurring outside the country.

For most of its duration, the Ming Dynasty enjoyed a prosperous economy and booming commerce. Unlike its predecessors, it had tied its own hands on monetary policy, and this had been salutary for economic improvement. Had it maintained disciplined government finance and social management under a commodity money system, it would not have been toppled by a domestic revolt and would not have let China once again be conquered by a rising foreign power.

Emperor Hsien-feng's monetary adventure

Knowing the lessons from earlier dynasties, the Qing (Ching) Dynasty (1644–1911) managed to be restrained by not resorting to paper currency throughout its entire ruling period of over 200 years. There were only two brief exceptions. The first was the decade 1651–61, when the Qing army was on the way south to crush residual Ming forces. Little detail is known about this instance and its impacts on prices and daily life.[58]

The second episode was from 1853–61, when Emperor Hsien-feng became almost desperate in fighting the Taiping Rebellion. As the Yangtze River valley, by that time the richest region in China, fell into the hands of rebel forces, shortfalls in government finance became dangerously large. Hsien-feng decided to go for a paper currency scheme. By his order, military expenses were all paid in newly issued paper notes.

Meanwhile, Hsien-feng required the recasting of copper coins, apparently following the example of Wang Mang: larger denominations containing smaller proportions of the metal. This was another deceptive debasement. He also ordered the casting of iron coins, apparently due to shortages of copper.

What differentiated Hsien-feng from his Chinese predecessors in monetary conduct was that, upon advice from his treasury ministers, he consented to establish special government agencies for recalling paper notes. These agencies – called Silver Houses or Coin Houses – supposedly performed the function of exchanging paper notes and coins. In principle, there was a two-step conversion: first, holders of paper notes could exchange them for silver notes; second, holders of silver notes could exchange them for silver or copper coins. This way, the government intended to let people believe that paper notes were ultimately convertible to silver or copper coins.

In reality, when receiving requests for note conversions, the government agencies demanded large discounts when supplying silver notes or coins to note holders. As a result, the value of the paper notes could not possibly be sustained.

There were numerous reports describing how prices jumped. Indeed, prices of goods in terms of the paper currency surged when they became available in markets. The values of paper notes in terms of coins and those of coins in terms of silver all fell drastically. The rapid devaluations in the paper notes and debased coins, with the former happening much faster than the latter, should be no surprise.

Nevertheless, estimates based on consistently compiled data indicate that between 1853 and 1856 there was merely a moderate rise in rice prices and general price levels in terms of silver. The year 1857 saw large inflation in both measures; 79.7 percent and 44.3 percent, respectively.[59] One possible cause of this inflation was output losses due to the military campaigns against Taiping revolts.

It is pretty certain that Hsien-feng's paper currency plan was basically unsuccessful right from the outset. Many provinces were reportedly hesitant in following the Emperor's order, and the most affected region was the capital city, Beijing, and its neighboring areas. When a new Emperor was enthroned in 1862 upon the death of Hsien-feng, he immediately renounced the paper currency scheme. The Qing Dynasty remained in a mixed, largely unregulated, commodity money system until its fall in 1911.

Wan Mao-in was a court councilor who advised Emperor Hsien-feng to issue paper notes. His main idea was to maintain the existing mixed monetary system, while the government could seek to issue a convertible paper currency. The latter step was a reflection of the practice adopted by the first emperor of the Yuan Dynasty in his earlier years. Wan went a step further by suggesting the establishment of partnerships with private financial institutions in note issuing and underwriting. This proposal was unprecedented in China at the time. When writing his *Das Kapital* in London, Karl Marx noted reports that mentioned Wan's policy recommendation and suspected he would be punished by the court. Indeed, Wan was subsequently censured and removed from his position.[60] Hsien-feng's paper currency scheme did not follow any improvement in social institutions or economic thought, and this was why he achieved much less than his predecessors in the conduct of monetary policy.

To summarize the many episodes of inflation and monetary adventures in China, we should first recognize that they occurred in a very distinctive cultural and political environment, so they may not be readily comparable to what happened elsewhere. China has had a long history of money and finance, but credit markets remained basically primitive until the modern era. Interest rates in private markets tended to be high and volatile over time.[61] Up to the early twentieth century, there had been no case of a government borrowing, either internally or externally, to finance its budgetary needs, except for a few occasions when the Late Qing requested a few loans from foreign banks. The idea of government securities bearing interest never came into the minds of Chinese rulers until the end of the nineteenth century. In the West, issue of convertible banknotes commenced before circulation of paper currency began, but in China, these developments occurred in the reverse order. Rulers of China in the past tended to believe that money is a handy, though sometimes also hazardous, instrument that they should make best use of whenever necessary and permitted by conditions. The incidence of hyper-inflation in China during the first half of the twentieth century further reflects the line of monetary thought.

Paper currency and the American Revolution

When people in the British colonies in North America sought to gain independence and waged war against the British expedition army in the 1770s, they resorted to a paper currency scheme to finance their budget. Almost a century later, when civil war broke out between the Federal North and Confederate South in the first half of the 1860s, the two sides both took advantage of paper currency to fill financial gaps, though to different extents. In both cases, inflation soared. At one extreme, the Confederate South almost solely relied on paper currency issues to finance its budget deficits and inevitably fell into the trap of near-hyperinflation.

John Kenneth Galbraith, the noted American economist, remarks in his book on the history of money: "If the history of commercial banking belongs to the Italians and of central banking to the British, that of paper money issued by a government belongs indubitably to the Americans."[62] He obviously speaks in the context of the Christian world, but nevertheless highlights an unusual tradition in U.S. monetary history. Inflations in the United States before the twentieth century had historical roots in addition to current reasons.

Like many of their European counterparts, the English Monarchy and subsequent British Empire ferociously pursued mercantilist policy in their international and colonial endeavors from the seventeenth century onward. A strong view of mercantilism was that money – gold and silver – constituted national wealth, and a country could be better off only if she maintained a trade surplus. This view, also known as bullionism, greatly affected Britain's policies towards her colonies in the New World. The notorious Navigation Acts in the 1650s, which prohibited the colonies in North America from trading with other European countries, were largely motivated by mercantilist considerations.

For many years before the 1770s, the colonies in North America had had trade deficits with England. Even in years when the colonies had trade surpluses with England, no payment in specie was allowed to be disbursed to exporters in America. With the population growing and the economy expanding in New England and other colonies in North America, people there were increasingly encountering problems of money shortage.

Throughout the seventeenth century, many goods were used as forms of money in the colonies, from nails to wampum (a shell bead fashioned by indigenous North Americans) and from playing cards to tobacco.[63] Tobacco was a popular currency in Virginia and Maryland, where it had become a staple export. In regions where there was a scarcity of suitable candidates for payments in kind, people had to barter with each other. In commerce, a system of debits and credits was also invented to overcome the trouble of money shortage and inconvenience of barter.

With this system, sellers of goods could keep balances on accounts which they would use to buy at later dates, and buyers had to either first sell or acknowledge their indebtedness in the accounts.

In 1690, the Massachusetts Bay Colony issued paper notes to its soldiers and promised to redeem them in gold or silver. A historian has acclaimed the event as "not only the origin of paper money in America, but also in the British Empire and almost in the Christian world."[64] Indeed, it was 15 years earlier than John Law's publication and 25 years earlier than his monetary experiment in France. Two decades later, "tobacco notes" were issued and used in Virginia as a substitute for money. In plain words, these were tobacco-convertible paper currency.

In order to earn specie and minimize exploitation by British mercantilism, colonial people increasingly engaged in smuggling with the Dutch and Spanish, among others. This caused numerous conflicts between the locals and their overlords.

By British regulation, colonial governors had no right to make coins on their own. Therefore, no debasement was possible at all. In the 1750s, the Board of Trade – a body in London dealing with colonial economic and trade affairs on behalf of the Kingdom – issued orders to disallow paper money issues in the colonies. Monetary conflicts between the colonies and the Kingdom were thus further aggravated, in addition to the already heated disputes over policies pertinent to economy, trade, and taxation.

Despite opposition and oppression from the Kingdom, the idea of paper currency had already spread in the colonies, and it gained support from educated merchants and intellectuals. Benjamin Franklin published a pamphlet in 1729 titled "*Modest Enquiry into the Nature and Necessity of a Paper Currency*," urging Great Britain to allow colonial provinces to issue paper notes as a form of money. In 1746, he actually conducted a "personal" paper-note experiment by printing an IOU to give to a merchant as evidence of his borrowing.[65]

When hostilities with Britain began in the mid-1770s, the nascent regime in North America had no financial resources available. Trade was largely cut off by the British navy. Foreign aid from France and Spain had to wait a few years. There were virtually no domestic banking system and securities market by which formal and large-scale borrowing could be sought. There were numerous voluntary contributions from revolutionaries and occasional lending by rich merchants who sided with independence, but they were small in amount. Most importantly, the leaders of the Revolution were loath to impose taxation – the very thing they saw as the reason for their rebellion against British rule.

When the Continental Congress met in 1775, it was decided that bills of credit should be issued in order to fund George Washington's military campaigns. A special committee – the Board of Treasury – was created to supervise the financial conduct of the new regime. The body immediately took charge of regulating the exchange rates between the bills and the various foreign coins that were circulating in the 13 colonies. It also stipulated that the amount of the issue should not exceed two million Spanish silver dollars.[66] Because subscriptions for the bills were supposed to come from individual colonies, and some of them were reluctant to deliver specie in full, the Continental Congress and Washington faced severe difficulties in finance. The value of Continental bills outstanding had exceeded 30 million dollars by 1778, 150 million dollars by 1779, and 240 million dollars by 1780.

Initially, the Continental Congress promised to redeem the bills with specie in the future, and continental bills issued then did not bear interest, which was the reason why Benjamin Franklin opposed the initiative at that time. Later on, as the difficulty of raising funds in specie became increasingly clear, the promise of specie convertibility broke down. The Continental Congress had to agree to pay interest on all bills of credit it issued. The interest rate was set first at 4 percent then later at 5 percent or 6 percent. In order to make continental bills widely acceptable, the Congress and individual colonies (states from 1783 onward) endeavored to make them legal tender. But these efforts achieved mixed results and only limited success before the mid-1780s.

Inflation began to soar from 1776, the year when independence was declared and war started. Measured with a wholesale price index, the annual inflation rate reached 38 percent that year and jumped to 205 percent the next year. After decelerating in 1778, it surged to 396 percent in 1779.[67] At one time in 1779, 70 dollars in paper were worth less than one dollar in silver. In 1781, as it turned out, the cost of printing a Continental dollar exceeded its value as currency.[68] This was obviously a situation similar to hyperinflation by modern definitions.

Severe inflation caused many problems to the new regime and its fight against British force. Many local people tried to avoid accepting the bills and to use old metal coins if they had them. Retail businesses went from place to place to barter. Supplies to Washington's army sometimes became unstable, in part due to financial distress related to monetary problems.

In dealing with rising inflation, the Congress and various regional governors and later states resorted to price controls. Price regulation was used in several colonies as early as the seventeenth century, but it had not become mainstream policy. It was severity of inflation that prompted many opinion leaders to call for it. Even Thomas Payne, a most liberal political activist, advocated for price controls.[69] Public announcement of price ceilings for essential goods was common practice when price controls were implemented during the Revolutionary period. Because authorities did little to regulate supply and demand as well when price controls were introduced, the effort did not stop inflation, although it may have helped slow its pace. In June 1778, the Continental Congress resolved to lift price controls, as it believed that the measures were not effective and to make them effective, more harmful measures would be required.[70] As a result, inflation exploded in the following year.

Speculation, hoarding, and paper-note counterfeiting were ubiquitous in the emerging republic. As price inflation sharply outstripped the interest rate on Continental bills, their value fell endlessly.

Four factors are believed to have contributed to stabilization from 1781. First, aid and loans from France and other European countries arrived. French loans to America amounted to several million livres by the early 1780s, and part of them could be repaid in tobacco exported to France. A large proportion of the funds was used to establish a federal-affiliated bank, which later helped stabilize credit to the United States government.

Second, a debt-for-debt swap program was undertaken, and the government thence became able to return to specie convertibility. From 1781, old Continental bills were required to be exchanged for new ones at the compulsory rate of 40:1.[71] New bills also bore interest of 5 percent. They were silver convertible as well, largely thanks to the government having increased its silver holdings considerably by way of foreign aid and resumed trade flows.

Third, the Congress agreed on taxation, which soon became a stable source of revenue for the government. This also helped reduce its reliance on note-issue financing significantly. For most of the time, the interest burden of 5 percent on its bills could also be sustained, as revenue kept growing and pressures of expenditure became alleviated as the war approached its end and peace returned.

Fourth and perhaps most importantly, the military situation shifted toward the American side before the end of 1781, and victories on the battlefield greatly reinforced people's confidence in the new currency notes issued by the new republic. The public's trust in government promises also increased. Needless to say, the large deflation in 1781 – wholesale prices went down by 52 percent that year – meant that interest of 5 percent on new paper notes was really a tremendous gain.

In short, paper currency and its resultant inflation were, in this case, a short-lived experience that an emerging regime had to resort to when it was reluctant to use explicit tax methods. In doing so, it gained financially at the start, but encountered numerous problems later on. At certain times, it was even in danger itself, as the paper notes were rapidly losing value and being rejected by people who were suppliers to the Revolution and the cause of independence. Had the inflation become worse or been coupled with a few other mishaps, it is possible that the North American colonies might have had to wait for another opportunity to rise up in pursuit of independence.

Assignats and hyperinflation during the French Revolution

The hyperinflation that occurred in France in the last decade of the eighteenth century created a record in the history of inflation in Europe before the twentieth century. The level of price inflation in revolutionary France was considerably higher than that in the American Revolution a decade previously or that in the American Civil War in the 1860s.

The French hyperinflation in the mid-1790s was the first one in Europe to derive from paper currency. Before that, a paper currency system on a national scale had been tried in the country early in the same century, largely by a financier and adventurer named John Law, who was originally from Scotland. The experiment was a debacle. Yet, the revolutionists decades later seem to have had no alternative in dealing with financial emergencies other than the use of a paper currency. The second exercise of paper currency in France – actually together with its third, in 1796 – ended up with even higher, explosive inflation. The aftermath of the hyperinflation rendered Napoleon in pursuit of a different financial policy, which did not help him gain victory over the British.

John Law and his paper currency experiment in France

John Law (1667–1729) was born into a family of bankers and goldsmiths in Scotland. Between 1695 and 1705 he lived in the Netherlands and France, having escaped from likely retribution in England for his mischief there. In 1705, he had a pamphlet published in Edinburgh entitled *"Money and Trade Consider'd with a Proposal for Supplying the Nation with Money."* In essence, it was a prospectus presented to the Scottish Parliament outlining his grand plan for a national bank and paper currency scheme.

The book demonstrated his innovative thinking in the economics of monetary theory. Right from its start, he challenged the view of John Locke – an influential thinker and opinion leader in Britain – on the role of money. Locke spoke of money's "imaginary value" as a repudiation to mercantilism. Law, however, praised the role of money in industry, trade, and employment. He is quoted as saying, "When blood does not circulate throughout the body, the body languishes; the same when money does not circulate."[72] With regard to metals, he believed silver superior to gold and copper. But he also believed that the value of silver was on the decline. It is from this point that he formed his idea of paper currency – a form of money with value guaranteed by a security whose value shall never fall. Such a security may be either a claim to the yields of land or an interest-bearing government bond, for the latter of which money should be invested into lucrative projects.

Unlike all previous episodes of paper currency in China or elsewhere in the Mongolian Empire, John Law's idea was largely based on a monetary theory that ties the function of money with the work of the banking system. Also different from the previously existing fully convertible banknotes mainly used as a means of payment for the sake of convenience, Law actually suggested a new type of banknote – one that could and should bear interest, so that it was superior to other ones. Probably for this reason, Joseph Schumpeter, a great economist in the first half of the twentieth century, eulogizes him by saying that he "worked out the economics of his projects with a brilliance and, yes, profundity, which places him in the front rank of monetary theorists of all time."[73]

Nevertheless, he did not achieve anything in Scotland or in England – the two were undergoing unionization to form the United Kingdom in 1707. He turned to France but had to wait until about ten years later, when the Duke of Orleans, the then Regent following the death of King Louis XIV, agreed to his grand plan in 1716.[74] Louis XIV's lavish lifestyle and aggressive foreign policy had left royal France hugely indebted. Under the auspices of the Duke of Orleans, Law was able to establish a bank, Banque Générale, which was renamed Royal Bank two years later, and to start issuing interest-bearing and silver-convertible paper notes. Meanwhile, Law bought or acquired several companies, with royal charters for monopolies, which aimed to explore lucrative opportunities in French colonies in North America – notably, the Mississippi Company to engage in business in

Louisiana (this is the cause of the later incident known as the Mississippi Bubble). With a note-issuing bank and several commercial companies under one umbrella, Law proudly called it the "System."

Apparently upon Law's recommendation, the French government decided to debase gold and silver coins by 40 percent in 1718. It was believed that debasement would help to promote exports. Law was further appointed as chief financial officer of France (Controller General) in 1720, when he promised to underwrite the entire public debt of the French government.[75]

Before 1720, share prices of the Mississippi Company soared to a high level, and note issues by the Royal Bank went extremely well. From early in that year, however, the situation started to reverse. Depositors began to use the paper notes to buy shares of the Company and then sell them for gold coins. In order to support the share price, Law issued more notes, but that resulted in more withdrawal of deposits and conversion into gold coins. Law requested the French government to limit the use of gold coins in the economy, but it was in vain. By the end of 1720, Law had been dismissed from all of his positions in France. He had to run away again, and the System fell apart.

Prices in France gradually moved up from 1719 onward, partly due to other, unrelated events such as poor recent harvests. An unweighted arithmetic index of wholesale commodity prices rose 63 percent year on year in September 1719.[76] France returned to her metallic currency regime.

The French Revolution and assignats

Ironically, John Law's scheme of paper currency was recalled into service seven decades later in France, despite having left a bad memory in the minds of French people. Before the Revolution, King Louis XVI endured great financial difficulties and once consulted people about reintroducing paper currency. But, the proposal was rejected outright.

The new regime that emerged in the first months of the Revolution faced fiscal problems similar to those experienced by the North American colonists seeking independence and was also loath to increase taxation. After some hesitation and debate, the National Assembly finally agreed to issue a new type of paper note – interest-bearing *assignats* collateralized on the land and properties confiscated from churches all over France. Initially, the notes were issued in large denominations such as 200, 300, and 1,000 *livres*. Later, the denominations were made as small as 50 *livres*.[77]

These notes were irredeemable but securitized on the value of land and properties seized by the new regime that were to be sold in the market. The total value of the land and properties was expected to be 2,000 million *livres* at the time the issuance of *assignats* was contemplated.[78]

Some economists see the *assignat* as a "land standard,"[79] and others, a "tax-backed money" scheme.[80] The latter refers to the way in which the government supported the notes (*assignats*) by its effective tax revenue. More precisely, they were short-term securities initially issued for debt service, not as a medium of exchange, for the purpose of increasing government spending until 1792. The *assignat* actually became a medium of exchange from 1792, when France was at war with a number of European powers.[81]

A strong supporter of the *assignat* publicly remarked: "Paper money under despotism is dangerous; it favors corruption; but in a nation constitutionally governed, which itself takes care in the emission of its notes, which determines their number and use, that danger no longer exists."[82]

Assignats were issued with a date of maturity, and they bore interest of 3 percent.[83] At the start, the total amount of the issue was said not to exceed 1,200 million, and they were to be immediately burned once returned to the treasury for land and properties.[84]

From late 1791, price inflation started to rise, and the market value of *assignats* also fell. The value of the 100 *livres* note was down to about 80 *livres* in Paris and soon fell to about 68 *livres*. At the end of February, 1792, it was further down, to 53 livres.[85] Certain provinces and districts in France also began to issue their own *assignats* in small denominations.[86]

In the year when the First Republic of France was established, the new regime tried and executed King Louis XVI, which enraged many European monarchs. War occurred first with Austria but eventually escalated to such an extent that France stood alone against almost the whole of Europe. At home, the Jacobins seized power and instigated their "Reign of Terror," which lasted less than two years. The new leaders, however, desperately needed finance, and they expanded *assignat* issues to ever greater scales.

By the end of 1795, the total value of *assignats* issued amounted to 45,000 million *livres*, though 6,000 million *livres'* worth of the notes had been annulled and burned earlier. Prices rose from an index number of 100 in 1790 to 3,100 in September 1795 and, more explosively, to 38,850 in May 1796.[87] Meanwhile, of their original value, *assignats* were worth half in early 1793, 25 percent in June-July that year, less than 1 percent in November 1795, and finally, a mere 0.36 percent in February 1796, when they were officially withdrawn by a new regime.[88] In May 1793, price controls on food were announced by the government, which tried to impose price ceilings for major food staples produced in the country. The regulation was revised twice in September and once again in November.[89] The year 1793 produced good harvests in France, but that did not prevent food prices from rising fast. The price controls are believed to have contributed to decline in agricultural output in 1794.[90]

In August 1795, France passed a new constitution, and the Directory took power. The Directory sought to secure "forced loans" from the wealthier classes, but did not achieve anything in this regard. In 1796, it turned to a new paper currency, named *mandats*, which replaced *assignats* with a form of land warrants. The *mandats* promised to pay their holders in terms of public real estate, whose transfer of ownership should take place "without the formalities and delays previously established in regard to the purchase of lands with *assignats*."[91]

In March 1796, when *mandats* were first issued, their price fell to 35 percent of the face value. Soon afterward, it dropped to 15 percent. Subsequently, it declined further to 5 percent. And finally, in August, 1796, the price reached 3 percent of its original level.[92] In 1795, when price controls were abolished, industrial output continued to decline, by as much as 30 percent in some regions,[93] largely due to the effects of rising inflation and war. Neglecting the procedural problems holders of *assignats* or *mandats* experienced when using them to purchase properties, fixed interest rates for the notes of 3 percent or 5 percent would make them sufficiently appealing economically if price inflation remained at low levels. But when price inflation rose above such levels, it inevitably resulted in the public shunning these paper notes. Once that occurred, inflation probably accelerated. John Law and revolutionary regimes in France invented securities-backed paper currency, but they failed to adjust the interest rates on the securities that underwrote paper note issues. Among all the factors that contributed to the failure of either *assignats* or *mandats* and the subsequent occurrence of rising inflation, the inability to adjust interest rates would be one of technical significance.

In 1796, prices in France rose 4,235 percent compared with those of the previous year and also reached a level 24,060 percent above those of 1789.[94] Later in 1796, the Directory decided to abandon the *mandats* and effectively let France return to a commodity money system. In the words of a noted American economist, *assignats* "have at least as good a claim on memory as the guillotine."[95]

A footnote: French and British experiences in financing the Napoleonic wars

The Napoleonic wars, if counting their start from 1796, lasted 20 years and ultimately ended in 1815. France was almost completely alone in fighting an array of continental European monarchs and, in particular, from 1803 onward, against the British on a global scale. The costs of the wars were undoubtedly huge for both sides.

A monetary economist in the late nineteenth century once wondered why Napoleon had never resorted to paper money to finance the wars at any time during such a long period. Milton Friedman replied to the question a century later by referring to the "*assignat* hyperinflation" that helped bring Napoleon to power and the credibility he would have lacked if he had opted for paper currency again. On the other hand, Friedman believes nations necessarily resort to currency depreciation when waging major wars. Britain during the Napoleonic wars was such an example in his view.[96]

"Currency depreciation" may also be interpreted as a policy of "inflationary finance," two economists note.[97] They examined the record of British and French financial performance during the Napoleonic wars and found a striking picture: "A financially strong nation" abandoned the gold standard and borrowed heavily, whilst "a financially weaker country" followed more "orthodox" policies by restraining herself from any inflationary means and primarily relying on taxation. They believe it was Britain's strong credibility that allowed her to adopt more flexible policies in financing budget deficits that were growing ever larger due to the effects of the wars.

As noted in their study, France and Britain both suffered a blow in the early 1720s, when the former was hit by the Mississippi Bubble and the latter by the South Sea Bubble. The two followed divergent paths, however, in financial development in subsequent decades. The French government, whether monarchy or revolutionary, defaulted several times on its debts. Each default necessarily resulted in higher interest rates for later bond financing. On the other hand, the British government substantially improved its fiscal system and behaved well in the domestic money markets. It increased transparency in budget and debt management and never defaulted on bonds it had issued. "Britain did not default on its debt during the 100 years following the Glorious Revolution of 1688, which reflected the existence of mechanisms intended to make the state creditworthy."[98]

Therefore, interest rates on British government bonds were significantly lower than those on French ones. Throughout the period, the average yield – the rate of return to bond investors, which also indicates the cost of bond financing – on long- and short-term British government bonds was approximately 5 percent, while that on French ones was over 7 percent. The interest rate difference between the two was at least 2 percentage points.[99]

The disparity in reputation and credibility between Britain and France may well explain why Napoleon did not resort to paper currency, since doing so would quickly re-ignite the flames of hyperinflation and demolish all efforts he had made to win the wars.

What is also interesting is why Britain did not suffer serious inflation when it discarded her *de facto* gold standard in 1797. In that year, specie payments were suspended, which means that banknotes issued by the Bank of England, as well as other notes issued by other banks, could no longer be exchanged for gold or silver. This effectively made the British monetary system one based purely on paper currency. As many episodes in other countries suggest, a pure paper currency system is believed to be highly prone to inflation.

Inflation in England – measured by a wholesale price index (WPI) or a retail price index (RPI) – did rise enormously in 1799 and 1800, with WPI figures of 15.7 percent and 20.8 percent and RPI reaching 13.7 percent and 34.2 percent, respectively.[100] Had the British government lost control of its financial and monetary policy, these high levels of inflation – whether or not they were caused by temporary supply shocks such as trade stoppages – would inevitably have led to even higher levels in later years.

What actually happened, however, is that WPI and RPI turned to disinflation quickly the following year, decelerating to 3.3 percent and 4.5 percent, respectively. Then in 1802, both indicators turned negative. Throughout the period 1797–1815, the annual average rate of WPI was 1.7 percent, and that of RPI was 2.1 percent.[101] Both were below the rates of interest that the United Kingdom government paid on its bonds in that period.

How was Britain able to experience low inflation, when it had conducted "inflationary finance" during the Napoleonic wars? First, the credibility the government had established made the majority of British people largely believe that sudden rises in inflation were truly temporary and would not last. Second, the government did not primarily rely on seigniorage ("inflation tax") for its war finance during the period, which, it is estimated, never rose above 5 percent of the budget deficit, except in 1810 alone, when it reached a little more than 10 percent.[102] Third, the government started to collect income tax – the first instance of such a tax in the modern world – and the new levy was quite successful, as the funds it raised accounted for about 20 percent of total tax revenue toward the end of the war. Last, but not least, as we have already seen, the prevailing interest rates on British government bonds stood above the average inflation rate during the period.

In short, the British example of war finance during the Napoleonic wars demonstrates that a pure paper currency system itself does not necessarily result in hyperinflation and that preventing an inflation explosion requires a number of conditions including transparency, credibility, and prudence in monetary policy.

Contrary experiences of inflation during America's Civil War

When civil war broke out in the United States in 1861, the North (the Union) appeared to be the stronger side: it had a larger population – 21 million against the South's 9 million; a more industrial economy; and a navy that could patrol the entire Atlantic coast of North America. On the other hand, the South (the Confederacy) also had certain advantages: the majority of white people there seemed to be more willing to fight for her cause and, therefore, more "patriotic" than northerners; it had staples of cotton and tobacco that could earn foreign exchange if their export was not obstructed for any reason – the South accounted for half of the United States' total exports before the Civil War; and preparation for a major confrontation started much earlier in the South than in the North. At the time they split, however, it was not absolutely certain which side would win. The outcome hinged on many factors, one of which was finance – what magnitude of financial resources could be mobilized, and how they could be used effectively.

In July 1861, President Lincoln informed Congress that he needed at least $400 million to suppress the southern rebellion.[103] The largeness of this figure can best be seen when it is compared to the federal revenue in previous years: $56 million in 1860 and an annual average of $62 million from 1855–59. In addition, in the years 1858 and 1859, the Federal Government had had budget deficits of $27.5 million and $15.6 million, respectively, and by 1859, the debt accrued by the Federal Government had amounted to $58.5 million.[104] The gross national product of the United States was about $3,500 million in 1859, so the funding suggested by President Lincoln was more than 10 percent of this figure.

As a legacy of the Revolution in the late eighteenth century, taxation in the United States had been kept rather small and rudimentary. The Federal Government had had three main sources of revenue: excise duties on commodities such as liquor and tobacco, tariffs on imports, and land sales. The first was the most important, as it usually accounted for more than half of total taxes before the Civil War. The third was minimal and never became a significant source of revenue. The Homestead Act that was passed in 1862, when southerners withdrew from the Union, helped accelerate land sales in western parts of North America, but the proceeds generated still remained small in amount.

At the request of President Lincoln, Treasury Secretary Salmon Chase immediately began to seek increases in taxation and initiated a number of tax schemes that were known as wartime tax. They included surcharges on stock transactions and stamp duty on bank deposits, as well as inheritance and income taxes. For income tax, the initial flat rate was set at 3 percent for people with yearly income of at least $800. Later, the rate was raised to 5 percent for people with income between $600 and $5,000. A top rate of 10 percent, much less than those of the 1930s and the present day, was also added. In addition, tariffs were enhanced enormously, which gave America a notorious, protectionist reputation in international trade. As it happened, foreign trade flows – both imports and exports – actually stagnated during the Civil War.

Overall, taxes and their overall increase did not contribute much to war finance. An estimate shows that tax revenue accounted for only 20 percent of the Federal Government's wartime budget, while 70 percent was raised through borrowing, and 10 percent came from greenback issues, approximately.[105] Clearly, the secret of the success in wartime finance – the raising of sufficient funds without causing high inflation – lay with the Federal Government's borrowing.

Where did it borrow? It attempted to obtain funding from abroad, but the efforts did not achieve much. Many European governments remained basically neutral to the civil war, and they could not lend significantly to either side. Britain was a possible source of external borrowing, but the United States' relationship with Britain was under strain during the period, and so Washington could secure just a small, private loan from London.[106] Mostly, the United States government borrowed in domestic financial markets.

America's financial system made great progress during the first half of the nineteenth century. Alexander Hamilton, one of the Founding Fathers of the young republic and perhaps the first American statesman to realize the importance of financial markets to the running of government, endeavored to promote the establishment of a central bank and securities market in the United States. Though the government bank system – reflected in the First Bank and the Second Bank of the United States up to the 1830s – did not survive for political reasons, the banking industry and securities market flourished following independence.

Prior to the 1860s, there were more than a thousand banks in operation throughout the continent. Many of them were indeed small ones. Some large private banks emerged, providing credit services to industry and commerce. Securities markets also expanded, with corporations and governments (both federal and state) regularly undertaking bond issues. During the Second American-British War (1812–14), the United States Government borrowed in the domestic money market to finance its ballooning budgets. Bond finance – borrowing funds by issuing tradable debt securities – had become the principal way of funding budget deficits in the United States.

Treasury Secretary Chase relied first on banks to complete his mission to market new bond issues. Soon, he also called upon private agents to sell treasury bonds to the public at large, a mass marketing strategy which became quite successful.

Of the total $400 million worth of bonds planned for issue in 1861, a proportion had to be priced with an interest rate as high as 7.30 percent.[107] The cost was obviously too high. Moreover, the large shipment of specie sent to the government by subscribing banks would inevitably cause severe problems for them, as they were likely to suffer shortages of reserves and operating funds. To overcome these problems, a new system of bank reserves and, indeed, banking was invented; the national banking system, which formally came into effect in February 1862.

Under the new system, banks were required to hold a minimum amount of treasury bonds or notes, which they could use as part of their reserves. They were subject to regulation by the Federal government instead of by the state administration. The banknotes they issued had to be redeemable in, and on par with, "lawful money" – either specie or new government currency. In return, prospective founders of a national bank could obtain a license from the Treasury instead of from their state government.

At the same time, a new law was passed in Congress that authorized the Treasury to issue a national currency, whose notes gained the nickname "greenbacks." The currency, which bore interest at the annual rate of 5 percent, was declared as legal tender in the United States, although it could not be used to pay customs duties, since for that the government still wanted to receive specie. The law stopped short of saying the new currency was convertible to specie but did specify that it was on a par with treasury bonds. The total value of greenbacks issued amounted to $450 million in 1862.

Like Continental bills, greenbacks bore interest, but they differed in that the former lacked the support of a banking industry. Like John Law's "System" or the French revolutionists' *assignats*, greenbacks were backed only by securities that were more or less of a similar nature. But unlike them, the circulation of greenbacks did not require the government to outlaw specie. Rather, the new currency operated in a competitive monetary environment where specie, government currency notes, and private banknotes were all in use. In this mixed monetary environment, government monetary policymakers were necessarily constrained by economic laws. Moreover, Congress – as the legislative branch of the United States Government and an institution inherited from the Revolution – had acted as the ultimate comptroller in deciding the total amount of new currency issued, which in effect prevented the onset of explosive inflation. Without these newer institutional elements, the greenbacks' fate would have been no different at all from those of Continental bills or *assignats*.

A measure of the aggregate money supply – the sum of greenback issues, other U.S. government not issues and short-term bank deposits – increased from $554 million in 1860 to $1,351 million in 1864, followed by a slight increase of $34 million to $1,385 million in 1865.[108] A consumer price index rose 6 percent in 1861, 14.2 percent in 1862, and about 25 percent in each of the following two years before decelerating to 3.7 percent in 1865.[109] From any view, inflation in the North was quite moderate during the Civil War, and this can partly be seen by the fact that the Federal government resorted to no means of price control throughout the period of the war.

The Southern extreme of inflation

As the war unfolded and inflation became increasingly severe in the South, many people in the North then believed that they were on the winning side and the southerners were losing the war. "Northern writers of an economic turn of mind have oftentimes attributed the collapse of the Confederacy to its paper money."[110] After more than 150 years, it remains interesting to see how exactly the Confederate government came to rely almost solely on paper-currency finance and generated hyperinflation unparalleled in the nineteenth-century world.

Largely thanks to the bitter experience of Continental bills and their resultant inflation, the United States Constitution passed in the mid-1780s firmly bestowed power over monetary affairs to the Federal government – no state government could produce its own coinage or paper notes. Immediately after the split, the Confederacy found itself newly free to dictate every aspect of money and finance. It hired a northerner with technological know-how to mint coins for the new regime, but he later refused to carry through the project.[111] Had the coinage program been undertaken successfully, the Confederacy might have gone for debasement rather than paper currency inflation.

At the start of hostilities, the South had a financial position not significantly inferior to that of the North. It seized properties and coins belonging to the Federal government and also detained payments that were on the way to merchants in the North. The southerners believed that their exports of cotton and tobacco to Europe could generate huge revenue. Cotton was even deified as "King Cotton" because the South was then the world's only major source of supply. At one time, they even held up exports with the hope that rising prices of cotton and tobacco could bring in more hard currency as well as coerce Europeans to become their supporters. But the situation quickly turned worse, as the North's navy started blocking the South's sea trade routes. Then later on, Europe eventually found new sources of cotton elsewhere.

Like the North, the Confederacy introduced various new taxes and counted on them in financing its ever-increasing budget needs. Property tax at a rate as low as 0.5 percent and income tax at 1 or 2 percent were first imposed on residents in 1861. At one point, it was estimated that there was $5.2 billion worth of property in the Confederate states, and that a tax of 54 cents on each $100 worth of property would raise $26 million.[112] But the Confederacy lacked an efficient mechanism of collection and enforcement, and hesitance and even resistance in several states in the South hindered effective implementation of the property tax. In the end, taxes contributed merely 5 percent or even less of the Confederacy budget.[113]

Private financial markets in Europe remained open to both the North and the South during the Civil War. Delegates and agents of the Confederacy in Paris and London sought vigorously to sell bonds that were guaranteed by cotton deliveries to Europe. Much of this was conducted through private placement in a network connecting a number of industrial and financial European cities. Yet, the effort achieved only partial success. Some southern states had already defaulted on earlier bonds in Europe, which undoubtedly scared away many prospective investors. In addition, prices and deliveries of cotton had become so unstable that to many private investors, the risks loomed increasingly large and unacceptable.

Being a little more innovative than their northern counterpart, the Confederacy issued two types of long-term government securities to the public: bonds and "stock." Both were interest bearing, but each differed in the method of payment and transfer – bonds were readily transferable, but transfer of stock required prior endorsement. Most of the long-term securities were promised with an interest rate of 8 percent or less, though a few had interest rates as low as 4 percent. At a time when price inflation was already in double digits, the continued subscription by the public indeed suggests that patriotism played an important part in war finance in the South. Overall, bond finance contributed less than 30 percent of the Confederacy budget by October 1864.[114]

A more frequent borrowing practice of the Confederacy was its direct requests to banks in the South for advances. Though much fewer in number and smaller in size than those in the North, the several hundred banks in the South appeared to be quite willing to assist the Confederacy with its war finance. When they lent to the government, they received paper notes or "call certificates" from its treasury department. In turn, the banks lent the notes to business borrowers, who were willing to accept them partly because they could repay the loans with the same notes, despite their great devaluation. The banks had thus become accomplices in the Confederacy's inflationary finance. Bank credit accounted for about 30 percent of the regime's budget.[115]

Apart from direct borrowing from banks, the Confederacy also issued short-term, interest-bearing treasury notes to the public. Initially, the Confederacy stated that the total value of the new notes issued would not exceed $100 million. In the end, $2 billion worth of notes were printed and circulated in the South, which included those delivered to banks in the first instance. The total budget spending by the Confederacy was about $2.3 billion, of which 68.6 percent is believed to have been created on the printing press.[116]

During the four years between April 1861 and April 1865, a general price index for the entire South rose 90 times, at an average monthly rate of 10 percent. In certain months, the monthly inflation was much higher – 40 percent, for instance, in April 1864.[117] Inflation was so severe that debtors were chasing creditors in order to settle dues with paper notes rapidly losing their value.

Real money balance – nominal growth in money stock relative to price inflation – had fallen considerably from 1862, which means that the Confederacy had slipped into the vicious trap of having to print more and more paper notes to maintain its budget in real terms. Money and prices were chasing each other. Under the effect of rising inflation, real wages in the South had been falling, which must have had a negative effect on patriotism in the later stages of the Civil War. Adding to the problem, cotton prices fell soon after the outbreak of the war, when prices of other commodities were rising, and this caused serious difficulty for the Confederacy in raising both tax and non-tax revenues.

The Confederacy attempted price controls in order to slow down inflation. Price ceilings were published for numerous commodities. Needless to say, they basically failed to fulfill their purpose.

There were some similarities in war finance between the North and the South, but significant differences also existed between the two sides. With regard to the latter, the tax revenue base proved much weaker in the South compared with not only the North, but also what the southerners had expected.

And the effectiveness of the "economic weaponry" of cotton and tobacco was greatly reduced by both the North's blockade and European pursuit of alternative sources of supply. Furthermore, direct borrowing from banks in the South opened a wide door for paper note issues and budget finance. This contrasted sharply with the situation in the North, where banks could use treasury notes only as a reserve instrument, and their credit expansion remained constrained by deposits in specie from the public. Last but not least, members of the Confederate Congress were too "patriotic" and too desperate in allowing their treasury department to keep breaking promises on note issues.

When the war came to an end in May 1865, Confederate notes stopped being currency in the South. Specie resumed wide circulation, and the North's treasury notes (greenbacks) also spread to some extent. The Federal government agreed to redeem greenbacks and other treasury securities in specie. The United States returned to a bimetallistic monetary system from the second half of the 1860s, and inflation left the country.

Notes

1 *Genesis*, 37:28, Authorized Version, 1611, as cited by Eagleton and Williams, p. 16.
2 Historians believe that the events related to the story occurred during the period toward the end of Egypt's New Kingdom, approximately around the eleventh century BC (Wilkinson, p. 336).
3 Eagleton and Williams, p. 18.
4 Homer and Sylla, Chapter 2.
5 Farber, Graph 14, p. 38; also cited in Fischer, Figure 5.01, p. 259.
6 Schuertinger and Butler, pp. 9–12, with Appendix A on the Code of Hammurabi involving price and wage controls, pp. 153–4.
7 Davies, pp. 61–5.
8 Galbraith, p. 8, where it also indicates that coins of a decimal division were in use in India even a few hundred years earlier than Herodotus narrates in the case of Minor Asia.
9 Reinhart and Rogoff, p. 137, where the origin of the event is referred to in another contemporary book. There were actually two Dionysius, father and son, both of whom were rulers of Syracuse from the second half of the fifth century to the first half of the fourth century.
10 Certain high inflation in the past may have been caused by neither "natural" factors nor debasement policy. Greece (Athens) witnessed a surge in the price of barley, in terms of drachma, around the time of the 320s BC (Fischer, Figure 5.02, p. 260). It was probably a result of sudden floods of electrum brought back by Alexander the

Great from his expedition in Asia and the Near East. A research paper by Temin (2002) indicates that the sudden death of Alexander in 323 BC resulted in a large, unexpected rise of money supply, which in turn caused the inflation.

11 A historian notes that when Wang Mang saw that impoverishment of the Han nobility had been achieved, gold circulation was permitted from AD 10 (Bielenstein, p. 233).
12 Ye, p. 73.
13 Bielenstein, p. 232, with footnote 27.
14 Peng, p. 127.
15 Peng, p. 127.
16 Qian and Guo, Chapter 3, details coins cast by rebel forces in various dynasties from the first century to the nineteenth century, pp. 98–108.
17 Jones, p. 296.
18 Julius Caesar found in 45 BC that almost one-third of citizens were receiving their wheat at government expense. See Schuettinger and Butler, p. 19.
19 Davies, p. 96.
20 Jones, p. 294. "To the pound" refers to equal division of a pound in weight. *"One aureus worth 25 denarii"* means that the silver-gold price ratio (parity) was approximately at 12.5:1.
21 Jones, p. 294. Michell tabulates the silver content of Roman coins from Nero, AD 54, to Claudius Victorinus, AD 268, the last of which was merely 0.02 percent of the original full standard (p. 2).
22 Jone, p. 298.
23 Schuettinger and Butler, p. 21.
24 Davies, p. 98.
25 Jones has noted evidence of hoarding in several cases, pp. 295, 298.
26 Schuettinger and Butler, p. 20, where the estimates' original source is given.
27 Michell, p. 1.
28 Davies, pp. 101–6.
29 Jones, p. 305.
30 The *Guinness Book of World Records* in the 1990s attributed the invention of paper currency in China to AD 980. Many Chinese scholars, however, believe this happened in the early years of the second millennium.
31 Ye, p. 210; also Peng, p. 315.
32 Lui, Table 1, p. 1070. The article also regards the episode as "the first nationwide inflation of paper money in world history."
33 Ye, p. 285.
34 Tan, p. 148.
35 Ye, p. 331.
36 Peng, p. 411.
37 Marco Polo's remarks are cited in Davies, 182–3; also in Eagleton and Williams, p. 167.
38 Weatherford, p. 127.
39 Yule, Vol. II, p. 240, footnote; cited in Peng, pp. 409–10 and footnote 27.
40 Davies, p. 183. He also holds that "the world's first paper currency hyperinflation" occurred in China and Persia under the Mongols, apparently neglecting those of the Jurchen and Sung.
41 Fischer, Sahay, and Végh, Table 1, p. 838.
42 Reinhart and Rogoff, Table 11.1, p. 139, summarizes episodes of debasement in Europe between 1258 and 1799. Braudel and Spooner, p. 380, also highlight several cases in this regard.
43 Davies, p. 198.
44 Chown, Tables 5.2 and 5.3. pp. 56–9, which is a citation from Gould, Table 2.
45 Davies, p. 198.
46 Chown, p. 49.

47 Davies, p. 202, as a citation from Challis, pp. 254–5.
48 Fischer, Figure 2.04, p. 74, where original sources of the estimates are given.
49 Fischer, *ibid.*
50 Chown, pp. 42–3.
51 Homer and Sylla, p. 99.
52 Homer and Sylla, p. 100.
53 Ouithwaite (1966, p. 289).
54 Some economic historians hold that it is "[p]rotests against rising prices, and financial difficulties of the governments of Henry VIII and then of Edward VI" arising from foreign debts that led Elizabeth I to depart from the earlier policy of debasement. Braudel and Spooner, p. 383.
55 Ye, p. 394.
56 Peng, p. 492.
57 Bernholz (2003, Table 4.1, p. 57).
58 Estimates of price rises and general price levels indicate that the former rose 117 percent over one year, the latter climbed 45.1 percent over the same period, and the two indicators decelerated in subsequent years. See, Peng (2006, Table A5.1, p. 168).
59 Peng (2006, Table A5.1, p. 173).
60 Zhang (2005).
61 Yang.
62 Galbraith, p. 45.
63 Markham, pp. 43–5.
64 Citation in Galbraith, p. 51.
65 Markham, p. 50.
66 Markham, p. 60.
67 U.S. Bureau of the Census, p. 1196.
68 Markham, pp. 66–7.
69 Markham, p. 67.
70 Schuertinger and Butler, p. 49.
71 The program is noted as a "predecessor to the Brady Plan," which helped resolve the foreign debt crisis in Latin America in the 1980s. Markham, p. 68.
72 Kindleberger, p. 96.
73 Schumpeter, p. 281.
74 The consent of the Duke of Orleans to Law's plan was apparently motivated by the situation of extreme indebtedness and huge budget deficits facing France largely due to earlier foreign wars. Hamilton (1936, pp. 43–4).
75 Hamilton (1936, pp. 47–8).
76 Hamilton (1936, Table 1, p. 52).
77 White, p. 3.
78 White, p. 4.
79 Galbraith, p. 66.
80 Sargent and Velde, p. 496.
81 Brezis and Crouzet (pp. 10–12) hold that assignats were "interest-bearing promissory notes" from December 1789 to March 1792, and it was the war that caused sharp increases in the French government's budget deficits and therefore changed the role of the assignats from 1792.
82 This is a remark made by M. Matrineau in 1790, when he was a member of the National Assembly (White, pp. 3–4).
83 White, p. 7.
84 White, p. 20.
85 White, pp. 33–34.
86 White, p. 20.
87 Capie, p. 124, citation of Harris. The same information is also in Chown, Table 25.1, p. 231.

88 Capie, Table 1, p. 123.
89 Schuettinger and Butler, pp. 45–7.
90 Brezis and Crouzet, p. 16.
91 White, p. 55.
92 White, p. 56.
93 Harris, p. 144.
94 Fischer, Figure 3.17, p. 152; these figures are slightly different from those shown in Fischer, Sahay and Végh, Table 1, p. 838.
95 Galbraith, p. 66.
96 Friedman (1992, p. 135).
97 Bordo and White (1991).
98 Sargent and Velde, pp. 478–9.
99 As shown in Homer and Sylla, the yield on long-term British government bonds was between 4.4 percent and 5.75 percent in the 1800s and 1810s and was actually declining from the mid-1800s (Chapter 13, Tables 6 and 19); while that on short-term ones remained at 5 percent throughout the period (Table 23). In France, the same indicator averaged 8.66 percent in the 1800s and 7.29 percent in the 1810s (Chapters 14, Table 25).
100 Mitchell, *Europe*, Tables H1 and H2.
101 Mitchell, *Europe*, Tables H1 and H2.
102 Bordo and White, p. 311.
103 Markham, p. 208.
104 These federal government finance figures all come from Carter *et al*, Table Ea584–587, pp. 5–80.
105 Sylla, p. 528.
106 Markham, p. 209.
107 Markham, p. 210.
108 Rockoff, Table 14.2, p. 657.
109 Carter *et al*, Table Cc1–2, pp. 3–158. Whole prices actually fell by 4.3 percent in 1865, see Rockoff, Table 14.2, p. 657.
110 Cited in Galbraith, p. 95.
111 Markham, p. 223.
112 Markham, p. 224.
113 Markham, p. 226.
114 Lerner, p. 180.
115 Markham, p. 226.
116 Markham, p. 226; and Lerner, p. 181.
117 Lerner, Table 2, p. 184.

3 The first wave of hyperinflation in the twentieth century

Germany, Russia, and CEE countries in the 1920s

"If there be fuel prepared, it is hard to tell whence the spark shall come that shall set it on fire."

Francis Bacon, "Of Seditions and Troubles," *Essays* (1625)

"The decades from the outbreak of the First World War to the aftermath of the Second, was an Age of Catastrophe for this society. For forty years it stumbled from one calamity to another. There were times when even intelligent conservatives would not take bets on its survival."

Eric Hobsbawm, The Century: A Bird's Eye View, *The Age of Extremes: The Short Twentieth Century, 1914–1991*, 1994

Entering the twentieth century, the world began to see waves of hyperinflation. The first arrived almost immediately after the end of the First World War, in Germany, Russia, and several other Central and Eastern European countries. Many others came during and after the Second World War and in the second half of the century. The frequency and scale of hyperinflation during the twentieth century are unparalleled in history.

Several new megatrends separated the twentieth-century world from that of the past and made occurrences of hyperinflation both more likely and more severe in magnitude than ever before. First, thanks to the Industrial Revolution and globalization, many national economies had been considerably commercialized, and the use of money had permeated almost every aspect of economic and social life. Second, banking industries and financial markets had grown up, and money growth could no longer rely merely on the running of printing presses or manipulation of specie currency. Credit supply became a new way of monetary expansion, and governments could simply draw on their state or central banks to finance their budget deficits. Third, progress in population literacy and mass media helped to accelerate the flow of information and enable people to respond quickly to any news related to price movements. Fourth, in an ever-globalizing modern world, events concerning international relations, politics, and economics exerted far more influence in domestic affairs than before, and both the beginning and end of hyperinflation in a country could be tremendously affected by "outside" events.

Because of this common background, hyperinflations in the twentieth century often occurred simultaneously in a number of countries, though they all had distinctive national features for domestic reasons. Germany, Russia, Austria, Hungary, and Poland were the five countries that experienced hyperinflation during the early 1920s, when they all shared in common the legacy of the First World War and the experience of its immediate aftermath. Table 3.1 highlights the periods and maximum monthly inflation rates of these episodes. Notable among the five, Germany saw two instances of hyperinflation during a short period, the second of which was the first hyperinflation in recorded history to reach an astronomical level, and Russia had the longest-lasting episode. Except for Russia, all the countries have detailed historical records of prices and other monetary and financial data, which can be used for the study of hyperinflation.

An episode not shown in Table 3.1 is the hyperinflation in 1923–24 in the Free City of Danzig, which was a small, semi-autonomous area created by the Treaty of Versailles in 1919 to enable newly established Poland to have access to the Baltic Sea. After Danzig's separation from Germany, the city's currency in circulation continued to be the German papiermark. Hyperinflation started in August 1923, and the currency had devalued 2,400 percent against the U.S. dollar by September 1924.[1] This episode ended in mid-October 1924, when an international aid program was adopted.

Before the end of the First World War, there were actually two isolated episodes of hyperinflation in Latin America. One was in Colombia in 1902–03, and the other occurred in Mexico in 1913–16. Each country was embroiled in a civil war during the respective period, and the troubled governments both resorted to printing non-convertible paper notes to finance their wartime budget deficits. It is not known exactly how Colombia's instance of inflation developed,[2] but the Mexican case has been well documented. In a period of 47 months to December 1916, general prices rose 107-fold, with the annual increase rate reaching as high as 7,716,100 percent at one point.[3] Both countries soon returned to specie standards (mainly silver) afterwards. The two episodes are essentially reminiscent of the hyperinflation in the American South's Confederacy in the 1860s.

Hyperinflation during the twentieth century, however, can best be exemplified by the five episodes of the 1920s.

Table 3.1 Hyperinflations in Germany, Russia, and CEE countries during the 1920s[4]

	Start date	End date	Highest monthly inflation rate	Month with highest inflation rate	Currency	Indicator of inflation
Germany	Jan 1920	Jan 1920	56.9 percent	Jan 1920	Papiermark	WPI
	Aug 1922	Dec 1923	29,500 percent	Oct 1923	Papiermark	WPI
Russia/USSR	Jan 1922	Feb 1924	212 percent	Feb 1924	Ruble	CPI
Austria	Oct 1921	Sep 1922	129 percent	Aug 1922	Crown	CPI
Hungary	Mar 1923	Feb 1924	97.9 percent	Jul 1923	Crown	CPI
Poland	Jan 1923	Jan 1924	275 percent	Oct 1923	Marka	WPI

Five basic facts of hyperinflation during the 1920s

Figure 3.1 shows the monthly price movements in Austria, Germany, Hungary, Poland, and Russia during the period, and it is clear that Germany witnessed the highest level of inflation, and Russia the longest, among the five countries. Compared to Germany and Russia, the hyperinflations in Austria, Hungary, and Poland were "moderate" in either magnitude or duration.

What is interesting to the student of hyperinflation is how economic relations change during a period of rapidly rising inflation. Based on observation of the hyperinflations in the early 1920s, we can summarize five basic facts cconcerning such changes. In our examination of the data below, only Russia has been neglected, due to data unavailability.[5]

Fact I: real money balance was declining

By definition, real money balance is the ratio of the nominal money stock to a price indicator, with each of the two figures indexed at a certain level at a base period or point in time. In Figure 3.2, the respective base periods for Germany, Hungary, and Austria are January 1921, July 1921, and January 1923 (when the country started a stabilization program).

As shown in Figure 3.2, real money balance was declining in both Germany and Hungary during the period of hyperinflation, with a little more fluctuation in Germany. In the first half of 1921, when Germany was in a relatively stable period, the money balance actually climbed. In Austria, after a stabilization program came into effect, the money balance started rising.

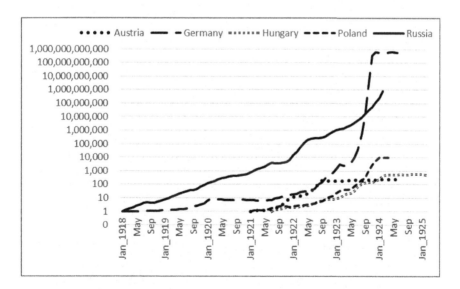

Figure 3.1 Monthly price movements in Austria, Germany, Hungary, Poland, and Russia, 1918–25[6]

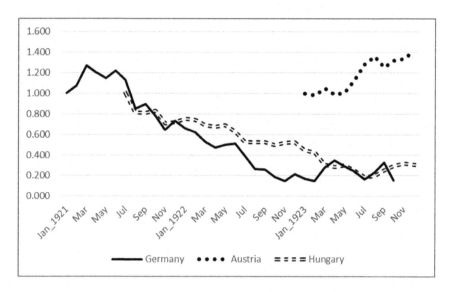

Figure 3.2 Real money balance, Germany, Austria, and Hungary, January 1921–December 1923[7]

A declining real money balance means that prices were rising faster than nominal money stock. In other words, price-setters were moving more quickly than money and credit creators – the Central Bank, banks and other lending agencies, and the government. Price-setters in the private sector were acting entirely on their expectations of future inflation, and the purchasing power of money fell accordingly.

The declining real money balance also suggests that money had largely lost its illusion. People no longer believed that the value of money was stable and that any increase in their money holdings would benefit them. Instead, they tended to spend money as quickly as possible whenever they received payments of it.

A declining money balance has vast implications for an economy. First, the real value of government revenue diminishes in the course of collection and spending, which obviously has a negative impact on government finance. Second, the real value of public debt diminishes as inflation rises. Old debts can be replaced by new ones which, although equal in nominal amount, have much smaller values in real terms. This, of course, has a positive effect on government finance. In the case of Germany, her total treasury bills outstanding in October, 1923 amounted to 6,907,511,102.8 billion mark – a 2,707,938,930-fold increase over the 262 billion mark in January 1919. When discounted by wholesale price inflation, the first figure merely equaled 23 billion mark in the value of January 1919, or less than one-tenth of the original amount.[8] This was effectively a "saving" in the German government's debt servicing outlay, but it was achieved at the cost of sacrificing public trust in the German currency.

The ostensible fluctuation in the real money balance trend in Germany may be explained by unbalanced movements in prices and money supply during the period. In principle, prices could not rise to an extent that the money supply could not accommodate. This also suggests that the race between price-setters in the private sector and money supply decision makers in the public sector is never a smooth process.

Fact II: deposits tended to shrink in the money supply

Under normal conditions, bank deposits facilitate payments and money transfers, in addition to generating interest gains for deposit holders. When inflation starts to surge, people have much less incentive to keep deposits at banks, except for the sake of making payments and money transfers.

As can be seen in Figure 3.3, Hungary saw bank deposits steadily shrink as a proportion of the money stock in the second half of 1922, down from 0.18 to 0.08. In Austria, even when her money market became more or less stabilized from early 1923, bank deposits' share of the money supply remained at a low level – less than 0.10.

In Germany, bank deposits as a share of the money stock fell only briefly, mainly in the middle of 1922. For most of the time during the periods of hyperinflation, the share actually went up, though with a certain amount of fluctuation. The unusual movement of bank deposits in Germany was probably a result of the overwhelming importance that the German banking industry had taken in payments and funds transfers. It could also be partially attributed to

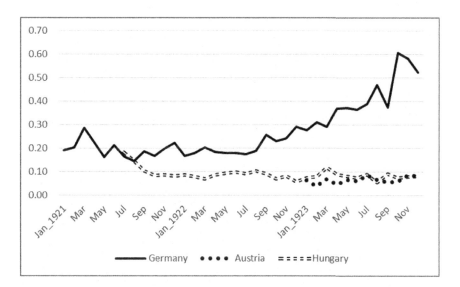

Figure 3.3 Deposits as a proportion of money supply, Germany, Austria, and Hungary, January 1921–December 1923[9]

the rapid credit expansion pursued by German banks. It is certain that German banks played a much greater role in the process of hyperinflation than did their counterparts in other, similar countries. This is also the reason why Germany's hyperinflation was the highest among all of those in Europe in the early 1920s.

Fact III: exchange rates depreciated faster than domestic prices rose

In this regard, Figure 3.4 shows the changes in four countries' domestic prices relative to their exchange rates. The four curves are indexed exchange rates – all expressed in units of domestic currency per U.S. dollar – relative to indexed domestic prices (wholesale or retail prices). A rise in a curve indicates that domestic inflation rose faster than the currency depreciated, and a fall indicates the reverse.

In 1921, three countries – Germany, Hungary, and Poland – all had upward moving curves, which suggest that inflation was more severe than currency depreciation in all three countries that year. Early in 1922, the ratio of domestic inflation to exchange rate began a downward trend in all three states, though with certain fluctuations in each of them. Notably, the German curve plummeted almost to zero, which indicates that depreciation of the German currency – *Reichsmark* – was so severe that domestic inflation lagged far behind.

There are no comparably useful data for Austria before 1923, when the country had already started a stabilization program. Therefore, changes in the Austrian curve were remarkably smaller than those in all of the other three countries.

The fact that the currency depreciated faster than inflation rose suggests that people in these countries were chasing foreign currency for the purpose of

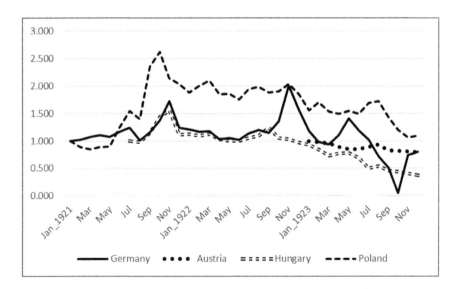

Figure 3.4 Domestic inflation relative to exchange rate change in Germany, Austria, Hungary, and Poland, January 1921–December 1923[10]

maintaining the value of their money holdings and that the domestic currency could no longer perform this particular function. Chasing foreign currency was without doubt largely motivated by domestic inflation expectations and would, in turn, further drive up domestic inflation.

An immediate effect of the faster currency depreciation would be that prices of imported goods rise to a larger degree than would prices of domestically-made goods. If the economy relied significantly on imports – either daily essentials, such as foodstuffs, or key industrial inputs, such as raw materials or equipment – the faster rises in prices of imported goods would cause considerable problems in the economy. Government budget expenditure might soar irresistibly, and business operation costs could override any possible profit.

In theory, when a country sees its currency depreciate more than domestic prices rise, assuming foreign prices remain unchanged, real devaluation occurs which helps improve the country's trade balance by making domestic products more price competitive in foreign markets. Yet, this could hardly be the case during hyperinflation. Orderly supply conditions in the domestic economy are needed for export industries to reap the benefits of real devaluation, but such conditions become difficult to maintain when inflation appears to be unbridled and unpredictable.

Ultimately, currency depreciation outpacing inflation renders a country's people poorer in international terms and foreign capital more valuable to them than before.

Fact IV: real interest rates became negative

Generally speaking, the real interest rate is the nominal interest rate minus the inflation rate over a given span of time. In practice, the concept of real interest rate is most relevant to businesses, because they need credit frequently, have access to credit markets, and constantly consider the real cost of credit in the light of price changes. If the real interest rate becomes negative, holding other things equal, business demand for credit increases explosively.

Monthly nominal interest rate and price data are available for Germany in the 1920s. The discount rate of the Reichsbank – the most important source of credit for German businesses – was the benchmark interest rate in nominal terms. Its daily money rate, for collateralized short-term loans between banks and credit agencies, was usually lower than the discount rate.[11] German wholesale price inflation, meanwhile, was measured here as a "forward" rate rather than as a conventional "backward" rate. The "forward" rate of 14 percent in January 1920, for instance, indicates that wholesale prices rose by that proportion between January 1920 and January 1921 such that it is correspondent to the interest rates in an exact same time horizon. As a matter of fact, all interest rates are a "forward" one.

As can be seen from Figure 3.5, the discount rate was kept unchanged at 5 percent by the Reichsbank throughout 1920 and 1921, whilst the daily money rate moved a little upward during 1921 but stayed below the discount rate. Meanwhile, the "forward" interest rate started to ascend in June 1920 and rose

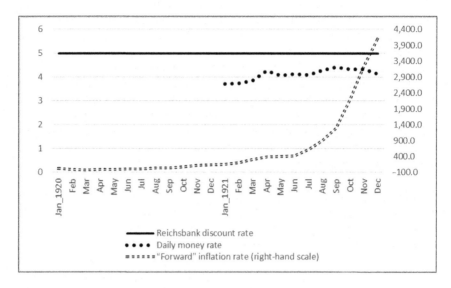

Figure 3.5 Reichsbank discount rate, daily money rate, and "forward" inflation rate, January 1920–December 1921[12]

above 1,000 percent in September 1921, with later figures so large that they cannot be effectively displayed on the same scale and therefore have to be omitted. As the "forward" inflation rate rose to 32 percent in August 1920, with the discount rate virtually unchanged, real interest rates in German money and credit markets became significantly negative.

When the Reichsbank began to raise the discount rate as late as in August 1922 (from 5 percent to 6 percent), the money rate had become higher than the discount rate (5.4 percent in July, 1922 and 6.5 percent the following month), indicating market perception of rising risks, and the "forward" inflation rate had already jumped to as high as 73,509 percent in July and 491,588 percent in August. In April 1923, when the discount rate was raised to 18 percent and the money rate 12.7 percent, the "forward" inflation rate escalated to an astonishing 23,800,844,106 percent.

Under new leadership, the Reichsbank began to adopt a new anti-inflation policy from 1923, and its discount rate was raised to 90 percent in September that year, with the money rate climbing to 1,606 percent the same month. The monthly rate of German wholesale price inflation continued to be much higher than these interest rates. But with falls in the price index from January 1924, the "forward" inflation rate turned downward from December 1923. As a result, real interest rates in German money and credit markets returned to positive, normal levels from then on.

Negative real interest rates were both an effect and a cause of rising inflation. The German experience in the early 1920s clearly indicates that hyperinflation coincided with negative real interest rates.

Fact V: real wages tended to fall

Changes of trend in real wage levels during hyperinflation are another important issue in the study of hyperinflation. But, there are problems in data collection and compilation with regard to assessment of real wages and their changes, especially at a national level covering many different regions and industrial sectors over time. Showing the development of real wages during the early 1920s, Figure 3.6 below displays money wages and the cost of living in the German city of Frankfurt and surrounding districts.

Three observations can be made from Figure 3.6. First, money wages continuously rose closely in line with the cost of living index. Second, during the three-and-a-half year period, real wages in the region fluctuated with basically no definite declining trend. Third, there are a few periods when the extent or pace of change was greater than average. For example, real wages fell more than 30 percent in the four months August to November, 1922 and more than 10 percent in the month of February, 1923. Coincidentally, these were periods when German wholesale prices rose most rapidly.

These observations suggest that real wages did not fall over the course of a few years, even when there was hyperinflation. In other words, hyperinflation itself may not change the long-term trend of real wages. On the other hand, rising inflation – at various speeds – significantly drove down real wages over short periods lasting from one to a few months.

A plausible explanation of what happened to real wages in Germany during the early 1920s is that there was actually a price-wage spiral during the hyperinflation. When workers faced the threat of falling real wages, they would protest and demand compensation. When their demands for rises in nominal wages were met,

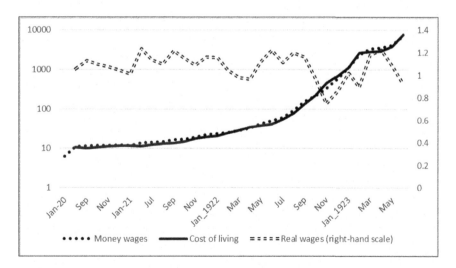

Figure 3.6 Money wages, cost of living, and real wages in Frankfurt and surrounding districts, January 1920–June 1923[13]

the money and credit supplies would expand and, in turn, stimulate new rounds of price inflation.

Given the fact that the unemployment rate was rising in Germany in 1923 – from 0.7 percent in 1922 to 4.5 percent in 1923[14] – falls in real wages, whether temporary or not, can be seen as having had no immediate and stimulating effect on employment. Their most significant and immediate effect, therefore, would have been increased uncertainty about the well-being of workers and macroeconomic conditions in the economy.

Among all of the Central and Eastern European countries in the early 1920s, Germany probably had the strongest trade union movement. The fact that hyperinflation did not lead to a fall in real wages in German industry over the long term should be attributed to strong labor rights. Despite this, as noted above, hyperinflation still led to short-run falls in real wages. In countries where labor rights were not comparable to those in Germany, therefore, falls in real wages over both short and long terms were possible.

The gold standard and the rise of the banking industry

The first wave of hyperinflation in interwar Europe occurred against a background in which every government in the region had suspended the gold standard and implemented a non-convertible paper currency regime. The pattern was partly repeated in the 1980s, when a number of Latin American countries were left out of the Bretton-Woods System – a gold exchange system based on U.S. dollar pegging – and fell into hyperinflation traps. During the last three decades of the nineteenth century and early years of the twentieth century, many countries that had moved to the gold standard witnessed relatively stable price and exchange rate environments in which modern banking industry grew and seeds of inflation – such as rapid expansion of deposits, which became an increasingly important component of the money supply – were sown.

Before 1870, only two countries in the world – Britain and Portugal – had adopted a "true gold standard."[15] The conventional definition of the gold standard emphasizes the establishment of gold parity for paper currency and rules of convertibility between paper currency and gold, which often involve free shipment of bullion across borders. In practice, an operational gold standard usually requires a specialized government agency – a central bank – to provide financial services for the government and business as well as the public service of issuing paper notes. The German experience of moving toward the gold standard from the 1870s best shows the importance of a central bank.

With victory in the Franco-Prussian war in 1871, Germany became a unified nation. Partly thanks to the large sum of French reparations – 5 billion francs at a fixed exchange rate – Germany was able to complete her transition to the gold standard. In 1876, the Reichsbank was formally established with the responsibilities of issuing paper currency, maintaining gold reserves, and providing credit to the government and business. By law, the Reichsbank was required to hold reserves (mainly gold) amounting to no less than one-third of its total liabilities, and it would be subject to punishment if the reserves fell below the minimum requirement. From the early 1880s to 1913, the reichsmark maintained a remarkably stable exchange rate with the U.S. dollar.[16]

The Austro-Hungarian Empire was economically weaker than Germany, and she moved to the gold standard rather slowly. For much of the nineteenth century, the country effectively operated a bimetallistic system, with both gold and silver coins in circulation, and there were no explicit and consistent rules for paper currency issue. On several occasions, the convertibility of paper currency was suspended, and this was quickly followed by rises in inflation.[17] By 1887, the government managed to revise the law and restructure the Austro-Hungarian National Bank, which apparently followed the example of the Reichsbank and helped finalize the transition to the gold standard.

Czarist Russia had gained notoriety for often debasing its paper currency.[18] It was as late as 1896 that a reformist minister of finance, Sergei Witte, took the bold move of standardizing Russia's currency system and establishing the nation's gold standard. A new, centralized state bank was formed to perform the functions of currency issue, reserve management, and credit supply. The value of the ruble was fixed in terms of gold at a level maintained until the outbreak of the First World War.

From the late nineteenth century, the gold standard helped the growth of international trade because of the exchange rate stability it intended to safeguard. The period also coincided with the spread of the industrial revolution, mainly across Europe and North America. Expansion of trade and industry resulted in growing, strong demand for modern financial services, especially banking. Prior to the First World War, there were hundreds of modern banks of various types in each of Germany, Austria-Hungary, and Russia. Even in the occupied territories of Poland, there were branches of German, Austro-Hungarian, and Russian banks, mainly state-owned ones. Many banks in these countries had close relationships with business through mutual stock holding arrangements and directorships. Unlike in Britain or America, many large banks in Germany and Austria had evolved from the mid-nineteenth century into what is called "universal banking," i.e., the same banking firm could provide a great variety of financial services to its clients. In the case of conventional lending, the term of a loan was usually much longer than in the Anglo-Saxon world. The closer relationship between banks and businesses in countries like Germany and Austria may have facilitated the rapid developments in railway construction and other heavy industries during the period. A hidden consequence, however, is that when the market environment experiences a shock, such as rising inflation, this type of financial relationship may exacerbate the problem.

In many of the rapidly industrializing European and North American countries, a profound monetary and financial development under the gold standard during the late nineteenth century and early twentieth century was the fast growth of bank deposits and their rising importance in the money supply. An estimate shows that between 1872 and 1913, for the United States, United Kingdom, and France as a whole, the share of gold in the money supply fell from 28 percent to 10 percent, and that of silver dropped from 13 percent to 3 percent. Meanwhile, the share of demand deposits rose from 27 percent to 68 percent, while that of paper notes went down from 32 percent to 19 percent. For 11 countries including Germany, the share of demand deposits was 63 percent in 1913, and that of paper notes was 23 percent.[19] All this shows that the rise of the banking industry revolutionized the concept of money in those industrializing countries. The fact that demand deposits gained primary importance in the money supply in the years before the First World War suggests that banks had become the center of finance for the economy and business, and people increasingly relied on banks to handle payments and make investments.

Developments in bank-dominated finance also enabled governments to expand their budgets, in part by borrowing on securities. From the late nineteenth century, the governments of many European countries, including Germany and Austria-Hungary, frequently issued long-term bonds to finance their budget deficits whenever there was a need. Government bonds were bought by the public and by domestic financial institutions, including banks.

Against this backdrop, methods of war finance became a crucial issue for belligerent governments during the First World War. There were three main ways to finance the increases in government military spending and other war costs: raising taxes, borrowing from domestic sources, and borrowing abroad. For the first, needless to say, all governments tried to raise taxes in order to reduce budget shortfalls. Invariably, though, they were afraid of losing domestic support by hiking taxes too much. For external borrowing, efforts were made to explore foreign sources, both private and official, but results were considerably different between the Allied States (the Entente Powers) and the Central Powers. Britain successfully borrowed large sums from American sources, which amounted to 4.1 billion U.S. dollars in 1918, equivalent to 854 million pounds sterling or 16.4 percent of the United Kingdom's gross domestic product in that year. French foreign borrowing was more than that of the British, and her creditors were America (more than half) and Britain (less than half).[20] On the other hand, the foreign borrowing of Germany and Austria-Hungary was insignificant compared to that of Britain and France, though they made similar efforts.

As a result, the German and Austro-Hungarian governments had to rely much more on domestic borrowing than did the Allied States during the war. Between 1913 and 1918, Germany's outstanding national debt in domestic currency increased 13.7 times, whilst those of Britain and France rose 7.3 times and 2.8 times, respectively.[21] With regard to the debt-to-GDP ratio, the German figure probably rose from 9.4 percent to 70 percent during the period, while that of Britain increased from 30.5 percent to 110 percent.[22] Though Britain's level continued to be higher than Germany's throughout the war period, it was Germany's debt ratio which rose much faster.

The inability to borrow considerably from abroad and the probably-resulting rising interest burden on domestic debt presumably prompted the Central Powers to resort to inflationary deficit financing during the war period, at least to a

Table 3.2 Consumer price index in four belligerent countries, 1913–18[23]

	Germany	Austria	Britain	France
1913	100		100	100
1914	103	100	98	102
1915	129	158	120	120
1916	169	337	143	138
1917	252	672	172	162
1918	301	1,163	199	210

significantly larger extent than did the Allied States, whose financial pressures were partly reduced by the availability of foreign funds.

Table 3.2 compares the consumer price indexes in four belligerent countries from 1913–1918. The rise in CPI in Germany or Austria was much higher than that in Britain or France. Among the four countries, the occurrence of the highest level of inflation in Austria probably suggests that she was the one that had the most difficulty in securing external funds for war spending and costs, and therefore she had to use inflationary means more than the others during the period.

In a sense, the wartime inflation experiences in Germany and Austria were the prelude to the episodes of hyperinflation in the interwar period. Many elements of hyperinflation were already planted in these countries prior to the outburst of hyperinflation: state control of central banking and currency issue, suspension of the gold standard, rising burdens on public finance, political unwillingness or inability to raise taxation, and a hostile external environment for borrowing. When these "fuels" continued to be in store after the end of the war, only a few sparks were needed to set off a forest fire of hyperinflation.

A caveat is need to understand the events which lead to hyperinflation in interwar Europe: although the suspension of the gold standard – unlocking the "golden fetters," as a prominent economic historian described it[24] – during the First World War and early years of the interwar period indeed removed a hard constraint on domestic monetary policy, it remained up to individual governments to decide the manner and magnitude of how exactly they would conduct the policy in coping with challenges and seeking international financial cooperation. Additional failures in these dimensions would make hyperinflation inevitable.

Alarm bells for hyperinflation: Lenin *vs.* Keynes

The October Revolution in Russia in 1917 had not only profound impacts on the world's politics, economics, and international relations in the twentieth century, but also an immediate effect towards the end of the First World War: the popularity of Lenin and his revolutionary thinking.

John Maynard Keynes, a British economist who was among the United Kingdom's delegation to the negotiation process leading to the Treaty of Versailles in 1919, was perhaps the very first intellectual who publicly warned of the danger of hyperinflation in postwar Europe and its devastating effects on economy and society. To buttress his view of the menace, he quoted Lenin as a living antithesis of capitalist monetary policy advocates:

> Lenin is said to have declared that the best way to destroy the Capitalist System was to debauch the currency . . . Lenin was certainly right. There is no subtler, no surer means of overturning the existing basis of society than to debauch the currency. The process engages all the hidden forces of economic law on the side of destruction, and does it in a manner which no one in a million is able to diagnose.[25]

"To debauch the currency" is obviously synonymous with instigating hyperinflation, and an intent of Keynes's writing was presumably to highlight a new threat to the economic and political establishment brought by revolutionaries' use of monetary instruments. Keynes admitted that he did not effectively exert influence on policy making during peace negotiations for the Treaty of Versailles and elsewhere, but his works were well received internationally. The book entitled *The Economic Consequences of the Peace* – where Keynes first referred to Lenin's remark – was soon translated into Belgian, Chinese, Danish, Dutch, Flemish, German, Italian, Japanese, Rumanian, Russian, Spanish, and Swedish.[26] No doubt, people became increasingly aware of the danger of hyperinflation in the interwar period.

Yet, the authenticity of Keynes's reference to Lenin's remark was challenged by an economic historian some five decades later. Frank Whitson Fetter published an article in 1977 in which he reported that no evidence of any such remark made by Lenin could be found. Instead, he had discovered that Lenin made a statement about the "evil" of inflation in 1917, which Professor Fetter believed was precisely opposite to what Keynes had indicated. Moreover, Fetter quoted from a well-known British historian – E. H. Carr, who wrote a substantial book on the Bolshevik Revolution – on the perceived relationship between the Revolution and inflation:

> None of the Bolsheviks wanted, or planned, inflation. But, when that happened (since the printing press was their main source of revenue) they rationalized it ex post facto by describing it as (a) death to the capitalists and (b) a foretaste of the moneyless Communist Society. Talk of this kind was widely current in Moscow in 1919 and 1920. . . . Keynes in 1919 had no special knowledge of Lenin; everything that came out of Moscow was automatically attributed to Lenin or Trotsky, or both.[27]

Although E. H. Carr mentioned "a famous dictum" by a high-ranking Russian revolutionary who described the printing press as the "machine-gun of the Commissariat of Finance, which poured fire into the rear of the bourgeois system," his reflection of "unintended consequences" raised questions other than whether Lenin made the kind of statement Keynes had suggested. Did the Russian revolutionaries really passively respond to inflationary pressures for which they were not accountable at all? And, is there any distinctive theory that Lenin and his associates followed in dictating monetary policy during the period immediately after the October Revolution? From a broader, international perspective, would the Bolsheviks' monetary practice influence that in other countries undergoing radical political and social change? To answer these questions, one first needs to find out what Lenin said about money and monetary policy, and whether Keynes was right in quoting him.

Helpful in this regard is the work of two economists who dug into archives and located the exact same media sources that Keynes must have accessed. Two newspapers – the *Daily Chronicle* in London and the *New York Times* – both published a long interview with Lenin, conducted by their international correspondents through a representative in Russia, in April 23, 1919. Above a section about the monetary situation in Russia, the article contains the subtitle "Lenin is obsessed at present by a plan for the annihilation of the power of money in the world."[28] In light of its unusual "archaeological" value, it is worthwhile quoting a large part of the original text here, which did not appear in the complete works of Lenin compiled by Soviet Communists:

Hundreds of thousands of rouble notes are being issued daily by our treasury. This is done, not in order to fill the coffers of the State with practically worthless paper, but with the deliberate intention of destroying the value of money as a means of payment. There is no justification for the existence of money in the Bolshevik state, where the necessities of life shall be paid for by work alone.

Experience has taught us it is impossible to root out the evils of capitalism merely by confiscation and expropriation, for however ruthless such measures may be applied, astute speculators and obstinate survivors of the capitalist classes will always manage to evade them and continue to corrupt the life of the community. The simplest way to exterminate the very spirit of capitalism is therefore to flood the country with notes of a high face-value without financial guarantees of any sort.

Already even a hundred-rouble note is almost valueless in Russia. Soon even the simplest peasant will realize that it is only a scrap of paper, not worth more than the rags from which it is manufactured. Men will cease to covet and hoard it so soon as they discover it will not buy anything, and the great illusion of the value and power of money, on which the capitalist state is based, will have been definitely destroyed.

This is the real reason why our presses are printing rouble bills day and night, without rest.[29]

Therein lie several points of interest to us. First, Lenin was frank about the ultimate objective of the pursuit: eliminating the capitalist system. Second, he believed that running printing presses was a better means of achieving the goal than confiscation or expropriation. Third, when paper notes became worthless, he reckoned this would be the end of the market economy, and a planned economy could arise.

Furthermore, the two economists found that Lenin replied to Keynes's work, *The Economic Consequences of the Peace*, during a talk given to the Second Congress of the Third Communist International (Comintern) in July–August 1920. Lenin was well informed about Keynes's publication as well as his participation in the peace negotiations in Paris. Lenin would unhesitatingly have rebutted Keynes had he believed that Keynes had distorted his view. In fact, Lenin's long speech did not refer to the matter, even indirectly.[30]

As a leading revolutionary at an unprecedented time, Lenin was obviously besieged by an enormous number of pressing matters. Nevertheless, he constantly took on issues related to money. In November 1921, when inflation was surging in Russia, he wrote for *Pravda* – at that time, the official newspaper of the Communist Party of the Soviet Union – an article titled *The Importance of Gold, Now and After the Complete Victory of Socialism*, in which he suggested that gold should be used to build public toilets in the future and that its present role was mainly to pay for imports.[31] Lenin obviously held a vision of a moneyless society consistent with the principles of Marx's communism. "To debauch the currency" was therefore possibly one of his tactics to achieve his ultimate goals.

It is clear that Lenin articulated the view of debauching the currency, as referred to by Keynes. Also, Lenin's view was not anything like an inadvertent remark or immature thought. On the contrary, it followed the logic of Marxist thought on class struggle and state control of the economy. More importantly, Lenin effectively put the theory into practice, and hyperinflation in Russia during the early 1920s was largely an outcome of the Bolsheviks' monetary policy. By no means was it an "unintended consequence."

It is also known that Lenin's view of money and inflation reverberated among the Bolshevik power circle. For example, Leon Trotsky, probably the Bolsheviks' No.2 figure then, spoke of the growing paper money and inflation as a result of the decline of "commodity and money relations."[32] This view was clearly shared by many of the revolutionary leaders.

Joseph Schumpeter, an influential economist during the first half of the twentieth century who was briefly finance minister in Austria during the inflationary period, wrote a book in the early 1940s theoretically summarizing the struggles between capitalism, socialism, and democracy. He noted several "merits" of inflation by saying:

> Inflation is in itself an excellent means of smoothing certain transitional difficulties and of effecting partial expropriation. . . . Finally, it must not be forgotten that inflation would powerfully ram such blocks of private business as may have to be left standing for the moment. For, as Lenin has pointed out.[33]

He is apparently in line with Lenin's and Keynes's thoughts on inflation. This is also a reminder that the idea that inflationary policy could be discretionarily sought in certain circumstances had spread among economists and politicians across Europe in the aftermath of the First World War with, or perhaps without, either Lenin's or Keynes's remarks. The exact political and economic justifications of inflationary policy may have actually arisen for different reasons in different countries, but they may also have shared certain common elements of theory and practice.

The Treaty of Versailles, reparations, and Germany's reaction

Reparations were a central issue in the interwar German political and economic processes, and many German people believed that the harsh conditions imposed by the Allied powers on Germany were the root cause of its adversities in the 1920s. No less important were the uncertainties that were created and aggravated on the German side during the process of determining and settling reparations.

The armistice between the Entente and Central Powers in early November 1918 included a term stating that "compensation will be made by Germany for all damage done to the civilian population of the Allies and their property by the aggression of Germany by land, by sea, and from the air."[34] Aware of the Allies' financial demand, the German government instructed its treasury office to estimate the amount of aggregate liabilities that Germany could owe, and the figure came out as 30 billion gold mark in December 1918.[35]

Britain and France were both highly indebted due to the effects of war, and most of their debts were ultimately owed to the United States. The three Allied powers were unable to reach an agreement on the exact amount of German reparations by the time the Treaty of Versailles was ready for Germany to sign, in June 1919. As a result, the Treaty of Versailles only determined three things with regard to reparations. First, Germany had to accept responsibility for the losses and damages caused by the war "as a consequence of the . . . aggression of Germany and her allies" and compensate the Allied powers. Second, a "Reparation Commission" was to be established to determine the exact amount of German reparations and work out a concrete scheme for payments and related financial arrangements by May 1921. Third, in the interim, Germany was required to pay the equivalent of 20 billion gold mark (5 billion U.S. dollars) in gold and in kind. The money would help to pay for Allied occupation costs. To Germany, the Treaty was a Carthaginian peace settlement. In hindsight, the Treaty was indeed "an ill-designed and ill-executed postwar settlement."[36]

In the midst of massive protests at home, the German government acquiesced to the Allied powers' ultimatum and accepted the Treaty. As it appeared, Germany was prepared to take the pains and move along with postwar reconstruction. In fact, the time between June 1919 and May 1921 was a relatively "stable" and calm period in German macroeconomics.

Figure 3.7 shows the monthly changes in German wholesale prices and exchange rate, between the German papiermark and the U.S. dollar, between February 1920 and July 1923. The numbers in the months following June 1923 cannot be displayed properly here because they are too large: wholesale prices rose 1,162 percent in August, 2,437 percent in September, 29,525 percent in October, and 10,129 percent in November, when the German mark depreciated 785 percent, 1,703 percent, 2,665 percent, and 158,039 percent, respectively.

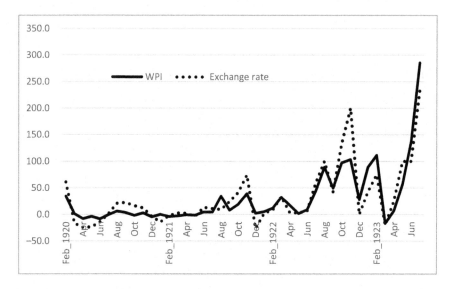

Figure 3.7 Monthly changes in wholesale prices and exchange rate (marks per U.S. dollar), percentage, Germany, February 1920–July 1923[37]

The four years from mid-1919 to late 1923 can be divided into three periods: from the Treaty of Versailles to the London Schedule in May 1921; from then to January 1923, when French and Belgian troops occupied the Ruhr region; and when German inflation culminated in hyperinflation in 1923.

The first period: from the Treaty of Versailles to the London Schedule, 1920–May 1921

During the first period, from mid-1919 to May 1921, wholesale prices in Germany and the mark's exchange rate had some fluctuations, but the movements were quite "moderate" compared to what happened later. In no single month did wholesale prices rise more than 50 percent monthly. Overall, wholesale prices rose merely 8.7 percent between January 1920 and June 1921, with an average increase of 0.6 percent per month in the one and half years. Meanwhile, depreciation in the mark against the U.S. dollar was small; the exchange rate fell only from DM59 to DM69 per dollar, although it did move somewhat turbulently in certain months of the period.

The fact that the mark's exchange rate had sharper fluctuations than wholesale prices should be largely attributed to the uncertainty and anxiety in German foreign exchange markets, which were greatly affected by news related to the ongoing work of the "Reparation Commission" in London and the progress of negotiations between German representatives and the Allied governments and others. From the second half of 1920, "bad" news began to surface that the

Commission might suggest a figure for German reparations much higher than what Germany could afford. The Commission indicated a figure of 226 billion gold mark in January 1921, and Germany soon appealed to the United States president for reconsideration.[38]

At home, the German government continued to run budget deficits, and its efforts to reform tax revenue did not achieve significant results. In the fiscal year 1920–21, the Reich government had a deficit of as much as 60 percent of its total expenditure, which amounted to 6,050 million gold mark.[39] The good news was that Germany's economy was recovering at a pace significantly higher than those in Britain or France. There was a belief that as her exports continued to grow, Germany would be able to pay war reparations. Exports growth together with other issues related to the balance of payments – such as depreciation or appreciation of the mark – were thus the focus of policy debates during the period.

The second period: May 1921–January 1923

In May 1921, the figure of Germany reparations was fixed at 132 billion gold mark (equivalent to 31.5 billion dollars) plus a few "small" items. It was still far larger than what Weimar Germany was willing to accept, but she had to accept the ultimatum once again.

Distribution of the sum among the Allied States was to be thus: France would receive 52 percent, Britain 22 percent, Italy 10 percent, Belgium 8 percent, and all others the remaining 8 percent.[40] The United States was not on the list of recipients.

According to the London Schedule, for the first 50 billion gold mark of the total reparations bill, Germany would pay 3 billion each year, including payments made for the fixed 5 percent interest rate by amortization. After the completion of this part, known as A and B bonds, payment of the remaining 82 billion gold mark (C bonds) would begin, probably in the second half of the twentieth century.[41]

An estimate shows that Germany's immediate annual payments toward the bill were equivalent to 13 percent of her national income or 80 percent of her exports then, which may be compared to the 11 percent of national income or 32 percent of exports that France had to pay in reparations to Germany after the Franco-Prussian war in 1871.[42] The high level of reparations was a result of mixed factors. Both Britain and France had an economic setback in 1920–21, and they wanted to utilize German funds to improve their balances of payments, so that they could ultimately return to a gold standard. Aware of Germany's non-action in disarmament, the two countries wished to cap her capacity for industrial expansion and military development as well.

With great dissatisfaction of the London Schedule, Weimar German representatives undertook a number of diplomatic initiatives with the aims of renegotiating the terms and seeking new credit arrangements, both bilateral and multilateral. At home, social unrest had grown, and public opinion was divided over how to deal with the demands of the Allied powers. At times, the German government made efforts to cut its budget deficit and deliver payments in cash and in kind toward the reparations bill.

From the second half of 1922, how much Germany had paid in reparations since 1919 and how much had been received by the Allied States and acknowledged by the Reparations Commission became a seriously contentious issue. For the former, the German figure was 51 billion gold mark up to the end of 1922, yet that of the Commission was merely 8 billion gold mark.[43] In particular, France began to criticize Germany's slowness in delivering goods in payment of reparations and threatened to undertake military action should the delay continue. Against this backdrop, German money markets became increasingly unstable as people saw signs of rising inflation momentum at home and mounting difficulties in German diplomatic efforts. The mark depreciated 100 percent monthly in August and 200 percent in November. More importantly, Germany's trade balance did not improve at all after the mark had devalued significantly.[44] Domestic industry and commerce had great shortages of funds that could be used for imports. When the Reichsbank decided to increase its discounting of government and industry bills, an immediate effect, nevertheless, was rises in domestic prices, which further fueled mark depreciation pressures.

The third period: 1923

Meanwhile, public opinion in German society was widely divided on many pressing issues, including how to deal with reparations. Germany and France were increasingly in dispute over the timing and amounts of payments, which consisted of both cash and goods. France threatened to use force to make Germany fulfill the Treaty and pay. As it turned out, French and Belgian troops occupied the Ruhr area in January 1923, a move which ignited a full-blown diplomatic, political, and economic crisis in Germany and paved the way to hyperinflation later in the year.

A German response to the crisis was to let her people desert their work in the Ruhr – a tactic known as the "Passive Resistance." As a result, the earlier self-restriction on budget spending had to be suspended. The Reich government provided financial support to all workers who walked out from their posts.

In the process of rising inflation, the German government – both at the central and state levels – found an unexpected "gift"; old domestic debts rapidly evaporated. The higher inflation became, the more rapidly the old debts were replaced by newly issued government securities, which in turn became increasingly devalued and worthless. Moreover, as most of the old domestic debts that the German government had were owed to the German public, new debts were issued to German banking institutions only, mainly the Reichsbank. Public subscription to government securities had become impossible when inflation skyrocketed.

Despite the fact that rising inflation helped eradicate German government debts to the German people, the German government continued to run budget deficits, and the size of the deficits became increasingly large, even in real terms. As mentioned above, after the French occupation of the Ruhr, the so-called "Passive Resistance" movement, encouraged by the Reich government, aggravated the pressure on German government spending. With the resultant rising inflation, the budget balance situation became worse than ever. As has been noted by economists who previously studied German hyperinflation, the Reich government's revenue in real terms started to decline from the second half of 1921, when inflation picked up considerably.[45] To sustain their budgetary obligations, the German government had to resort to further inflationary means by increasing securities issues at an ever faster pace. This was effectively a race between maintaining budget spending in real terms and price inflation.

The race between government spending and price inflation has occurred many times in history. The uniqueness of the German experience in the 1920s was that the banking industry had joined the process of credit expansion; banks provided credit to both government and business. When receiving credit from banks, both government and industry were able to chase price inflation by expanding their borrowings in various ways – for the government, it was mainly issues of treasury bills that were subscribed to by the Reichsbank, and for corporations, it was issues of commercial paper that were first discounted by banks and later re-discounted by the Reichsbank.

Of course, not all firms were able to borrow from banks. Those who could borrow were mainly large German firms that had long-term relationships with German banks. For this reason, there were people who believed a conspiracy theory suggesting that the German industry-bank complex was behind the hyperinflation.[46] It is undeniable that without banks' involvement, the hyperinflation would hardly have reached the high levels it did in the late months of 1923.

Technically, the skyrocketing level of inflation needed to be accommodated by an almost equally rapid expansion of paper note printing. At the heyday of inflation in the early 1920s, the Reichsbank alone ran 30 paper factories and 29 plate factories, employing 7,500 shift workers manufacturing paper notes for the country.[47] Despite this, shortages of currency notes frequently occurred. Many German states issued their own currency notes to catch up with the exploding need for the means of payment. They were called *Notgeld* – emergency money.[48] In Hamburg alone, there were about 70 currency notes of different kinds in circulation in August 1923, when inflation reached an astronomical level.[49] Germany's currency union was under threat of disintegration.

The German government did attempt a number of countermeasures to check the momentum of inflation. It sought external borrowings from America and Britain through official and private channels. It conducted an issue of securities in foreign currency – the U.S. dollar. It reintroduced and tightened foreign exchange controls. The Reichsbank raised its discount rates many times from July 1922 and offered gold for sale to the public. A new law on the autonomy of the Reichsbank was passed in May 1922, but as its president revealed, "For limiting inflation, today's autonomy of the Reichsbank is but a very small expedient."[50] The conduct of the Reichsbank during the hyperinflationary period made it notorious as a "partner in catastrophe."[51]

The German economy was in deep recession in 1923, largely due to the effects of hyperinflation. Her gross domestic product in constant prices fell by 16.9 percent over the previous year, whilst Britain and France had growth of 3.2 percent and 5.4 percent, respectively, in the same year.[52] "Hyperinflation proved an exhausting climax, but it furnished the basis for a new start," an economic historian noted.[53]

Currency reform: October 1923

The German government introduced a currency unit called *rentenmark* from mid-October 1923. It was not legal tender, but its value was guaranteed by securities on industrial and commercial land that were held in a new banking institution called the Deutsche Rentenbank, which by legislation was independent of government. The exchange rate between the *rentenmark* and the *papiermark* was set at 1 to one billion, with a total issue of 2.4 billion – half to the government, and half to the public.[54] Later, the issue of *rentenmark* increased to 3.2 billion.

In April 1924, the German government decided to establish another central bank, the Golddiskontbank, in order to restore the credibility of state banking institutions. The capital of the bank was provided in part by loans from abroad (mostly Britain), and its work was mainly to offer hard currency loans to German businesses. It also had the right to issue currency, which was never formally executed. By mid-1924, there were three central banks in Germany: the Reichsbank, which issued the currency of legal tender; the Rentenbank, which issued notes that were not legal tender but had a stable value; and the Golddiskontbank, which made loans in foreign currencies (mainly sterling).[55] The top leadership of the Reichsbank had been changed in November 1923, with a new, conservative governor who began to tighten up loan policy toward the government and business.

The *rentenmark* resembles French *assignats* in some ways, and it would certainly have failed had it not been accompanied by a number of other reforms and supporting measures. In fact, after several cabinet reshuffles, the German government returned to an austerity policy in public finance and required the Reichsbank to suspend its note issues and discounting practice. More importantly, Germany was assisted by the Dawes Plan – a multilateral schedule that was agreed in August 1924, and came into effect from the next month, which brought back financial inflows to Germany. With the Dawes Plan, France agreed to withdraw from the Ruhr, the amortization of German reparations was elongated and alleviated, and the United States and Britain promised to offer a large sum of loans to Germany. The Dawes Plan helped end both the diplomatic crisis and the currency crisis in Germany.

Soon after seeing solid signs of stabilization, Germany returned to a gold standard in September 1924, ahead of the United Kingdom (May 1925) and France, which first attempted the move in August 1926 and finally succeeded in June 1928.

Soviet Russia: hyperinflation under "New Economic Policy"

The October Revolution in 1917 was quite unexpected by many people. Lenin and other Bolshevik leaders quickly took advantage to seize power from the old regime in Russia. They soon found themselves surrounded by three daunting challenges: to end the war with Germany, to suppress massive internal rebellions, some of which were mixed up with foreign interventions, and to transform the economy and society into a new, socialist-communist model.

For the first, the Bolsheviks signed the Treaty of Brest-Litovsk with Germany, Austria-Hungary, and the Ottoman Empire in March 1918, under which Russia agreed to cede territories and pay Germany six billion gold mark in reparations. Meanwhile, revolutionary Russia defaulted on its debts to Entente countries, especially that to France. In the Treaty of Brest-Litovsk, Germany appeared to get more than she had expected, and Russia suffered enormously. It was by Lenin's insistence that Russia finally signed the Treaty after some hesitation, as he believed it a necessary cost for internal power consolidation in the country. Luckily, as the First World War ended in November 1918, the Treaty was effectively terminated. A new, bilateral treaty between Russian and Germany – the Treaty of Rapallo – was signed in April 1922, under which the two nations forfeited all earlier territorial and financial claims against each other.

The five years between the start of 1918 and the end of 1922 were a bitter time for the new regime as it fought against numerous rebellious forces in all directions. During the period, Soviet Russia even engaged in armed conflict with Poland, from February 1919 to October 1920, with a peace treaty reached in March 1921. Eventually, the Bolsheviks managed to win all battles on the domestic front in 1921 and 1922 and began to establish formally what later came to be called the Union of Soviet Socialist Republics (USSR) and to receive recognition in the international community.

Immediately after the October Revolution, the Bolshevik regime started to overturn the economic establishment in Czarist Russia. Following the doctrine of the *Communist Manifesto* published by Karl Marx and Friedrich Engels in 1848, the revolutionaries quickly nationalized all major banking institutions and took over management of all major industries, including the railways. Later, all major industrial firms were nationalized and consolidated into a state-dictated economic system. A central economic planning committee was established, and its power started to expand month upon month.

In rural areas, land redistribution from landlords to peasants was encouraged. Domestic commerce and foreign trade were increasingly put into the controlling hands of Soviet agencies. Needless to say, the Bolsheviks confiscated all property of the Czars and enemies of the revolution and also defaulted on internal government bonds. In an assault on the Russian State Bank, the Bolsheviks amassed gold reserves worth as much as 600 million gold roubles. Separately, a Czars' treasury of gold bullion, worth over 560 million roubles (300 million U.S. dollars), was captured by the Czechoslovak Legion in Kazan in late 1918 and later handed over to the Red Army when the Legion finally left Russia from Siberia the next year.[56] The bulk of the gold was put into Soviet vaults until 1922, when a new currency reform was undertaken in order to bring down hyperinflation.

Looking at the patterns of price movement in post-revolution Russia, as shown in Figures 3.1 and 3.8, it is interesting to note several aspects in which they differ from those in other countries over the same period. First, the Russian inflation was the longest one in Europe during the period. It started from early 1917, when the revolution began, and lasted until early 1924, when a major currency reform was carried through. By the strict definition of hyperinflation, the Russian episode in the early 1920s is the world's longest one, lasting 26 consecutive months from

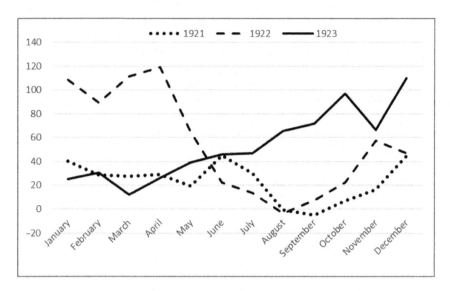

Figure 3.8 Monthly rises in general prices, percentage, Russia, 1921–23[57]

January 1922 to February 1924. Second, it is in the later years of 1922 and 1923, plus the early months of 1924, that inflation accelerated considerably. In other words, inflation during the War Communism period (1918–20) was much more moderate than that in the New Economic Policy (NEP) period (1921–24). Third, in each of the years, it is after autumn that prices turned to a surging trend through to the early months of the next year. As shown in Figure 3.8, the only exception to this was the year 1923, when inflation continued to escalate from March to October, which unambiguously indicates that inflation had then reached a new height.

The first aspect can be easily explained by the fact that Bolshevik policy never seriously attempted to kill off inflation until early 1924. Despite numerous price-control measures adopted in cities and the countryside, the new regime never ceased issuing non-convertible notes to meet the need for Soviet disbursements – wages, procurement costs, and credit provided to state-run businesses, among others. Foreign exchange markets remained closed throughout the inflationary period. Specie was used for imports and other international transactions, but it was not used for domestic payments.

The second aspect appears to be somewhat perplexing. The budget situation facing the Bolsheviks was certainly considerably worse in the War Communism period than in the later NEP period, as the regime was besieged by various internal and external forces. From early 1921, all major military conflicts were approaching an end. The Russian economy should have been on a path to recovery, despite the regime change that had taken place a few years previously. In particular, 1920 was reported to be a great harvest year in agriculture, and many other sectors of the economy were showing positive signs of turnaround.[58]

War Communism was notorious for its forced procurement of grain products in rural areas. This was undertaken through either a "grain tax" or compulsory purchases at below-market prices.[59] Its results were understandably the emergence of black markets and insufficient supplies to cities and industry. The New Economic Policy initiatives were supposed to correct such harsh measures by relaxing grain-price controls and reintroducing markets in the economy.

An immediate effect of the more or less liberally inclined NEP was naturally a surge in prices. If the liberalization were truly an output-friendly program, the inflation or hikes in inflation should have been short-lived. In fact, what happened after the NEP was put in place was a synchronization of three things: famine, accelerating inflation, and intensified price controls.

Famine in 1921 took about 5 million lives,[60] partly because of the chaotic railway system, which was now managed by incompetent Bolsheviks and trade union members. A general retail price index rose 10.5-fold in 1921 after rising 5.7-fold in 1920. Moscow decided to set up the Committee of Prices in 1921 to enforce price ceilings in the markets. In the meantime, other planning agencies were working hard to allocate and distribute goods.

Experts working with the League of Nations estimated that usual revenues accounted for merely 16 percent of Russian government expenditure in 1921, and note issues covered three-fourths of the budget deficit.[61] These figures per se, however, do not necessarily suggest that the budget deficit was the chief cause of accelerating inflation. In theory, causality may run in the opposite direction – a rise in inflation causes a budget deficit to enlarge as the purchase power of revenue declines.

The acceleration in Russian inflation from 1922 should be at least partly attributed to the introduction of a parallel currency system, despite the possibility that the policy move was intended to stabilize the country's economy and finance.

The third aspect of Soviet hyperinflation – monthly price increase rates tended to escalate after the autumn each year – suggests that agriculture lay at the center of the issue of inflation. By the early 1920s, the main industries, together with the major organs of trade and commerce in cities, had been nationalized and largely restructured into a burgeoning centrally planning system. The Russian government should have had no incentive to use inflationary policy, since that would inevitably disturb the work of national industry and trade, which had become part of the government system. Yet, one thing stood outside this broad structure: farming in rural areas. The earlier land redistribution had created millions of new private owners in the countryside (although millions of them had already died of various causes), who undoubtedly preferred a market system for their business and living. War Communism had intensified tensions between the new regime and the peasants, and the NEP – implemented from 1921 – appears to be a concession made specifically to the peasants, albeit one which was obviously a deviation from orthodox Marxist doctrine.

It was perhaps due to the mastermind of Lenin and his associates that a solution was found to the new challenge: let the peasants continue to have their private property and businesses and meanwhile supply them with rapidly depreciating paper notes. As the state now controlled industry and major commerce, together with the prices of goods from these sources, peasants would inevitably and increasingly lose their bargaining power in the markets. In the article by Lenin referred to earlier, about the role of gold in socialist Russia, he blatantly suggested that the Russian government adopt price discrimination between public and private establishments, e.g., by selling goods to the latter at higher prices.[62]

An estimate shows that the ratio of industrial prices to agricultural prices rose more than four-fold between March 1922 and September 1923.[63] The widening trend in the relative prices of industrial goods to agricultural ones was often called the "scissors" effect in Soviet economics, and this also reverberated in post-1949 Chinese economics. Peasants lost their bargaining power in markets as trade was increasingly controlled by monopolistic state agencies. In principle, for the "scissors" effect to occur, an economy need not have hyperinflation.

The Soviet Union began to take measures to reform the currency and stabilize prices. Its first attempt was to introduce a currency known as the *sovznak*, a promissory note that was linked to the paper rouble but whose issue and circulation were subject to the dictates of Soviet central planning agencies. The practice of using the token money probably began in 1919 or 1920, but it proved completely ineffective at checking inflation. A more serious attempt was made in June 1922, when a new currency, the *chervonets*, was issued.

By decree, the coin of *chervonets* was minted to contain 7.74234 grim pure gold and was thus equivalent in value to 10 old rouble. Paper *chervonets* notes of equal value were also issued, and they were supposedly convertible to specie. The policy intention was to let paper *chervonets* be used in domestic transactions and reserve gold *chervonets* for foreign trade. By regulation, holders of paper *chervonets* notes could exchange 25 percent of their holdings for specie and the remaining 75 percent for government securities and state-distributed commodities.[64]

The convertibility of *chervonets* to specie – both gold and silver coins were minted during the brief period until 1928 – was enough to keep the currency at a relatively stable value. The new issue suggests that the Soviet government held significant gold reserves and it was willing to use them to back its new paper currency.

For a period, two kinds of currency – *chervonets* and paper roubles – both circulated in the economy. The government published exchange rates between *chervonets* and paper roubles on a regular basis, with the latter continuing to depreciate over time. This was the period of the parallel currency system, and it is no surprise that the one which had the certain backing of specie pushed out the one which had no such backing.[65] Perhaps surprising to some of the policy designers, however, the immediate effect this parallel currency system had of accelerating the pace of inflation. When the people had a choice between the two currencies, they would necessarily strive to get rid of the inferior one more quickly than in settings where there was no such option. As a result, the share of paper roubles in the total currency stock shrank over time after *chervonets* were introduced. Apparently, as the Russian people quickly spent their paper roubles, the pace of inflation become higher. Perhaps due to unavailability of small denominations of *chervonets,*[66] the use of *chervonets* could not be further enhanced in transactions and savings, which in turn might have helped slow the pace of inflation. The Russian episode thus provides an example of currency substitution, in which parallel currencies of unequal value caused people to switch to the one of higher value.

The Soviets also undertook a number of other measures to consolidate the banking industry and budget management. In November 1921, a state bank of Soviet Russia was established, which was later restructured into the State Bank of the USSR – known as the Gosbank. The bank had monopolistic power to issue paper notes and provide credit. The new bank was cheered by its founders, as they saw it as a "powerful apparatus." Lenin ridiculed the self-acclaim by saying that the bank's function up to that time was utterly incomplete, as the real value of its work was minimal.[67]

Several so-called specialized banks – an industrial and commercial bank, an electricity bank, and a foreign trade bank – were set up from 1922 as part of the NEP program. Regional banks and mutual trusts were also established, apparently to renew the banking industry. These banking institutions were all under the auspices of Soviet central planning agencies, and they operated on discriminatory interest rates. In 1923 for instance, monthly interest on loans given to state agencies, cooperatives, and private firms was 8 percent, 10 percent, and 12 percent, respectively.

Meanwhile, the Soviets started to issue government bonds from 1922. The first issue was a one that was payable in kind, with a term of 8 months. The second issue, in 1923, was a bond payable in grains. Long-term bonds payable in roubles were also issued, with one in 1924 that bore an 8 percent fixed interest rate and a maturity of six years.

With these measures at hand, the Soviet government decided to discontinue the issue of old paper roubles in February 1924. Beforehand, new roubles were issued to replace the old ones at a ratio of 1 to 15,000. Convertible *chervonets*, which were at least partially convertible, had become the sole currency in circulation in the preceding years.

March 1924 was the time when hyperinflation ended in Russia. In retrospect, it took at least two years to bring down the inflation to a stable level, and this was achieved with restructuring in the banking system and budget management. Gold reserves of the Soviet government were called upon to help restore public confidence in the new currency – this also suggests, in hindsight, that the Bolshevik/Soviet implementation of inflationary policy did not result from a lack of specie reserves and that a paucity of financial resources was not the true cause of the hyperinflation in Russia in the early 1920s. If the Russian experience of ending hyperinflation in 1924 is to be judged a success, it should also be noted that it was achieved by heavy-handed state controls over large parts of the economy whose market foundations had already been destroyed.[68]

Soviet Russia gained enormously from its hyperinflationary experience. Lenin had earlier called for "rapid industrialization" as an inspiration to the Russian people in supporting the revolution. Indeed, industrial reconstruction was undertaken at a pretty fast pace from the early 1920s. As noted earlier, Russian industrialization was pursued at a huge cost to the nation's peasants, significantly through an inflationary policy and price discrimination. Continuation of the inflationary policy would have not only inevitably further jeopardized the relations between peasants and the state, but also caused unmanageable complications in the operations of industry and commerce, which had been largely nationalized and put under a central planning system by the early 1920s. In other words, the additional benefits of hyperinflation for the state were rapidly disappearing, and by the early 1920s, it was economically and politically right to decide to bring it to an end. To a certain extent, the decision to bring down inflation in Russia at that particular time might also have been affected by the stabilization programs in neighboring countries, where signs of economic recovery and progress were surfacing.

A question that may be interesting is why hyperinflation in Russia in the early 1920s did not reach a level similar to that in Germany, when the former perhaps had stronger intent to implement an inflationary policy than the latter. A plausible explanation is a relatively backward banking industry in Russia and the Bolshevik/Soviet government's suppression of the private sector's access to credit. The Russian Revolution had not only nationalized the banking system, but also paralyzed its function considerably, at least in the years immediately after the Revolution. Had credit activity taken place in a way similar to that in Germany, Russia's hyperinflation would certainly have contested Germany's record.

Finally, it should be noted that although hyperinflation in Russia ended from March 1924, the Russian economy under the central planning system continued to display certain instability throughout the latter part of the 1920s and the 1930s.

The political economy of hyperinflation: Austria, Hungary, and Poland

These three Central and Eastern European countries shared the same general background with Germany and Russia: they were active, belligerent participants in the First World War, had complicated relations with major victory powers and neighboring states, and had new political regimes that were frequently challenged from the inside. Besides, large-scale population displacement and trade reorientation immediately following the end of the war handicapped economic recovery and reconstruction, with food-supply stabilization and infrastructure restoration being the overriding economic tasks. Nevertheless, in each of the three countries, both hyperinflation and stabilization had their own "national identities," just as much as did those in Germany and Russia.

Austria: devaluation preceded inflation

As the First World War approached its end, the Habsburg Monarchy – the dual political entity which ruled the Austro-Hungarian Empire at the heart of Europe from the 1860s – fell apart. The German-speaking, mostly Catholic, people formed the Republic of German-Austria in November 1918, apparently with a wish of merging with Germany in the future. The Entente powers quickly opposed the drive and explicitly required Austria to remain independent from Germany. Meanwhile, because of the postwar split of the Austro-Hungarian Empire, Austria lost her access to many of her traditional agricultural and industrial supplies in Hungary and Czechoslovakia. She became an "orphan republic," alienated by many of her neighboring countries, old and new.[69]

The Treaty of Saint-Germain, signed in September, 1919 between Austria and the Entente states, defined her new borders and also imposed clauses on reparations. Similar to Germany's situation under the Treaty of Versailles, the amount and method of payment of reparations were not specified for Austria in the first instance. In particular, the Treaty provided the Allied States with a first charge on all assets and revenues of the Austrian government for the purposes of meeting the costs of occupation and paying reparations.[70] This clause effectively deprived Austria of access to international financial markets and hampered revenue restructuring in the country until the issue was renegotiated and the situation clarified.

Austria experienced serious inflation during the period 1918–20, with consumer prices doubling each year therein. Many Austrians were unemployed, rationing was adopted in cities, and many people's living standards were reduced to a subsistence level. To meet growing demands for expenditure, the government continued to run sizable budget deficits throughout the period.

These three years were the most critical time for political transition in Austria, but she managed to maintain a Vienna-centered parliamentary system and overcome her hardest economic distress. Yet, hyperinflation occurred in the following two years. A retail price index rose to 70 percent monthly in November 1921 and jumped to nearly 130 percent in August the following year (Figure 3.9). Overall, the consumer price index rose 95 percent in 1921, and 2,500 percent in 1922.[71]

Looking closely at Figure 3.9, we may immediately find that prior to the surges in retail prices in the two months, there were earlier, and somehow larger, depreciations of the Austrian currency – *crown* (also spelled *krone*) – which fell by 133 percent in September, 1921 and 124 percent in July, 1922. The latter change seems smaller than the inflation rate in the next month (130 percent), but depreciation greatly exceeded inflation on a cumulative basis over the three months to July, 1922 (409 percent vs. 323 percent).

This pattern has made observers believe that hyperinflation in Austria in 1921– 22 was very much "exchange rate-driven." A senior expert who worked at the League of Nations between 1918 and 1924, J. van Walre De Dordes, believed that disappointing news of the negotiations between Austria and the Allied States, which took place from March 1921 – August 1922, shocked the Austrian money market and fueled hyperinflation. The chain of causality was thus: when the crown's value fell in the market, the Austrian government had to expand its spending to cover the additional costs of imports – much of the Austrian government's spending then was on imported goods such as food and energy – and therefore, it had to issue more paper crown notes in the absence of alternative

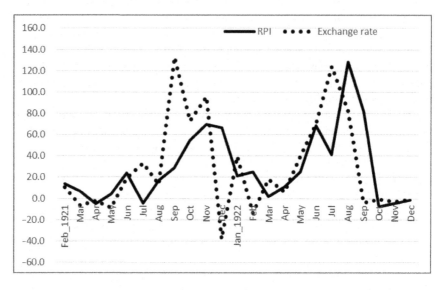

Figure 3.9 Monthly changes in retail prices and exchange rate (Austrian crowns per U.S. dollar on the New York market), percentage, Austria, February 1921–December 1922[72]

sources of revenue and access to credit. The view was also shared by many who were working at the League of Nations.[73]

In particular, Walre De Dordes noted an effect of inflation on the budget deficit: when prices were rising, the real value of taxes paid to the government became considerably less in the interim few months between assessment and actual collection, especially in the case of direct taxes on property.[74] This is an example of the Tanzi Effect: fast inflation tends to cause the real value of tax revenue to decline during the process of collection and spending.

Moreover, the process of negotiation over more than one and a half years was never smooth. Demands of a merger with Germany from certain political groups in Austria were heard from time to time during this period. The Allied States, together with the League of Nations, finally agreed to offer a multilateral aid program to Austria in August 1922, which was signed in October and finalized with legal procedures in early 1923. The crown's exchange rate was first stabilized, and this was followed, with a lag of one month, by a fall in inflation (Figure 3.9).

With the program, all signatory countries assured the political and economic independence and territorial integrity of Austria and agreed to contribute a pool of loans and guarantees to Austria. In return, Austria agreed to restructuring of her internal public finance and allowed the League of Nations greater monitoring of the work of the budget system inside the country. The Austrian success of stabilization with an international supporting program provided an exemplary model for a number of countries in Eastern Europe, including Hungary, a year later.

As a result, the Austrian government began to be able to borrow on private markets. It also started to reorganize the state banking system by forming the Austrian National Bank, which replaced the old Austro-Hungarian National Bank. In March 1925, the crown was replaced by a new currency, the *Schilling*, when Austria formally returned to a gold standard.

During the interwar period, several leading economists took senior positions in the Austrian government. Of them, Joseph A. Schumpeter was its first Finance Minister, though only for six months. As noted by Galbraith, many of them "shared with Schumpeter a profound mistrust of any action that seemed to risk inflation along with an even greater distaste for anything that seemed to suggest socialism."[75] In latter decades of the twentieth century, after a majority of them had migrated to America in the 1930s, they gained influence, and their philosophy became known as the Austrian School of Economics.

Hungary: inflation-led devaluation

When the First World War ended in November 1918, the troubles of Hungary appeared to be just beginning. As a successor state to the Austro-Hungarian Empire, she had to engage in peace talks with the Entente powers with the hope of minimizing losses. Hard bargaining proved unsuccessful, and a provisional government had to resign. Then it was followed by a left-wing rise, a "Red Terror," and a "White Terror." Meanwhile, new regimes in the country had to fight, from time to time, with several new neighbors – all of them were either claiming land or ethnic minorities in parts of the old Empire. This was a time of "postwar convulsions," which lasted approximately from 1918 to mid-1920.[76]

With improved signs of political stability in the country, the Treaty of Trianon was made ready by the Allied States for Hungary to accept. Under the terms of the Treaty, signed in June 1920, Hungary lost about two-thirds of its population and three-fifths of its territory. Like the two cases of the Treaty of Versailles with Germany and the Treaty of Saint-Germain with Austria, the Treaty of Trianon did not spell out the total amount of, or payment schedule for, reparations. The Allied States' Reparation Commission held a lien on the assets of the Hungarian government, and this obviously crippled its financial capacity. Conflicts and tensions with neighboring countries also impeded trade and economic recovery.

Before the end of the war, the currencies circulating in Hungary were the crown and paper notes issued by the Austro-Hungarian Bank in Vienna. After the split, old notes were stamped in Hungary until August 1921, when a Hungarian-run banknote printing agency started to operate. The new currency, Hungarian *krone*, replaced all earlier ones. Note issues became a chief source of the Hungarian government's budget deficit financing.

Of the monthly data available for 1921–22, the changes in retail prices and the exchange rate between the krone and U.S. dollar are displayed in Figure 3.10. Compared to the case of Austria (Figure 3.9), there is a similarity in the level of inflation. Between January 1921 and December 1923, retail prices rose 289.7-fold in Hungary and 218.5-fold in Austria. With regard to monthly rates, Austria had a

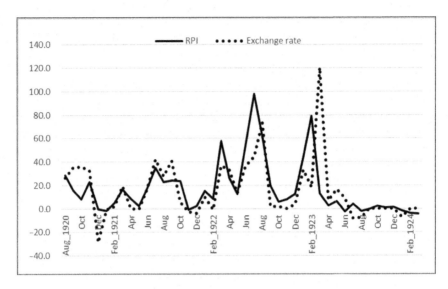

Figure 3.10 Monthly changes in retail prices and exchange rate (Hungarian *krones* per U.S. dollar on the New York market), percentage, Hungary, August 1920–March 1924[77]

higher level of inflation (129 percent in August 1922) than Hungary (97.9 percent in July 1923), as shown in Table 3.1. The difference in the monthly rate between the two countries may suggest a gap in private sector access to credit. In both countries, banking institutions lagged behind those in Germany, and the ones in Hungary were possibly more rudimentary than those in Austria.[78]

There are two other differences between Hungary and Austria. First, the rate of change in prices shows a stronger zig-zag tendency in Hungary than in Austria, which perhaps suggests that short-run political and policy instability was more prevalent in Hungary than in Austria. Second, inflation moved more closely together with depreciation of the currency in Hungary than in Austria. As discussed earlier, the pattern in Austria looks like a "depreciation-driven inflation," but in the case of Hungary, it is more like a "co-movement of inflation and depreciation" in both timing and magnitude. To be precise, depreciation moderately lagged behind inflation. So, in a sense, this may be regarded as an "inflation-led depreciation."

A possible explanation of the difference between the "inflation-led deprecia-tion" in Hungary and Austria's "depreciation-driven inflation" lies in trade dependence. In theory, in an economy greatly reliant on external trade, exchange rate movements tend to exert major influence on both real and expected trade flows. Surrounded by several hostile or nervous neighbors – some of them equally as politically and economically unstable – Hungary could hardly be expected to recover and grow its external trade in a normal way. In fact, data show that by 1924, Hungary's total turnover of import and export of goods, measured in U.S.

dollars per capita and based on the country's interwar territory, remained 25 percent less than the level in 1913.[79]

Similar to what happened in Austria, Hungary finally managed to receive an aid program from the League of Nations. When the talks between the two sides showed positive signs from early 1923, domestic inflation and foreign exchange rates quickly returned to more normal levels. Finalized in 1924, the deal was meanwhile accompanied by the establishment of the Hungarian National Bank and budget system restructuring. Also like in Austria, Hungary issued a new, convertible currency – the *pengő* – to replace the previous one in 1925 and returned to a gold standard.

Poland: inflation and devaluation in parallel

After more than a century of partition, mainly by Prussian Germany and Czarist Russia, Poland had the opportunity to regain her independence after the First World War. Many Poles had joined Entente armies and fought against occupying forces of Germany and the Austro-Hungarian Empire. Soon after the establishment of the Second Polish Republic, toward the end of 1918, the country was at war with Bolshevik Russia for three years, up to 1921, and briefly engaged in border conflicts with Czechoslovakia. But unlike many others, as a newborn republic, Poland did not owe war reparations or any significant debt. What she needed most was to heal the war-torn land and move to build new infrastructure.

In a sense, what happened in the territories of the Austro-Hungarian Empire after the First World War was disintegration of a monetary union, and what happened in Poland at that time was monetary union. There were four or five currencies in circulation prior to the founding of the new republic: Austro-Hungarian crowns, German marks, German ostrubles (ruble-equivalent currency issued by German authorities in the Baltic region), Russian rubles, and markas (also known as marks) issued by the German-controlled Polish State Loan Bank. A new currency – the Polish marka – was issued by the young republic in 1920 in the midst of the Polish-Bolshevik war. Inflation had already become severe in the two-year period 1919–20.

Monthly price movement and exchange rate data, available from early 1921, are shown in Figure 3.11. Like in Hungary, the movements in prices and exchange rate were closely associated, except for a few months in 1921 when changes in the exchange rate lagged behind those in prices. Also notable is that during 1922, there was a trend of accelerating inflation, which was followed by a distinctive disinflation in the first half of 1923. Then, inflation galloped to a new height, with the monthly rate over 100 percent in each of the last three months of 1923.

Apparently, the level of inflation in Poland in October 1923 – 275 percent – was much higher than the highest monthly inflation experienced by either Austria or Hungary. But, the Polish figure (based on wholesale prices) is not entirely comparable with those of Austria and Hungary (based on retail prices). By and large, the hyperinflation in Poland in late 1923 was not lesser than those in Austria or Hungary some time before.

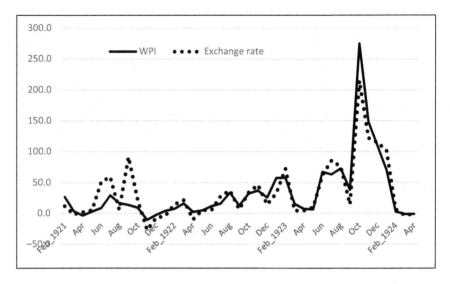

Figure 3.11 Monthly changes in wholesale prices and exchange rate (Polish marka per U.S. dollar), percentage, Poland, February 1921–April 1924[80]

The fundamental cause of the rising inflation and hyperinflation was the inflationary policy adopted by the Polish government during the period. As in the cases of Austria and Hungary, the competing political parties in Poland all needed to expand their budgets, but many of them were afraid of raising taxes. Several attempts to stabilize the currency failed. Stability in politics and policy was a severe problem in the early 1920s. There was an assassination of the president-elect in December 1922, and four years later, a *coup d'état*.

A major currency reform took place in early 1924, when the nominally gold-convertible *zloty* replaced the *marka*. Meanwhile, the Bank of Poland, the republic's central bank, was established. Several restrictive measures were adopted, including maximums on credit to the government and a reserve scheme for central banking. Both prices and exchange rates returned to stable patterns in early 1924.

The 1924 currency reform was an undertaking without direct foreign aid, though there was an Italian loan of 400 million lira (equivalent to $18 million by then exchange rate) arranged soon after the start of the reform).[81] The Polish prime minister – the same person also assumed finance minister at the time – apparently wanted a quick success without diplomatic complications.

In fact, the success did not last long. From 1925, rapid domestic credit expansion and relaxation on exchange controls, together with the central bank's direct lending to the private sector at "insufficient" interest rates, caused a renewed threat of inflation.[82] The *zloty* depreciated significantly in the summer that year. This time, the Polish government could no longer refuse international offers of aid. An international banking syndicate, under the aegis of the French and American governments, provided a large sum in loans to Poland in 1927, and a seconded senior American official was appointed as financial advisor to the Polish government and director of the Bank of Poland.[83] The new par value of the *zloty* was set to be 58.14 percent of its original level in early 1924.[84] With trade and economy recovered eventually, Poland's monetary and financial system gained true stabilization. She subsequently moved to a gold exchange standard.

Czechoslovakia: a silver lining to the cloud of hyperinflation during the 1920s

Czechoslovakia, also an Eastern European nation newly born after the end of the First World War, did not experience serious inflation in the later 1910s and 1920s, despite the fact she then had hyperinflationary neighbors in virtually all directions. Thomas Sargent, a Nobel Prize winner in economics, highly praised Czechoslovakia for her unusual monetary conduct in his study of hyperinflationary episodes of the 1920s.[85] Another eminent macro-economist has cited Czechoslovakia as the country that "stopped inflation before it even started."[86]

Like other successor states of the Austro-Hungarian Empire, Czechoslovakia had to manage the disintegration of monetary union. Stamping crown paper notes previously issued by the Austro-Hungarian Bank and currently circulating inside the country was the first necessary step. At the time of the introduction of a new currency, the *koruna*, conservative institutional arrangements for monetary and financial conduct were put into effect.

The *koruna* depreciated considerably against the U.S. dollar in 1919 but started to stabilize from early 1920. Throughout the first half of the 1920s, the *koruna* remained a stable currency. Measured in wholesale prices, there was no significant inflation at all in the period.[87] Like Czechoslovakia, several other Eastern European countries – Romania and Yugoslavia, for instance – somehow did not have hyperinflation during the period as well. A British historian believed that it was French protection that helped the Danubian states avoid the worst outcomes of the economic disorder after the war.[88] In fact, it was Czechoslovakia alone that had the lowest and most stable inflation, and all the others experienced serious inflation of one degree or another at the time.[89]

Moreover, with a fast economic recovery and strengthened financial resources, Czechoslovakia was even able to participate in the international aid programs to Austria in 1922 and to Hungary in 1924, among others.

Professor Sargent believes that the Czechoslovakian government successfully maintained self-imposed fiscal and financial discipline, so that it had to finance its spending – including that for capital improvement – by either taxation or borrowing on securities, i.e., not by issuing currency notes.[90] Budget deficits were not absent in the early 1920s, but they were small in amount and mostly covered by government loans.

A deeper question is, what possibly contributed to Czechoslovakian success in establishing conservative policy rules for monetary and financial conduct at that time? There are several candidate explanatory factors, but each of them alone seems inadequate.

First, Czechoslovakia engaged in no major conflicts with neighbors, but this factor was shared by Austria. Second, Czechoslovakia maintained good diplomatic relations with major powers, especially Britain, France, and the United States, and consequently, she received an enormous amount of international credit for food imports in the early years of the postwar period, which helped reduce inflationary pressures. Yet, this factor was more or less shared by Poland.[91] Third, unlike Austria or Hungary, Czechoslovakia had no obligation for war reparations, nor did she inherit any significant public debts from earlier regimes. This was again shared by Poland. Fourth, compared to other successor states of the Austro-Hungarian Empire, Czechoslovakia had better industrial capacity and infrastructure and a more educated population. This was obviously shared by Germany, to no lesser extent.

It must be a combination of internal and external factors that worked in a coordinated, yet unrelated, way for Czechoslovakia to be able to first commit to a conservative institutional framework and subsequently sustain its functions in the realm of monetary and financial conduct. At times, maintaining macroeconomic stability came at a cost, but with some luck, the country managed to get through adverse circumstances.[92]

After a period of stability, Czechoslovakia in April 1926 joined the wave of nations returning to the gold standard.

The League of Nations: an emerging role of multilateralism

The wave of hyperinflation in interwar Europe became a center of attention in the World, and its deepening impacts on economies and societies posed threats to the international economic and political order that was largely restored and pursued by the Allied States during and after the Versailles peace process. Many people feared the possibility that Bolshevik-style revolutions would quickly gain strength in Europe as a result of economic disasters. Before the end of the First World War, U.S. President Woodrow Wilson made a popular declaration – the Fourteen Points – concerning postwar world peace and international relations. He appealed for the principle of national self-determination, demanded the removal of economic barriers between nations, and called for "[a] general association of nations" that "should be formed on the basis of covenants designed to create mutual guarantees of the political independence and territorial integrity of States, large and small equally."[93] The last point later effectively catalyzed the establishment of a new intergovernmental institution, the League of Nations, which was endorsed by the Treaty of Versailles in 1919 with the intent to make it, unprecedentedly, become a truly global authority for world peace and security. Thus, the world began to have a prototype body for global governance for the first time. Despite the fact that the United States Senate did not ratify the Treaty of Versailles, the League of Nations played a constructive, though sometimes also controversial, role in international affairs during its short life, mainly in the 1920s and 1930s, and thereby set an example for the United Nations and the Bretton-Woods Institutions that were established for world peace and international economic order after the Second World War.

As part of the large international institution, which was somewhat ambitious in its early years, the Economic and Financial Organization (EFO) – sometimes alternately called the Economic and Financial Section or Department – assumed a leading function in policy consultation and coordination in the field of international monetary and financial affairs. Its primary work was to convince the international community of the importance of currency stability and orderly flows of international capital. For this purpose, the EFO organized a large international economic and monetary conference in Brussels in the summer of 1920 which was attended by 34 countries, including some who were former enemies.[94] Participating countries were required to submit information on currency, public finance, international trade, retail prices, and coal production.[95] This was obviously the beginning of international macroeconomic surveillance, an endeavor entirely inherited and currently conducted by the International Monetary Fund. The need for macroeconomic monitoring prompted the League of Nations to hire a large number of experts of different nationalities, mainly economists and statisticians, to provide international civil service. Unlike diplomats and delegates, who were largely constrained by national interests and ideologies, these professionals could work together in a more transparent manner, albeit in an "absence of accountability."[96]

Austria was the first country that received a multinational aid program to end hyperinflation through the coordination of the League of Nations. The EFO had no financial resources of its own to do the job, and it had to obtain consent from the leading members of the League, mainly Britain and France. In addition, any aid program to successor states of the former Austro-Hungarian Empire required permission from the Reparation Commission, which had already placed certain conditions on the use of state-owned assets. Thus, international politics would necessarily complicate the work of the League of Nations in the field of international financial arrangements. In the end, when a consensus emerged in October, 1922, the League of Nations – through its EFO – quickly seized the opportunity to implement the aid program to Austria.

With guarantees from a number of participating governments, syndicated securities were marketed by major Austrian banks in New York and London. The Austrian government had agreed to back up the scheme with its revenue from its monopoly on tobacco and custom duties as collateral.[97] In addition, Austria agreed to restructure its public finance, strictly following the principle of austerity. In the event, food subsidies were cut, and 5,000 civil servants were laid off.[98] Moreover, a foreigner, a Dutch national, was appointed by the League as a commissioner in Vienna to oversee Austrian government finance. He had the power to approve or override budget plans for the young republic for more than three years until 1926.

Ludwig von Mises, a leading Austrian economist and then principal officer of the Austrian Chamber of Commerce, once recalled his experience of working with League representatives while hyperinflation was brought to end in the country:

"Austria did not need a foreign loan at this time; what it did need was a foreign finance commissioner whom the government could, if necessary, hold responsible for the odium; a vetoing of an increase in outlays."[99]

The successful experience of ending hyperinflation in Austria encouraged Hungary to receive a similar aid program under the auspices of the League of Nations, when it fell into the vortex of hyperinflation in 1923. Like Austria, Hungary had to agree to a number of fiscal and monetary conditions set by international lenders. An international commissioner – this time, a U.S. national – was stationed in Budapest to monitor Hungarian public finance and its reform. Compared to Austria, austerity was implemented to a lesser degree, and the amount loaned was only half.[100]

Apart from Austria and Hungary, the League of Nations arranged financial aid for the Free City of Danzig, Greece, and Bulgaria in the mid-1920s, when they encountered great troubles in their monetary and financial systems. Through these cases, a pattern of international financial aid emerged with characteristics such as multilateral guarantees for securities issued by recipient governments, fiscal austerity, and resident international surveillance. They appeared to become a standard package for governments dealing with a monetary crisis.[101]

Notably, not every country that had a currency problem appealed to the League of Nations for help. Poland managed to implement domestic reform on her own to bring down inflation in 1924, but the situation deteriorated two years later. The country was in need of foreign financial help. But for diplomatic reasons, Poland accepted aid mainly from France. In 1926, when the country needed foreign financial aid once again, Britain insisted that she go to the League of Nations, but France managed to offer internationally syndicated credit instead.[102]

In the case of Germany, the issue of whether and how to receive an international credit program was more complicated than elsewhere. Technically, Germany was not a member of the League of Nations until 1926, and for this reason no action could be undertaken within the framework of the League. Second, a central issue under dispute was reparations, which were also outside of the reach of the League. Third, in the absence of United States involvement, the financial resources the League could use were so limited that the issue of German hyperinflation looked just like an elephant in the room.

In practice, the presence of international superintendents appointed by the League of Nations sometimes caused frictions and frustrations in countries where a League-coordinated aid program was underway. The finance commissioner from the Netherlands in Austria, who had a demanding and uncompromising personality, indeed provoked enormous negative sentiment among the Austrians who were working with him. He later even became a symbol of "unwelcome international interference" in the country.[103]

Admittedly, the League of Nations, with its EFO, had many limitations in its work dealing with issues related to stability of the international financial system and in providing a helping hand to countries to end hyperinflation. In fact, many lessons were taken from the League of Nations' interwar experience when the world once again had an opportunity to rebuild the architecture of the international financial system at the end of the Second World War. Elements of multilateralism remain today in the work of the International Monetary Fund and the World Bank, among others.

Hyperinflation and the rise of the Nazi Regime

The wave of hyperinflation in interwar Europe exerted vast impacts on the economy and society in countries where it spread. One of the profound questions concerning its consequences is whether and how hyperinflation in Weimar Germany actually caused the rise of the Nazi Regime, which remains somewhat puzzling.

Costantino Bresciani-Turroni, an Italian economist who once worked with the League of Nations on German financial issues, wrote a large volume on German hyperinflation in the 1920s. When the book was translated into English and published in 1937, Lionel Robbins, a leading British economist of the time, stated in his foreword to the book,

> It was the most colossal thing of its kind in history: and, next probably to the Great War itself, it must bear responsibility for many of the political and economic difficulties of our generation. It destroyed the wealth of the ore solid elements in German society: and it left behind a moral and economic disequilibrium, apt breeding ground for the disasters which have followed. Hitler is the foster-child of the inflation.[104]

The view that links hyperinflation and the rise of the Nazi regime is clearly not an isolated one. At the end of 1924, when currency reform was undertaken in Germany, a British diplomat stationed in Munich – a city in southern Germany, where Hitler first attempted a political hijacking (the Munich Putsch) in November, 1923 – observed, in an insightful note:

> National Socialism had thrived in the existing depression of 1923. There was a don't-care feeling in the air. The greater fiasco of the trial disillusioned the minds of more reasonable people, although Hitler's party a little later got one-fifth of the Landtag votes . . . Hitler's greatest enemy is the Rentenmark. It is impossible to overestimate the beneficial effect of the stabilization of the currency on Bavaria, and I suppose also on the whole German outlook. When the London Conference [on the implementation of the Dawes Plan] assembled in July 1924, six months of stabilization had already had a calming effect on the Nationalist hotheads.[105]

Upon reflection, one may wonder that if hyperinflation were indeed a hotbed of extremists like the Nazis, why could they continue to grow after the successful currency reform that obviously had "a calming effect" on the German economy and society from 1924? An American economist who won a Nobel Prize in 2008,

Paul Krugman, disputed the view in 2013 by saying that "the 1923 hyperinflation didn't bring Hitler to power; it was the Brüning deflation and depression."[106]

Heinrich Brüning was German Chancellor in 1930–32, when the German economy, as well as the world economy, slid into recession. He responded to the worsening situation by adopting a deflationary policy package, including cuts of government expenditure and hikes of tax revenue. The unemployment rate in Germany rose to 13.9 percent in 1931 and 17.2 percent in 1932, the highest level in Europe.[107] Prices fell also considerably between 1929 and 1933, much more so than in Britain and France. Meanwhile, he devoted great energy to persuading the Allied Powers to reduce German reparations, and for this purpose, he assumed the post of foreign minister from 1931. In the end, when an international conference in Lausanne, Switzerland in June, 1932 agreed to finalize the last reparations Germany was obligated to pay at the amount of 3 billion *reichsmark*, Brüning had already resigned from his government posts due to increased rifts in domestic politics. At the time of his resignation, the Nazis seemed already an unstoppable force in German politics.

In a sense, Brüning's deflationary policy was an outcome of the hyperinflation in earlier years. After the return to the gold standard and financial reforms at the end of 1924, politicians of Weimar Germany became scared of inflationary policy measures. More importantly, many of them had lost the trust and confidence of the German public, who had become increasingly discontent and impatient, politically and socially.

William L. Shirer, an American journalist and war correspondent, who was reporting in Europe from the mid-1920s and in Germany from the mid-1930s, witnessed the interwar German economic depression and the rise of the Nazi regime. He believed that when Weimar Germany resorted to inflationary policy, the hyperinflation in the early 1920s destroyed the political and social foundations of the democratic government system. As he observed, after the bitter experience of hyperinflation,

> The masses of the people, however, did not realize how much the industrial tycoons, the Army and the State were benefiting from the ruin of the currency. All they knew was that a large bank account could not buy a straggly bunch of carrots, a half peck of potatoes, a few ounces of sugar, a pound of flour. They knew that as individuals they were bankrupt. And they knew hunger when it gnawed at them, as it did daily. In their misery and hopelessness, they made the Republic the scapegoat for all that had happened. Such times were heaven-sent for Adolf Hitler.[108]

In retrospect, 1923 was probably a turning point for the rise of Hitler:

> Down in Bavaria, the young firebrand Adolf Hitler grasped the strength of the new nationalist, antidemocratic, antirepublican tide. He began to ride it. He was greatly aided by the course of events, two in particular: the fall of the mark and the French occupation of the Ruhr.[109]

These events seemed to have given him a springboard to jump into the German political arena, though there was still a long way to go to the top of power:

> No doubt, the hardships and uncertainties of the wanton inflation were driving millions of Germans toward that conclusion [dictatorship], and Hitler was ready to lead them on. In fact, he had begun to believe that the chaotic conditions of 1923 had created an opportunity to overthrow the Republic which might not recur. But certain difficulties lay in his way if he were himself to lead the counterrevolution, and he was not much interested in it unless he was.[110]

A dedicated historian of modern Germany has also taken up the issue of how hyperinflation in the earlier years and deflation (the Great Depression) in the later years contributed to the rise of the Nazi regime. As he first reflects, "There is no contesting the fact that it was the Great Depression and not the inflation that was the driving force in making it possible for National Socialism to come to power in January 1933."[111] He then shows evidence that German society and politics were paralyzed and altered under the impacts of hyperinflation, and that the Nazi movement made gains by propagandizing the "devil of inflation." A final conclusion he arrives at is, "Surely, the German inflation is one important reason why so many Germans defaulted not only on democracy, but also on civilization itself."[112]

In this light, the electoral victory of the Nazis in 1933 was their gain in the second chance provided by the deflation from the early 1930s, as they had the first some ten years ago. Brüning's economic policy might be held at least partially accountable for the magnitude of the distress, but the root causes of the economic depression in Germany in the 1930s were both international and historical. For the latter, the hyperinflation in the early 1920s was certainly the one to blame.

Again, in retrospect, one can say that the currency reforms in 1924 saved the German economy from falling into an abyss and helped to restore the German public's trust in the currency and to stabilize the economy. But they could not cure the pains inflicted on the German populace and elite by the Treaty of Versailles and its aftermath of reparations. Despite the Dawes Plan, the Young Plan, and the Lausanne Conference – all of which substantially reduced the burden of reparations on German shoulders, Weimar Germany never really had rapprochement with the Allied Powers.

The fact that Italy did not have hyperinflation in the 1920s but also experienced a rise of Fascism suggests that hyperinflation itself was not a necessary and sufficient condition for the rise of the Nazi regime in Germany. Yet, in many ways, the hyperinflation helped facilitate social changes in Weimar Germany which the Nazis took advantage to gain support. In a sense, Hitler's rise in the 1930s may be an "unintended consequence" of the hyperinflation in the early 1920s. And, this also suggests that the impacts of hyperinflation on an economy and society do not die instantly with a stabilization program, even one that is successful. Memories of hyperinflation were acrimonious. Like Napoleon, Hitler appeared to be greatly mindful of the inflationary effects of expansionary financial policy in his pursuit of the "Millennium War," even at his neediest time.[113]

Notes

1   Hanke and Krus, *ibid.*
2   It is briefly mentioned in Cagan, Hyperinflation: Theory, in *The New Palgrave Dictionary of Economics*, Vol. II.
3   Fischer, Sahay and Végh, Table 1, p. 838. Kemmerer (1940) and Cáardenas and Manns (1987) provide detailed studies on the Mexican episode of hyperinflation. As documented in Cáardenas and Manns, in the last two months of 1916, the Mexican peso devalued with U.S dollar by 134 percent and 115 percent, respectively (Table 2, p. 384).
4   Hanke and Krus, Table 30.1 "The Hyperinflation Table," p. 371.
5   There is little data available for Russia other than a monthly retail price indicator. Increases in paper currency in circulation in Russia every half-year between January 1918 and December 1920 have been documented in one source: Davies (1989, p. 995), but no other continuous data concerning deposits, interest rates, exchange rates, and wages, among other items, are traceable.
6   Data of Austria, Germany, Hungary, and Poland are from Sargent (2013); and that of Russia is from Paarlberg, Table 2.9, p. 70. The German and Polish curves show WPI, and the others show RPI. For Germany and Russia, January 1918 = 1; for Austria and Poland, January 1921 = 1; and for Hungary, July 1921 = 1.
7   Uses the same data source as Figure 3.1. Poland is excluded because of the lack of data on money supply (deposits and currency in circulation). Both of the price indictor (WPI or RPI) and money supply are indexed to 1 in the initial month (Germany: January 1921; Austria: January 1923; and Hungary: July 1921).
8   The amount of German treasury bills is given in Holtfrerich, Table 20, pp. 67–8. Between January 1919 and October 1923, German wholesale prices rose by a factor of 117,875,616.
9   Uses the same data source as Figure 3.1. Poland is excluded because of the lack of data on money supply (deposits and currency in circulation).
10 Uses the same data source as Figure 3.1.
11 Holtfrerich, p. 72.
12 The Reichsbank discount rate and daily money rate (both annualized) are from Holtfrerich, Table 23, p. 73. The "forward" inflation rate is the year-on-year percentage change in wholesale prices, with raw data from Sargent (2013).
13 Holtfrerich, Table 46, p. 243. The index of hourly money wage rates comprises 29 categories of workers and is based on collective agreements at the beginning of each month, with a fixed base period of 1914; and the cost-of-living index is an average for each month, with a fixed base period of 1913–14. The real wage is the money wage index divided by the cost-of-living index each month.
14 Maddison (1982, Table C6, p. 206).
15 James, p. 4.
16 The exchange rate varied between 4.18 and 4.21 reichmarks per U.S. dollar in the 34 years (Sommariva and Tullio, pp. 231–2). The exchange rate of 4.20 in 1913 was thereby regarded as the standard value of "gold mark," which was frequently referred to in subsequent years including in the calculations of German reparations stipulated in the Treaty of Versailles.
17 An episode of hyperinflation occurred in the Austro-Hungarian Empire during the Napoleonic wars in the early 1810s (Kindleberger, 1984, p. 130).
18 Chown, p. 258.
19 Cippolla, p. 181.
20 Kindleberger (1984, p. 296).
21 Kindleberger (1984, Table 16.2, p. 296).
22 There are no official figures of aggregate output in Germany for 1914–18 and several years after 1918, but it is known that the net national product in Germany in real terms contracted by 35.1 percent during the period (Sommariva and Tullio, Appendix 2,

pp. 226–7). Using a likely inflation rate of 300 percent for the period – a simple average of the changes in CPI and WPI, we derive a nominal NNP for 1918 and therefore the debt ratio in the text.

23 Mitchell, *Europe*, Table H2.
24 Eichengreen (1992).
25 Keynes (1919[2009], p. 43); also cited by Fetter, p. 78.
26 Fetter, p. 77.
27 Fetter, p. 78.
28 White and Schuler, p. 217.
29 White and Schuler, p. 217.
30 White and Schuler, p. 219.
31 *Lenin's Collected Works*, 2nd English edition, Volume 33, pp. 109–16, Moscow: Progress Publishers, 1965. The text is also available online at www.marxists.org/archive/lenin/works/1921/nov/05.htm.
32 Full citation of Trotsky's speech in July, 1920 is given in Nenovsky, p. 4.
33 Schumpeter (1994[1942], pp. 226–7).
34 Holtfrerich, p. 140; citation of Keynes (1919).
35 Holtfrerich, p. 141.
36 Toniolo, p. 24.
37 Sargent (2013, Tables 3.3 and 3.4, pp. 72–3).
38 Kindleberger (1984, p. 298).
39 Bresciani-Turroni, p. 56.
40 Toniolo, p. 26; also Hardach, p. 25.
41 Germany finally paid off the last bit of the reparations in 2010, 20 years after German Reunification.
42 Webb (1989, Figures 6.1a and 6.1b, pp. 106–7).
43 Holtfrerich, p. 149.
44 Ferguson (1995, pp. 239–54), where it is shown that German exports grew at a fast pace in many months in 1921–22, while her imports increased at an even higher pace.
45 Graham, Chart 11, p. 39; also Bresciani-Turroni, pp. 64–7.
46 Ferguson (1995, pp. 274–5).
47 James (1999, p. 17).
48 Webb, p. 14; and MacGregor, Chapter 23, "Money in crisis," pp. 420–37.
49 Ferguson (1995, p. 286).
50 Marsh, p. 99.
51 Marsh, Chapter 4, pp. 91–121.
52 Maddison (1982, Table A8, pp. 176–7).
53 Kindleberger (1984, p. 327).
54 Kindleberger (1984, p. 326).
55 James (1999, p. 23).
56 Mohr, p. 118, 205.
57 Raw data from Paarlberg, Table 2.9, p. 70.
58 Davies (1989, p. 1007).
59 Paarlberg, p. 74.
60 Paarlberg, p. 75. During the civil war period (1918–20), about 7 million Russians died, which was four times the number of Russian deaths during the First World War.
61 Paarlberg, p. 76.
62 The original text of Lenin is a bit long, but worth recounting here: "The proletarian government can control trade, direct it into definite channels, keep it within certain limits. I shall give a small, a very small example. In the Donets Basin a slight, still very slight, but undoubted revival in the economy has commenced, partly due to a rise in the productivity of labour at the large state mines, and partly due to the leasing of small mines to peasants. As a result, the proletarian government is receiving a small additional quantity (a miserably small quantity compared with what is obtained in

the advanced countries, but an appreciable quantity considering our poverty-stricken condition) of coal at a cost of, say, 100; and it is selling this coal to various government departments at a price of, say, 120, and to private individuals at a price of, say, 140. (I must say in parenthesis that my figures are quite arbitrary, first because I do not know the exact figures, and, secondly, I would not now make them public even if I did.) This looks as if we are *beginning*, if only in very modest dimensions, to control *exchange* between industry and agriculture, to control wholesale trade, to cope with the task of taking in hand the available, small, backward industry, or large-scale but weakened and ruined industry; of reviving trade on the *present* economic basis; of making the ordinary middle peasant (and that is the typical peasant, the peasant in the mass, the true representative of the petty-bourgeois milieu) feel the benefit of the economic revival; of taking advantage of it for the purpose of more systematically and persistently, more widely and successfully restoring large-scale industry."

63 Paarlberg, p. 77, where original sources of the estimate are given.
64 Nenovsky, p. 9.
65 Hanke (1998) and Bernholz (1996).
66 Bernholz (1996, p. 311).
67 Lenin, *Letter to A. L. Sheinman*, February 28, 1922.
68 Nenovsky gives a detailed analysis on this point.
69 Beller, pp. 198–212.
70 De Bordes, p. 24.
71 Maddison (1982, Table E3, p. 238).
72 Sargent (2013, Tables 3.3 and 3.4, pp. 72–3).
73 De Bordes, p. 24.
74 De Dordes, pp. 20–1.
75 Galbraith, pp. 151–1.
76 Molnár, pp. 250–61.
77 Sargent (2013, Table 3.10, p. 80).
78 Sargent (2013, p. 55) indicates that government loans – via agencies – to the private sector were growing considerably in Hungary during the early 1920s, and terms were usually extremely favorable to borrowers. Boross (1984) also shows that loans from the government benefited large firms enormously and enabled them to expand investment in land, machinery, buildings, and inventory.
79 Z. Drabek, Table 7.1, p. 380.
80 Sargent (2013, Tables 3.15 and 3.16, pp. 80–1).
81 Smith, p. 148.
82 Sargent (2013, p. 59).
83 Teichova, p. 932.
84 Smith, p. 158.
85 Sargent (2013, pp. 64–5).
86 Dornbusch, p. 401.
87 Sargent (2013, Tables 3.26 and 3.27, pp. 109–10).
88 Carr, p. 61. He referred to the "Little Entente" that formed in 1920–21 between the Central and Eastern European states – excluding Bulgaria, Hungary and Poland – with France through a series of bilateral treaties of alliance and friendship (pp. 38–43). Notable is also that the French involvement had made the country not become one like Switzerland as some earlier hoped (Hoover, p. 402).
89 Teichova, pp. 927–8. CPI rose 212 percent in Bulgaria between 1919–22 and 226 percent in Romania in 1921–24 (Mitchell, *Europe*, Table H2).
90 Sargent (2013, Table 3.24, p. 65).
91 Between the last day of 1918 and that of 1923, Czechoslovakia received 78.5 million gold dollars in credit under arrangements by the League of Nations for food imports, and Poland received 151.5 million gold dollars. The total amount of credit extended by the League of Nations to Eastern European countries during the period was 330.1

million gold dollars (Teichova, Table 125, p. 927). In per capita terms, Czechoslovakia and Poland each received $9, whilst Bulgaria and Hungary each got $1 (Z. Drabek, Table 7.6, p. 387).

92 It has been noted that when hyperinflation started in Germany, the Czechoslovakian *koruna* began to suffer from overvaluation, but the French occupation of the Ruhr unexpectedly generated huge quantities of new orders for Czechoslovakian exports (Teichova, p. 929).

93 Quoted from "Wilson's Fourteen Points, 1918", an online article on https://history.state.gov/milestones/1914-1920/fourteen-points.

94 Kindleberger (1984, pp. 333–4).

95 Clavin, p. 19.

96 Clavin, p. 21.

97 Clavin, p. 27.

98 Clavin, p. 27.

99 Mises (2009, p. 90).

100 Clavin, p. 30.

101 Economists still believe they are relevant in contemporary world (Dornbusch, pp. 420–1).

102 Teichova, pp. 931–2.

103 Clavin, p. 28. Mises also remarks on him, 2009, p. 90.

104 Bresciani-Turroni (1937, p. 5).

105 Cited in Fergusson, p. 129, with explanatory words inserted within brackets.

106 Paul Krugman, "The Conscience of a Liberal.It's Always 1923," *The New York Times*, 12 February 2013.

107 Maddison (1982, Table C6, p. 206).

108 Shirer, p. 57.

109 Shirer, p. 58.

110 Shirer, p. 58.

111 Feldman, p. 854.

112 Feldman, p. 858.

113 As it has been noted, Nazi Germany was constantly short of resources during World War II and had to resort to expansionary monetary policy in general. Leaders of the Nazi regime were, however, "sensitive to the dangers of currency inflation," and "had learned the lesson of hyperinflation well" (Petrov, pp. 32, 39).

4 The Second World War and the upsurge of hyperinflation in the 1940s

> "[T]he best remembered lesson of our World War [I] experience concerns infla-
> tion . . . . [W]hatever the state of feeling about the present war, any sort of poll
> would show a grim [sic] determination to defeat inflation."
>
> John Kenneth Galbraith, an article published in 1941

Like the First World War, the Second World War (WWII) brought huge distortion and destruction to the economic resources of all belligerent countries. Unlike the First World War whose battlefields were mainly in continental Europe, the Second World War had a much larger geographical spread, with the Asia Pacific region experiencing conflict as well. Moreover, hyperinflation did not occur during the First World War; it was largely an outcome of the bitter ending of the war and the revolutions that arose from the war. But, before the end of the Second World War, several countries had already fallen into hyperinflation. After the end of the war, more countries, including defeated Axis countries and ones engaged in civil war, joined a wave of hyperinflation in the second half of the 1940s. The five countries that experienced hyperinflation in the wake of WWI – Germany, Russia, Austria, Hungary, and Poland – had a total population of approximately 280 million in the early 1920s. In the second half of the 1940s, the countries in Europe and East Asia that endured hyperinflation or were under the shadow of hyperinflation had a total population of at least 662 million.[1]

On a list of "World Hyperinflations,"[2] defined as episodes of monthly inflation exceeding 50 percent, Greece had one (May 1941 to December 1945), Mainland China had two (July 1943 to August 1945 and October 1947 to May 1949), Hungary had one (August 1945 to July 1946), and Taiwan had three (between August 1945 and May 1949). It is clear that hyperinflation either occurs during a war – external, internal, or a mixture of both – or immediately at the end of or after a war. Of these countries, Hungary set the world record for highest inflation in the summer of 1946, and throughout the 1940s, Mainland China withstood the world's longest high inflation. As the nature and causes of inflation in wartime China were substantially different from those of cases elsewhere, her experience of hyperinflation is discussed separately in Chapter 5.

Not shown in the list are the three defeated Axis states: Italy, Japan, and Germany. Their records do not qualify by the strict criteria of monthly inflation, but nonetheless fit the annual standard – a yearly rise in prices of over 500 percent, except Germany. Inflation began to climb in Italy when major military conflict had halted in the country, although battles continued in Europe. Japan rather successfully kept down inflation during the war, but the end of the war appeared to ignite the flames of hyperinflation. In wartime Germany, like in Japan, inflation was extremely low, and she seemed to have many reasons to suffer another hyperinflation after the end of the war. In fact, post-1945 Germany had an inflation that was much lesser than hyperinflation by any usual criterion. Germany's monetary experience then had profound implications for her later development as well as for postwar European development.

Without doubt, war was the common reason for the spate of hyperinflations involving many countries during the 1940s. WWII "nurtured" almost every condition for rising inflation, from ever-enlarging budget deficits to sharp falls in output and economic resources. To cope with the pressures of rising inflation, countries like the United States and Britain had to resort to price controls during the war. Once again, it was policy and institutions that fundamentally determined the course of each particular inflation and economy, even in the midst of fighting among or within nation states.

Greece: wars and long stabilization

The drachma, probably the world's earliest currency unit, originated in the eastern Mediterranean region in the tenth century BC. After Greece regained her independence in the 1820s, the drachma was reborn as the new nation's currency, largely linked to silver for most of the time until the First World War and tied to the gold standard in the late 1920s and early 1930s. In 1940, a British gold coin – the sovereign – could be exchanged for 1,100 drachma in Greece, and by December 1944, it could fetch 19,900,000,000,000 drachma – an 18,090,909,091-fold increase (roughly 18 billion-fold). But the story of the Greek hyperinflation does not end there: between December 1944 and January 1946, when the old drachma had been replaced by a new drachma at the ratio of 50 billion to one, the price of the sovereign in new drachma increased another 37-fold. After 1946, hyperinflation was largely past, but the momentum of inflation continued. Greece endured the longest process of stabilization in postwar Europe.

Figure 4.1 shows the monthly changes in the drachma prices of gold sovereign and the real money balance in Greece between January 1941 and June 1946. Because of limited space, the graph omits two months, October and November of 1944, when the drachma price of sovereign rose 12,620.8 percent and 4,085.6 percent, respectively (the break in the solid line). From what can be seen in Figure 4.1, hyperinflation started in Greece in June 1941, when the drachma price of sovereign rose 177.8 percent, and culminated in October 1944. Between 1942 and 1946, there were several attempts to suppress hyperinflation. Differing both in nature and degree of effect, none of them achieved complete success in stabilization.

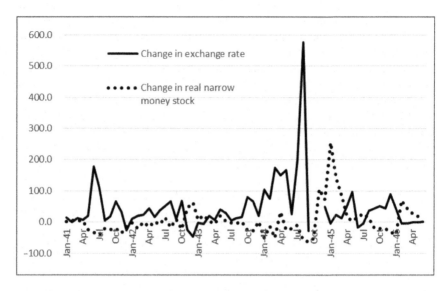

Figure 4.1 Monthly changes in drachma price of gold sovereign and real money balance, percentage, Greece, January 1941–June 1946[3]

The dotted curve of changes in the real money balance in Figure 4.1 is displayed to show how hyperinflation destroyed the value of the money stock for its holders. As can be seen from the figure, for most of the time, the dotted line stays below zero, indicating falls in the real value of the money stock. In particular, there is apparently a negative association overall between the rise in the drachma price of sovereign and the fall in the real money stock during the period under observation, which suggests that money holders necessarily suffered from the hyperinflation.[4]

The development of the Greek hyperinflation and the pursuit of its stabilization were greatly affected by international events. A dedicated researcher identifies "four ends" of the Greek hyperinflation between 1941 and 1946:[5] the first was undertaken by a German high commissioner in occupied Greece in late 1942; the second, by a British special envoy in November 1944; the third, by a returned Greek government in June 1945; and the fourth – the most successful one – by a joint Greek-British initiative, the "Anglo Greek Financial Agreement," in January 1946. In the end, the Greek stabilization had a long tail, through into the 1950s, when American influence superseded that of the British in the country.

When the Second World War broke out in 1939, Greece was a neutral state. It was Mussolini's invasion of Albania in October 1940 that eventually brought Greece into the war on the Allied side. When a British army entered Greece to aid her fight against Italian invasion, Germany launched a blitzkrieg on Greece in April 1941 which drove the Greek government into exile almost within a month. The German invasion kicked off hyperinflation in Greece.

Late that month, "even eggs became a luxury," noted a diplomat who remained in a Greek city.[6] Monthly double-digit consumer price rises first occurred in May (35.5 percent) and continued in July (71 percent). Three occupation zones were formed: the Germans mainly in Athens and the central north, the Bulgarians in the northeast, and the Italians in the rest of the country. The three Axis states ruled the country brutally, expropriating tremendous amounts of resources from Greece during their occupation.

The puppet government in Greece was required to pay costs of occupation to the Axis powers but was considerably short of revenue in the midst of a shattered economy and the populace's increasing disobedience. Hundreds of thousands of Greeks joined resistance forces that were associated with different political factions. Tax revenue covered less than 6 percent of fiscal expenditure in the final year of the occupation.[7] The Bank of Greece – the country's Central Bank, which was established in 1928 at the suggestion of the League of Nations – appeared to be the only important source of finance for budgets. Between 1941 and 1943, the number of notes issued rose 72-fold, and prices in terms of the gold sovereign multiplied 155-fold.[8] As hunger and resistance spread in the country, the Germans initiated a stabilization program in late 1942 and early 1943. It scaled down the amount of the indemnity imposed on Greece and credited the puppet government with payments in arrears. The main effect of these actions was temporary falls in prices in the following months.

When Italy withdrew from the war and started to exit from Greece in September 1943, prices in the country resurged. The drachma price of sovereign rose 79.9 percent in October, 104.2 percent in January 1944, and 174.3 percent in March, two months later. Hyperinflation-induced poverty, restricted movement due to the Axis occupation, the Allied blockade of Greece, and a harsh winter together led to a great famine: one-quarter of a million Greeks had died of starvation by the end of the Axis occupation in 1944.[9]

How hyperinflation impoverished the Greek people can be seen partly from Figure 4.2, where two indexes of real wages – for Bank of Greece staff and Greek government Class A secretaries – are shown for the period from late 1944 to January 1946. The two curves each averaged in 1945 about half the level they had in 1940. The lowest levels in real wages for the two categories of employee, reached in December 1944, were merely one-fifth of the levels in the base period. This should be largely attributed to the effects of hyperinflation during the German occupation, which ended in September 1944.

Nonetheless, the fact that the two indexes of real wages fluctuated remarkably throughout the first year after liberation, 1945, suggests that stabilization programs adopted by the Greek government were not successful at all, and real wage levels in early 1946 were still far below the prewar levels.

Supported by British troops, the exiled Greek government returned to the country in October 1944 and soon started a currency reform with technical assistance from the British. In November 1944, holders of old drachma were required to convert them into new drachma at the rate of 50 billion to 1. The new drachma was set to be convertible to British Military Authority pounds at the rate of 600 to

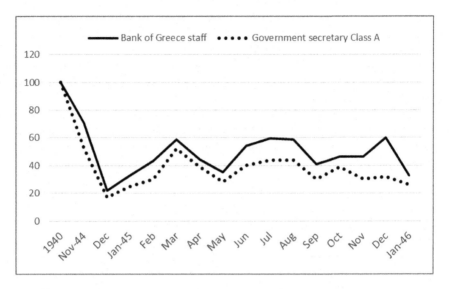

Figure 4.2 Real wage indexes, percentage, Greece, 1940–January 1946[10]

1, but only in large amounts. The fixed, low value of the new drachma was aimed at promoting Greek exports, though the military pound was neither legal tender in the United Kingdom nor convertible into ordinary pounds.[11] The hope was that the currency reform would quickly help restore the economy and trade when it was supported by arrivals of foreign aid in kind.

Yet, it did not. A civil war broke out in Athens in December, which paused only due to forceful intervention by the British. As the Greek government continued to expand its budgets, price inflation returned to double digit levels in April and May 1945. Meanwhile, recovery in the economy was not significant, partly because the rise in inflation was largely fueled by fiscal expansion rather than credit growth.[12] Realizing the need for further reform, the Greek government appointed an "economic czar" as part of implementing a comprehensive reform and stabilization program in June 1945, which aimed at seeking more aid from abroad, increasing domestic production, and imposing price and wage controls. New tax schemes on property and rent were also introduced, and a special "market police force" was formed in order to enforce them. The latter, however, encountered great resistance from urban citizens. When the key leader of the reform had to resign, with major measures effectively abandoned in two months, price inflation started to accelerate, and CPI inflation escalated from 45.3 percent in September to 113.8 percent in January 1946.[13]

Monetary disorder and slow economic recovery apparently made the British worry about political stability in Greece in the context of postwar security in Europe. The "Anglo-Greek Financial Agreement" was reached in January 1946, under which the British consented to provide an interest-free loan of 10 million pounds to Greece and also waived 46 million pounds of debt Greece had incurred in 1940 and 1941. A "Currency Committee" consisting of three Greek cabinet ministers, one Briton, and one American, was empowered to have the last say on matters of currency issue. In addition, the Greek government agreed to improve its budget system and taxation, and the Bank of Greece began to operate an open market for gold transactions as part of its efforts to establish drachma convertibility and restore public confidence in the drachma.[14]

With these measures in place, Greece's economy and finance showed several signs of improvement in 1946. Consumer prices stopped rising, and exchange rates of the drachma became more or less stable. Government budget deficits were smaller than before, with revenue increased. Tentative evidence suggests that unemployment fell and real national income grew considerably in that year – 62.1 percent compared to 5.5 percent in 1945 or 33.9 percent in 1947.[15]

In fact, the Greek stabilization program was not completed in 1946. New dramas in domestic politics and international relations soon emerged, in 1947, and greatly affected subsequent movements of inflation and outcomes of stabilization in Greece. As shown in Figure 4.3, price inflation surged again in 1947, with CPI and WPI at levels double those of 1946 yet much more moderate than those prior to 1946. That year, the so-called "third-round" of Greek civil war broke out, between the rightist government force and Soviet-linked communist rebels, concurrently with the announcement of the "Truman Doctrine," which aimed at containing Soviet expansion and influence in Europe.

When Greece inadvertently became a "frontier" in the nascent Cold War, huge quantities of American military and economic aid flooded into the country,

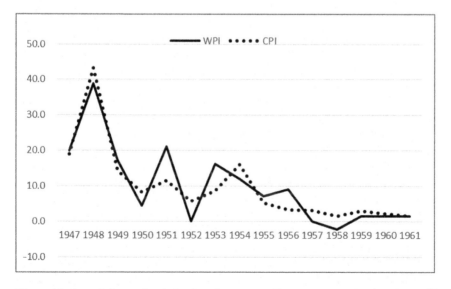

Figure 4.3 Annual changes in wholesale and consumer prices, percentage, Greece, 1947–61[16]

overwhelming the earlier British undertakings. But the old problems of corruption, black markets, tax evasion, social and political polarization, among others, continued to plague the country. Even during the period from the late 1940s through much of the 1950s, when strongmen took power and maintained a steady political regime, Greece's economy and finance remained far from attaining full growth and stability. In the late 1940s and early 1950s, when many Western European countries had recovered and moved into a stage of stable growth, intermittent rises in Greek inflation frequently resulted in overvaluation of the drachma, prompting the Greek government to devalue the currency on several occasions, which in turn caused turbulence in Greece's foreign exchange market and trade flows. As late as 1953, the country's multiple exchange rate regime was finally abolished and replaced with a uniform and transparent system, with the official exchange rate of the drachma devalued from 15,000 to 30,000 drachmas to a dollar.[17] In May 1954, another currency reform was undertaken; conversion of old drachmas to new ones at the rate of 1000 to 1. The rate was maintained through March 1961, when Greece declared a par value (30 drachmas to a dollar) to the International Monetary Fund,[18] which she and 28 other nation states had founded in 1945.

Italy: rising inflation in the last stage of the war

When the lira became the national currency of Italy in 1862, following her unification the previous year, its value was set at par with the French franc, mainly based on the silver parity and occasionally on the gold parity in a bimetallistic system; thereby the Latin Monetary Union was formed in 1865 among France, Belgium, Italy, and Switzerland. Prevailing exchange rates of the lira with major currencies in the late nineteenth century were 25.22 to a pound sterling, 5.18 to an American dollar, and 1.11 to a German mark.[19] On the first day of 1999, when the euro was launched, the exchange rate of the lira with the new currency was fixed at 1,936.27,[20] which was equivalent to 2,940.56 to a pound, 1,817.41 to a U.S. dollar, and 989.99 to a German mark. Much of the fall in the value of the lira occurred in 1944, when Italy was trapped in the last stage of her involvement in the Second World War.

Italy encountered serious inflation during the First World War, but was not blighted by hyperinflation afterward, partly because she was on the Entente side. The rise of fascism in the country was largely a result of soaring nationalist sentiment and dissatisfaction with the Anglo-French orchestration leading to the Treaty of Versailles, which denied many of Italy's territorial demands. Whether or not such ideas were illusive, Mussolini was determined to ensure a glorious rise for Italy on the international stage. In 1937, Italy's GDP per capita in comparable terms was 53.4 percent of Britain's, 74 percent of France's, 70.8 percent of Germany's, and 51.6 percent of America's.[21] Despite her apparently underdeveloped economy, Mussolini's Italy took on an aggressive foreign policy and invaded Ethiopia in 1934, which resulted in Italy's exit from the League of Nations the following year. These events occurred before Hitler's Germany annexed Austria and Czechoslovakia's Sudetenland.

In the second year of his dictatorship, which began in 1925, Mussolini pegged the lira's exchange rate with the pound at 90, equivalent to approximately 25 to a U.S. dollar. Over the next ten years, the lira appreciated from the early 1930s amid the Great Depression. The lira's rate with the U.S. dollar was less than 12 before the outbreak of the Ethiopian War in December 1934, but had fallen to more than 19 by the time the war came to an end in May 1936. The devaluation of the lira is believed to have been a policy move by Mussolini to make up for war costs, which became increasingly unbearable for the Italian people.[22] Throughout the period 1939–44, the military burden on Italy was the lowest among those of all the major belligerent countries, measured in military outlay as a percentage of national income.[23] Because of the mounting war costs, little of Italy's military outlay was used for military industry.[24] Unable to win any major battle on the fronts in the Balkans and North Africa and even to defend Sicily against the Allied landing, Mussolini lost his popularity in Italy. As he was expelled from power in July 1943 then a month later restored by the Germans in a puppet government in northern Italy, the country was split and went into the final stage of the war. It is during this period that inflation ballooned in Italy.

Like in other belligerent countries, price and wage controls were implemented in the country right from the start of the war. In addition, Italy under her fascist regime adopted an approach to economics and finance that has been called "direct capital circuit" and "indirect capital circuit."[25] The former refers to direct demands by the government to reduce private sector investment and consumption believed to be unrelated to military purposes. The latter specifically targeted the finance industry by requiring financial institutions to increase their reserves and deposits at the Bank of Italy – the country's Central Bank, which in turn could lend more to the government, whose deficit had grown large. The weakness in Italy's fiscal position at the time is evident in the facts that government revenue as a percentage of national income fell from 20.5 in 1939 to 8.0 in 1944[26] and the fiscal deficit amounted to nearly 30 percent of GDP in 1942–43.[27] Needless to say, all the budget deficits were financed by issuing debt securities to the Central Bank and a few other domestic banks, as Italy was unable to seek any international financial aid. Even Nazi Germany could not offer anything significant in finance to Mussolini's Italy.[28]

As shown in Figure 4.4, inflation first surged in 1943 and then culminated in 1944. CPI rose 67.9 percent in 1943 and 344.6 percent in 1944, and WPI climbed 50.7 percent in 1943 and 274.2 percent in 1944. As these are official figures published in wartime, they could underestimate the true rates of inflation.[29] Yet, the changing trend is clear: inflation was accelerating from 1943 to 1944. In fact, inflation started to escalate from the second half of 1943 and further soared after June 1944, when Allied troops entered Rome. At that time, old price controls imposed by the government became ineffective, first in south Italy, then later also in north Italy.

As noted by two Italian economists, inflation rose much faster and higher in Rome than in Milan in the first half of 1944, while from the later months of that year, it surged in both cities at a similar pace.[30] Disparities in price levels

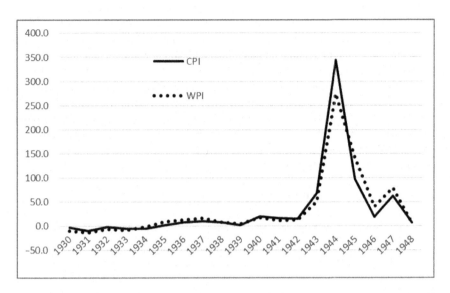

Figure 4.4 Annual changes in consumer and wholesale prices, percentage, Italy, 1939–48[31]

and paces of inflation would obviously create opportunities for people to conduct arbitrage transactions between the two zones, with the south occupied mainly by Americans and the north by Germans, which in turn would effectively drive price levels and inflation paces to converge. Of course, there were military barriers on the front lines because of the war which deterred the flow of goods between the zones.

An immediate result of the rising inflation was the declining real money balance. Shown in Figure 4.5, wholesale prices and cash at hand (cash held by the public) increased roughly at a similar pace, and consequently, the real money balance (the ratio between the two indexes) stayed basically unchanged between 1932 and 1938. Between 1938 and 1943, cash at hand increased faster than wholesale prices, which reflected the more intensified use of inflationary finance by the government and effective control of price inflation during the period, whilst the real balance actually ascended. The rise in the real balance implies that the Italian people, as money holders, accepted sacrifices to "support" the inflationary deficit financing by the government during that period.

But when inflation jumped to a high level in 1944, the real balance fell, nearly halving that year. An implication was that the government, as the cash (money) supplier, could no longer expect a steady inflow of inflation tax or seigniorage. If it wished to maintain the inflation tax in real terms, it had to increase the money supply, by printing currency notes, at an ever higher pace, which in turn would further drive up inflation.

It is likely that Italy encountered hyperinflation, probably very briefly, in the summer of 1944. Part of reason for the briefness was the aid work undertaken by

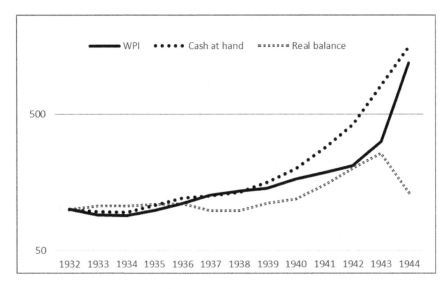

Figure 4.5 Indexes of wholesale prices, money stock, and real money balance, log scale, Italy, 1939–44[32]

the Allied forces when they were in the midst of liberating the country. Aware of the severe shortages and people's suffering in Italy, the Allies by August 1945 had brought more than 5.9 million tons of goods, worth 490 million U.S. dollars, for distribution in the country.[33] From then to the end of 1947, mainly under the auspices of the United Nations Relief and Rehabilitation Administration (UNRRA), such shipments had reached a total of 10 million tons, worth 418 million dollars. Except China and Poland, no other country received more aid from UNRRA than did Italy after the war.[34] The United States government also arranged other emergency aid programs for Italy in addition to releasing assets withheld during the war and facilitating remittances from American Italians to their motherland, both of which were worth tens of millions of dollars.

In retrospect, it should be also noted that the Allied forces were actually aware of the possibility of rising inflation and its harms to Italian people when they entered the country. In early 1944 they created the Allied Anti-inflation Committee, composed of high-level American and British economic experts.[35] But members of the committee often could not agree on the methods of inflation control, despite all urged Allied aid to speed up.

The disinflation in 1945 and 1946 did not last. Increasing inflation returned to the country in 1947, when consumer prices rose 62.1 percent and wholesale prices 78.9 percent (Figure 4.4). Monthly data show that wholesale prices rose 14.8 percent in May 1947 over the previous month, with the lira down by 30 percent against the dollar in the same month.[36] Direct causes of the return of inflation included coal shortages, due to a workers' strike in America, and sudden falls in exports to Britain. Indirectly, financial and monetary arrangements between the occupation authorities and Italy were also related factors. They required the Italian government to cover the costs of the occupation out of its budgets, which were already in bad shape. Italy's contribution to the costs of the Allied occupation was stopped from 1947.

On the other hand, when the Allied troops entered the Apennine Peninsula in September 1943, inflation remained relatively low in the country, and exchange rates of the lira with the dollar and pound were set at 100 and 400, respectively, at the suggestion of the British.[37] The artificially low value of the lira is believed to have stimulated inflation, as inflows of foreign hard currency generated huge demand for local goods and services. Later, when domestic inflation soared, the lira consequently became overvalued, and people chased foreign hard currency.

As part of the liberalization pursued by the postwar Italian government, a two-tier foreign exchange scheme was introduced in January 1946. An official rate of 225 lira to a dollar was set for Italian exporters, whilst for other transactions the exchange rate was allowed to float freely.[38] As it turned out, the official rate was too high to sustain, and the lira had to devalue by 54 percent that year.

The partial liberalization was also reflected in agricultural prices: when prices received by farmers tripled in May 1946, those paid by consumers remained unchanged.[39] This brought about two immediate impacts: a drain on public finance, which supported urban consumers with subsidies; and a stimulus to credit expansion, which flowed into procurement agencies and related businesses. For the latter, the impact was evident in the fact that bank credit rose 61.8 percent between June 1946 and September 1947, whilst money stock increased 40.5 percent over the same period.[40] The return of inflation in 1947 was thus largely a result of credit expansion.

With a change in the cabinet in May 1947, a task force was appointed to curb inflation. Several drastic tightening measures were taken from August onward which categorically targeted the banking and financial sector. The standard reserve ratio on deposits was raised to 20 percent, and would be raised higher, as high as 40 percent, as deposits increased. The official discount rate was hiked from 4 to 5.5 percent, with the official exchange rate of the lira raised to 350 to a dollar. Under these measures, Italy's economy and finance endured a "credit squeeze."[41]

There were certain short-term side effects of the stabilization program. Industrial output fell for several months after the policy shock, and unemployment increased. A more important issue was how to deal with balance of payment problems and make adjustment of the lira's exchange rate; since Italy was suffering a deficit in her balance of payments that year, imports or external payments were more than exports or external revenue in dollar terms. If the balance of payments deficit continued, domestic industry and commerce would possibly come under further strain, and people's confidence in the lira would be weakened.

To tackle the issue of balance of payments, the Italian government decided to devalue the lira further in December 1947 to the rate of 575 to a U.S. dollar. This was a large devaluation from the earlier level of 350. Markets were shocked once again, but Italian exporters gained an additional and significant stimulus.

Apparently unexpected by Italy, the Marshall Plan – officially, the European Recovery Program (ERP) – arrived as timely assistance from late 1947. Between 1948 and 1952, Italy received 1.47 billion dollars from the ERP, which accounted for 11 percent of the program's total disbursements in Europe.[42] How large the figure of 1.47 billion dollars was to Italy at that time can be seen by comparing it to her exports in the previous/subsequent five years, which totaled 3,867 billion lira, equivalent to 6.445 billion dollars when a flat rate of 600 is applied.[43] Between 1947 and 1951, Italy's revenue from exports in liras increased 31.8 percent each year.

Italy basically completed her stabilization program in 1948, and from then on, she experienced steady economic growth over the long term. With the lira further devalued to 625 to a dollar in 1950, Italy's postwar growth was an export-led success. The exchange rate was maintained through 1960, when the par value of the lira was finally established with the consent of the International Monetary Fund, which Italy had joined in 1947.[44]

In short, the postwar stabilization program in Italy was a monetary policy Big Bang without currency reform, and technically, that is the reason why the denomination of the lira was so large when Italy joined the Eurozone, together with the ten other founding member states, in 1999.[45]

Hungary: the world record hyperinflation

Hungary had a hyperinflation in the early 1920s after her disintegration with Austria at the end of the First World War (see Chapter 3). The second hyperinflation she endured, after the Second World War, created a world record of inflation, in terms of magnitude, which has not yet been matched by any other hyperinflation.

The second Hungarian hyperinflation started in June 1945 and ended in August 1946. During the 14 months, the monthly inflation rate – measured in a cost of living index, which is close to consumer prices in conception – escalated from 31 percent in July 1945 to 4.19×10^{16} percent in July 1946. When rent is included, the monthly rate of July 1946 was 1.29^{16} percent, slightly lower than that when rent is excluded.[46]

The colossal monthly rate of 4.19×10^{16} percent in July 1946 can be translated into an average daily inflation rate of 207 percent, which also means that consumer prices doubled every 15 hours.[47] In a more detailed study, the daily inflation rate – again, the cost of living index including rent – in July 1946 was as high as 75,655 percent,[48] which is equivalent to an average hourly rate of 60 percent.

As noted by a historian, when a popular Hungarian poet and writer received a royalty fee of 300 billion pengő from his publisher in the summer of 1946, he ran to a nearby market in central Budapest and spent the entire amount "on one chicken, a litre of olive oil and a handful of vegetables."[49] In July 1946, a one hundred quintillion pengő note (one followed by 20 zeros) was issued, which remains the largest denomination of paper note in the world today, and the Hungarian government was preparing to issue even larger notes, but did not actually do so.

Figure 4.6 displays a cost of living index and the official exchange rate of the pengő with the U.S. dollar in August 1938 and in the period April 1945 – July 1946, both on a log scale. Clearly, the two curves changed so precipitously from early 1946 that they look perpendicular in the several months just prior to July 1946, which indicates that inflation and devaluation were accelerating at an explosive pace in the last stage of hyperinflation. The large numbers shown in the figure are usually used only for describing the accelerating speed of a free-falling asteroid.

Looking more closely at Figure 4.6, it appears that the devaluation lagged behind the inflation. If this were the case, it means that the Hungarian pengő actually appreciated against the U.S. dollar in real terms over that period. In reality, this could have been the case for government-controlled trade flows and other external transactions, which were probably insignificant in size at the time, as the government had not yet started to monopolize the economy and commerce. For ordinary Hungarians, however, the pengő depreciated considerably in real terms. As revealed in the above-mentioned detailed examination, black market prices were usually 2.5 to 5 times official prices, exceptionally 7 times, from late 1945 to July 1946, whilst the pengő was often ten times lower in value on the black market than on the official one.[50] Even considering only the official exchange rate data, the real exchange rate of the pengő began to decline in the last month of hyperinflation in postwar Hungary.[51] Falls in the real value of the pengő were an additional factor in the hardship that Hungary had to experience at a crucial time, when she desperately needed imports of food and equipment for postwar recovery and reconstruction.

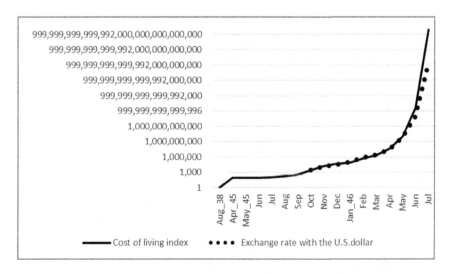

Figure 4.6 Cost of living index and exchange rate of the pengő with the U.S. dollar, log scale, Hungary, August 1938 and April 1945–July 1946[52]

Several obvious facts can easily explain why Hungary encountered a serious inflation in 1945–46: war damage, reparations and costs of occupation, lack of gold reserves, and reverse flows of currency notes from neighboring regions, among others.

Though Hungary was a "marginal" participant in the Second World War on the Axis side, her land became a major battlefield between the Germans and the Russians during the last stage of the war, until April 1945. When the Germans retreated, all the bridges on the Danube were blown up.[53] The Germans took away all they could physically move (including Hungary's gold bullion reserve), and the Soviets subsequently occupied the country. The Armistice, signed in January 1945, set the total amount of reparations Hungary should pay at 300 million dollars, in kind. This was exercised mainly through removals of industrial equipment by the Russians. Altogether, about 40 percent of Hungary's non-human wealth is estimated to have been destroyed or reduced by the war.[54]

In addition, Hungary was required to pay costs of occupation to Russia for her troops stationed in Hungary, who numbered between 500 and 700 thousand,[55] equivalent to 5.6–7.8 percent of the Hungarian population. According to estimates, the actual costs of occupation plus reparations totaled 600–900 million dollars, mainly for the two years 1945–46, when the national income of Hungary was about 1 billion dollars per year. Hungarian reparations to Russia could have been 19–22 percent of her national income at the time.[56]

During the war, Hungary expanded her territory into several neighboring countries, contravening the Treaty of Trianon, and the Armistice in 1945 required the return of these lands. Consequently, pengő-holders in these regions rushed to markets to purchase goods, which understandably pushed up inflation. However, it is estimated that reverse flows of the currency notes amounted in total to merely 1.2 percent of the pengő notes in circulation as of December 1945.[57]

Taking account of all these happenings, there is no doubt that in the immediate postwar years, the Hungarian government faced huge budget deficits, as revenue was slow to recover and colossal expansion of expenditure was needed. To rebuild bridges on the Danube and repair other infrastructure necessitated tremendous input, mainly through government budgets.

Unlike many other war-torn countries after the Second World War, Hungary was apparently unable to receive foreign aid in large quantities before 1946. Russia sent foodstuffs in early 1945 and signed a bilateral trade agreement with the Hungarian government in the summer of that year, which irked the Americans and British, who were presumably demanding the Hungarians to stand on a multilateral stance.[58] The first arrival of food assistance from the United Nations Relief and Rehabilitation Administration was as late as May 1946. At the request of the Hungarian government, the United States in December 1945 called for the Allied states to set up a special committee to consider finance, industry, and the economy in Hungary. But the Russians kept rejecting the American proposal, and blamed Hungary's economic woes on the U.S.'s holding of Hungarian property – mainly gold bullion discovered in Germany that was believed to have been taken out of Hungary before the end of the war. Facing strong objection from the Russian side in the occupation commission, the United States also found she could do little for most of 1946.[59] Hungary's economic isolation in 1945 and the first half of 1946 was more or less a result of Russian policy toward the country and the West.

As a result, the printing press became the only available primary option for the Hungarian government to finance its budget deficit. The fact that inflation in 1945 was not yet explosive was mainly because Hungary's note-printing plates had been taken away early that year, and even the paper and ink for note printing were unavailable until later that year.[60]

More or less similar to the case of Greece, government budget deficits, rather than credit growth in the private sector, primarily caused the expansion of note issuance through the nation's tightly controlled Central Bank (National Bank of Hungary). As recalled by one who once worked in the policy community in postwar Hungary, the Hungarian government spent almost recklessly to state-owned enterprises, whilst it also encouraged banks to lend to private businesses.[61] The re-discount rate set by the Central Bank remained invariably at 3 percent throughout the inflationary period, and Hungarian banks, which were only a handful in number then, could still profit by lending to private borrowers even at the time of rising high inflation.

Knowing the budgetary reason for the inflation and technical factors behind its timing, it remains interesting to ask why hyperinflation in postwar Hungary was so phenomenal. Two related explanations are most relevant.

The first is that Hungarians remembered the first hyperinflation, and their inflation expectations played an instant and powerful role in the process of inflation escalation. As pointed out by Ludwig von Mises, a well-known Austrian economist,

> [a] nation which has experienced inflation till its final breakdown will not submit to a second experiment of this type until the memory of the previous one has faded. . . . Made over-cautious by what they suffered, at the very outset of the inflation, they would start a panic. The rise of prices would be out of all proportion to the increase in the quantity of paper money; it would anticipate the expected increase of notes.[62]

These words were written in 1932 as a reflection on the German hyperinflation, yet they read like a perfect vision of what the Hungarians did in the country's second hyperinflation in the 1940s.

The second is that faulty policy design generated new impetus for an inflationary spiral. When inflation picked up in 1945, the Hungarian government faced a problem in maintaining the purchasing power of tax revenue: as prices rose, the real value of tax revenue tended to shrink in the periods between tax certification and collection and between revenue collection and spending. As a measure to counteract this effect, the Hungarian government launched a scheme known as Tax Pengő in January 1946: taxpayers were required to deliver the amount of tax that was stipulated on the initial notice plus an amount that was reckoned by a factor of price rise on the day of the delivery. For the scheme to be workable, the government published a price index daily, which would be used in calculating the total liability of each taxpayer. For this reason, information about prices in postwar Hungary was voluminously available at the time and is still so today. In theory, the scheme should have facilitated tax payments and safeguarded the real value of the tax revenue.

Yet, the government went a step further the same month by urging banks to open what were called "valorization accounts" under the Tax Pengő scheme: deposits in the accounts were entitled to receive a return that was linked to price rises. When daily inflation reached 100 percent, a hundred pengő deposit in a valorization account that day would become 200 pengő the next day. This way, price inflation – a time-changing index that the government used to calculate the return on deposits in valorization accounts – thus became the number of power in the exponential growth of money (pengő notes that were to be withdrawn from banks).

Reactions by the public to these policy measures are not hard to imagine: people took frequent trips to banks to make deposits and withdrawals, demanded rapid wage payments, and also spent what they received quickly. In short, the velocity of money accelerated as did the pace of inflation.

Moreover, the Hungarian government let the Tax Pengő become a currency in daily transactions from May, performing the same function of medium of exchange as the ordinary pengő. Again, this move pushed holders of ordinary pengő to spend as quickly as they could and meanwhile, enabled Tax Pengő-holders to spend more conveniently. Hardly anyone expected inflation to fall or the government to stop its inflationary policy. Banks were not where people saved their money. They became, essentially, places where money lodged overnight between bouts of exchange.

The Tax Pengő scheme was an early example of what economists call *Indexation*: a linking of the nominal value of an economic variable with price inflation. In Hungary in 1946, indexation was used firstly to tie tax liabilities with price inflation; and later, to link bank deposits with price inflation. No distinction was made between demand deposits and saving deposits in this regard. Economists believe this was a major fault in the policy design, and it was responsible for the second Hungarian hyperinflation becoming astronomical.[63]

During the period of rising inflation, the Hungarian government took several other measures in attempting to curb inflation. One was a tax (stamp duty) on pengő notes of large denominations, imposed in December 1945 apparently for the purpose of discouraging people from holding pengő and encouraging them to deposit the notes at banks. Another significant policy step was the so-called "calorie wages" scheme, introduced in May 1945, to link wages with workers' standard calorie needs and their market cost, for which compensation would be made in a mixture of money and kind. This proved difficult in practice right from the start.[64] Both measures had a limited deterrent effect on inflation, but neither was able to quell the momentum of rising inflation.

The fact that the Hungarian government did not resort to any significant price or wage control measures shows that it remained rather liberal in that period. It resorted, however, to big changes in both administration and policy in late 1947.

What the Hungarian government gained from the hyperinflation was the "disappearance" of its budget deficit and debt in real terms, as shown in Figure 4.7.

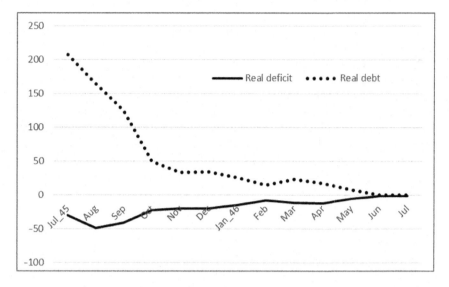

Figure 4.7 Government fiscal and debt positions in constant prices, millions of pengő, Hungary, July 1945–July 1946[65]

But the disappearance of budget deficit suggested here is deceptive because the purchasing power of government expenditure was also diminishing as prices rose faster than either nominal revenue or note issue. Moreover, in the process of inflationary finance, the government sacrificed its credibility, so few people really believed in the government regarding its intent and ability to control inflation. The loss of popularity of the coalition government, of which the communists were initially a nominal minority, effectively opened a window of opportunity for them to seize power in late 1947.

On the first day of August 1947, the Hungarian government announced a Big Bang currency reform with a number of fiscal and financial realignments. A new currency unit, *forint*, replaced the *pengő* at the rate of 1 to 400 octillion, and the Tax Pengő at the rate of 1 to 200 million. The forint was given gold content, though it was not gold convertible. Under a new regulation, the Central Bank could not lend to the government unless the latter deposited gold or foreign exchange of equal value to the loan. Banks were required to hold a 100 percent reserve for all demand deposits until further notice. On the fiscal side, new taxes such as income tax were introduced, and rates for certain existing taxes were raised. The government itself undertook an austerity plan, including cuts of staff and civil services together with reductions in regular army and state police force personnel.[66]

The austerity plan achieved remarkable results soon after its launch. Tax proceeds covered 21 percent of expenditure in August, but the level rose to 33 percent in September and 96 percent in October. Annually, the coverage ratio was 78 percent in fiscal year 1946–47 and 96 percent for 1947–48.[67]

A key element to success in the monetary reform was the return from the United States in August 1947 of gold bullion weighing 22 tons and worth 32 million dollars at the time. This was combined with 12 million dollars' worth of gold and foreign exchange from other sources to form a reserve that fully covered forint issues, though gold was never exchanged with forint in domestic transactions.

Prices fell quickly after August. In accordance with the government's Three-year Reconstruction Plan, announced around the same time, Hungary shifted to a path leading to socialism based on the Soviet model.

Japan: surge in inflation after the war

Like all other belligerent countries, Japan used every means to suppress inflation whilst constantly expanding the government budget during the Second World War. Between 1938 and 1945, retail prices increased 1.37-fold, at an average of 13.7 percent per year; and wholesale prices, 1.67-fold, 15 percent per year on average. These levels were moderately higher than those in the United States or Britain, partly reflecting the major resource constraints that Japan faced at the time, but looked like nothing compared to the high levels reached after the end of the war.

As shown in Figure 4.8, both retail prices and wholesale prices started to surge from 1945. Retail prices rose 47.2 percent in 1945, 513 percent in 1946 and 292 percent in 1947; and wholesale prices rose 51.7 percent in 1945, 363 percent in 1946 and 195 percent in 1947. The two years 1946 and 1947 stand as the time when Japan had the highest inflation in her modern monetary history.

After the Meiji Restoration in 1868, Japan started to modernize her monetary system, attempting to unify currency units and move to a gold standard.

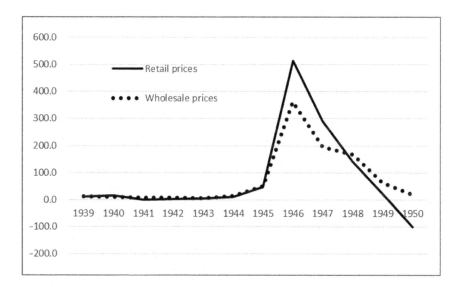

Figure 4.8 Annual changes in retail and wholesale prices, percentage, Japan, 1939–50[68]

The New Currency Act of 1871 stipulated that a Japanese yen be convertible to 1.5 grams of pure gold, a value which was at par with that of the U.S. dollar. Yet, up to 1897, Japan had a *de facto* bimetallic system of gold and silver, with the use of paper notes growing faster than that of metal coins. In 1882, the Bank of Japan was founded as the nation's central bank, taking charge of note issues and underwriting government securities. The gold value of the Japanese yen was halved in 1897, when the country finalized her transition to the gold standard.

Like many European countries, Japan suspended the gold standard during the First World War, and upon returning to the system in the interwar period, the yen's gold parity was reduced. From 1931, when the United Kingdom abandoned the gold standard, Japan followed suit, and the yen became non-convertible. On the eve of Japan's Pearl Harbor attack in December 1941, 4.26 yen could be exchanged for a dollar.[69]

While Japan waged war in 1939 and 1940, mainly against Nationalist China, her military spending accounted for roughly 22 percent of national income at the current prices. But, following the start of the Pacific War against the United States, the military burden soared, with its share of national income reaching 76 percent in 1944.[70] With regard to total central government expenditure, the share of military outlay is estimated to have been 14 percent in 1934–36 and 87 percent in 1944.[71] On the output side, Japan's gross domestic product increased about 30 percent during the war in China (1937–41), became stagnant during the Pacific War (1942–44), and fell sharply in the year of defeat, 1945, and the following year, 1946.[72]

The relatively low inflation in wartime Japan was due largely to tight price controls imposed by the militarist government and, to some extent, to obedient behavior by the Japanese people. After the unconditional surrender in August 1945, millions of soldiers became veterans and further millions of Japanese expatriates and colonists returned, together with their family members, mostly from Manchuria in mainland China, the Korean peninsula, and Taiwan. Severe food shortages soon emerged. The government had to further expand its budget spending by operating overdrafts on its accounts at the Bank of Japan. The total budget deficits of 1946 and 1947 – 76 billion yen and 65 billion yen respectively – were to be entirely financed by increases in currency issue.[73] Inflation quickly escalated, and black markets flourished in all large Japanese cities.

Figure 4.9 shows that the money stock increased at a faster pace than retail prices between 1939 and 1945, in general. This resulted in a steadily rising real money balance, which made it possible for the government to finance its ever-increasing budget deficits by monetary means. But the sharp drop in the money balance in 1945 and its continued fall in 1946 suggest that the practice of deficit financing by expanding the money supply had become unsustainable. The Japanese government's inflationary policy thus encountered great setbacks.

The impacts of inflation and inflation expectations on money-holding behavior are illustrated by the two curves in Figure 4.10: the cash-holding ratio turned upward from 1943 and accelerated in 1945, and the ratio of quasi-money to broad money stock plummeted in 1946 and fell further to a negligible level (7.9 percent)

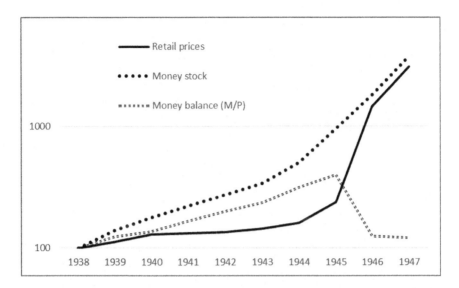

Figure 4.9 Indexes of retail prices, money stock, and real money balance, log scale, Japan, 1939–47[74]

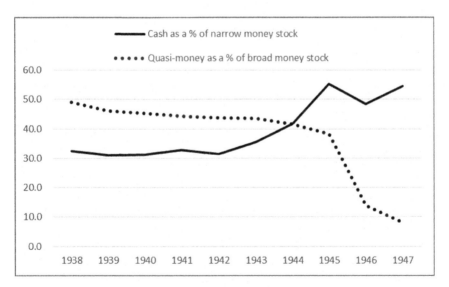

Figure 4.10 Cash as a percentage of narrow money stock and quasi-money as a percentage of broad money stock, Japan, 1939–47[75]

in 1947. The former indicates that people were shifting away from holding demand deposits or even increasing their withdrawal of such deposits, and the latter shows that bank deposits, which consisted mainly of savings, became unattractive. As explained in the introductory Chapter 1, large changes in these two ratios are evidence of hyperinflation.

The U.S. occupation authorities were busy with overhauling Japan's political system and de-militarizing her industry, and they paid little attention to the country's economic and inflation problems initially. Alerted by massive street protests and worried about possible famine, the occupation authorities started to offer support to the Japanese government to bring down inflation and normalize the economy. They helped arrange food imports and allowed the Japanese to resume ocean fishery, among other things. Coinciding with the announcement in March 1947 of the Truman Doctrine – the U.S. foreign policy aimed at containing Soviet expansion in Europe – the Supreme Commander of the Allied Powers in Japan, General Douglas MacArthur, urged the Japanese cabinet in the same month to strengthen price controls and set food distribution on a fair basis. He also convened the following month a high-level meeting of Allied representatives to tackle the issue of price and wage stabilization in Japan.[76]

Numerous inflation-curbing measures were undertaken by the Japanese government in 1946 and 1947 including food rations, price ceilings for key commodities, credit controls and allocation, and multiple exchange rates for imports and exports. Yet, none of these achieved anything decisive. Many of the Japanese elite then held the belief that the state should dictate credit flows and allocate resources into "priority" sectors in order to overcome bottlenecks in supply. For this purpose, the Reconstruction Finance Bank was set up by the Japanese government in January 1947 to provide business loans, with funds solely from the Bank of Japan, as directed by government officials. In hindsight, the Reconstruction Finance Bank's operations actually fueled rather than deterred inflation, according to a Japanese economist.[77]

The year 1948 saw a large disinflation, but the level of inflation remained high. Retail prices rose 141.7 percent; and wholesale prices, 166.7 percent. Meanwhile, the yen's exchange rates with the U.S. dollar rapidly devalued. From October 1947 to August 1948, the rate for Japanese exports fell from 140 yen to a dollar to 268 yen to a dollar, and that for Japanese imports dropped from 60 to 115.[78] In early 1949, the yen's exchange rate with the U.S. dollar fell further, to over 400 in some transactions. The situation was a far cry from stabilization.

As part of changing policy toward Asia and partly in response to Japan's economic crisis, U.S. President Harry S. Truman dispatched Joseph M. Dodge to Japan in December 1948 to engage in policy consultation and formation. He was a banker from Detroit and assumed a job in postwar Japan that was somewhat similar to that of Charles G. Dawes and Owen D. Young in interwar Germany, though not involving anything related to war reparations. After three months of extensive investigation and examination, he recommended a policy package, later called the "Dodge Line," in March 1949. It was a nine-point program mainly targeting budgetary systems and government intervention in the economy.[79] It called for the Japanese government to balance its annual budget; increase tax collection efficiency; improve the functioning of price controls, foreign trade and exchange controls, rationing, and food collection; reduce government intervention in credit flows; and sustain wages in real terms. With the support of General MacArthur, the policy recommendations were presented to the Japanese government. As it turned out, 1949 is the first year the government in postwar Japan has had a budget surplus.[80]

Apparently in accordance with the Dodge Line, the Supreme Commander dictated that the exchange rates of the yen be uniform and fixed at 360 to a dollar – the level that was subsequently maintained for more than 20 years in postwar Japan, until 1971. This ended the long-lasting practice of multiple exchange rates in Japan and also increased the international price competitiveness of Japanese products when domestic inflation stopped.

As shown in Figure 4.8, retail prices actually fell 100 percent in 1950, and wholesale prices rose 18 percent in the same year. Overall, the Japanese economy became stabilized that year. In a broader context, economic recovery and stabilization in Japan were also aided by factors other than the Dodge Line. Like in postwar Europe, with the United States-led pursuit of postwar world security and reconstruction, no financial claims were placed on Japan by other countries, and Japan herself became a recipient of U.S. foreign aid from 1946. Moreover, when the Korean War broke out in June 1950, foreign demand for Japanese goods exploded, and the Japanese economy became set on a path of export-led high growth throughout the 1950s and 1960s.

The Philippines and South Korea: hyperinflations before and after

Before and during the Pacific War, Japan established a yen block in East Asia. For the colonies or affiliated regions – the Korean Peninsula, Taiwan, and Manchuria – that Japan had annexed or controlled many years previously, a fixed-peg system was in place such that wartime inflation in these regions was relatively moderate. For new territories in Southeast Asia occupied from the early 1940s, a different currency policy was adopted by the Japanese military authorities. Often, the Japanese issued military notes (or army notes) for local use and outlawed indigenous currencies. There were several names for the notes: Japanese military yen, invasion money, or simply *gunpyō* (meaning military scrip).

A special financial institution – the South Seas Development Bank (SSDB) – was established in 1942, which also issued its own notes, although they were effectively the same as the military notes. There was no link between the military notes and the Japanese yen, and all the transactions between Japan and her newly acquired territories were handled through special accounts at the SSDB and its correspondent, Japanese-controlled corporations.[81] Such financial and monetary arrangements may suggest that the Japanese belligerents were uncertain about the fate of the war, and they tried to maximize economic gains in the short term.

The Philippines was largely under Japanese occupation from January 1942 to early 1945, and from mid-1944, the Japanese occupiers were engaged in fighting U.S. forces in major islands of the country. Right from the start of their occupation, the Japanese issued localized military currency notes to replace the country's original notes. The notes were printed on poor quality paper, without serial numbers, for much of the period of occupation.[82] Excessive issues were a practice from the outset, but they did not cause serious inflation, partly because price controls were imposed by the Japanese occupying authorities.

When the price controls became increasingly ineffective and the Japanese army was losing battles in the Philippines, inflation surfaced. May 1944 saw the first instance of monthly price inflation rising to a double-digit level (12 percent). It escalated to 60 percent in November that year and peaked at 120 percent in January 1945, when the Japanese army was desperately defending its last stronghold in the Philippines – Manila. Within a month, American troops reclaimed the Philippines.

An interesting footnote to the Filipino episode of hyperinflation is that when American military forces launched their offensive in the Philippines from 1944, they surreptitiously distributed counterfeit Japanese army notes to Philippine guerrilla groups, which undoubtedly added fuel to the flames of inflation in the country at the time.[83]

In fact, high inflation caused by Japanese occupation did not occur in the Philippines alone. In Southeast Asia, Malaysia, Singapore, Indonesia, Burma (Myanmar), and Hong Kong, all witnessed surges of high inflation of varying paces due to the debasement of Japanese military notes before the end of the war.

Unlike in many other places, hyperinflation did not break out in South Korea until after the end of the war. Between 1910 and 1945, the Korean Peninsula was under Japanese rule, and the currency, issued by the Japanese-controlled Bank of Chosen, was initially made convertible to gold or Japanese gold notes. As part of the yen bloc, Korea did not endure significant inflation even during the Second World War.[84] Wholesale prices in Korea rose 1.75-fold from 1938 to 1944, at an average rate of 9.7 percent annually. The year 1944 saw a moderate rise in wholesale prices, 11.5 percent, which was even lower than Japan's 13.7 percent that year.[85] When the war ended in August 1945, the situation changed drastically. Wholesale price rises jumped from double digits to quadruple digits in a matter of months.

Figure 4.11 shows three price indicators in South Korea covering the period 1944 to 1954 which come from different sources.[86] The WPI series, on the left-hand scale, omits the years 1950 and 1951; the PPI graph misses out the period 1950–52; and the CPI curve is continuous from 1945. WPI rose 1,852.6 percent in 1945, 1,900 percent in 1949, and 3,200 percent in 1952. The other two indicators – relatively recently compiled by South Korean experts – show more moderate changes than WPI: PPI rose 385.4 percent in 1946; and CPI, 280.4 percent in 1946 and 390.5 percent in 1951. The CPI figures in 1946 and 1951 also indicate that high inflation occurred both immediately after the Japanese surrender in 1945 and after the outbreak of the Korean War in mid-1950.

When Japan surrendered in mid-August 1945, American military authorities started to administer part of the Korean Peninsula, south of the 38th parallel (north latitude), and were soon joined by a newly formed provisional Korean government. More than two million ethnic Koreans returned to South Korea, while less than one million Japanese left. Rice output had declined before the end of the war due to shortages of chemical fertilizers. Rationing and price controls were believed to be imperative to maintain orderly distribution of necessities and avoid social unrest. But, the apparently inexperienced authorities did not succeed in

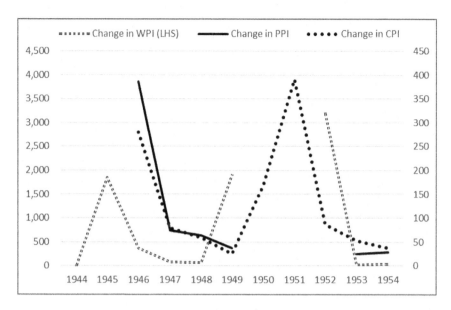

Figure 4.11 Annual Changes in WPI and CPI, percentage, log scale, South Korea, 1944–54[87]

establishing workable schemes for rationing and price controls in the first two years after the end of the war. By fall 1945, average food prices paid by authorities in their procurement had risen five-fold.[88] In contrast, though facing similar food shortages, North Korean authorities were able to enforce rationing and price controls, at least much more effectively than their counterparts in the South, and so inflation was rather moderate there.

The outbreak of the Korean War in June 1950 dealt a huge blow to the South Korean government, formally established in 1948, which seemed totally unprepared for the event. It lost control of many aspects of the economy, from key materials to logistics, and high inflation arrived in the country once again.

Germany: bitter escape from hyperinflation

From an economic point of view, there were three effects of the war on Germany's economy in the middle of the 1940s: First, a great bulk of economic resources were diverted from civil use to military purposes; second, the Allied counterattacks from 1942 caused great damage to the nation's infrastructure and industrial capacity; third, in order to finance its ever-enlarging military spending, the Nazi regime exploited various monetary means. All this would have resulted in a great inflation if it had not been offset by other counterbalancing factors.

An estimate shows that in 1943, Germany's military outlays accounted for 70 percent of her national income, as measured in either current prices or constant prices.[89] In that year, out of the Third Reich's total budget of 657 billion reichsmark, two-thirds are believed to have gone to the Nazi's military forces, the *Wehrmacht*.[90] Between 1943 and the end of 1944, the Nazi army conquered almost the entire European continent, and many occupied countries and territories paid huge amounts toward Germany's military spending, which is estimated to have been 25,000 billion reichsmark in 1943 and 28,000 billion reichsmark in 1944 (January to September).[91]

In 1944, the total budget expenditure of the Nazi regime was financed by several different methods: domestic revenue accounted for one-third, direct borrowing from the Reichsbank contributed another one-third, one-fifth came from loans, advances, and securities subscriptions from various financial institutions – commercial banks, savings banks, and insurance companies – and the remaining one-eighth consisted of war donations and levies on occupied territories.[92] By April 1945, when Hitler died, the Third Reich's total debts, which were only 31 billion reichsmark when the war broke out in 1939, amounted to 337 billion reichsmark.

Between 1932 and 1944, the money stock in Germany increased 437 percent, whilst wholesale prices rose merely 22 percent, according to official statistics.[93] This seems puzzling. The first figure suggests that prices should have risen much more for that period than the second figure indicates. Even if adjusted for more realistic price changes, inflation in wartime Germany remains extremely moderate, especially compared to that of other belligerent countries. It is believed that Germany's economy under the Nazi regime actually shifted toward a planned type, which consisted of price controls, strict rations, and state allocation of resources and products. In addition, the large-scale Allied bombings from 1943 destroyed many key facilities in Germany's transport systems and therefore resulted in greatly reduced transport and travel, which may also have been a significant factor in German people increasing their real money balance. In any case, the money stock increased faster than price inflation.[94]

Between May 1945, when Germany unconditionally surrendered, and June 1948, when a new currency reform was conducted, the reichsmark remained the legal tender in all occupied zones. The national net product in West Germany in 1946 shrank by 28.3 percent from its level in 1945, which had already fallen by nearly 40 percent from the previous year.[95] In addition, there were approximately six and half million ethnic Germans moving into West Germany from neighboring countries and territories.[96] The Allied occupation authorities invalidated all the price controls implemented earlier by the Nazi regime, except for food supplies which were put into a new rationing scheme. Shortages of daily goods were widespread, and Germany was once again under the threat of hyperinflation.

Yet, there was no hyperinflation at all. In fact, inflation in postwar West Germany was quite moderate, as measured by conventional price indicators. A consumer price index rose only 9 percent in 1946 – the most difficult year for millions of ordinary Germans. In the following two years, it rose 7 percent and 15.4 percent, respectively. Again, these were low levels compared to those in Italy and Japan, and they were also lower than those in France.[97]

The juxtaposition of massive shortages and moderate inflation in the absence of effective price controls and totalitarian-styled income policy is quite unusual. To see how it actually occurred, we need to look at the broad background of the postwar reconstruction of West Germany under the Allied occupation, which was distinctively different from the experience after the First World War. As noted by historians, there was a fundamental change in United States policy toward Germany in the matter of weeks or months at the end of the war. Earlier in September 1944, U.S. military directives stipulated that "Germany will not be occupied for the purpose of liberation but as a defeated enemy nation."[98] What later happened is that Germany had been liberated from her older political and economic system.

The Potsdam Agreement in the summer of 1945 directed the Allied Control Council to take over management of Germany's transition to postwar reconstruction.[99] The U.S.-led organization followed an approach that was in many ways opposite to that of the Treaty of Versailles in 1919. War reparations that were sought were not only small in size, but also non-financial. They were pieces of industrial equipment from German factories, mostly in heavy industries. Meanwhile, the costs of occupation were largely borne by the occupying powers, which is again in sharp contrast to the situation after the First World War. In addition, through the work of the United Nations Relief and Rehabilitation Administration (UNRRA), more than ten million Germans received help in relocation and settlement, though many ethnic Germans were not granted direct aid of food and medicine like people in other war-torn countries.

The U.S.-led campaign of German reconstruction – known as "new nation building" in postwar Germany – had a strong intent to destroy the social and economic foundations of the Nazi regime. The measures undertaken by the occupation forces are often referred as the "Four De-s." "De-nazification" was a direct political drive, purging Nazi activists from social organizations. Demilitarization required Germany to ensure sufficient industrial disarmament by cutting her industrial capacity, especially in heavy industry. Decentralization moved political powers to subnational levels, suspending many functions of the central government. Finally, "de-monopolization" in economics targeted three specific sectors – banking, chemicals, and heavy industry – and forcibly dismantled cartels and *konzerns* (a German word meaning syndicates) and broke up many German business conglomerates.[100]

In the banking industry, the largest three German banks – Deutsche Bank, Dresdner Bank, and Commerzbank – were all broken down into 30 separate regional units. All bank accounts were subject to strict examination for the purposes of "denazification." Many banks had to suspend their business operations until they had obtained approval from the occupation authorities. More importantly, the Reichsbank – the central banking institution that had played the pivotal role in the 1920s' hyperinflation – was deprived of many of its functions and disintegrated into a regional structure. It could no longer discount bills for commercial banks or underwrite government securities, although it was allowed to provide technical assistance in the areas of interbank payments and currency notes replacement. Decentralization and "de-monopolization" were both applied to this once colossal and omnipotent organization in Germany.

Without central bank support, the banks in West Germany that remained in operation found themselves unable to expand their businesses despite the availability of plenty of liquidity. In fact, demand for credit from the private sector was limited, and market interest rates – the discount rate and Lombard rate – remained unchanged at 3.5 percent and 4.5 percent, respectively, until 1948. There was no "true monetary policy" in West Germany in the immediate postwar period.[101]

Besides the partial functioning of the banking industry, there were certain other economic factors that contributed to the changing role of money and depressed inflation in postwar West Germany. First, the economy had switched to a system of barter to some extent. It is estimated that half of production in the Anglo-American occupied zones in 1947 and the first half of 1948 was used in "countertrade" – firms traded goods in kind, and market prices were used only for measurement and settlement. The reasons for the phenomenon were several: it was a practice inherited from the later years of the Nazi regime; it bypassed regulations imposed by the new authorities; it avoided accumulation of *reichsmark*, whose value and stability were uncertain; and it controlled the costs of raw materials, which were rising faster than output prices.[102]

Ordinary Germans faced a subtle dilemma: commodities they wanted to buy were in short supply in shops and department stores, and what was available was mostly highly priced and hardly usable. *Reichsmark* were mainly used for purchasing foodstuffs under the strict rationing scheme and for paying rent, taxation, and public utility bills. Again, many ordinary Germans had to use grey and black markets and started to barter for goods. A worker in a cigarette factory could receive 800 cigarettes as part of their wages, which could be exchanged for 1,500 *reichsmark* on the black market. The value of this sum can be gauged by comparing it to the wages of workers in coal minefields: a typical worker was paid only 60 *reichsmark* a week. Cigarettes, especially those that were made in America and brought to Germany by soldiers and staff of the occupation authorities, became a currency on the grey and black markets.[103]

The most important reason for the depressed inflation in postwar Germany was the lack of an effective central government and the consequent absence of state budget expansion. As mentioned earlier, many functions of the old Reich government were delegated to regional and local levels as part of the decentralization drive pursued by the occupation authorities. There was no capital in West Germany until 1948. The handful of remaining administrative offices had to keep working with much-reduced staff numbers.

To a certain extent, the low inflation – especially that which was reflected in published price indexes – was helped by price controls, despite the fact that they had been weakened by regime change and economic collapse. After mid-1945, German officials reapplied many price controls and attempted to exercise their power to punish those who were found to have contravened the rules. Worried about possible hyperinflation, the occupation authorities agreed to the price controls. Many German people actually showed a good deal of cooperation and suffered from the unpopular practice. Yet, the widespread existence of black markets and bartering in many spheres of the economy also suggest that in the absence of an authoritarian regime, price controls were ineffective in keeping prices down.

In short, it was the combination of dysfunctional central government, suspended central banking, debilitated banking industry, partially-functioned price controls, and retreat to barter that helped check the momentum of inflation in the early years of postwar Germany, either intentionally or unintentionally. In addition, basic food supplies, overseen by the occupation authorities through rationing schemes and foreign aid, also played a positive role. If Germany had continued to operate her political and economic systems after 1945 in ways similar to how they were run after the First World War, hyperinflation would certainly have once again haunted the country.

Recognizing the distortional effects of price controls in the economy, several German economists and officials called for price liberalization. Ludwig Erhard, a German official who worked closely with the occupation authorities and later became German Chancellor during the 1960s, played a leading role in the drive. He managed to obtain the green light from the Anglo-American authorities to implement sudden price decontrol a few days before a major currency reform in June 1948. In many other countries, when a currency reform is combined with price decontrol, inflation tends to emerge or accelerate. But this was not the case in Germany in 1948.

The currency reform was initiated by the occupation authorities in consultation with German officials and economists. The reform's main motivation was to serve the new nation-building objective and break monetary linkages with the old regime. In finance, institutional restructuring had already started in late 1946. First, several "Land Central Banks" ("land" in German means "state" or "province") were established, first in the American zone and later in the British zone. They assumed many functions of a central bank in the regions, except for note issuing. Second, the Bank deutscher Länder was formed in the spring of 1948 to act as the central bank for all Land Central Banks, again without the right to issue currency notes. With these new institutions functioning, the Allied authorities believed conditions were right for a major currency reform.

There were three main elements of the currency reform: first, a new currency unit, deutsche mark (D-mark or DM), replaced the old *reichsmark* at the rate of 1:10; second, securities denominated in *reichsmark* were not eligible for conversion; third, new currency issues had to be authorized by the Allied Control Council.[104] The cancellation of old debts was obviously very deflationary, with the resultant losses largely borne by German people who were relatively rich and by German savings and investment institutions. The third condition imposed on the new currency by the occupation authorities was apparently a device for checking expansionary monetary policy.

Externally, the new D-mark's exchange rate with the dollar was set to be 3.33:1,[105] effectively a large devaluation in real terms. The nominal exchange rate between the old *reichsmark*, which had lost much of its utility either before or after the end of the war, and the dollar was 2.5:1. But given the two facts that price inflation in Germany was relatively low during the period – even lower than that in the United States – and that the new D-mark had a designated value ten times that of the old *reichsmark*, the exchange rate of 3.33:1 was a great discount of the D-mark in international transactions. At that time, Germany had to import a lot of essential goods from abroad, and the much devalued D-mark would have necessarily driven up domestic prices of the imports if no countermeasures had been taken to offset the negative impacts.

As a countermeasure, following the currency reform, West Germany maintained exchange controls, which lasted for a long time. More importantly, as the Cold War began to unfold from 1947, the United States made changes to her foreign policy in Europe, particularly towards the postwar reconstruction in West Germany, which brought new foreign aid to the country from 1948. The Marshall Plan (officially the European Recovery Program) was proposed in 1947, and its implementation started from 1948. West Germany was one of major beneficiaries of the program, with hundreds of millions of dollars received each year between 1949 and 1952. As a result, the currency reform encountered only temporary setbacks, lasting a couple of months, in markets and the economy. By the end of 1948, prices had become stabilized, and industrial output in the Anglo-American zones had turned to growth.[106]

Almost a year later, the Federal Republic of Germany – formally incorporating all elements of a modern, democratic political system – was established in West Germany, with her capital in Bonn. In 1957, a new law was enacted to establish the Deutsche Bundesbank, with its headquarters in Frankfurt, as a replacement for the Bank deutscher Länder. The central bank enjoyed a high degree of institutional independence in conducting its monetary policy, keeping Germany away from any serious inflation throughout the postwar period. West Germany experienced the fastest economic growth in Europe between the 1950s and the 1970s, which was dubbed an "economic miracle" by many. The reputation that the Deutsche Bundesbank earned helped Germany play a pivotal role in the process of European monetary integration towards the euro during the 1980s and the 1990s.

Appendix note on Austria: earlier currency reform and higher inflation

Like Germany, Austria was stunned by hyperinflation after the First World War. Under the Nazi regime, she was merged with Germany and her older currency absorbed into the *reichsmark*. Upon the end of the Second World War, the Allied powers all agreed to make Austria an independent nation. They quickly helped an interim central government form and a general election take place soon afterward. An agreement reached among themselves in June 1946 effectively reduced the power of Russia as a dissenter in the postwar transition period,[107] so Austria's coalition government could undertake a currency reform from the end of November 1945, again with help from the occupation authorities.

The new schilling could be exchanged with old *reichsmark* at the rate of 1 to 1, up to a limit of 150 schilling per person. Holdings of old *reichsmark* above that limit had to be deposited in banks, where their use was subject to certain restrictions. Records at the National Bank of Austria (Austria's central bank) indicate that the nation's total money stock amounted to 899 million schilling in March 1939, yet the bank had recalled 8,659.8 million schilling by February 1946.[108] The disparity between these two figures suggests that the money stock expanded enormously during the period of Nazi rule and that the currency reform was successful in retiring a huge portion of the money supply and, therefore, in reducing inflation pressures.

Nevertheless, inflation started to climb from 1946. CPI in Austria rose 6.4 percent in 1945, 26.7 percent in 1946, and 95.9 percent in 1947.[109] From 1948, CPI inflation decelerated but remained in double digits until 1953, when Austria was finally in a position to consolidate her currency market and she fixed the schilling's unified exchange rate with the dollar at 26:1.[110] An immediate cause of the serious inflation was that the Austrian government ran budget deficits right from the start, and the costs of occupation were mainly covered by Austria. In 1946, Austria's payments to the four Allied powers accounted for 25 to 35 percent of her central government budget, which totaled 2.5 billion schilling. For the next year, the payments were reduced to 130 million schilling, a figure which was still a significant burden on the nation's public finance.[111]

Historians believe that it was the Marshall Plan that came to Austria's economic rescue and laid the foundations for her postwar recovery and prosperity. Between 1948 and 1952, Austria received about 1 billion dollars under the Plan, an amount equivalent to $137 per person, which was much higher than West Germany's $19 per capita average.[112] Without such foreign aid, Austria might have slipped once again into an inflationary trap in the late 1940s and early 1950s.

Notes

1 In 1945 or 1946, Greece had a population of 7.3 million, Italy, 45 million, Hungary, 9 million, West Germany (later Federal Germany), 46 million; and in East Asia, China (excluding Hong Kong and Taiwan), 455 million, Japan, 75 million, South Korea (later the Republic of Korea), 19 million, and Taiwan, 6.1 million (all figures from Mitchell, *Europe* and *Africa, Asia and Oceania*, Table A5, respectively).
2 Hanke and Krus, p. 372.
3 The drachma price of British sovereign is from Palariret, Table A2, and the real money balance (the nominal value of M1 divided by price inflation) is from Table A5. In November 1944, the new drachma was introduced, so the monthly change from December that year is expressed in the new drachma price. M1 is paper notes of drachma in circulation plus demand deposits at banks.
4 Because of the lack of data for the years 1942–44, many researchers of the Greek hyperinflation have used the drachma prices of gold sovereign to indicate the underlying price inflation, which should be treated with caution. As noted by Karatzas (1988), for the period June 1940 – May 1941, the drachma price of the sovereign and consumer prices had "a poor relationship" (also see Makinen, 1988 for his response to this note).
5 Palairet (2000). The last three Greek stabilization programs are also reviewed in Makinen (1986).
6 Mazower, p. 2.
7 Makinen (1986, p. 797).
8 Makinen (1986, p. 797).
9 Sebestyen, pp. 256–7.
10 Palariret, Table A7. Each of the two series has the base index value of 100 in 1940 and continuous monthly figures only for November 1944 through January 1945.
11 Makinen (1986, p. 800).
12 Makinen (1986, p. 797).
13 Palariret, Table A1, p. 121.
14 Makinen (1986, p. 802).
15 Makinen (1988, p. 1071).
16 Mitchell, *Europe*, Tables H1 and H2. For figures prior to 1958, "consumer prices" are actually an index of cost of living in Athens.

17 International Monetary Fund, *Annual Report*, 1953, p. 73.
18 De Vries and Horsefield, Vol. II, p. 48.
19 Kindleberger (1984, pp. 137, 475) (Table 5).
20 Online information from the European Central Bank at www.ecb.europa.eu/euro/intro/html/index.en.html.
21 Derived from Maddison (2003, Tables 1c and 2c).
22 Sullivan, p. 187.
23 Harrison, Table 1.8, p. 21. The highest figure of Italy was 23 percent in 1941.
24 Sullivan, pp. 189–90.
25 Fratianni and Spinelli, pp. 163–5.
26 Fratianni and Spinelli, p. 162.
27 Zamagni, p. 200.
28 Nazi Germany was actually in debt to all of the "occupied" countries and "friendly" countries during World War II and there was no financial resource available for aid to Italy (Petrov, p. 31).
29 It is noted, for instance, that retail prices of foodstuffs in Rome were more than 30 times those in 1938 when the war ended in April 1945 (citation in Toynbee and Toynbee, pp. 440, of Bruno Foa, *Monetary Reconstruction in Italy*, New York: King's Crown Press, 1949, p. 15). Most of the rise in prices likely occurred in 1943–45.
30 Fratianni and Spinelli, pp. 166–7 and Figure 6.1 therewith.
31 Mitchell, *Europe*, Tables H1 and H2.
32 Raw data from Klein, Table 2, p. 134. The real money balance is the ratio between the two indexes in each year (M/P).
33 Toynbee and Toynbee, pp. 441–2.
34 Toynbee and Toynbee, p. 445. Also Hitchcook, Table on p. 220.
35 Petrov, p. 86.
36 Fratianni and Spinelli, Table 6.4, p. 172.
37 Toynbee and Toynbee, p. 440.
38 Fratianni and Spinelli, p. 170.
39 Fratianni and Spinelli, p. 170.
40 Fratianni and Spinelli, Table 6.3, p. 172.
41 Fratianni and Spinelli, Table 6.3, p. 174.
42 Castronuovo, p. 408.
43 Exports figures are from Mitchell, *Europe*, Table E1.
44 De Vries and Horsefield, Vol. II, p. 48.
45 The lira's exchange rate with the dollar of 625 was maintained throughout the 1950s and most of the 1960s. It started to fluctuate from the late 1960s, with substantial depreciations in the 1980s and 1990s, which ultimately resulted in the lira's international value when Italy joined the Eurozone in 1999.
46 Siklos (1991, Table 2.3, p. 30).
47 Hanke and Krus, Table 30.1, p. 372.
48 Siklos (1991, Table 7.1, p. 98).
49 Sebestyen, pp. 166–7, footnote.
50 Black market prices relative to official ones from Siklos (1991, Table 2.7, p. 34), and comparison of depreciation between the black market and official rates from Table 2.9, p. 36, *ibid*.
51 Siklos (1991, Figure 7.6, p. 119).
52 The cost of living index including rent is from Siklos (1991, Table 2.4), last column, p. 29; and the exchange rates – also from Siklos (1991, Table 2.3, pp. 25–6) – are official ones that were on dates close to the last day of the month.
53 Molnár, p. 296.
54 Bomberger and Makinen (1983, p. 803).
55 Bomberger and Makinen (1983, p. 804).
56 Bomberger and Makinen (1983, Footnote 18, p. 813), citation of other authors. Siklos (1991, Table 5.1, p. 80) shows that the proportion of Hungarian reparations payments

to government expenditure was 33 percent in 1945, 33 percent in 1946, 39 percent in 1947, and 32 percent in 1948. Also p. 79 in Siklos, *ibid.*

57 Siklos (1991, p. 99).
58 Toynbee and Toynbee, p. 324.
59 Toynbee and Toynbee, pp. 325–6.
60 Siklos (1991, p. 87) and Bomberger and Makinen (1983, Footnote 10, p. 807).
61 Grossman and Horváth, pp. 417–8. Horváth was in the Hungarian government during the period. The two authors believe three factors had prevented Hungarian banks from directly engaging in goods hoarding and rendered them instead remaining in the business of lending: the fewness of the banks made it easy for the government to regulate; the tradition of bank-business relationship as exemplified in the German model of banking; and "altruism" (p. 419).
62 Citation in Siklos (1991, p. 97).
63 Bomberger and Makinen (1980).
64 Siklos (1991, pp. 100–2) for tax on pengő, and pp. 114–7 for calorie wages.
65 Siklos (1991, Table 7.3, p. 109).
66 The August reform is documented in detail in Bomberger and Makinen (1980, pp. 813–8).
67 Bomberger and Makinen (1980, p. 816).
68 Mitchell, *Africa, Asia and Oceania*, Tables H1 and H2. The retail price data before 1946 is for Tokyo only. An alternative estimate gives higher figures for retail price changes during the war period (Hara, Table 6.13, p. 260).
69 Cater *et al*, Table Ee646–661, pp. 5–576.
70 Harrison, Table 1.8, p. 21.
71 Hara, Table 6.11, p. 257.
72 Hara, pp. 226–7. In Maddison (1982), GDP figures of the two years are missing, and 1957's level was only 56 percent of 1939's – Japan's highest in the first half of the twentieth century (Table A7, p. 175).
73 Jones, Borton, and Pearn, pp. 391–2. The issue of more currency in 1947 than in 1946 was a result of rising inflation and its shrinking effect on revenue in real terms.
74 Retail prices from Mitchell, *Africa, Asia and Oceania*, Table H2; the money stock (cash plus demand deposits) from Hara, Table 6.12, p. 258; the real money balance is the ratio between the two indexes in each year (M/P).
75 Hara, Table 6.12, p. 258. Narrow money is cash plus demand deposits, and quasi-money is the difference between the narrow and broad money stocks.
76 Jones, Borton, and Pearn, p. 390.
77 Yoshio, p. 531.
78 Yuji, p. 75. The differential exchange rates for imports and exports could benefit trading firms enormously, and in prewar Imperial Japan, many trading firms were affiliated to *zaibatsu*, family-based or family-linked industrial and financial conglomerates that were subject to dissolution by the American occupation authorities after the Second World War.
79 Savage, p. 270.
80 The budget surplus amounted to 156.9 billion yen for the fiscal year of 1949, from April 1 through March 31, and the previous year's budget deficit was 88.7 billion yen (Savage, Table 1, p. 268). The author believes that Dodge contributed significantly to the Japanese Ministry of Finance's "postwar penchant for fiscal conservatism" (p. 267).
81 Hara, p. 259.
82 Sicat, p. 20.
83 Hanke and Krus, p. 369.
84 Mizoguchi (1972) provides a detailed account of price inflation and real wages in Korea and Taiwan under Japanese rule, though does not cover the years after 1939.
85 Mitchell, *Africa, Asia and Oceania*, Table H1B.
86 A paper published by Makinen in 1971 (in Makinen, 2014, pp. 1–32) cited the data of RPI covering the period from December 1947–December 1953 (Makinen, 2014,

Table 2, p. 4), which are basically same as the changes in the CPI shown in Figure 4.11, but they are different for 1951 (390.5 percent vs. 300.2 percent) and 1952 (86.6 percent vs. 146.3 percent).

87 Figures of WPI are from Mitchell, *Africa, Asia and Oceania*, Table H1B; and those of CPI and PPI are from *Sixtieth Anniversary of Korean Recovery in Statistics* (in Korean), edited by the Bank of Korea, Seoul, 2003, p. 83.

88 Jones, Borton, and Pearn, p. 453.

89 Harrison, Table 1.8, p. 21. An alternative estimate indicates that Germany's military spending was 18.9 percent of her national income (net national product at factor cost) in 1938 (Abelshauser, Table 4.5, p. 138).

90 Hardach, p. 90.

91 Abelshauser, Table 4.7, p. 143.

92 Hardach, p. 90.

93 Klein (1956).

94 Klein (1956).

95 Sommariva and Tulio, p. 227.

96 Hardach, p. 103.

97 CPI in France rose 63.9 percent in 1946, 59.7 percent in 1947, and 58.5 percent in 1948 (Maddison, 1982, Table E3, p. 238).

98 Hitchcook, pp. 208–9.

99 In West Germany, there was the Supreme Headquarters of the Allied Expeditionary Forces (SHAEF), under the direction of the Anglo-American authorities. The SHAEF issued a large handbook with detailed guidelines for how the military government should deal with various matters, including banking and finance, in occupied zones (Buchheim, p. 63).

100 Hardach, pp. 99–100.

101 Buchheim, p. 66.

102 Hardach, pp. 106–7.

103 Hardach, p. 104, Footnotes 1 and 3; and p. 107. Another example of "cigarette currency" emerged in POW camps in Germany toward the end of the Second World War, which involved the use of cigarettes as a unit of value and a means of exchange among prisoners, who obtained goods from rations and then traded them. A description and economic analysis of the situation was given by a British POW who later became a professional economist in America. See Radford (1945).

104 Buchheim, p. 89.

105 The D-mark was further devalued to 4.2 to the dollar in 1950, a level which was sustained for the following decade. Sommariva and Tulio, p. 233.

106 Buchheim, pp. 95–7.

107 Beller, p. 254.

108 Mair, p. 349.

109 Maddison (1982, Table E3, p. 238, and Table E4, p. 240).

110 The Austrian schilling exchange rate with the dollar experienced several large changes from 1945. That year, it was 10 schilling to a dollar, but this ratio was hardly used in practice. A multiple exchange rates scheme was implemented, and intermittent devaluations followed. Unification of the exchange rates was completed in 1953, when domestic fiscal and credit policies were also reformed. The 1953 Annual Report of the International Monetary Fund, which Austria joined in 1948, gives a detailed description of the monetary developments in Austria (pp. 63–4).

111 Mair, p. 350.

112 Beller, pp. 252–3.

5 War finance and its aftermath
China in the 1940s

> Seldom if ever in a brief span of years has any country seen changes as swift and
> dramatic as those affecting China during the second quarter of this century.
>
> Arthur N. Young, *China's Nation-building Effort, 1927–1937:*
> *The Financial and Economic Record*, Preface, 1971

China played a distinctive role in the Second World War. A bilateral war against
the Japanese invasion commenced in 1937, whilst European powers and the
United States remained basically neutral about this Asian conflict until September
1939 or December 1941. After the end of the Pacific War in August 1945 massive internal conflicts in China reemerged, which ultimately led to collapse of the
Nationalist regime in mainland China in 1949. During the 1940s, China endured
high inflation followed by hyperinflation.

In both of these periods – the first half of the 1940s during the Pacific War
and the second half of that decade when internal war erupted – Nationalist China
was weakened and exposed to many kinds of threats, displaying how fragile an
authoritarian regime could be when it came to financing its budgetary needs *and*
controlling inflation. In hindsight, it is not surprising that the regime would suffer
both military failure and monetary fiascos from time to time, despite the many
advantages and resources it had once held.

War finance and high inflation in the first half of the 1940s

Nationalist China lost many battles in fighting against Japanese military aggression
that began in July 1937, and its armies had to retreat inland by 1938. A stalemate
occurred at that point, which continued almost until the end of the Second World
War. Inflation rose violently in many parts of China. In the end, Nationalist China
won the war against Japan, but the victory required massive economic and social
sacrifices, and throughout, China struggled unsuccessfully to contain rising inflation.

China split into multiple currency areas

Several different political entities and currency areas in "Greater China" existed
before 1937, including Manchuria (northeast China), West China (Xinjiang),

Tibet, Taiwan, Hong Kong, and Macau, in addition to Nationalist China, which had successfully conducted a major currency reform in 1935. In the early 1940s, three more currency areas surfaced: East China, where a Japanese puppet government had formed in 1941, North China where another Japanese puppet regime was in place from the late 1930s, and a Communist regime that was active mainly in parts of northern China from the late 1930s. Each of these three regimes issued one or more paper currencies of its own, backed by nothing that was acknowledgeable at a later stage. The former two regimes (East and North China) initially attempted to link their currencies to the Japanese yen and become members of the yen bloc, but their exchange rates versus the yen were never maintained, whether intentionally or unintentionally.

In addition to numerous Chinese currencies circulating in mainland China, in late 1937, the Japanese issued military notes (*gunpyo*) throughout occupied China, mostly in East and South China, in parallel with the currencies of the Japanese puppet regimes. *Gunpyo* was unpopular with the Chinese people as well as with the puppet governments in the occupied regions. As in other parts of Southeast Asia, there was little link in practice between the Japanese military notes and the Japanese yen.

Table 5.1 summarizes the currency regimes that existed in Greater China during the first half of the 1940s. With a few exceptions, all of the major regions endured high inflation during this period. Of them, the puppet regime based in Nanking (Nanjing) – which also controlled Shanghai – witnessed hyperinflation. A wholesale price index in Shanghai rose more than 50 percent every month beginning in July 1943; this escalated to 302 percent per month starting in June 1945.[1] The year 1943 was when Japan began to lose the Pacific War and could no longer lend economic support to her puppet regimes. Japan's domestic economy was in disarray, and the puppet regime in Nanking was unable to collect revenue due to the effects of both its internal conflicts and the Pacific War.

There are several regimes for which information about price inflation was not available at the time it was happening, nor is it available to us now. It is possible to guess how much inflation occurred in these currency areas by analyzing signs of exchange rate movements. For example, one Communist currency, measured in terms of the *fabi* – Nationalist China's legal tender since 1935 – was equal to 1.21 *fabi* in 1937, 1.5 in 1941, 2.2 in 1943, and 8 by official quotation in 1944.[2] The Communist currency was evidently on a steady path of depreciation versus the *fabi* during the first half of the 1940s, which should indicate that inflation in the currency area was no less severe than it was in the *fabi* areas during the same period. Of course, the economy of most Communist-controlled regions was more rural and more self-sufficient than other parts of China, so that high inflation may have impacted them less severely.

Many observers have referred to the monetary situation in China during the period from 1937 to the early 1940s as a "currency war" or "monetary warfare," especially when considering the interactions between the Nationalist government and the Japanese puppet regimes.[3] Two main factors defined the monetary

Table 5.1 Currency regimes and levels of inflation in "Greater China," 1941–45[4]

	Population million	Political status	Currency regime	Level of inflation
Free China	210	Independent, nationalist government	Suspended peg; unbacked currency	High inflation
East China	130	Japanese puppet, also self-called "Republic of China"	Unbacked currency; nominal link with Japanese yen	Hyperinflation
North China	110	Japanese puppet, "autonomous regions"	Unbacked currency; nominal link with Japanese yen	High inflation
Communist China	1–10	Communist military regime	Unbacked currency	High inflation
Manchuria (Manchukuo)	40	Japanese puppet since 1931	Pegging Japanese yen	Significant inflation
West China (Xinjiang)	4.5	Autonomous region	Unbacked currency	High inflation
Tibet	1	Semi-independent region	Mixed specie currencies	Significant inflation
Taiwan	6.5	Japan-ruled region since 1895	Pegging Japanese yen	Significant inflation
Hong Kong	1.6	British colony occupied by Japan	Suspended silver money; Japanese military notes	High inflation
Macau	0.4	Portuguese colony	Largely silver-based currency	Significant inflation

Note: Categories of "Hyperinflation," "high inflation," and "significant inflation" here refer to annual inflation rates, occurring mainly in 1944–45, of quadruple, treble, and double digits, respectively. North China, West China, and parts of Communist China may possibly have endured hyperinflation.

interaction between the Japanese and Nationalist China. First, while the Nationalist government continued to operate with an exchange-rate pegging system – which involved sustaining the *fabi*'s exchange rates with the U.S. dollar and the British pound sterling, mainly from the late 1930s to the early 1940s – the Japanese tried to deplete Nationalist China's foreign exchange reserves to shake the foundations of her monetary system. Chinese operation of the peg was conducted at money markets in venues known as Concessions located in Tientsin (Tianjin) and Shanghai. Both of these cities were besieged by the Japanese starting in 1937 but had remained autonomous, with extensive connections in Hong Kong where Nationalist China's banking agencies could freely conduct business. The currency pegging policy helped to boost the confidence that the domestic public and the international community had in Nationalist China, despite the fact that her trade relations with the outside world had been largely cut off by Japanese blockades.

Japanese sabotage efforts included amassing *fabi* notes to buy foreign exchange from Chinese banking agencies, as well as demanding that British and French authorities that engaged with the Concessions stop helping the Chinese. At one point, the Japanese were able to obtain a significant portion of China's reserves; in the six months leading up to February 1938, Nationalist China lost nearly one-fifth of her foreign exchange reserves.[5] The outbreak of the Second World War in Europe in September 1939 made the operation of the Concessions impossible to maintain, and the Japanese occupation of Hong Kong in December 1941 finally ended it. However, fortunately for Nationalist China, she was able to attract a certain amount of capital inflow from Hong Kong and Southeast Asia and to receive financial support from the British and American governments until the end of the peg system in late 1939.

The second aspect affecting currency interactions between the Japanese and Nationalist China is that Japan encouraged its puppet regimes to issue their own currency notes, establishing currency areas in which the *fabi* could be marginalized and the yen bloc could be extended. Forced conversion of the *fabi* into puppet currencies helped the Japanese gather *fabi* funds by purchasing foreign exchange from the Chinese until late 1939. In addition, if the *fabi* notes that had been circulated earlier in the occupied regions flowed into Nationalist China in certain ways, this could generate additional inflationary pressures in the currency areas.[6] Enlargement of the yen bloc was perhaps a more important part of the Japanese strategy in the early stages of Japan's expansionist pursuit of China and greater Asia. The degree to which resources were available to them ultimately decided the fate of the puppet currency regimes.

Nonetheless, the complex variety of currencies that largely resulted from the Japanese invasion of China complicated Nationalist China's monetary management. Harry D. White, an American Treasury official who once worked with a Chinese counterpart in 1940 and later became the United States' chief negotiator at the Bretton-Woods conference leading to the establishment of the International Monetary Fund and the World Bank, remarked in 1940 that the person who had to untangle China's currency situation had the world's "really most difficult monetary job."[7]

A possible outcome of the multiple currency areas in wartime China was that many of the monetary authorities did not consider the consequences of trade deficits in intraregional trade relations between areas that were mutually hostile to each other. Put simply, when a regime experienced an excessive currency issue that resulted in its having higher inflation than other regimes, as well as a trade deficit, it did not worry about "indebtedness" or "finances" as it would in a case of normal trade relations. In wartime China, a trade deficit with other currency areas might actually have been regarded an advantage in terms of resource flow. It is also possible that the existence of multiple currency areas and the occurrence of widespread inflation in many of these regions increased political tolerance of inflation: politicians did not worry overly about inflation as long as their region's inflation was not worse than that of other regions.

Deficit financing by low-yield bonds

When the Nationalist government retreated to China's heartland in 1938, it lost access to revenues from custom duties and salt tax, which once served as major revenue sources. Meanwhile, large-scale industrial relocation and infrastructure construction required tremendous amounts of new fiscal input. As a result, the Nationalist government began to incur a budget deficit that expanded rapidly from 1937 onward.

Borrowing was one obvious solution. Before the outbreak of the war, the Nationalist government made some successful efforts to improve its reputation in the domestic bond market. The average yield on its bonds and short-term treasury notes fell to 8.7 percent in June 1937 from 13 percent in 1935 and 11.6 percent in 1936.[8] During the period from 1928–37, the total issue of government securities amounted to C $1,998 million, but only C $1,530 million could be used for fiscal purposes, with the rest going to debt service and allowances for marketing, etc. The average "discount rate" was as high as 23.4 percent. This suggests that the Nationalist government had already been highly indebted and had significant debt financing costs to sustain. However, the decline in the yield rate on government bonds in 1937 suggests that public acceptance of government indebtedness had improved by then.

Had the Nationalist government continued to improve its behavior and reputation in terms of debt financing, it is less likely that it would have ignited the inflationary spiral that haunted the country and the government itself.

Throughout the period from 1937–45, the Nationalist government conducted or seriously attempted to conduct bond issues each year. In each issue, the interest rate (coupon rate) was invariably set at 6 percent, and in a few cases it was set at 4 percent.[9] The Liberty Loan – a bond scheduled with a maturity of 30 years and a total amount of C$500 million – was the first government security issued in China since July 1937, and its interest rate was set 4 percent. Between January and August 1937, the cost of living index had risen 5 percent already,[10] meaning that public subscribers of the bond were likely to suffer a loss in real terms.

The result of the marketing of the Liberty Loan was C$146 million domestic subscribers to the bond, and C$37 million came from overseas Chinese.[11] The combined amount that the bond raised was 36.6 percent of the planned amount. The reaction of the Nationalist government was to order that the entire remaining, publicly unsold, amount was to be bought by Chinese banks. When the banks did not have enough funds to purchase the government bonds, they borrowed from the Central Bank. As long as the interest rate on the funds borrowed from the Central Bank was below the yield on the government bonds, banks were able to make a profit and survive.

Technically, this type of budget deficit financing was the root cause of China's inflationary spiral throughout the 1940s. Between 1937 and 1945, the total amount of government bonds issued was C$15,522 million.[12] It is believed that approximately 80 percent of this amount was actually bought and held by banks.

Direct lending to the government by the Central Bank was of course another factor.

Either way – the government directly borrowing from its Central Bank or selling its bonds to banks that were using funds borrowed from the Central Bank to buy them – had in effect opened a new way of debt financing: namely, debt financing through money creation.

In addition to its flawed policy in terms of determining the interest rate for bond issues, the National government also behaved inappropriately in conducting the sales of bonds. Recognizing the difficulties in marketing the bond issues, the Nationalist government resorted to certain compulsory and distributive measures from the early 1940s on. At a time, the Ministry of Finance assigned quotas for individual provinces in terms of contributing to the sales of the bonds. Wealthy people and sometimes public servants as well were required to purchase government bonds.[13] However, the government did not have enough information to determine who was wealthy and thus obliged to subscribe to the bonds.[14] As social dissatisfaction with government bond policies grew, the government bonds became increasingly unpopular.

Moreover, the Nationalist government also tried to market issues of bonds denominated in foreign currencies to Chinese people at home, and sometimes also to those scattered around the world in the Chinese diaspora, starting in 1938. This proved to be unwise and damaged the public's confidence in the domestic currency.

The foreign currencies that were used in the denomination of certain bond issues were the U.S. dollar, the British pound sterling, and Customs Gold Units – an artificial device invented in 1930 to try to protect the economy against falling silver prices. Interest rates on these bonds were often 5 percent. The exchange rates that the government determined in the process of transactions involving bond sales and repayments became increasingly different from market levels.

From 1942, dollar-backed securities were launched. They were payable in the *fabi*, and receivable to the holders in dollars at the official exchange rate. A flat interest rate of 4 percent was applicable. At a time when the official exchange rates were diverging from market levels, these dollar-backed securities became attractive to some, and especially to the American army personnel who were in China at the time.[15] A dollar could buy more than C$50 in the market, and if invested in the securities, C$20 would return a dollar according to the official rate in approximately one year. By the end of 1943, public subscriptions of the dollar-backed securities amounted to US$150 million, with the remaining $50 million bought by government banks.[16]

To its credit, the Nationalist government successfully sought foreign aid from the British and the Americans soon after the hostilities with Japan began in 1937. A Sino-British Stabilization Fund was established in March 1939, aiming to support China's exchange rate management in a market that had become ever more turbulent since August 1937. In April 1941, the United States joined the Sino-British cohort by contributing $50 million to the British £5 million and the Chinese banks' subscriptions of $20 million. The total amount raised in that effort in

U.S. dollars was 90 million. Again, the main purpose was to support the *fabi*'s exchange rates with the U.S. dollar and the pound sterling. In December 1941, the United States decided to give China $630 million in lend-lease funds, followed by another $500 million loan – all to the Nationalist Government in Chungking (Chongqing). Upon requests from Chungking for help in checking inflation, in March 1942, Britain and the United States agreed to provide credits of £50 million and $500 million, respectively. China during the wartime was not really short of foreign aid or foreign funds.

Hans Morgenthau, the U.S. Treasury secretary who worked extensively with the Nationalist government at that time, once reported to the U.S. president about an American loan of $200 million to China by saying that it "had little effect except to give additional profits to insiders, speculators, and hoarders and dissipate foreign resources," and "made no significant contribution to the control of inflation."[17]

In short, market-based domestic borrowing played little role in China's deficit financing during the war period. As shown in Figure 5.1, domestic borrowing – exclusive of borrowing from banks or foreign borrowing – accounted for 45.7 percent of the Nationalist government's fiscal deficit in 1937, and this ratio dropped to as low as 1 percent or less between 1938–42, with higher levels in later years of 10.1 percent in 1943 and 5.7 percent in 1945. In a mature economy, 100 percent of government budget deficits should be financed by market-based domestic borrowing and would not necessarily result in an inflationary spiral regardless of the level of budget deficits. From 1938 on, the Nationalist government's fiscal deficits were financed primarily by inflationary means.

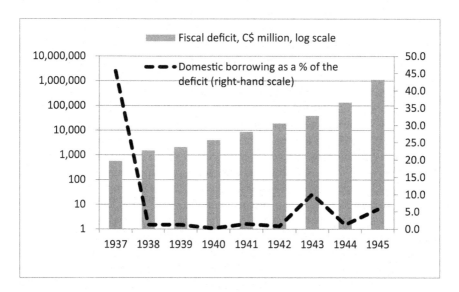

Figure 5.1 Fiscal deficit and domestic borrowing, Nationalist China, 1937–45[18]

Rising inflation and declining seigniorage

A huge number of people rushed to Chungking (Chongqing) and other inland Chinese cities starting in 1938. The population in Chungking was 261,000 in 1937, and it was more than a million by the end of 1939.[19] Other inland cities witnessed similar rises in population during this period. Food and other necessities quickly became scarce in these areas. Had the government implemented effective ration schemes that matched basic need for supplies of the ever-growing population, price inflation would have been much slower than it was.

Somewhat ironically, the Nationalist government struggled to control key resources and industries on the one hand, and adopted a rather laissez-faire stance to its fragile economy on the other hand. In order to finance its ever-increasing fiscal spending, it turned to banknote issues as a financial means. In 1938, the currency issue totaled C$2,310 million, which was a C$670 million or 40.9 percent increase over 1937. The year 1939 further saw an increase of C$1,980 million, or 87.7 percent, over the previous year.[20]

China at that time did not have conventional price indexes, like a retail price index or a consumer price index. Instead, it had a wholesale price index (WPI) and a cost of living index (CLI). Hereinafter in this chapter, unless otherwise indicated, any referral to inflation or price inflation is based on WPI.

There was no single year from 1938–45 in which fiscal revenue made up more than half of actual fiscal expenditures. The four years from 1938–42 were particularly difficult times, during which revenue accounted for less than one-third of expenditures.[21] Currency issues had thus become an unconventional way to finance wartime budget deficits. Thanks to the currency reform in 1935 that gave the government monopolistic power over currency issue, the Nationalist government could conduct currency issues at its own discretion.

The way in which the government financed its budget deficits involved more than forcing banks to purchase bonds, as described above. Indeed, bank purchases of government bonds were relatively small compared to the direct credits that the banks provided to the government.

Between 1939 and 1945, the total credit extended by banks to the private sector rose from C$1,092 million to C$132,046 million – an increase of 120.9 times. Over the same period, the credit advanced to the government rose from C$2,310 million to C$1,043,257 million – an increase of 451.6 times. The percentage of total credit borrowed by the government rose from 68 percent to 89 percent.[22] Credits provided to the government were not based on any tangible assets, and was simply the government overdrafting its accounts at the banks.

These overdrafts gave the government purchasing power to buy goods and services in the economy, and this essentially constituted seigniorage (profit made by a government through credit or money creation) in nominal terms.

When credit was used for real-time purchases, currency notes were needed as the means of payment. Checks and other non-cash instruments of payment were not readily available in China at the time, so the amount of currency in circulation best reflects the monetary movement on the supply side.

Before 1942, currency notes were issued by four government-controlled banks, and afterward the issue rights were concentrated at the Central Bank alone. The Central Bank stopped publishing figures regarding the amount of currency notes issues from mid-1940, but this move was believed to have undermined public confidence.[23]

Despite the lack of timely information about currency issues, many Chinese people were still able to form their expectations about inflation and respond to the monetary situation in a basically correct way. Figure 5.2 shows the annual increases in currency issues and the wholesale price index from 1938–45. During the first two years of high inflation (1938–39), currency issues expanded faster than the wholesale price index; this is an indication that people may not have been able to predict the pace of inflation. However, over the next five years (1940–44), price inflation outpaced currency issues, suggesting that people were reacting more rapidly to price adjustments than the rate at which the government was expanding its currency issues. The last year shown in the figure – 1945 – saw a reverse relationship between the increase in currency issue and that in WPI. The main reason for this reversal was probably that during the previous year (1944), the Nationalist government had tried hard to bring inflation down using a mix of policy measures, including large sales of gold reserves, ceilings on wages and prices, and promises of self-restraint in currency issue and credit provision.

An implication of the fact that the wholesale price index was rising faster than currency issues from 1939–44 was that the purchasing power of new currency issues was decreasing. Because most of the acceleration in currency issues was driven by fiscal purposes and uses, the declining purchase power of these currency issues means that the government's seigniorage in in real terms fell during the period.

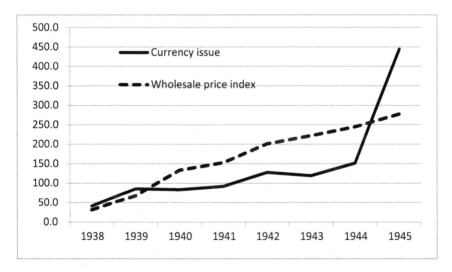

Figure 5.2 Annual increases in currency issues and wholesale price index, percentage, Nationalist China, 1938–45[24]

The Nationalist government's fiscal expenditures amounted to C$3,063 million in 1939 and rose to C$1,266,438 million in 1945. Meanwhile, when adjusted for price inflation – changes in the wholesale price index during these years – fiscal expenditures in 1945 calculated in terms of 1939 prices amounted to C$1,222 million only. This is equivalent to slightly more than 30 percent of the 1939 level. The worst year was 1944, when the amount of fiscal expenditures in 1939 prices was C$770 million, merely one-quarter of its level in 1939.[25]

The calculation of fiscal expenditures in 1939 prices may overestimate the situation in the years from 1941 on, because from that year, the Nationalist government started to collect Land Tax in kind, which should not have been subject to changes in the wholesale price index. If one considers the yield of the in-kind Land Tax in monetary terms – C$280, 000 million in 1945[26] or 22.1 percent of the total fiscal receipts (including borrowing) in that year – then the estimate of fiscal expenditures in 1939 prices for the years between 1941 and 1945 should not be too severe. Ultimately, the declining trend in the purchasing power of the Nationalist government's fiscal expenditures due to rapidly rising inflation was certain.

To finance government budget deficits by directly borrowing from banks, or in other words, by "printing money," is often regarded as quiet and invisible.[27] It may help reduce debt service for a government that is already highly indebted. Debt service or loan service – repayments of principal and interests – accounted for approximately 6 percent of the Nationalist government's fiscal expenditures in 1940–43, falling to 3 percent in 1944 and 1 percent in 1945.[28] Yet, compared to the huge losses in seigniorage in real terms due to accelerating price inflation, the benefits for the government of inflationary budget-deficit financing were much smaller than what may have been expected, and they diminished rapidly.

There were two other types of costs of wartime China's inflationary policy: the cost of printing notes and the cost of exchange rate pegging.

The cost of printing notes is often believed to be small in terms of the overall process of issuing currency and conducting inflationary deficit finance. However, this cost was not small in China in the 1930s and 1940s. The Nationalist government had at many times resisted the temptation to print large notes (i.e., notes of higher denominations), and as a result more notes were needed in the economy. "Of the US$500 million loan of 1942, no less than US$55 million went for banknotes, paper, and ink," an inside witness noted.[29]

With regard to maintaining exchange rate targets, the costs were much higher. The start of hostilities with Japan in July 1937 did not stop the Nationalist government from constantly intervening in China's foreign exchange markets. When its foreign exchange reserves approached exhaustion, it repeatedly requested financial aid, first from the British government and later from the Americans. Hundreds of millions of dollars were spent for the purposes of maintaining the *fabi*'s exchange rates with the dollar and sometimes with the sterling. At this time of heavy intervention in currency markets, Free China's external trade flows had virtually halted due to hostilities and the effects of the war. In a real sense, there was little if any need to continue to play a heavy hand in maintaining exchange rate targets.

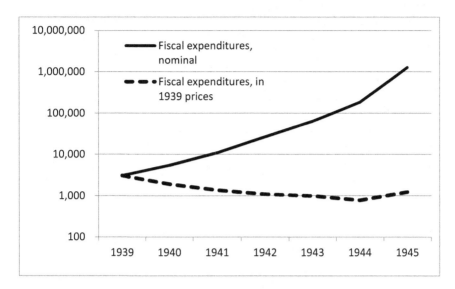

Figure 5.3 Fiscal expenditures, nominal and in 1939 prices, C$ million, log scale, Nationalist China, 1939–45[30]

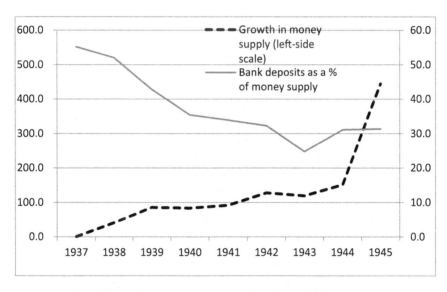

Figure 5.4 Annual growth in money supply and bank deposits as a percentage of money supply, Nationalist China, 1937–45[31]

One main reason for the Nationalist government's foreign exchange intervention during this period was understandably to maintain the *fabi*'s function as a store of value. However, this motivation also created policy conflicts. The *fabi*'s function as a store of value was important for the government to sustain its seigniorage, yet the *fabi* had been hurt by the government's inflationary policy and its effects. Foreign exchange-funded interventions could help shore up the *fabi*'s function as a store of value, but these interventions could not eliminate the problem when the government continued to run its inflationary policy. After all, playing the monetary game was not favorable for the Nationalist government's side.

Changes in the *fabi*'s function as a store of value may be seen in the share of bank deposits in the money stock and its change over time. In theory, when the value of a currency rises, deposits tend to increase faster than cash holdings, so that the share of deposits in money stock (cash in circulation and deposits) goes up. Otherwise, this share would tend to go down. As shown in Figure 5.4, between 1937 and 1943, the share of bank deposits in Nationalist China's money stock fell considerably, from 55.2 percent to 24.7 percent. It picked up moderately in 1944 and 1945, but remained lower than its level in 1942.

The rampant inflation had a consequence on monetary union even within the framework of Nationalist China. Chen Cheng, a provincial chief of Hubei in central China in the later 1930s and later premier in Taiwan in the 1950s, decided in 1942 to switch the entire province of 20 million people to the barter system in the midst of rising inflation in the *fabi* zone. Under his direction, a complex scheme of certification and exchange was formulated and put into use. Tax liabilities in the province and those owed to Chungking (Chongqing) were all delivered in kind. He called it a New Deal in Hubei.[32] The *fabi* remained in use there as a unit of account, but apparently no longer as a medium of exchange and store of value.

Ineffective price controls

Attempts at price controls in Nationalist China began as early as December 1937, but they were nominal and insignificant then. The Ministry of Economic Affairs was authorized in October 1938 to undertake measures to fix prices, but no significant steps were actually taken. Beginning in 1939, a series of price control measures were planned and implemented. Local authorities were required to set up price stabilization committees and coordinate with the central government in stabilizing prices. From July 1940, the Price Stabilization Bureau of the Ministry of Economic Affairs began direct operations of purchases and sales. The agency ran supply lines of coal and charcoal to residents of Chungking (Chongqing), a city that had already become the capital of the Nationalist government.[33]

Later, the coverage of price controls was extended, and it sometimes came with new priorities. Rent controls were introduced in some large cities, especially Chungking. Japanese bombings in that city and the poor crops of 1940–41 caused food shortages. As a response, the National Food Administration was established to stabilize the supply and pricing of food. This governing body was elevated as the Ministry of Food in June 1941.[34]

Starting in early 1942, the Ministry of Economic Affairs had a special operational unit called the Bureau of Commodities. The body was given a fund of

C$450 million, of which C$200 million came from budget allocation and C$250 million was a loan from four government banks. It could directly buy goods at controlled prices and sell them to public employees.[35] Meanwhile, there were other government agencies being newly established, and they were also empowered to undertake price-controlling measures in various areas. For instance, a government body called the Cotton, Yarn, and Cloth Administration was operating for these commodities, taking charge of procurement and distribution.[36]

The Nationalist government adopted many other measures during this period, including credit rationing, interest rate controls, foreign exchange allocation, and trade restrictions.

Generalissimo Chiang Kai-shek once made a personal appeal to the public, asking them to exercise restraint in price setting. He ordered a comprehensive price-control program to be introduced in early 1943. In this new program, more than 1,000 commodities were subject to government price ceilings in Chungking. Black markets were illegalized. People found violating government regulations were severely punished, often by the confiscation of their merchandise and other possessions.[37]

However, Chiang's view toward inflation was fundamentally different from conventional wisdom. He made a remark at the end of 1942 when high inflation had become a menace to Chinese people's ordinary lives: "The seriousness of the problem of commodity prices is not due to the effect of currency but to the divergence of social psychology and spirit and will." Further, he believed that "the gentry, rich business men and social leaders should be stimulated to a high pitch of patriotism and induced to abandon their mean designs of profiteering."[38]

John King Fairbank, a long-time China expert who worked for the U.S. government in wartime Chungking, had many contacts with Chinese intellectuals at that time. He recalled a remark made by a Chinese economist about Chiang's anti-inflation policy: "It was like a folly, but he acted as if he were able to change economic laws."[39] In Fairbank's own observation, 1943 was the year that Chiang and his regime were losing the trust of the Chinese people, and uncontrolled inflation played a part in that process.[40]

Like in any other economy, in wartime China, many goods were produced in one place and required for consumption in another place. Coordination and cooperation from local governments were necessary for successfully implementing price controls and supply stabilization. Unfortunately, many local authorities behaved in a manner that created new dilemmas for the central government. One contemporary observed:

> Local governments placed increasingly severe restrictions on the movement of goods to prevent the escape of commodities subject to price control. Trade barriers sprang up between provinces and even between different cities in the same province as the local governments endeavored to maintain their own price systems. Eventually, internal trade in Free China was threatened with disruption, and the central government was forced to issue a regulation prohibiting the local governments from installing barriers to inter-provincial

trade. This action immediately furnished an opportunity for official to abandon their efforts to control prices without losing prestige in the eyes of their constituents.[41]

It was reported that at times the prices of cotton cloth were lower than those of cotton yarns, and pork supplies disappeared from the market after price ceilings were installed for them, yet restaurants continued to serve pork dishes.[42]

Hoarding – which prevailed throughout most of the cities under Nationalist control – was believed to be the main culprit for the failure of the anti-inflation policy. Though it had been illegalized and heavy punishment measures were in place for anyone caught hoarding, offenders were numerous. Many of the worst offenders were actually military and civil. Even the "government itself was a hoarder of food and other supplies."[43]

In essence, the root causes of the failure of the anti-inflation policy lay in the deficiencies in the government system. As reflected by a witness, "The fundamental weakness of price controls in Free China was that the government had neither the administrative strength to regulate prices at the retail level nor the ability to prevent dealers from exploiting inflationary conditions."[44]

Rising inflation and the incompetence of the Nationalist government in containing inflation resulted in a great deal of discontent among the public toward the leadership. An official in Chungking was quoted as saying in January 1943 that "The problem of inflation is more severe than the war."[45] A popular Chinese writer published a novel in 1944, in which the hero murmurs at the end of the story, "Victory is theirs, not ours."[46] This is a reference to the war with Japan, and implied the great disappointment felt among the populace then in its own government.

As a senior consultant to the Nationalist government on financial and monetary affairs in the late 1920s, Arthur N. Young had intimate contacts with Chinese officials throughout wartime in Chungking. His book on the Chinese anti-inflation experience concluded: "The government's inability to deal with the inflation, coming along with the disruption and suffering from enemy invasion, had a major part in making China ripe for revolution."[47]

Internal war and hyperinflation waves during the late 1940s

The Nationalist government won the war over Japan in August 1945, but soon found itself submerged by new threats of high inflation. Meanwhile, its conflicts with the Communist army gradually escalated into a full-scale war. In the end, the Nationalist government lost control over inflation, lost its credibility, and ultimately lost the war. When it fled to Taiwan in the later 1940s, high inflation occurred there, too. In the Chinese mainland, the triumphant Communists also encountered hyperinflation, and they fought hard by all means to press it down. From that point on, political and economic developments on the Chinese mainland and Taiwan took divergent routes.

Temporary cooling-down

Inflation in Nationalist China accelerated during the first half of 1945. A wholesale price index rose 32.4 percent month-over-month in March, and the cost of living rose 29.1 percent in the same month. Though this is still below the standard definition of hyperinflation (a 50 percent rise in a month), the situation was so devastating that the economy was chaotic, and people were largely demoralized. A witness account puts it this way:

> In the last few months before the end of the war Free China was on the verge of exhaustion. All the saving and marketable possessions of the average consumer had been used in the struggle to subsist. The depredations of tax collectors and soldiers had left the peasants disheartened and embittered, and the list of deserters from the army grew daily. Throughout China the spirit of resistance was being smothered by the relentless inflation. If victory had not come when it did, the economy of Free China would have disintegrated rapidly.[48]

Against this backdrop, it is not surprising that under severe constraints in terms of fiscal resources, the Nationalist army did not undertake any major offensive against the Japanese forces in mainland China from 1944 through to the end of the war. The only large battles that the Nationalist Chinese army engaged in were part of the joint offensive along with British and American forces in Yunnan and Burma that successfully drove out the Japanese from the region. The supply line on land from India to China was reopened in January 1945.

The news that Japan surrendered in mid-August 1945 was a huge relief to the Chinese people, who had suffered from high inflation and various government controls for many years. Massive amounts of consumer goods flooded the market, and shortages that used to be everywhere in the economy rapidly disappeared.

The wholesale price index fell 15.7 percent monthly in September 1945, and the cost of living fell 7.1 percent in the same month. Meanwhile, the price of gold dropped by 90 percent in Shanghai, a city that had recently come back under the control of the Nationalist government. The *fabi* appreciated by 100 percent against the dollar in the market in Chungking (Chongqing),[49] the city that continued to be the Nationalist government's capital until the end of the year. The decline in the value of gold and the U.S. dollar were indications that fears about high inflation in the *fabi* were largely gone.

September was a good month for bringing down inflation. Decreases in price indexes had not been seen in the country since the late 1930s. Disinflation continued in October, when wholesale prices fell 2.2 percent over September, and the cost of living index fell 2.8 percent. The magnitude of this decrease was smaller than in the previous month, but it was still good news that ordinary people might be able to buy a larger quantity of goods and services by spending the same amount of money.

Nevertheless, the disinflation process lasted for only two months. In November, prices began to rise. Wholesale prices rose 16.5 percent, and the cost of living went up 5.7 percent in the month. The increases in both measures remained in single-digits in December, but they climbed to double-digit levels for many months in 1946.

There were several factors that curtailed disinflation in postwar China. First, the country lacked fundamental political stability. The Nationalist government and the Communist leaders held talks in October 1945, and they reached merely a nominal agreement for truce, disarmament, and political reconciliation. No one really believed that the agreement would be honestly implemented. Political uncertainty actually increased. Before the end of the year, news reports of military conflicts between the two sides resurfaced.

Second, regime change in regions that had been occupied by Japan caused certain disruptions in production and supply. Many senior officials in the puppet governments and members of the elite were caught up for punishment or tried to escape. Factories and businesses were often found under-staffed in the months immediately after the war.

Third, demand for goods and services had been sharply "liberalized" and quickly soared. Consumer behavior in wartime was regulated by various policy and non-policy restrictions, and it quickly changed to a "normal," liberated pattern after the war. Limits on prices and sales of luxuries were largely lifted or became ineffective soon after the end of the war. While the supply of many consumer goods in the market increased, the increase in the demand outlasted the increases in supply.

Meanwhile, in preparation for occupying entire territories and in anticipation of military confrontation with the Communist forces, the Nationalist government continued to expand its budget expenditures by all means. Military spending accounted for 60 percent of the Nationalist government's fiscal expenditures in 1946 and 55 percent in 1947.[50] Though these figures are smaller than the 80 percent of total budget spent on the military during the wartime period, they remain conspicuously large.

The Nationalist government also undertook a campaign of "currency reunification" in the newly acquired regions. It ordered the forceful conversion of puppet currencies into the *fabi* in September 1945. The two currencies that were previously issued by the Central Reserve Bank in central China and the Federal Reserve Bank in north China were required to be withdrawn from the market within four months, and any person who held the puppet currencies was allowed to exchange them for up to C$50,000. The conversion rate was set at 200 to C$1 for CRB notes and 5 to C$1 for FRB notes. An economic analysis shows that according to the principle of purchasing power parity, a more reasonable conversion rate would have been between 48 to C$1 and 35 to C$1 for CRB notes and 2 to C$1 for FRB notes.[51] Because of this severe undervaluation, puppet currency-holders had to rush into the markets to buy goods and services in order to minimize their conversion losses. It was cruelly ironic that the purpose of undervaluing the puppet currencies was to avoid the over-issue of the *fabi*;

however, the actual effect was to stimulate puppet currencies-holders to run into the market and drive up prices.

Before the outbreak of internal war with the Communists, the Nationalist government seemed to have a strong confidence in its military. It quickly started to liberalize the economy by undoing or relaxing many restrictive measures that had been undertaken during the wartime period. An estimate shows that at the end of 1945, the Central Bank of the Nationalist government held foreign exchange reserves amounting to $858 million; this consisted of dollar- and sterling-denominated deposits, proceeds of loans from the United States government, and gold and silver obtained largely from confiscated assets that had been held by the Japanese and puppet governments. By the official exchange rate – approximately C$20 to a dollar then, the foreign reserves were equivalent to C$17,160 million in *fabi*, or 1.4 percent of fiscal revenues in 1945. Yet, by the prevailing market rate – approximately C$1,222 to a dollar, the foreign reserves were equivalent to 84 percent of the fiscal revenue. "The Chinese government had never had so much foreign exchange and would probably never have so much again," noted a contemporary witness.[52]

With the large volume of foreign exchange at hand, the Nationalist government decided to liberalize foreign trade when it resumed political control over port cities along China's coasts. It also hoped that increased imports would help reduce inflationary pressures in the domestic market. Partly due to strong demand in the domestic market, the trade turned out to be deficit in 1945 and the trade deficit further widened in the first half of the next year.

A decision was made in February 1946 to devalue the currency and relax trade restrictions. The official exchange rate changed from C$20 to 1 dollar – the level from the end of 1943 – to C$2,020 to a dollar, which was closer to the prevailing market levels. As before, the government pledged that it would return to a peg system; that is to say that it would be willing to engage in unlimited trading in foreign exchange to defend the exchange rate target. In principle, this is analogous to an "exchange standard," or a kind of currency board system. To make such a system work requires the monetary authority to give up its maneuver on monetary policy, or at least to substantially reduce its expansionary stance of money and credit supply to domestic economy. In reality, the Nationalist government was never truly preparing for such a system. With the new currency system, what it really wanted was to win the trust of the Chinese people in the money market, and at the same time to continue its expansionary monetary policy. Therefore, it is not surprising that the exchange rate target was frequently under attack and had to be realigned from early 1946 on.

In external trade, new regulations stated that except for luxuries and certain listed items, the import and export of all "essential goods and raw materials for industry" were permitted without restriction. The proceeds from exports were to be surrendered to the Central Bank via its designated state-owned banks. The aims of this new policy were to promote export growth and to make imports a means of reducing domestic inflation. Imports were believed to have two roles: increasing supply in the domestic market and absorbing the money stock held by domestic households.

What happened subsequently was that exports did not accelerate and imports rose considerably. In 1946, China's merchandise exports actually contracted by $20 million, while merchandise imports tripled. The country had a little trade surplus in 1945, but it had a large deficit of $416 million in 1946. The amount of the trade deficit in that year was almost half of the foreign exchange that the Nationalist government had held in reserve at the end of 1945.

The exchange rate target was not sustainable after all. From the second half of 1946, it became increasingly clear that the country was on a path to creeping devaluation and ever-deteriorating inflation.

Battles to contain inflation, 1946–47

The story of inflation that began in 1946 was in a way a repeat of China's experience during the Sino-Japanese war, but on a much larger scale. Nationwide price inflation had already started to pick up in the early months of 1946. As shown in Figure 5.5, prices rose 29.2 percent monthly in February and 23.6 percent in March; in Shanghai they rose 70.6 percent monthly in February and 25.9 percent in March. These increases were largely the result of market panic, temporary supply shortages, and workers strikes, among other factors. The high levels suggest how sensitive the public had been to negative news and shocks.

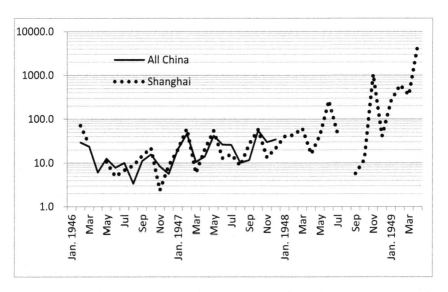

Figure 5.5 Monthly changes in wholesale prices, percentage, log scale, for all of China and Shanghai, February 1946–April 1949[53]

Note: Because of the use of a log scale here, the negative figure of −5.3 percent for Shanghai in April, 1946, cannot be displayed in the figure. Also, a new currency reform took place August 1948, and therefore no comparable figures are available for that month.

The new commitment made by the Nationalist government to maintain the exchange rate target had a positive effect in reversing inflation expectations, though only temporarily. A direct price the government had to pay for maintaining the exchange rate target was the eventual depletion of its foreign exchange reserves. Between February 1946 and February 1947, the Nationalist government's dollar reserves decreased $347 million to $199 million, and its gold reserves fell $116 million to $83 million in value.[54] Total foreign exchange reserves diminished to $347 million from $834 million.[55] The government found itself increasingly unable to safeguard its old exchange rate targets, and it had to devaluate the levels as time went on.

As before, the root causes of this new inflation were the absence of market-based deficit financing, the unstoppable expansionary monetary policy that had been employed to finance ever-increasing budget deficits, and the lack of trust that the Nationalist government encountered internally and externally.

As discussed earlier, the government's budget authorities had resorted to means such as bond issues and external borrowing to deal with budget deficits. In April 1947, the Nationalist government issued a dollar-denominated bond worth $100 million to domestic investors. This was an indication that by this time, the government did not dare to try issuing a bond in its own currency, which further suggests that the government itself lacked confidence in the domestic currency.

At the time of the new bond issue, the official exchange rate between the *fabi* and the U.S. dollar was already devalued to the ratio of C$12,000 to US$1. The result of the issue after four months was, however, that only $25.8 million had been received from subscribers. Another attempt to issue a *fabi*-denominated bond was made soon after the dollar-denominated issue. The Central Bank guaranteed that the proceeds of the latter could be converted into foreign currency at the official exchange rate when the bonds came due. Again, this seemed to be attractive to domestic investors. Yet, both plans failed in later months when the public heard the news that the Nationalist government could not come to agreement on budget deficit controls and would not support the Central Bank's cautionary policy recommendations.[56]

Externally, the Nationalist government constantly sought aid from the United States, but the pursuit had been complicated by divergent views toward China's postwar political developments. Shortly after the end of war, the United States offered a loan of $3,750 million to the United Kingdom with a maturity of 50 years. Upon hearing this news, the Nationalist government immediately instructed its delegation and other connections to persuade Washington to offer China similar loans. The amount that the Chinese delegation later requested was $500 million. The United States apparently saw this as an opportunity to urge Generalissimo Chiang to seek political reconciliation with the Communists and other political parties. An American mission led by General George Marshall (later U.S. Secretary of State) arrived in China as the prime negotiator between the Nationalist and Communist sides. He and his delegation insisted that the Nationalist government produce a detailed plan for China's political reform. The effort was unsuccessful. Marshall left China in January 1947. In the summer of 1947, another American mission visited China for a month, led by General Albert C. Wedemeyer. He made requests of the Nationalist government similar to what Marshall had sought, and he found similar results.[57]

In the end, the Nationalist government was unable to secure any new deal for borrowing from the United States until early 1948. During 1946 and 1947, the Nationalist government continued to draw on earlier unused credits granted by the United States in 1942. In addition, it received shipments of supplies arranged by United Nations Relief and Rehabilitation Administration (UNRRA). The total value of the supplies that China received equaled $235.1 million, and the delivery was completed in the first half of 1947.[58] In addition, the United States had given the Nationalist government certain quantities of military equipment.

By and large, the Nationalist government had proven unable to finance its budget deficits either by market-based bond issues or through external borrowing. As before, it continued to rely on overdrafting its accounts at the Central Bank.

As a result, prices continued to rise. Levels of inflation were often driven by particular events such as news from a military front or an especially bad accident somewhere. At times, inflation reached new heights. The nationwide price index rose 46.1 percent monthly, and in Shanghai it rose 60.2 percent in February 1947. These figures, again nationwide and for Shanghai specifically, were 41.6 percent and 54.1 percent, respectively, in May, and 54.6 percent and 57.3 percent in October. The general trend was clearly an accelerating one. Inflation was usually higher in Shanghai than nationwide, mainly because speculation was the most intense in that commercial and financial city.

An emergency plan for price and wage controls was made in February 1947, targeting key consumer goods for urban residents. The new regulation prohibited eight "daily necessities," including rice and flour, cotton yarn and cloth, fuel, salt, sugar, and edible oil, from being sold above their price ceilings in cities. Meanwhile, wages in cities were frozen in accordance with the January 1947 level of cost of living.

In order to make this work, the government began to acquire suppliers of key consumer goods and raw materials, and to take charge of distribution. Yet, once again, it had not established an effective operational system to do so. Many municipal authorities, however, found themselves unable to acquire and distribute adequate quantities of supplies to fulfill promises made to workers in need of the rationed goods. They had to instead pay workers a living allowance as a compensation for the rising costs of rationed basics. As such, the maintenance of the living standard of the workers was more or less left to the forces of the market, and this weakened the effectiveness of the price ceilings. The schemes for price ceilings and wage controls largely broke down in the later months of the year.

Municipal authorities in Shanghai asked the Central Bank to step in and assist in the process of inflation controls. Trapped by its inability to cut credit supply to the Nationalist government, the monetary policy agency undertook an unusual job in history: it set up a special organization to procure listed commodities and make them available for distribution in July 1947.[59] The reason for this unprecedented move was apparently that the Central Bank had the power to supply funds to the procurement agency, which in effect channeled the funds into the market. In so doing, money supply was effectively in a race with prices, and neither monetary expansion nor price inflation could be expected to slow.

Moreover, speculation and hoarding behavior became prevalent in society, which helped fuel further inflation. Resources were shifting away from production and moving into areas where profiteering became more possible, such as speculating and hoarding. Incentives to run a normal business may have been greatly reduced. Industrial output was reportedly in decline from late 1947 in many categories of essential goods and areas.[60] Shrinkages in supply would have aggravated the pressure for price inflation.

During the second half of 1947, a number of anti-inflation policy measures were launched. In August, government banks were required to stop providing loans to anyone who did not belong to one of five categories that had been deemed "most essential." In December, government banks were prohibited to lend to private banks. Also that month, a Banking Control Bureau was set up with the aim of preventing capital outflows.[61] Perhaps seeing all these measures as undesirable, Generalissimo Chiang personally ordered an all-stop to credit provision in January 1948, just at the time the Chinese New Year arrived. The money market in China was once again in chaos, and business and everyday life were enormously disrupted.

At times, the Central Bank did raise its discount rate – an important interest rate instrument in monetary policy – in order to catch up with market movements. However, it obviously failed to do this in an effective or powerful way. An episode in April 1948 shows how feeble its policy conduct had been: it decided to sell short-term treasury bills to the public, with a yield of less than 24 percent per annum.[62] At the time, nationwide and Shanghai-based price inflation had already reached more than 1,000 percent per annum.

A special agency set up by the Central Bank in August 1947, the Foreign Exchange Stabilization Fund Committee, admitted, "The Central Bank's foreign exchange reserve was nearly exhausted, and there was no prospect of foreign aid. The Committee did not have access to significant amounts of gold and foreign exchange to stabilize the market."[63]

Since June 1946, the Chinese exchange rate regime had become a *de facto* crawling peg that the authorities used to conduct devaluation repeatedly over time. Between August 1947 and May 1948, the official exchange rate between the *fabi* and the dollar went down from C\$38,636 to C\$399,000, falling by C\$36,000 every month.[64] Moreover, each time a new devaluation was announced, the level was still far behind what had been occurring in the market. The difference between official rates and market rates became increasingly large. The momentum behind devaluation expectations gained strength, helping to fuel inflation expectations in the domestic money market. Runaway inflation was threatening to cause a total collapse of the currency system.

Weird banking industry and its role in hyperinflation

The end of the war in 1945 appeared to have ushered in a golden time for the Chinese banking industry. When Kuomintang representatives returned to Shanghai that

year, they shut down 74 modern banks and 92 native banks on charges of cooperation with the puppet governments during wartime. In the subsequent two years, the
number of modern banks in Shanghai rose from 74 to 145, and that of native banks
from 48 to 78.[65] Many of these new banking firms are believed to have been short of
capital and deposit resources, but they could actively engage in the short-term lending market. Bank regulation was rather lax. They often paid an interest rate close to
black-market levels in order to attract deposit customers. Many customers regarded
the banks as a source of funds for their speculative operations.[66]

Thus, credit flowed into speculation and hoarding, fueling inflation. As long as
interest rates on lending of this type lagged behind price inflation, the default risk
for speculators and hoarders could remain low.[67] In fact, the Central Bank was often
either unwilling or unable to decide on interest rates in its own right. As of January 1946, the Central Bank's re-discount rate was fixed at 1.8 percent per month,[68]
approximately equivalent to 23.9 percent per annum. However, the annual inflation
rate in terms of wholesale prices had already reached as high as 270 percent in
December 1945. In August 1947, the Central Bank began a kind of deposit reserve
scheme with the commercial and native banks, paying an interest rate of 5 percent
per month on the deposit reserves, which was raised to 12 percent per month in
November. The monthly price inflation rate was 15 percent and 13 percent, in October and November, respectively, with October's level at 57 percent.[69]

In 1947, the Central Bank's proposals to raise official interest rates "to more
realistic levels" were rejected by the Board of Joint Administration of Government Banks,[70] a policy decision-making body set up by Chiang Kai-shek personally in 1939; he served as its chairman until 1948.[71]

It is also known that the Kuomintang had been using its power and influence to
place senior party members in leading positions at various banks and enterprises
after the end of the Sino-Japanese war. Many party members who controlled
industrial and commercial firms had relied on "cheap and easy credits" from government banks,[72] and it was obviously in their interest to resist any attempt to raise
interest rates. The Board of Joint Administration of Government Banks had intimate relations with government banks in this regard.[73] Seen in this light, one may
see that political connections played a part in weakening the ability of the Central
Bank to make proper decisions on matters of interest rates and credit supply.

As a result, the Central Bank's monthly re-discount rate had remained
unchanged at 1.8 percent throughout the period from January 1946 to December
1947, while monthly market interest rate rose from 7 percent to 19.5 percent.
Meanwhile, the monthly black-market interest rate rose from 11 percent to 23 percent, and the average monthly increase in Shanghai's wholesale prices rose from
20.8 percent to 26.4 percent.[74]

It is interesting to note that from 1946–48 the use of checks was rapidly spread-
ing in China, as it became increasingly regarded as a means of making late payments in light of rising inflation. Check use became like a glut. During these two
years, the monthly number of cleared checks tripled, and the monthly value of the
cleared checks multiplied by more than 520 times.[75]

Savings accounts as a share of total deposits at government banks shrank from
10.6 percent in 1945 to 3.1 percent in January–June 1948, while current and

fixed-term deposits as a share of total deposits at commercial and provincial banks fell from 11.6 percent to 4 percent. However, the ratio of fixed-term deposits to total deposits at commercial and provincial banks did not decrease, between 1946 and 1948; rather, it increased.[76] This category of deposits was the most important supporting factor for the overall growth in deposits during the period. These deposits were not savings. The fixed term was usually one week, one month or 100 days; thus, they were still a short-term type of deposits. For these fixed-term deposits, much higher interest rates could be offered,[77] though perhaps they were still lower than corresponding inflation rates.

Banks – mostly non-state and smaller banks – could offer an interest rate that was catching up with black-market levels and inflation rates; this likely strongly supported the growth in deposits. Also, the ability of these banks to provide payment services in the form of checks and bill-clearing for their customers likewise must have attracted considerable fund inflows from the business community when inflation soared. All of this helps explain why the share of deposits in terms of the money stock did not decline during the second half of the 1940s. Yet, it also suggests that with the continued large inflows of funds, Chinese banks were able to increase the credit they extended to undertakings such as speculation and hoarding, which further fueled inflation.

To the extent that the weird banking industry had played a bigger part than it had before in fueling inflation during the second half of the 1940s, the pace of inflation rose in China. As a result, the real money balance shrank rapidly beginning in 1946, falling from 3.38 to 0.47 in the first half of 1948 (Figure 5.6). Another implication of the rapidly shrinking real money balance was that the

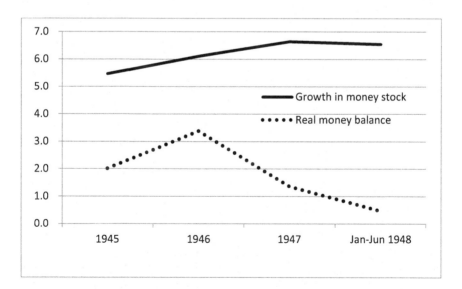

Figure 5.6 Growth in money stock and real money balance, China, 1945–48[78]

Note: Real money balance is defined as the change in money stock divided by the change in price index, with the base year being 1944.

Nationalist government's seigniorage – and thus the amount the government could raise through printing money and expanding credit in order to support its deficit financing – was diminishing just as rapidly over time. The stage was being set in China for a return of hyperinflation.

1948: Gold yuan program and hyperinflation

Historians believe that it was Chiang Kai-shek's own initiative to pursue another major currency reform: namely, one that would forcibly introduce a new currency unit – the Gold Yuan – to replace the old one (*fabi*) in August 1948.[79] At the time the decision was made, his troops were trapped in Manchuria, and the Communist army was preparing a full-scale offensive on all fronts in northern China. Within the Nationalist government, key positions such as the Finance Minister and the Governor of the Central Bank had recently been replaced with new faces. As an "outsider" to the currency issue, Chiang received little resistance in his cabinet to carry out the plan within one month. He used his special power in the capacity of President to bypass the Congress and issue an emergency ordinance for the regime change in the currency.

According to the new regulation, *fabi*-holders were required to convert their old notes, together with their holdings of gold, silver, and foreign exchange, into the Gold Yuan before the end of September 1948. The unit of value of the new currency was defined as 0.22217 centigram of pure gold, and its exchange rate with the old *fabi* was set at C\$300,000 to 1. The ordinance also stated that the maximum amount of Gold Yuan note issues could not exceed GY200 million, and the authorities pledged to maintain 40 percent of that amount in gold, silver, and foreign exchange. One interpretation of this new policy is that China was attempting to establish a "gold standard."

In order to make this change, sometimes called the Big Bang, succeed, the Nationalist government adopted a series of new measures. It promised to cut budget deficits and impose self-restraining disciplines in deficit financing, which it had never succeeded in doing before. Many reports and estimates at the time indicated that the government covered only 30 percent of its fiscal expenditures using normal revenue streams. Its borrowing from abroad, mostly from the United States, continued to encounter difficulties and ultimately proved to be insufficient.

After many rounds of internal debates and long delays, the United States passed the China Aid Act in April 1948. The total amount was \$400 million, much less than what the Nationalist government had requested. Of this, \$125 million was intended for military purposes; the government believed its use of these funds would be "unconditional." The remaining amount was "conditioned" on terms supervised by the U.S. Economic Cooperation Administration in China (ECA), which placed priorities on importing and distributing food, cotton, petroleum, and fertilizer in China.[80] It may have been that Chiang's decision to instigate currency reform was contingent on the availability of the U.S. aid program to China at that time. Nonetheless, the resources that the Nationalist government had in hand to mobilize and put into use for reform were inadequate for dealing with the massive shortages that surfaced soon after the currency reform.

In pursuing the "Big Bang" program, the Nationalist government resumed its harsh controls over prices, interest rates, and exchange rates in large cities. Workers strikes and demonstrations were banned.[81] Anticipating negative reactions from urban residents, the Nationalist government sent high-ranking officials onto the cities to implement the plan and stood ready to punish those who were deemed disobedient. Generalissimo Chiang's own son, Chiang Ching-kuo, who later became president in Taiwan, was dispatched to Shanghai to sit at the Central Bank office, and he was empowered to catch "tigers" (corrupt high-ranking officials and business moguls). A number of business people who were found hoarding were sentenced to prison terms.

Some witnesses believed the program a success, at least in financial terms or in the short term. Then U.S. Ambassador in Nanking, John Leighton Stuart, who had been a long-term China expert and pro-China pundit, recalled in his memoir about the event that the plan was carried out without a leak, and that middle-class Chinese people had responded positively to the new initiative. As such, the government was able to collect gold, silver, and foreign exchange with a total worth of more than $200 million within a month.[82] According to Stuart, the major problems facing reform were resistance from wealthy people and military failure on the front lines against the Communist forces.

In fact, intensified fights against the Communists made it impossible to cut budget deficits. The Ministry of Finance promised to cut the budget deficit from 70 percent to 30 percent of fiscal expenditures in August, and it managed to reduce it to 50 percent in October. Nevertheless, the ratio had climbed back to 75 percent by November.[83] Any remaining and/or newly increased budget deficits at that point had to be financed by credit from the banks, and/or by new Gold Yuan notes that had been issued in late August of that year.

October 1st was a date on which a new, higher sales tax came into effect. On this day, people rushed to department stores and shops in a panic, eager to buy goods before the sales tax rose. This phenomenon quickly spread from city to city. Retailers ran out of inventory, and shortages resurfaced in the country. In particular, a lack of sufficient food supplies was reported in several cities. Faced with a severe situation and the potential starvation of urban residents, some municipal authorities were forced to relax their implementation of price controls.

On the last day of October, the Nationalist government decided to suspend price ceilings for foodstuffs and lift restrictions on the trade and distribution of food-related goods. Ten days later, in November, the Ministry of Finance announced it would cut the gold parity requirement of the Gold Yuan by 80 percent. Along with this announcement, a gold convertibility measure for Gold Yuan-holders was proclaimed. According to the proclamation, people were granted the right to exchange Gold Yuan notes for gold; this move was diametrically opposite to what had happened in August, at which time the same measure had been proposed and denounced.

The Central Bank was instructed to manage the gold conversion for Gold Yuan-holders. They were asked to place a deposit of Gold Yuan notes at the Bank for a year and then receive an equal amount of gold coins or silver dollars. This in effect created a further, large discount of the value of the Gold Yuan. Despite the unfavorable terms, people lined up to deposit their Gold Yuan notes with the Bank. The inevitable drain of the Central Bank's gold reserves looked unstoppable.[84]

Soon after this transpired, a quota scheme to allocate gold sales was put into effect. Again, this measure could not reduce the crowds of applicants lining up to purchase gold. Fights erupted between people waiting in the lines in front of government banks in Shanghai, waiting for endorsement of their applications. Dozens of people were killed or injured.[85] The government suspended gold sales and, in late December, decided to sell gold at the ongoing market prices.

In January 1949, with the Communist army already approaching the north bank of the Yangtze River, the Ministry of Finance conducted an open sale of treasury bonds with a maturity of two years. They were backed by 2,000,000 ounces of gold, repayable in monthly installments of gold payments. The selling price was fixed by the Central Bank on the basis of the market price of the U.S. dollar. By mid-February, the government had sold an amount of bonds equivalent to 4,000 ounces of gold, or 0.2 percent of the original planned offer.[86]

At the end of November 1948, the total amount of Gold Yuan notes that had been issued was GY3,204.3 million, nearly ten times the level sold at the end of August. This amount had expanded a further 18.6 times by the end of February 1949. Since early 1948, compiling national price indexes had become impossible, which is why Figure 5.5 displays price inflation information only for Shanghai after 1948. As shown in the figure, wholesale prices in Shanghai rose 264 percent monthly in June 1948, and 1,054 percent monthly in November. April 1949 was the last month in which Shanghai remained under the Kuomintang's control; in that month, the price index rose 5,070 percent monthly, a record-breaking level in China's history that has also earned China the dubious honor of sixth place on the world's table of hyperinflation.

When the hyperinflation occurred, Generalissimo Chiang was in Taiwan and the Nationalist government had split again. Chiang's successor to the presidency, a long-term rival of his, assumed control over some of the functions of the government. Apparently obsessed with old Chinese traditions, he ambitiously launched another currency reform in February 1949: the Silver Yuan Program. The plan set the value of a new silver yuan (or silver dollar) as having the worth of 320 Gold Yuan, and the government pledged to maintain at least 50 percent of the silver reserves needed to back the new notes. At the time, the outstanding amount of Gold Yuan in circulation was approximately SY60 billion. In principle, to have enough silver to back the Silver Yuan, i.e., to allow Silver Yuan notes to be convertible into silver, the government would have needed a minimum reserve of 60 million ounces of silver. It had just 25 million ounces.[87]

It is not surprising that from the beginning, the public was reluctant to accept the new currency despite strong demands made by the government. The new acting president appealed to the United States for a silver loan, and the request was promptly denied.[88]

In October 1949, when the Nationalist government relocated its functions southbound, approximately 25 million Silver Yuan notes were in circulation. By the end of that year, before the arrival of the Communist army, even that small amount of notes was withdrawn from the market. The life of this new currency lasted less than a year.

Both the Gold Yuan and the Silver Yuan were short-lived. Both schemes were highly risky ventures into monetary reform, and each was a monetary fiasco. Lack of political coalescence and economic resources, loss of policy credibility, uncooperative banking and business activities, and deficient and corrupt administration were common causes of the failure in each case of attempted currency stabilization.

Economic and political impacts of hyperinflation, 1946–49

Rising inflation in 1946–47 and hyperinflation in 1948–49 had a great impact on Chinese society in all aspects. Against this background, it can be seen that the Nationalist government was eventually on the losing side of this particular period of history, while the Communist regime emerged the winner. The ultimate result was that the former was driven out of China's mainland and was only able to survive by retreating to Taiwan. The Communist regime, meanwhile, was able to establish itself in 1949 as a new, vast power ruling China's mainland.

During the second half of the 1940s, China remained largely a traditional rural economy, with more than 85 percent of the population living in the countryside. Farming was mostly subsistence (but it was also largely self-sufficient), and in many cases, peasants and their families felt the least negative effects of rising inflation and hyperinflation during the 1930s and 1940s. For some of them, rising inflation may indeed have had a positive effect on real income, as the demand for foodstuffs and other necessities continued to grow during the period of hyperinflation. This does not necessarily mean that their living standards improved, however. Faster increases in input prices, transaction costs, and general uncertainty likely counterbalanced any monetary benefit a farmer gained from the elevated prices driven by the hyperinflation. As noted earlier in this chapter, the gains of hyperinflation went most often to merchants who were able to speculate successfully, to hoard without being caught, and to readily access a cheap credit supply.

Hyperinflation tended to affect mostly people in cities and towns, and the effects were greatly uneven among different levels and members of the society. From time to time, the Nationalist government provided allowances or pecuniary support to wage-earners in the public sector. These measures were helpful in alleviating workers' loss of purchasing power. Nonetheless, the allowances and pecuniary support often lagged behind inflation, as did the interest rate subsidies that were sometimes given to bank depositors. Indexation had not become a popular practice in China, nor was the trade union movement strong enough to mobilize any sustained action.

A notable development in inflationary China was that despite the switch to barter and to various other alternative means of payment, dollarization likely had little influence. A survey that was undertaken in a province under the Communist regime before August, 1950, revealed that 55 percent of its trade was conducted in old silver dollars, 20 percent by barter, and 25 percent in the new paper currency.[89] An estimate based on a comparison of studies done on the Nationalist government's Central Bank and the United State Treasury reveals that the private dollar holdings of the Chinese declined steadily, from $150–190 million in 1945 to $40–50 million in late 1949, while the amount of net short-term dollar assets held by Hong Kong residents increased from about $23.7 million in 1945 to $80.2 million at the end of 1949.[90] Capital flight from China's mainland may have begun as early as 1946 or 1947 as the civil war escalated. With a diminishing supply of dollars assets, and also possibly of other hard currencies, the use of the U.S. dollar in domestic transactions could not spread as much as it may have otherwise. It is possible, on the other hand, that the increased scarcity of the dollar in China accelerated the decline of the value of the *fabi*, which in turn caused inflation to intensify.

Most of all, runaway inflation had outraged the public and demoralized the civil society in Nationalist China. Public support was what the Nationalist regime most needed in the fight against the rising Communists. Yet, uncontrolled inflation had effectively made people increasingly discontent and politically indifferent. As noted by a Chinese-American author writing about the history of China during that period, the middle class in Chinese cities comprised those who had been effectively "expropriated." A question they asked frequently was "could the Communists be any worse than the Kuomintang?"[91]

It was increasingly clear to Chinese people that the Nationalist government was not only unable to solve inflation and inflation-related economic problems, it was also politically incompetent to the point that it could not increase administrative efficiency and reduce corruption. Invariably, the Nationalist government kept "attacking symptoms rather than causes."[92]

Chang Kia-ngau was briefly the governor of China's Central Bank during the late 1940s. He also assumed several senior positions in the Nationalist government before and after the Sino-Japanese war. When the Kuomintang was defeated on the mainland, he went first to Australia and later to America for academic research. He wrote a book on the inflationary experience in China. At the end of the volume, he summarizes his observations and reflections by saying: "Inflation was no less an enemy of the free society than Communism and, as we have seen in China, may be the harbinger of a Communist triumph."[93]

Related to all of this is the question of why the Communists were able to grow and ultimately outshine the Nationalist regime? It is known that the Communist "red army" was much smaller than the Nationalist force in size, and it was also inferior in equipment and weaponry, at least up until the end of 1947. As the scale of the fighting increased over time, the Communists' need for economic and financial resources would have been the same as that of the Nationalist government. Were Communists immune from the sins of high inflation? The answer of course is no. As we can see in Table 5.1, the Communist regime had experienced high inflation in the territories it controlled at least as early as in the first half of the 1940s. It is now well known that the Communists held several isolated base areas before 1948, and in almost every one of these localities, they issued separate currencies. The amounts of notes issued often multiplied within a year or so.[94] High inflation was no doubt widespread in all of the regions controlled by the Communists, and it was perhaps only marginally less severe than it was in the Nationalist-controlled areas.

But there was a significant difference in the economics of the two contending regimes. The Nationalist regime was largely based in cities, and the Communists were mostly rooted in rural areas. The Communists' economic dependence on commerce and industry was significantly smaller than that of the Nationalists'. When the Japanese army withdrew from northern China in August 1945, Communist forces quickly moved in and soon started a "Land Reform" in these newly acquired areas. It was a forceful campaign, much more than simply demanding "rent cuts." Land and other possessions of landowners were often seized and redistributed to the poor. As a result, the Communists won "hearts and minds" of the lowest spectrum of rural society and gained their support in the uprising against the Nationalists. Massive use of voluntary labor in logistics for large-scale battles was evident in 1948.[95] Within the Communists' revolutionary camps, ration systems – supported by centralized procurement organizations – were deployed to their full potential, but this did not occur in areas controlled by the Nationalist regime. It is of course also true that before their overwhelming victory in the late months of 1949, Communist commanders and soldiers had lower living standards than their counterparts in the Nationalist army.

The specter of hyperinflation haunted the new Communist government from its very first days to an extent that was quite comparable to its effect on the Nationalist government. Shock therapy was called upon when the new regime wanted to bring about stabilization.

Ending hyperinflation in China mainland and Taiwan

In early 1949, both the Nationalist and Communist regimes faced hyperinflation in their own regimes. As the Nationalist regime had been increasingly shifting to Taiwan, its economic undertakings were somewhat different than they had been on the mainland. The Communists, on the other hand, were essentially following an approach that was unprecedented and unique in many ways.

Ending hyperinflation in China mainland

Perhaps in anticipation of its forthcoming triumph over the Nationalist government, the Communists decided to establish the People's Bank of China in December 1948. The Bank was actually a merger of several "regional" banks that existed in different locations. It performed basically two functions: to issue notes – the *Renminbi* (or RMB) which translates literally in Chinese as "the People's Currency" – and to grant loans under the direct instruction of the Communists. One immediate job that it undertook was to force out the Gold Yuan in any newly "liberated" areas.

The decreed conversion rate between the RMB and the Gold Yuan was 1RMB to 6GY with a deadline of 20 days in Tientsin (Tianjin) in January 1949; 1RMB to 10GY with a deadline of 20 days in Peiping (Peking or Beijing) in February; 1RMB to 2,500GY with a deadline of 10 days in Nanking (Nanjing) in April; and 1RMB to 100,100GY with a deadline of 7 days in Shanghai in May.[96] As recalled by an official who participated in the process of forced conversion in Peiping, the conversion rate for ordinary citizens in the city was 1RMB to 6GY within a maximum that was reckoned for covering living expenses of a half month, and that for business owners was 1RMB to 30GY.[97]

By April 1951, currency conversion into the RMB or currency unification had been largely complete in China mainland, including Manchuria and Inner Mongolia where the Communists issued separate currency notes in parallel with the RMB during the transition period. An estimate indicates that call-backs of old notes issued by the Communists amounted to 82.95 percent of the total issues by the time.[98] Currency conversion later also took place in West China (Xinjiang) in October 1951 and in Tibet in August 1959.[99]

Under the new regime and in the new currency, however, hyperinflation continued. In Shanghai, wholesale prices rose 104.6 percent monthly in July, and food prices rose 202.5 percent. November saw a further rise of 132.7 percent in the wholesale price index and 137.6 percent in food prices. The increase in February 1950 reached as high as 46.2 percent in wholesale prices and 42.1 percent in food prices.[100]

A number of anti-speculation and anti-hoarding measures were employed in large cities, and especially in Shanghai and Tianjin where private businesses had been strong. Hundreds, if not thousands, of "speculators" were arrested during the campaigns. Authorities in Shanghai forced 407,000 people to leave the city and return to their hometowns or villages in August and September 1949 alone; this was 9.7 percent of the total population of Shanghai.[101] Massive population relocation, sometimes in conjunction with de-urbanization and sometimes not, seemed to be employed as a powerful means to deal with economic difficulties under the new regime.

Price ceilings and ration schemes for key commodities were adopted beginning in mid-1949. Securities trading and foreign exchange markets were suspended or utterly terminated. Gold, silver, and foreign currencies were banned from circulation. Multiple exchange rates were introduced into a highly regulated currency market. The RMB's exchange rates were revalued several times in 1950 and then devalued in December 1951.[102] Increasingly, many activities in domestic commerce and external trade were required to be licensed by the government, or to be nationalized or monopolized by the state. Communist agencies mobilized a plethora of resources and production methods in order to assemble "key" goods, including rice, flour, cotton, cotton yarns, coal, and fuels, and government economic and monetary authorities engaged in game-playing battles with "speculators" in the market.

Moreover, tight credit controls were placed on financial firms that continued to operate, and the drive to nationalize the banking industry was underway. State-controlled banks were able to quickly adjust interest rates on deposits and loans. In November 1949, the People's Bank of China in Shanghai raised its monthly interest rate on private business deposits from 75 percent to 360 percent, and it raised the rate on loans to such businesses from 240 percent to 1,000 percent[103] amidst of a new wave of soaring inflation. By the end of the month, wholesale prices in Shanghai had risen 132.7 percent monthly, partly as a result of the inability of Communist agencies to maintain a supply of goods to the market at lower prices.

The new regime continued to run a fiscal deficit at least as late as 1950, and its budget plan had been made in a non-monetary measurement rather than in usual monetary terms. A retrospective published in 2009 indicates that the total fiscal revenue in 1950 was equivalent to 52,542.6 million *qin* (500 grams) of grain, while expenditures totaled 59,490.2 million *qin*, with a deficit of 6,947.6 million *qin*.[104] Massive assets left by the old regime and seized by the new must have helped enormously as 1951 was the first year in which the new regime reported a fiscal balance.[105] To its credit, it quickly normalized the transport systems in China's mainland and forcefully reorganized production systems in agriculture and industry. As domestic conflicts largely faded in 1950, political uncertainties also reduced significantly. Levels of output appeared to be recovering.

Some have claimed that hyperinflation in mainland China ended in March 1950, citing the rise in wholesale prices in Shanghai – the only available price indicator from that time – had slowed to single digits (6.9 percent) in March, with food prices decelerating to 2.5 percent in the same month. In April, the wholesale prices fell at a rate of −16.6 percent monthly, and food prices declined by −7.8 percent. In several of the remaining months of the year, these two price indexes continued to fall. By these measures, disinflation had apparently begun in mainland China.

However, this claim requires qualification. It is known that bank deposits decreased considerably in October 1950, and the Chinese began a cycle of panic purchasing again.[106] In response, the government rushed to freeze deposit withdrawals for all non-private deposits and introduce indexation measures for personal deposits. In the end, government-compiled price indicators did not rise above the double-digit level in subsequent months.

A notable financial practice that seems to have supported the economic stabilization of mainland China was indexation, which was used with perhaps obscure effects. The People's Bank of China launched a so-called "in-kind saving deposit" program in several cities in April 1949, which linked the value of the principal – the original amount of a deposit – with price inflation. A difference versus the practice of postwar Hungarian indexation is that the Chinese did not index the interest rate in this case; they were apparently unaware of the Hungarian episode of hyperinflation in 1946. Interest rate indexation was adopted in China in October 1950, but the indexing did not include the principal at that time. With the "in-kind saving deposit" program, branches of the People's Bank of China in Shanghai saw a 4.4-fold increase in deposits in 20 days in November 1949,[107] a month in which inflation soared to a new height, and authorities temporarily suspended the supply of goods to the market.

A government bond in kind – payable in the *Renminbi* or on the gold, silver, or foreign exchange, with the amount of receivables linked with price inflation – was also issued by the new regime in January 1950. With a coupon interest rate of 5 percent, the bond appeared to be well received by the public.

Yet, the banking system did not record any significant amount of deposits from ordinary Chinese residents until 1952. Data about the banking system for that period, some of which was released as late as in 2006, shows that deposits held by urban households amounted to RMB 860 million yuan at the end of 1952, accounting for 9.2 percent of the total deposits of the banking system. Deposits held by rural households were first shown in 1953, and they amounted to RMB 10 million yuan. Together with deposits made by urban households (RMB 1,220 million yuan), they accounted for 11.4 percent of total deposits in that year.[108] Interest rates on loans to private businesses fell in August 1950 from 400 per thousand to 39 per thousand in monthly terms, with the latter figure equivalent to 52.3 percent in annual terms, which is obviously not a normal level. The lending interest rates were cut to 10.5–16.5 per thousand monthly, or 12.2–19.7 percent annually, in 1952,[109] which may be regarded as approaching more normal levels.

It is likely that stabilization succeeded in mainland China somewhere between 1951 and 1952 when the function of the new currency as a store of value was finally recognized by the Chinese people. Needless to say, successfully ending hyperinflation was accompanied by a recovery in the levels of output, along with forceful price controls imposed by the new regime and the rapid expansion of nationalization and a state monopoly.[110] With the benefit of hindsight, we may also see that inflation stabilization ushered in a socialist transformation of the economy from 1953 onward.[111]

Ending hyperinflation in Taiwan

The end of hyperinflation took a somehow different trajectory in Taiwan during the second half of the 1940s. When Japan surrendered and renounced its rule in Taiwan in August 1946, hyperinflation immediately broke out, with wholesale prices in Taipei rising 399 percent monthly in September. The Bank of Taiwan – a Japanese-styled commercial bank established in 1899 that sometimes assumed the partial functions of a central bank – was instructed by the Nationalist government in Nanking to conduct a currency reform and stop hyperinflation. Taiwan remained a separate currency area from the mainland. Yet, inflation in Taiwan continued to rise, after a brief period of moderateness. Wholesale prices in Taipei rose 50.8 percent monthly in February 1947, which coincided with large-scale social unrest that spread over almost the entire island at the end of the month. This has been remembered as the "February 28 Incident." Greatly tightened societal and economic controls helped to suppress the momentum of inflation afterward, but it was never eliminated. From 1946 to 1948, the average monthly rate of the increase in Taipei's wholesale prices was 11.3 percent, 18.5 percent, and 22.5 percent, respectively.[112] From the summer of 1949 on, hundreds of thousands of Kuomintang-affiliated personal, together with its troops, flocked to the island. Taiwan was once again facing hyperinflation.

To Chiang Kai-shek and his power circle, Taiwan represented "streams in the desert" from early 1949 on. During his time in Taiwan that began in May 1949, there were three priorities on his agenda: follow Leninism to transform the party-state system, strengthen the military defenses of the island, and stabilize the Taiwanese currency.[113]

He arranged a shipment from the mainland to Taiwan of hard assets totaling $300 million, mainly in the form of gold bullion,[114] which he planned to use for another currency reform on the island. In June 1949, a Big Bang in the currency system was announced in Taiwan. The main points of the plan were (1) to issue a new currency unit called the New Taiwan Dollar (NT$) and retire the old one (at a conversion rate of NT$1 to 40,000 yuan of the old); (2) to repay advances the Nationalist government had taken from the Bank of Taiwan with gold, silver, or any other hard assets; (3) to place a ceiling of NT$200 million on the issuance of new notes, which was to be fully backed by gold, silver, and other hard assets; (4) to allow the NT$ to be partially convertible at a rate of NT$5 to US$1, with the government promising to supply foreign exchange support to certain external payments at the exchange rate; (5) to establish a Gold Savings Deposit Program that allowed deposit holders of NT$ to receive repayment in gold at maturity.[115]

In certain aspects, the new program reflected what the Nationalists had done in the mainland before. Yet, it was greatly different from what the Communist government was doing at the same time on the mainland.

After the announcement of the new program, inflation decelerated but did not fall to a low level. Between June and December 1949, wholesale prices rose 82 percent, a sharp contrast with their rise of 729 percent in the first five months of the year.[116] Other indications that hyperinflation was not yet over were the persistence of black markets for credit and foreign exchange. For instance, unofficial exchange rates reached NT$8 to the U.S. dollar in December 1949.

In March 1950, a further monetary policy measure called the Preferential Interest Rate Deposit (PIR) was launched; this was a scheme to make pecuniary compensation to time-deposit-holders when the nominal interest rate fell behind inflation. At the time, the interest rate was set as high as 7 percent per month (225 percent in annual terms).[117]

Trade balance was not in Taiwan's favor in these years, and the NT$ continued to feel the strains of devaluation. Unexpectedly, the outbreak of the Korean War in June 1950 resulted in a resumption of aid from the U.S., which helped reduce the pressures on the currency.

Finally, the Nationalist government started a Land Reform in Taiwan in early 1949. Its first step was a large-scale rent cut, which was followed by privatization of land that was once occupied by the Japanese when they occupied Taiwan. The land distribution was restricted to indigenous people only, i.e., mainland Chinese were not allowed to participate. Land redistribution was conducted in mid-1952 and largely financed by the government. The Land Reform was completed by the end of 1953, and it is notable that crop output steadily increased over those three years.

Wholesale prices in Taipei rose 53 percent in 1951, and then plummeted to 3.4 percent in 1952. It is believed that 1952 marked the end of hyperinflation in Taiwan.[118] Thereafter, Taiwan began to experience macroeconomic stability that lasted a few decades and supported its transition to a modern, market-oriented, industrial economy.

Appendix note: Friedman's view on FDR, silver, and China

Milton Friedman, a Nobel Prize laureate in economics for his study on monetary theory and history, published a large volume in 1963 with his collaborator on monetary developments in the United States since the late nineteenth century. In this analytical narrative, they wrote that U.S. President Franklin Delano Roosevelt's silver purchase program in the 1930s had little effect at home but exerted a profound influence on certain other countries. FDR's silver purchase program was largely driven by domestic political events and resulted in silver price surges in the world market; these led to massive silver outflows from China. Deflation and economic setbacks subsequently prompted Nationalist China to abandon her silver standard and move to a paper currency system in 1935 that ushered in a path that ultimately led to hyperinflation.[119]

Several later scholars have gathered new data and proposed a certain antithesis. A paper published in 1989 by another Nobel Prize laureate in economics, Thomas Sargent with his co-author, established three key observations: first, China's money stock did not decline after the U.S. silver purchase program in the 1930s; second, there was no significant downturn in the Chinese economy during the first half of the 1930s; third, there was no banking crisis or its widespread contagion in then China.[120] Their findings have been supported by several other studies on prewar Chinese economy.[121]

Friedman revisited these studies but questioned the robustness of the data. He insisted on the deflationary effects of the U.S. silver purchase program on China and believed that the Chinese transition toward a paper standard had to occur earlier because of them. Furthermore, he related monetary movements to political change in China in the conclusions of his 1992 essay:

> [T]he U.S. silver purchase program was responsible for the [Chinese] hyperinflation's occurring earlier and being more severe than it would have if the price of silver had not risen sharply. In that way the silver purchase program contributed to the ultimately triumph of communism in China.[122]

Friedman's view was unambiguously shared by Arthur N. Young, who published a book in 1963 on wartime China's international economic and financial relations; Young was at that time apparently unaware of Friedman's work on American monetary history. With extensive working knowledge of the Sino-American relations and Chinese systems, Young's 1963 work provided a powerful narrative about a similar chain of events:

> [U]nder the managed currency system [the foreign exchange-linked *fabi*], which had started out with so much promise, made it easy to issue paper currency for war needs. Under stress of war, an inflation followed which the government found itself unable to control. Although Japan was ultimately defeated, galloping inflation became a major cause of the government's downfall. If by staying on a silver basis China had found herself unable to make prolonged resistance to Japan, the latter events of World War II and its aftermath would certainly have been different. Whether for better or for worse is an interesting intellectual speculation.
>
> Thus it is ironic and indeed frightening that an American policy promoted by special interests, and apparently when adopted of rather minor importance to the United States, changed world history in a way that could not have been foreseen.[123]

It is certain in all studies on prewar China that the U.S. silver purchase program and the resultant increase in silver prices enabled the Nationalist government to swiftly establish the *fabi* system, by which China's economic and financial ability to counterattack Japanese invasion was considerably increased. The Nationalist government had long yearned for currency reform in order to have stronger control of China's banking industry, and it would seem that the timing and exact mechanism of such a reform were shaped by events related to Roosevelt's silver policy. Yet, the Nationalist government's inability to curb high inflation during the Sino-Japanese war, and its apparent hopelessness in the face of hyperinflation during the Chinese civil war, should be attributed to institutional and policy deficiencies more than to a paper currency system that it was pushed hurriedly into adopting.

Notes

1 Young (1965, Table 57, p. 357). It is also recorded in the international table of hyperinflation compiled by Hanke and Krus, Table 30.1, p. 372.
2 Young (1965, p. 188).
3 "Currency war" is referred in Chang (1958, pp. 20–4); Young (1963, pp. 154–60); Young (1965, pp. 165–88); Hara (1998, p. 259); and "monetary warfare" is in Campbell and Tullock (1954, p. 236).
4 The population data of all regions except Communist China and West China (Xinjiang) are from Mitchell, Tables A1, A2 or A5. Figures of Free China, Manchuria, Central and Eastern China, and Northern China are based on provincial ones of the nearest years and have been adjusted for certain territorial "losses and gains," but they remain preliminary. There were significant changes in the population in the Communist-controlled areas, and a range of numbers is given therefore.
5 Chang, p. 22.

6 An estimate is that the *fabi* notes circulating in occupied regions accounted for about 10 percent of total amount outstanding in 1938 (Chang, p. 22).
7 Citation in Young (1963, p. 155), from *Morgenthau Diaries*, vol. 334, p. 13, December 1, 1940.
8 Young (1971, p. 152).
9 Young (1965, p. 76).
10 Chang, Appendix B. Prices, Table 52, p. 352.
11 Young (1965, p. 76).
12 Young (1965, p. 75).
13 Chang, p. 148.
14 Young (1965, p. 77); and Chang, p. 258.
15 Young (1965, p. 83).
16 Young (1965, p. 84).
17 Quoted by Young (1965, p. 86).
18 Figures showing the fiscal deficit are from Chang, Table B-1, p. 374; figures showing domestic borrowing (exclusive of that from banks) are from Young (1965, Table 40, p. 332).
19 Combs, p. 260.
20 Chang, Table B-3, p. 376.
21 Chang, p. 80.
22 Young (1965, Table 20, p. 158).
23 Young (1965, p. 161).
24 For currency issues, see Chang, Table B-3, p. 376; for wholesale price index, see Chang, Table A-2, p. 371.
25 Chou (pp. 269–70) has concluded that loss of fiscal revenue in real terms due to rising inflation in wartime China was extremely large.
26 Young (1965, Table 9, p. 29). Also in the same book, costs related to the collection of the Land Tax appeared to be substantial. The government employed as many as 200,000 persons to do the job (*ibid.*, p. 24); misreports, abuses, stealing, and adulterating, and waste and losses in the process of storage and distribution, were vast. The Ministry of Food, a body in charge of the tax and price controls related to foodstuffs, had adopted "a policy of holding unduly large amounts of grain, thus becoming itself a hoarder." (*ibid.*, p. 25).
27 In wartime Germany, it was termed as "noiseless finance" (Kindleberger, 1984, p. 405).
28 Chang, p. 130.
29 Young (1965, p. 161).
30 Fiscal expenditures from Young (1965, Appendix A, Table 39, pp. 331–333); the underlying price deflator is the wholesale price index from Chang, Table A-2, p. 371.
31 Chang, Table B-3, p. 376.
32 Chen Cheng, pp. 224–40.
33 Young (1965, p. 143).
34 Young (1965, p. 143).
35 Young (1965, p. 144).
36 Chang, p. 348.
37 Combs, pp. 267–8.
38 Young (1965, p. 147).
39 Fairbank, p. 252; also quoted in Combs, 268.
40 Fairbank, Chapter 20.
41 Chang, p. 346.
42 Combs, p. 259.
43 Young (1965, p. 151).
44 Chang, p. 56.
45 Combs, p. 253.

46 Combs, p. 279.
47 Young (1965, p. 328).
48 Chang, p. 67.
49 Chang, p. 69.
50 Chang, p. 71.
51 Chang, p. 70.
52 Chang, p. 303.
53 Chang, Table A-3, pp. 372–3.
54 Gold sales were conducted in 1944, and they were resumed from March 1946. As the public demand for gold kept soaring and draining on the reserves, the government decided to suspend its gold sales in February 1947. Chang, pp. 258–61.
55 Chang, Table 86, p. 311.
56 Chang, p. 73.
57 Tang Tsou, Chapter XI "Partial Withdrawal, Limited Assistance, and the Decision to Abandon China 1947–1948," pp. 441–464.
58 Tang Tsou, p. 445.
59 Chang, pp. 345–6.
60 Chang, 353.
61 Chang, p. 77.
62 Chang, p. 78.
63 Chang, p. 313.
64 Chang, Table 87, p. 314; also Table 25, p. 79.
65 Chang, p. 193.
66 Chang, p. 194.
67 It has been estimated that monthly possible profits in investing in commodities – in terms of percentage rises in Shanghai wholesale price index – were significantly greater than that in securities investing or black-market interest rate during January-June 1948. Chang, Table 75, p. 268.
68 Chang, p. 75.
69 Chang, pp. 266–7.
70 Chang, p. 75.
71 Hong, pp. 385–6.
72 Chang, pp. 194, 266.
73 Members of the Board also consisted of government departmental heads, in addition to representatives of government banks. Chang, p. 266.
74 Chang, Table 73, p. 266.
75 Chang, Table 76, p. 270.
76 Chang, Table 57, p. 199.
77 Hong, p. 517.
78 Figures of money stock are from Chang, Table B-3, p. 376; figures of price index from Chang, A2–A4, pp. 371–3.
79 Hong, pp. 530–2.
80 Tang Tsou, pp. 485. The book has a sub-section (3) of Chapter XL, "American economic aid and the Chinese currency reform," pp. 484–6. Also, Chang believed that economic aid was linked to the calculated needs in China, but it might have been biased toward large Chinese cities (Chang, pp. 81–2).
81 Taylor, p. 386.
82 Stuart, p. 182.
83 Chang, p. 80.
84 Chang, p. 83.
85 Chang, p. 83.
86 Chang, pp. 83–4.
87 Chang, p. 84.
88 Chang, p. 84.

89   Campbell and Tullock, footnote 13, p. 243.
90   Chou, pp. 293–9.
91   Tang Tsou, p. 486.
92   Chang, p. 360.
93   Chang, p. 369.
94   Jiang, Chapter 8.
95   Pepper, pp. 755–6.
96   Yang *et al.*, p. 34.
97   Wang (2009, p. 13).
98   People's Bank of China, p. 140.
99   People's Bank of China, pp. 140–1.
100 Economic Research Institute of the Academy of China, and Economic Research Institute of Shanghai Academy of Social Sciences, p. 448. The data of wholesale prices, together with their categories, were discontinued in 1957. Alternative price data are not available either.
101 Sun, p. 47.
102 Dai, p. 99.
103 Shang (1989, p. 55).
104 Wang (2009, Table 4.6, p. 27).
105 Two economists have noted the particularity of the Chinese stabilization program in the absence of fiscal balance, which differs from many other episodes (Burdekin and Wang).
106 Shang (1989, p. 66).
107 Shang (1989, p. 55).
108 Su, Volume 2, p. 1058.
109 Dai, p. 58.
110 In early 1950, the Soviet Union provided a loan equivalent to $300 million at an interest rate of 1 percent for five years, mainly for Chinese imports of equipment from Russia for her urgent needs in industrial reconstruction, Shen (2001).
111 In March 1955 there was a denomination change in the currency that new notes replaced the old ones at a conversion rate of 1 to 10,000. The change was mostly of notational significance.
112 Makinen and Woodward, p. 91.
113 Taylor, Chapter 10, "Streams in the Desert," pp. 412–3.
114 Taylor, p. 405 and footnote 119.
115 Makinen and Woodward, p. 92.
116 Makinen and Woodward, p. 93.
117 Makinen and Woodward, p. 94.
118 Makinen and Woodward, p. 95.
119 Friedman and Schwartz, pp. 489–91.
120 Brandt and Sargent, p. 33.
121 In particular, in Rawski (1989), Appendix A shows the growth in manufacturing to 1936, and Appendix C summarizes monetary aggregates to 1936.
122 Friedman (1992, p. 188).
123 Young (1963, p. 34). The last paragraph is also cited in Young (1971, p. 319), and the latter was referred to by Friedman (1992).

6 Hyperinflation in an "age of inflation"

"The infant industry argument is a smoke screen. The so-called infants never grow up."

Milton Friedman and Rose Friedman, *Free to Choose*, 1979

"When prices take the lift, wages cannot take the staircase."

A remark likely made by Juan Perón,
Argentine politician (1895–1974)[1]

In a comprehensive survey of the "conditions in which very high rapid inflation has appeared," published in 1986, a notable economist of monetary history focused on the factors that might lead to a collapse of tax revenues. The study was an investigation of why, when the government of a country experienced sharp declines in tax revenues, its budget deficits inevitably soared, forcing the government to resort to inflationary deficit finance that ultimately led to hyperinflation. His conclusion was that

> [social] unrest [leads] to government difficulties and deficits and on to rapid inflation. No doubt the inflation produced further social disorder, and the causality can be seen to run both ways, but in seeking the origins of these extreme examples, [they run] from social disorder to inflation.[2]

"[T]hese extreme examples" to which that economist referred are episodes of hyperinflation that occurred in the years leading up to the 1940s; i.e., those years covered in previous chapters of this book. It is true that most of the hyperinflation did occur in close proximity to a war, either external or internal. In particular, in countries that experienced internal conflict during the first half of the twentieth century, any regime that had the power to print paper currency often tended to do so. This appears to have continued in the second half of the twentieth century, as the cases of Nicaragua in the 1980s and Congo (Zaire) in the 1990s will demonstrate.

Several episodes of hyperinflation or near-hyperinflation occurred in the last three decades of the twentieth century that did not involve external or internal conflict. Bolivia in the 1980s is the first example of this kind. That country's political system had certain weaknesses, but it never verged on collapse during the 1980s. However, a consumer price index in Bolivia rose 11,750 percent in 1985, ushering in a wave of hyperinflation or high inflation across most of Latin America. Brazil and Argentina, which are politically and economically similar, each encountered hyperinflation the later years of the 1980s. Outside of Latin America, rapid inflation also occurred in countries like Israel and Turkey, although to a lesser extent.

A survey of the postwar world based on a large database compiled by the International Monetary Fund concluded that there were no episodes of hyperinflation between 1947 and 1984, and that since 1984, there have been seven such episodes (in six countries) in market economies.[3] The survey looked at more recent periods as well, and found that between 1987 and 1996, there were 25 episodes in 23 countries of an annualized inflation rate of 100 percent or above, lasting 45.9 months on average. The shortest was 12 months and the longest lasted 100 months. There were 20 episodes in 19 countries with an annualized inflation rate of 400 percent or above, lasting 39.7 months on average; 13 months was the shortest and 59 months the longest.[4] The heavy incidence of hyperinflation on this scale obviously suggests that many of the episodes of hyperinflation in the 1980s and 1990s were not accidental.

Indeed, two types of factors contributed to the rather frequent occurrence of hyperinflation in the 1980s and 1990s. One was international in nature; namely, the world economy and international finance drifted into a stage of turbulence and oscillation in the 1970s, punctuated by the collapse of the Bretton-Woods System and the advent of an "Age of Inflation." Volatile world markets can easily damage the economies of countries with young or fragile economic systems and infrastructure. The other factor was domestic, and had to do mainly with economic policy in certain countries. For these countries, their strategies for internal development were not generating desirable results and had instead rendered the economy and domestic finance more vulnerable to external shocks. Moreover, when such external shocks arrived, the domestic policy response did not address the nature of the domestic economic problems, making these countries vulnerable to the trap of hyperinflation.

The collapse of the Bretton-Woods System and the advent of an "age of inflation"

The postwar world economy enjoyed a "Golden Age" in the 1950s and 1960s. Sixteen industrial countries combined had an annual average growth in terms of gross domestic product of 4.9 percent in 1950–73, while their consumer prices increased at a moderate annual average rate of 4.1 percent.[5] This impressive economic growth was not confined to the developed world during the "Golden Age." The developing world had had an accelerated growth as well. The world as a whole witnessed an average annual growth in terms of GDP per capita of 2.93 percent in this period, which lasted just over two decades. It was unprecedented in the economic history of the world and was not matched by levels of growth in the remaining decades of the twentieth century.[6]

There were many factors – policy- and non-policy-related – that contributed to world economic growth and stability during the Golden Age. One of them was the Bretton-Woods System, an institutionalized international monetary arrangement designed to maintain currency exchange rate stability and help adjust the balance of debt payments for nations in the postwar world. The system had two large institutional pillars: the International Monetary Fund (IMF) and the World Bank (its other and more official name is the International Bank for Reconstruction and Development); both have headquarters in Washington, D.C., with the former focusing on short-term issues and the latter on long-term and structural matters. An earlier version of the Charter of the IMF stipulated that each member state should establish a par value in terms of the gold parity of its currency, by which its exchange rates with other currencies could be determined and maintained. If a country temporarily suffered a shortage of liquidity or a payment imbalance or current account deficit, it could draw on lending facilities at the IMF that were in part automatic and in part conditional. If a country's balance of payment problems were deemed long-term, then the World Bank would step in to provide financial assistance related to economic development, or the country would be advised to undertake appropriate policy adjustments, including realigning its par value.

The Bretton-Woods System worked well for most of the later 1950s and early 1960s. Several countries – developed and developing – ran into balance of payments problems from time to time during this period, and most of these were solved rather quickly with help from the IMF. With a functioning par value system, exchange rates among member states of the IMF remained remarkably stable. Meanwhile, inflation and interest rates in many countries remained at low levels, which was conducive to economic growth.

In principle, the International Monetary Fund was devised as an international mutual fund: each member state made a financial contribution to it and was therefore entitled to the benefit of financial assistance from it. In reality, it was more than that. Member states' contributions were made in the individual national currencies, but most countries' need for international liquidity was in one "common" currency: the U.S. dollar. The par value system was essentially based partly in gold and partly in the U.S. dollar, with the latter playing a more important role in the flow of international liquidity. Thus, the foundation of the Bretton-Woods System was the fixed value of the American dollar in gold. The dollar's gold parity provided transparency in international transactions, as well as significant additional liquidity, to international finance through both private and official (intergovernmental) channels. The U.S. dollar had a pivotal role in international reserve and liquidity management, supporting the growth of international trade and investment.

However, a system with the dollar at the core of international reserves and liquidity had an inherent potential flaw. The demand for international liquidity – manifested as international demand for the dollar – tended to expand alongside world economic growth, which required proportional outflows of dollars from the United States. Outflows of the dollar tended to create two new problems: one involved the balance of payment deficits for the United States. The other was the gradual depletion of America's gold reserves (because other countries that held excessive dollar liquidity could legitimately exchange dollars for gold through official channels according to the design of the Bretton-Woods System). These two problems generated pressure on the stability of the dollar's gold parity.

Failing to secure concessions from her European partners regarding currency and gold standard concerns, the United States under the Nixon Administration suspended the dollar's gold parity in August 1971, and in so doing, the U.S. apparently offloaded her international obligations to sustain the Bretton-Woods System. Numerous subsequent negotiations did not achieve a consensus to return to the old system. Instead, the International Monetary Fund finally endorsed the practice of floating exchange rates in the second half of the 1970s, formally abandoned the par value system, and effectively demonetized gold.

World economy and finance dealt another blow to the Bretton-Woods system in 1973, when the Yom Kippur War broke out between Arab countries and Israel in October of that year. Some Arab countries imposed an oil embargo against the West at the same time. Crude oil prices soared abruptly, from $20 per barrel to $40 per barrel in the matter of a month. Because many industrial economies relied heavily on imports of petroleum oil from the Gulf region, this "Oil Shock" prompted them to relax monetary policy in order to accommodate increasing oil prices and other commodity prices in international markets. As a result, inflation surfaced and spread worldwide. Crude oil prices have since become a significant factor in the macroeconomic policies and movements of many nations.[7]

A senior economist at the World Bank published a book entitled *Inflation: A Worldwide Disaster* in 1974, in which he proclaimed: "The world is confronted by a persistent global inflation and there are strong expectations that it will continue for years to come. This poses a grave threat to all countries, irrespective to size, wealth, political structure, or social ideology."[8] He believed that it was a "new kind of inflation," saying that "modern inflation is persistent and worldwide, unlike its predecessors which, arising from very different causes and existing under very different conditions, were temporary and usually confined to a few countries at any one time."[9]

The Age of Inflation beginning in the 1970s was more than a general rise in inflation in many countries and worldwide for a period lasting more than a decade. It was also accompanied by frequent ebbs and flows in many other dimensions: interest rates, exchange rates, cross-border capital movement, and so forth. In short, world economy and finance had entered a time in which macroeconomic uncertainties had increased, and the forces of private capital gained ever-greater impetus around the globe.

Against this backdrop, business cycles and macroeconomic policy in leading economies like that of the United States began to exert greater impact on international finance, and in particular on financial flows to developing economies. When interest rates were low in the United States and the dollar was relatively weak, developing economies would find easy access to external finance. When the opposite occurred, it would be increasingly difficult for developing countries to sustain their position in international finance, depending in part on how much they had previously relied on external financing to support their domestic economies. Thus, variability in the international financial markets posed great challenges to the economic policy of many developing countries.

Six Latin American countries experienced hyperinflation by the standard definition in the 1970s and 1980s; namely (in order of the magnitude of the inflation) Peru twice in 1988 and once in 1990, Nicaragua from 1986–91, Argentina in 1989–90, Bolivia in 1984–85, Chile in 1973, and Brazil in 1989–90.[10] Except for Chile, Nicaragua, and to a lesser extent Peru, where hyperinflation was triggered by domestic conflicts, hyperinflation in Bolivia, Brazil, and Argentina was mainly the result of economic policies that did not achieve what had been pursued in the past *and also* did not respond properly to the current external and internal shocks.

Two other countries – Israel and Turkey – encountered extreme inflation in the 1980s, though it was not hyperinflation according to the standard definition. In the case of Turkey, the problem was more likely a mixture of near-hyperinflation and chronic inflation throughout the 1990s. Again, the root causes of these monetary crises were ineffective or inappropriate economic policies.

Bolivia: the first peacetime hyperinflation in the world

Bolivia's hyperinflation started in April 1984 and culminated in August 1985. In February 1985, the country's CPI rose 183 percent (as measured monthly), and over 66 percent each month thereafter from June to August. Between March 1984 and August 1985, consumer prices multiplied 623 times. Though the Bolivian government devalued its currency, the *peso*, many times since December 1983, the dollar value of the peso continued to fall more rapidly than the official rate. By August 1984, a dollar could buy a million pesos on the black market, which was 14 times the official rate. For comparison, the black-market rate was only 2.5 times the official rate in December 1983 (Figure 6.1).

The hyperinflation caused huge social unrest in the country. The president, a strongman general turned politician, was forced to step down. An unexpected "boon" during this time, however, was the disappearance of bank robbery. To transport peso notes worth $5,000 on the black market would have required 20 men to lift the bags of notes into a getaway truck in just a few minutes, which obviously would not have been a profitable venture.

Bolivia had a troubled political history. In the 172 years since her independence, the country experienced 189 coup d'états.[11] In the first half of the 1980s, however, the country had no wars, external or internal, no reparations, and no real diplomatic isolation. However, the fiscal position of the government rapidly deteriorated in just a few years after 1981. Revenue as a percentage of gross domestic product was 37 percent in 1981; it fell to 9.1 percent in 1982 and further declined to 3.6 percent in 1984.[12] Meanwhile, the government tried to keep expanding expenditures, although it eventually had to cut some of them. Expenditures as a percentage of GDP were 46.7 percent in 1981, 25 percent in 1982, 32 percent in

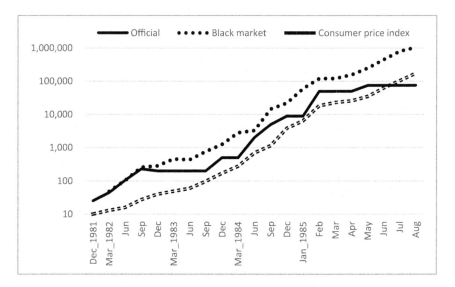

Figure 6.1 CPI and official and black-market exchange rates of peso/dollar, log scale, Bolivia, selected months in 1981–85[13]

1983, and 29 percent in 1984. As a result, the budget deficit as a percentage of GDP rose from 9.6 percent in 1981 to 24.4 percent in 1984.

Falling commodity prices in international markets was one factor behind the smaller revenues in 1981–82, but there were other reasons for the problem as well, perhaps more serious. Like many Latin American countries, Bolivia had a substantial public industrial sector due to her "import substitution strategy" in previous decades. This sector underperformed for many years, as it was unable to compete as a business unit internationally. When the dollar began to gain strength in 1981–82, the Bolivian peso was devalued accordingly. This led to a rise in the cost of production in the Bolivian industry, which rendered Bolivia's industrial sector an increasingly smaller contributor to government revenues. In 1983–84, when inflation accelerated, tax evasion became widespread in the country, dealing the government another blow in terms of revenue collection.

Meanwhile, the government kept supporting the public industrial sector, even as its revenue was falling behind. Though government expenditures decelerated in 1981–84 as the revenue fell, the pace of the contraction of expenditures was much slower than that of revenue. Naturally, without a change in economic policy, there was little hope of correcting the path of inflationary financing.

Externally, as interest rates in the international financial markets started to rise from the early 1980s, the debt service obligation of the Bolivian government increased significantly. Like many Latin American countries, the Bolivian government had borrowed heavily in the international financial markets during the 1970s, taking advantage of the cheap dollar and low interest rates then. By

1981, Bolivia's foreign debt amounted to 89 percent of GDP, with debt service on foreign loans alone equivalent to 26 percent of the country's export revenues.[14]

On the verge of defaulting on her foreign debt in 1980, Bolivia engaged in negotiations with its creditors, but it could not stop the inflation of 1981. The World Bank and the International Monetary Fund suspended lending to Bolivia that year.[15] These events not only prompted the Bolivian government to turn to internal inflationary finance, but also rendered it in desperate need of foreign exchange. Upon erroneous and unscrupulous policy advice, the government ordered all dollar deposits at domestic banks to be converted into pesos in 1982.[16] This triggered a public panic, caused a massive capital flight from the country, and set in motion an inflationary spiral. Capital flight had occurred to the country. An estimated shows that by the end of 1987, a time after the stabilization program, Bolivian assets that were held abroad totaled $2 billion,[17] equivalent to 46.5 percent of her GDP of the year. Before 1981, Bolivia was a country receiving net resources from abroad; after 1981, the country became plagued by the net outflow of resources, in amounts in excess of hundreds of millions of dollars.[18]

In Bolivia's domestic economy, dollarization had taken place. As noted by an American economist, Jeffrey Sachs, who was a leading member of an international advisory team to the Bolivian government for stabilization, the dollar was performing at least two classic functions of money in the country in August 1985: it was the unit of account and a store of value.[19] Many transactions were priced in dollars, though largely executed in pesos. There might have been a shortage in the dollar supply at the time, so that the dollar prices of Bolivian goods and services were fundamentally stable, or even somewhat deflated.

With a change in government and upon policy recommendations prepared by an international consulting team, a Big Bang was launched in Bolivia in late August 1985. It was a comprehensive program, combining currency devaluation and convertibility, fiscal austerity, trade liberalization, price de-controls, and privatization of public enterprises. A new currency, the *boliviano*, which was also the name of the Bolivian currency for a century until 1963, replaced the peso at a rate of 1 to a million. The *boliviano* was set at par with the dollar, which was basically the same rate as the black-market exchange rate immediately prior to the Big Bang. This was equivalent to a devaluation of more than 90 percent vs. the earlier official exchange rate. To prevent the reemergence of the black market, the government operated a crawling peg in later years, which allowed the *boliviano* to depreciate over time, and to appreciate only occasionally.

Another key element of the stabilization program was a program of cuts in government expenditures, and this was achieved mainly by raising public sector prices and freezing wages in the sector. As noted earlier, the public sector was the country's white elephant, consuming a good deal of government expenditure. Cuts in subsidies to, and investment in, the sector saved significant resources in the government's budget. The wage freezing in the sector also meant that the burden of stabilization was largely transferred to the shoulders of public sector workers. As a result, the government budget, net of its interest payments, returned to a surplus by the end of the year. With regard to tax revenue, an overhaul scheme was approved by the country's Congress and put into effect eight months later. Revenue as a percentage of GDP rose from 12 percent in 1985 to 19.5 percent in 1986.

Internationally, the Bolivian government started to renegotiate with international lenders over foreign debt restructuring. A loan from the International Monetary Fund was secured in the next year, and an agreement with international banks was reached two years later.

Was the Bolivian stabilization program a success? Categorically yes, considered in the context of Latin America. Bolivia's CPI inflation fell to 273 percent in 1986, and all the way down to 14.6 percent in 1987, although it did not fall to single digits until 1993. GDP growth was negative at 1.7 percent in 1985 and negative again at 2.5 percent in 1986, but resumed a positive trend in 1987, growing 2.5 percent. Currency account deficits as a percentage of GDP decreased considerably in 1988 and disappeared in 1989. Meanwhile, many other Latin American countries, including Brazil and Argentina, continued to suffer rampant inflation, currency crises, and foreign debt crises throughout the 1980s and into the 1990s.

The most difficult part of the Bolivian stabilization program was sustaining exchange rate stability and wage controls in the public sector. For the latter, the government mainly relied on political determination. For the former, the task was apparently quite risky, as foreign exchange markets had been liberalized. At the time the stabilization program was launched, the Bolivian government had no significant foreign exchange reserves on hand, or financial backup from abroad. Its policy credibility was obviously on the line, and it did not have a past record to encourage confidence in its present strategy. It therefore decided to devalue the currency heavily in the short term and to subsequently allow the currency to depreciate virtually in line with domestic inflation, which had largely been brought under control. In a sense, the Bolivian approach to stabilization was different from a traditional approach that would have prioritized fiscal austerity and the building of credibility.[20]

Against this backdrop, expectations regarding domestic inflation and currency devaluation continued, though demands for change in these areas become gradually subdued. Continued negative expectations were presumably one reason that inflation was not completely controlled in Bolivia in subsequent years. Moreover, long-standing problems of unequal income distribution and public sector inefficiency remained virtually intact, and these continued to strain government budgets and the country's economic growth.[21]

Nevertheless, the Bolivian experience of hyperinflation and stabilization set an example in Latin America that rampant inflation could be brought to an end with a bold, liberal-styled, and internationally assisted reform program.

Brazil and Argentina: hyperinflation in parallel

The World Bank has published its *World Development Report* with *World Development Indicators* each year since 1978. This report compiles national data on an internationally comparable basis. Gross national product or income per capita in current U.S. dollar terms is a widely used development barometer. According to the annual *Reports*, Brazil's GNI per capital in dollar terms was 67.5 percent of Portugal's in 1976, and Argentina's was 53.1 percent of Spain's in the same year.[22] Twenty-five years later, in 2001, Brazil's GNI had fallen to merely 28.7 percent of Portugal's, and Argentina's was 46.8 percent of Spain's. In 2015, Brazil's level recovered to 48 percent, still below that of its 1978 level, and Argentina's continued to fall, dropping to 43.7 percent that year. During the entire period of nearly half a century, Brazil and Argentina remained middle-income nations, while Portugal and Spain had each upgraded into the world's high-income group – the two countries are also among the 11 founding member states of the euro in 1999. The lagged development in Argentina for more than a century has been labeled the "Argentine paradox."[23]

In contemporary literature of economics that focuses on development and growth issues, there have been numerous discussions about the so-called "middle income trap," which is a situation in which a developing economy that reaches a level of middle income is unable to further progress to a high income level for various reasons. Brazil and Argentina have been frequently cited as examples of countries that fell into this "middle income trap."

Among all the factors related to the Brazilian and Argentine experience of unsuccessful economic development, the most conspicuous issues include persistent high inflation, occasional hyperinflation, and stop-and-go stabilization and reform.

The two countries both saw inflation beginning to rise in 1970, and further accelerated from 1980. Between 1980 and 1994, annual CPI inflation in Brazil and Argentina was not less than 100 percent each year and had exceeded 1,000 percent in both 1989–90 and 1992–93. In Argentina, the length of CPI inflation that was higher than 100 percent was shorter than in Brazil, but Argentina's overall level of inflation was much higher than Brazil's: 4,924 percent in 1989 (Figure 6.2). In monthly terms, Brazil's CPI inflation rate exceeded 50 percent between December 1989 and March 1990, with the highest monthly level being 82.4 percent in March 1990. In Argentina, hyperinflation occurred between May 1989 and March 1990, with the highest monthly level (197 percent) occurring in July 1989.[24] Overall, it took six years in Brazil, and five years in Argentina, for inflation to fall to single-digit levels from its peak.

In many countries that experienced hyperinflation during the first half of the twentieth century, the cause was either a sudden upsurge, or something that had been building as a result of inflation in earlier years. Hyperinflation in Brazil and Argentina had resulted from high inflation that persisted for decades. As indicated in the World Bank's first issue of the *World Development Report* in 1978, Brazil's average annual rate of inflation in CPI terms was 46 percent in 1960–70, and Argentina's was 21.8 percent; both of these rates were among the highest in the world during the "Golden Age." When entering the "Age of Inflation" in the 1970s, Brazil's average annual inflation lowered to 26.1 percent in 1970–76, and Argentina's rose to 88.7 percent; both of these rates again were among the highest among all middle-income nations except Chile, another Latin American country

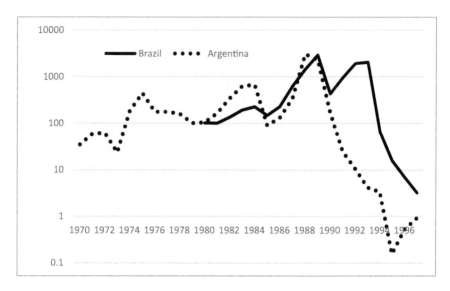

Figure 6.2 CPI inflation rate, percentage, log scale, Brazil and Argentina, 1970–97[25]

that experienced hyperinflation immediately after her civil war, which occurred in the first half of the 1970s. Brazil and Argentina, the two largest and most resource-rich countries in all of South America, apparently shared a common tradition of persistent high inflation.

From an international macroeconomic perspective, the two years from 1989–90 were not an unusual period. The Federal Reserve cut its benchmark interest rate in December 1989, and international oil prices remained moderate, at about $40 a barrel. Unlike Bolivia in the first half of the 1980s, when hyperinflation was triggered by certain external factors, the hyperinflation in Brazil and Argentina in 1989–90 was primarily due to domestic problems.

In response to rising inflation and mounting foreign debt in the first half of the 1980s, both countries undertook reforms and stabilization programs in the mid-1980s. Brazil announced the "Cruzado Plan" in February 1986, introducing a new currency unit (the *cruzado*) to replace an old currency (the *cruzeiro novo*), at a rate of 1 to 1,000, effectively devaluing the currency. To ensure the success of this plan, the government imposed a wide range of price freezing and suspended its erstwhile practice of indexation in many areas.[26] Interest rates on Brazilian federal treasury bonds were fixed, apparently as part of the effort to de-index. The result of these measures did not create stabilization at all. As can be seen from Figure 6.2, CPI inflation in Brazil decelerated marginally, from 226 percent in 1985 to 147 percent in 1986, and then accelerated again in 1987 (228 percent). The reform did not attempt to sort out problems of budget balancing or other economic fundamentals that would support external balance and exchange rate stability.[27] Public response to the reforms was immensely negative: a shift to the black market and barter, acquiring fixed assets such as land if possible, and capital outflows.[28]

In Argentina, a stabilization program called the "Austral Plan" was adopted in June 1985, several months earlier than the similar Brazilian plan. A new currency unit, the *austral*, replaced an old currency at a rate of 1 to 1,000. The currency devaluation was accompanied by exchange rate controls, arranged in a complex scheme. Unlike Brazil's Cruzado Plan, the Austral Plan did not call for price and wage freezing, but it did pronounce an ambitious goal of "tight fiscal policy and monetary restraint,"[29] from which the Argentine government proved unable to enforce or benefit. The disinflationary results of the Austral Plan seemed more impressive than those achieved by the Cruzado Plan: the CPI rate in Argentina fell from 385 percent in 1985 to 81.9 percent in 1986. Yet, this turned out to be more fragile than what the Brazilian program achieved: CPI inflation in Argentina climbed to treble digits from 1987: 174.8 percent in the year and 387.7 percent in 1988.

As stabilization in both countries left core issues of macroeconomic stability unchanged, inflationary momentum was merely temporarily suppressed for a short while. When events concerning the fiscal soundness of the government emerged, and public confidence in the creditability of various policies and reforms was damaged, the momentum of inflation once again was unleashed. Foreign debt crises and restructuring played an important role in the dynamics of inflation in both countries in the later 1980s.

Brazil declared a moratorium on foreign debt payments in late 1987 and reached a compromise with international lenders in early 1988, after intense negotiations. Though the new debt restructuring deal was a long-term one – 20 years for total repayment – it placed increased pressure on the fiscal position of the Brazilian government, which had to find ways to squeeze foreign exchange resources in the domestic market. Brazil had an account surplus in 1988 and 1989, partly reflecting the effect of the debt-restructuring program that reduced its foreign exchange payments in the early years of the agreement. To increase its position in the foreign exchange, the Brazilian government sharply expanded its issuance of securities in order to make purchases on the foreign exchange, which clearly signaled a shift toward an inflationary or re-inflationary policy. By February 1989, the market price of Brazilian government bonds was merely 34 percent of the bonds' face value.[30]

Foreign debt problems were more severe in Argentina than in many other Latin American countries in the 1980s. The country had already had a foreign debt crisis in 1982; the restructuring program she put in place to deal with this crisis only worked for a few years. The year of 1988 was a year in which Argentina needed to renegotiate with international lenders over debt restructuring once again, and this time the International Monetary Fund played a role in convening meetings and imposing conditions. As part of its long-standing doctrine, the IMF insisted that the Argentine government cut budget deficits and undertake austerity, and without seeing solid signs of improvement on these accounts the Fund could do nothing but walk away from negotiation.[31]

The Argentine government managed to produce a stabilization program known as the Plan Primavera in August 1988, focused on exchange rate realignment by allowing the peso to devalue over time within a predetermined limit. In the eyes of the IMF, however, the program stood short of emphasizing budget control and revenue consolidation, and they expected the budget deficit of the Argentine government to eventually deteriorate over 4 percent of GDP in the next year. The view on Argentine public finance held by the IMF in the negotiations did not square well at times with the staff at the World Bank or officials at the U.S. Treasury Department. In the end, the IMF continued to play a leading hand in the process of talks with the Argentines.[32]

The news of IMF demands and others had, however, provoked public outrage and social unrest in Argentina in 1989, a year in which a presidential election was being held, meaning the departing government was in a lame duck state. The Plan Primavera collapsed in February 1989, as the government was unable to keep the peso's exchange rates within the target zone, which was partly a result that Argentina's foreign exchange reserves approached exhaustion by then. A new multiple exchange rate system was introduced, which effectively means that exchange rates applied to financial transactions were no longer subject to government regulation and the peso had been drastically devalued. Capital flight reemerged in the country. As a result, CPI jumped to a hyperinflationary level in 1989, 4,924 percent, which is also considerably higher than Brazil's level (1,430 percent) in the year (Figure 6.2).

To people living outside Brazil and Argentina, it seemed inconceivable that these two resource-rich, upper-middle-income countries would endure secular budget deficits and heavy foreign debts. An obvious, political economy explanation is that like many Latin American countries, Brazil and Argentina had a long history of political instability and a lack of institutional constraints on fiscal expansion. In terms of economics, however, the two problems – persistent budget deficits and significant reliance on foreign debt – had a common origin: a highly inward-looking development strategy that had been pursued almost invariably by all politicians in virtually all Latin American countries – especially Brazil and Argentina – since the first half of the twentieth century. The strategy had several ingredients regardless of what the various Latin American countries may have called it:

- To place industrial development as the foremost goal of the nation's economic growth and the primary way through which to achieve "economic independence"
- To promote investment in industries that mainly targeted the domestic market
- To establish state-owned enterprises in key industrial branches
- To levy high tariffs on imports of industrial goods that were believed to be competing with domestic products
- To set exchange rates at a level that could help reduce the costs of imports that were used as intermediate inputs for domestic industries

- To provide subsidies and tax treatments for public enterprises when they were deemed necessary to sustain domestic industrial development; wherever applicable, credit supports were also given to public enterprises
- To erect barriers to foreign direct investment inflows, so national equity ownership could be protected and would prosper

Another term for this type of inward-looking development strategy is Import Substitution Industrialization; namely, promoting domestic production by replacing imports from foreign countries. The concept of pursuing industrial development with state protection and promotion is often called the "infant industry argument." In theory, such a strategy could boost a country's ability to interact with the foreign exchange by reducing the need for imports. In reality, when domestic industry did not sufficiently satisfy demands at home, the need for imports remained. Moreover, growing investment in domestic industry tends to generate new demand for imports and foreign exchange. In essence, whether import substitution industrialization can save foreign exchange or not depends on whether the domestic industry is efficient and competitive, domestically *and* internationally.

Unfortunately, many domestic industries pursued in postwar Latin American countries via public enterprises were not efficient, nor were they competitive internationally. Consequently, they did not contribute to government revenues significantly in net terms, nor did they help reduce the demand for foreign exchange.

A thorough investigation completed in the early 1990s of the relations between the public sector and the Latin American crisis of the 1980s confirms the view that "the overexpansion of the public sector has been at the root of . . . external indebtedness problem" to a varying degree depending on the country. The study also finds that public sector expansion resulted in fiscal deficits for several reasons: cheaper external credit generated an increase in current and capital spending; low world interest rates during the 1970s encouraged borrowing as a substitute for tax revenues and domestic sources of financing; and political pressures kept tax revenues low.[33] Moreover, in Brazil and Argentina, provincial and state governments spending was notably spendthrift.

Researchers have also found significant differences between Latin American and East Asian countries toward foreign borrowing. The ratio of external debt to exports was a weighted average of 134 percent in six Latin American countries, including Brazil and Argentina, in 1981; it was 82.1 percent in four East Asian countries. The debt service ratio – interest payments plus principal repayment as a percentage of export earnings – was a weighted average of 153.8 percent for the former countries in 1980–83, and 61.7 percent for the latter.[34] It is believed that the

> foundations for . . . import-substitution policies in Latin America are political. . . . In spite of an urgent need to spur exports to grow out of the debt crisis, movements towards export promotion in almost every Latin American country have been frustrated recently by countervailing movements of [the] further protection of domestic industry.[35]

The infant industry argument had apparently become an entrenched part of the ideology of many Latin American countries.

In the 1980s, Brazil and Argentina's resistance to foreign direct investment began to change, apparently reflecting a reluctant acceptance of the "Washington Consensus," a recapitulation of a set of liberal, rule-based policies regarding the role of market forces and international trade and investment; a positive opinion of most of these policies was presumably shared by the International Monetary Fund and the World Bank. Foreign direct investment did flow into Brazil and Argentina in the 1980s, but it remained too small in size to exert any significant impact on their economies.

In August 1987, a would-be finance minister in Brazil published an article in an English journal stating,

> when this article was written, one month after the Brazilian heterodox shock, everything seemed to indicate that inflation would be brought under control. If this prediction is confirmed, and the 1,000% inflation in Argentina and the 350% inflation in Brazil are eliminated with almost no cost, economic theory and policy . . . will have taken a great step forward.[36]

His remark was obviously overly optimistic from both a realistic and a theoretical perspective.

A new president came into office in Brazil in March 1990, and he promised to reduce inflation. He resorted to measures of price controls, bank deposit freezing, and suspension of foreign exchange transactions, amid strong political opposition in the Brazilian Congress and a reluctant public. CPI inflation decelerated from nearly 3,000 percent in 1990 to 432 percent in 1991, and then turned to climb through 1994, at which time it once again rose above 2,000 percent. The president escaped impeachment in Congress for corruption charges by resigning, and he left the office to his vice president, who later appointed Fernando Henrique Cardoso as finance minister in 1993 to take charge of stabilization. Cardoso, an outsider of economics, knew he faced an almost insurmountable task – in the prior eight years, Brazil had changed currencies seven times, and within the seven months before he became finance minister, three other finance ministers had been replaced.[37] To him, Brazil had many world-class fine economists working for the government, and they could invent stabilization programs that looked perfect in theory.[38] In the end, he was able to work out a new program of currency reform, with aid from a number of experts and professionals.

His plan was called the Real Plan ("real" in Portuguese is an equivoque of the *real* and *royal*), and it included several features that were unprecedented in the monetary history of the country. First, the value of the *real* was set at par against only the dollar on its first day of introduction in early 1994. This made the *real* look like a localized dollar to residents of the country. To make the new currency publicly acceptable, Brazil's Central Bank began to run an open market operation in a newly liberalized foreign exchange market by buying and selling the *real* at about its par value. Second, to limit oversupply of the *real*, which would undoubtedly have led to its devaluation, the program called for budget cuts, which were achieved mainly through political tactics. Third, in a transition phase lasting six months, all retailers were required to have dual pricing commodities: one in the new *real* and another in the old *cruzeiro real* (which had been introduced only a year earlier). A result of this double listing was that when *cruzeiro real* prices continued to rise, the *real* prices of the same commodities remained unchanged; in other words, the dollar prices of local goods remained stable. Public awareness of the stability of *real* prices made the new currency easy to accept when it was put into circulation in July 1994.

In retrospect, Cardoso's actions revealed that inflation in Brazil had many secret beneficiaries, from politicians to bankers and from bribers to indexed wage-earners in the public sector. Without a radical program, hyperinflation could not be separated from the country.

CPI inflation decelerated to 66 percent in 1995, 15.8 percent in 1996, and 6.9 percent in 1997 (Figure 6.2). The Brazilian economy resumed steady growth in 1994. The success of the Real Plan gained Cardoso timely popularity, and he won a general election and became president of Brazil in 1994. Brazil finally emerged as an influential emerging-market economy in the international arena in the second half of the 1990s and the first decade of the twentieth-first century.

Argentina's stabilization began earlier than Brazil's. A new president came into office in May 1989 and immediately attempted to quell hyperinflation; he was even able to reach a temporary compromise with the International Monetary Fund. However, the deal soon proved to be impossible to implement, and the IMF ceased negotiations. CPI inflation remained above 1,000 percent in 1990 (at precisely 1,344 percent). The president called upon Domingo Felipe Cavallo to assume the role of minister of the economy and tasked him with developing a stabilization program in February 1991. A trained economist and long-term politician, Cavallo soon launched a scheme known as the currency board system for Argentina.

A key issue in the currency board system concerned who would make decisions about the money supply, and how. Cavallo's scheme was to tie Argentina's money supply solely with the foreign exchange reserve that accrued to accounts in the Central Bank, effectively depriving the government of the power to print money. On the first day of 1992, after several months of preparation, a new currency unit, the *peso*, was introduced to replace the *austral* at a rate of 1 to 10,000. The value of the *peso* was fixed at par with the U.S. dollar, and it was convertible to the foreign exchange. As Argentina had a long past of foreign exchange control, the new scheme – together with its official name (the "Convertibility Plan") – sounded extremely appealing to the Argentine people. With the program, Argentina became the world's largest country ever to formally operate on a currency board system.

In order to increase its foreign exchange reserves and therefore the capacity with which the Central Bank was able to defend the *peso*'s par value vs. the dollar, the program also included a series of privatization and deregulation measures to attract foreign capital. This signaled Argentina's self-motivated consent to the Washington Consensus. Excepting banks, all state-owned enterprises were made available to private equity investors, including those from abroad. Massive foreign capital poured into the country following the stabilization program.

CPI inflation fell to 84 percent in 1991, and then fell further to 3.9 percent in 1994. The Argentine economy appeared to be steadily growing without the fuel of inflation during the first half of the 1990s. If time had stopped before the twenty-first century, the Argentine stabilization would have been a near-perfect success story. The currency board system managed to survive after the series of external shocks caused by the Mexican financial crisis in 1994, but it could not sustain another rounds of shocks – a combination of external and internal crises – that occurred at the turn of the century, first with the Brazilian devaluations in 1999 and second with domestic bank runs in 2001.[39] Argentina formally abandoned the currency board system in January 2002, when the *peso* was devalued by 40 percent and dollar deposits were forcibly converted to *pesos* at the earlier rates. Argentina returned to a period of double-digit inflation, and has since experienced zig-zag economic growth.

Israel and Turkey: contrasting experiences of high inflation

What Israel and Turkey witnessed since the 1970s would not be considered hyper-inflation by any conventional definition. The highest CPI inflation rate in Israel was 374 percent in 1984 and 305 percent in 1985, and in Turkey it was only 110 percent in 1980 and 106 percent in 1994, as shown in Figure 6.3. These figures are far below those of over 1,000 percent in a single a year in Brazil or Argentina. Yet, scholars have not refused to refer to the term hyperinflation in articulating the Israeli inflationary experience of the 1980s in particular. An IMF staff paper

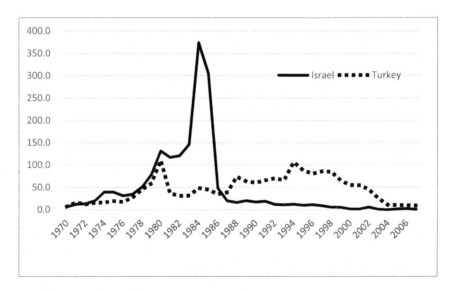

Figure 6.3 CPI inflation rate, percentage, Israel and Turkey, 1970–2007[40]

published in 1987 compared Israel with Argentina in terms of fighting hyperinflation.[41] Looking at the two countries from a long-term perspective, one can say that Turkey endured inflation more severe than Israel. As shown in Figure 6.4, Turkey's accumulative inflation – measured as a fix-based inflation level for a longer period under observation – surpassed Israel's in magnitude in 1997, and it was 20 times that of Israel in 2004 and 27 times higher by 2007. While Israel experienced near-hyperinflation in the mid-1980s, Turkey experienced a combination of chronic inflation and high inflation in the decades from the 1970s and following.

Despite many differences in history and culture, the economies of Israel and Turkey had much in common before the mid-1980s, which helps explain why the two countries had encountered serious inflation up to that point. In the 1950s and 1960s, both countries adopted import substitution industrialization, in a manner similar to that of many Latin American countries. Trade and foreign exchange were tightly controlled by the government. Because of the significant need for defense and a robust defense industry, the Israeli and Turkish governments constantly ran budget deficits. Foreign aid – especially from the United States – alleviated pressure on the budget balance in the case of Israel, to which Turkey did not have this same access. However, Turkey had an enormous amount of remittances each year from Turkish workers employed overseas, especially those working in postwar West Germany, which helped reduce pressure on Turkey's balance of payments. Finally, the two countries were neighbors with oil-rich Arab countries, but they themselves did not produce petroleum and were significant oil importers. Fluctuations in international oil markets thus had a significant impact on these two economies.

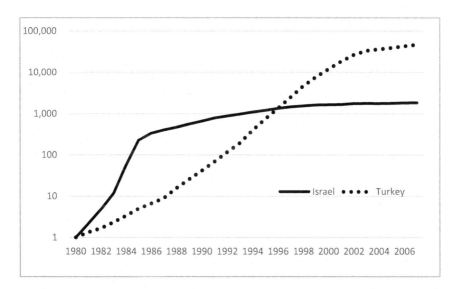

Figure 6.4 Index of CPI, 1980 = 1, log scale, Israel and Turkey, 1980–2007[42]

Beginning in the 1970s, both countries attempted to liberalize trade and foreign exchange, starting a shift from import substitution industrialization to export promotion. The Second Oil Shock in 1980 caused by the Iraq-Iran War aggravated the external trade balance and internal budget balance of both Israel and Turkey. The Israeli budget deficit increased during the Yom Kippur War of 1973, and did not fall significantly in subsequent years,[43] in part because Israel embarked on another major military venture in Lebanon in 1982–85,[44] and in part because the American aid policy toward Israel changed after 1973, to become linked to Israeli defense needs only.[45] Since the early 1980s, Israel and Turkey have been on different inflationary paths and stabilization programs, largely due to differences in their policies and institutions.

During the second half of the 1970s and the early 1980s, the Israeli government mainly relied on inflationary policy to finance its budget deficits; this is another form of debt monetarization. In order to relieve pressure on workers' real incomes, wage indexation was put into place from 1974 on, which prolonged the process of inflation. Relaxation in foreign exchange controls in the late 1970s, coupled with ongoing domestic inflation, invoked strong demand for foreign exchange, which in turn heightened domestic inflationary expectations. Beginning in the second half of 1984, the economic and financial situation in Israel rapidly worsened. Budget deficits and the balance of payments deficits were enlarging. Foreign exchange reserves were falling. Trade unions were demanding larger and more frequent wage increases. News that the U.S. government rejected Israeli requests for aid further drove up public inflation expectations. The Israeli currency, the *shekel*, began to devalue rapidly in the black market beginning in late 1984.[46] Even a hard-won deal with trade unions on wage determination in November 1984 could not prevent inflation from reaching the triple-digit level by the end of 1984.

In mid-1984, the Israeli government was preparing for a major reform and stabilization program, which was announced and implemented in July. Key elements of the program were (1) to cut government budget spending, mainly by reductions in subsidies given to public sector institutions; (2) to abolish wage indexation and grant a one-time wage increase; (3) to impose price ceilings for a definite period; (4) to suspend dollar-linked short-term deposits made by Israelis domestically; and (5) to let the Central Bank – the Bank of Israel – conduct a fixed-peg exchange rate, which would defend a specific a target in the *shekel*'s exchange rate vs. the dollar.[47] Further, a new *shekel* replaced the old one at a rate of 1 to 1,000 on the first day of 1986. Except for the last measure, all of the other tasks listed were a tough task, especially cutting budgets and maintaining an exchange rate target.

Budget cuts required a change in policy toward public sector development, which Israel managed to achieve. Public sector investments as a proportion of GNP decreased from 4.1 percent in 1973–84 to 3.1 percent in 1985–87, and that of government subsidies, including indirect subsidies for credit to public enterprises, decreased from 12.9 percent to 5.1 percent over the same time period. Budget deficits fell to 1.1 percent of GNP in 1985–97.[48]

For exchange rate management, the Bank of Israel was given the authority to conduct a peg system aimed at cooling down devaluation expectations and driving out black market premiums. This system supplied foreign exchange to a market that was initially highly controlled, without the use of additional funds from foreign sources. A U.S. aid package was granted several months later, when the stabilization program was in effect. At one point, members of an Israeli government task-force team worried that the American funds might arrive early and undermine the resolution of the Israeli government to cut budget deficits.[49]

CPI inflation in Israel fell to 48 percent in 1986 and 20 percent in 1987. In the years since 1988, CPI inflation has never again risen above 20 percent. In retrospect, it is fair to say that the success of the Israeli stabilization effort should not be attributed to the program itself. Instead, it was the determination and commitment of the Israeli government to budget balance, together with upholding policy credibility and respecting the independence of the central bank, which decisively helped to reduce and eliminate inflation expectations and win cooperation from trade unions and the public at large. For this reason, it was Israeli institutions that mattered the most for the country's success in stabilization. In comparison, the factors at play in Turkey were substantially different.

Like Israel, Turkey had a debt and inflation crisis in 1979–80, which it overcame with help from the International Monetary Fund. From then on, the Turkish experience of macroeconomic policy and inflation was incongruent with that of Israel. As indicated earlier, Turkey never had an annual inflation rate over 200 percent throughout the 1980s or the 1990s, although that does not mean that inflation remained low in the country. Quite the contrary, annual CPI inflation in Turkey averaged 61 percent in 1980–2002 (Figure 6.3). Very few countries in the world had such a long record of high inflation.

The official exchange rate of the Turkish *lira* with the U.S. dollar was 90 to 1 in 1980, 1,300 to 1 in 1988, 45,000 to 1 in 1995, and 1,650,000 to 1 in 2001. The *Guinness Book of Records* ranked the Turkish *lira* as the world's least valuable currency in 1995 and 1996, and again from 1999 to 2004. A new *lira* was introduced in 2005 to replace the old currency at a rate of 1 to 1,000,000.

One reason that Turkey did not slip into hyperinflation was the price controls that the government had maintained for a long period of time. The government also intervened in the pricing behavior of the public sector, which had been sizable in the country. But this practice came at a cost: the government could do little to enhance efficiency and productivity in the sector, even when general economic policy shifted away from import substitution industrialization to export-led growth in the early 1980s. In addition, government controls of banking institutions made it difficult for credit to flow into more efficient and productive sectors; and this tended to slow the growth of revenues to the government. Moreover, slow improvement in social institutions resulted, from time to time, in a lack of adequate respect for the independence of the country's central bank, which effectively enabled the Turkish government use inflationary means to finance its budget deficit when it felt this necessary.

Turkey had several currency and financial crises after 1980, with at least one in 1988, one in 1994, and another in 2001. Each time, a stabilization program was implemented to deal with rising inflation and currency devaluation, and/or with concurrent financial crises. Policy and institutional improvements took place at intervals during these periods, but nothing that could be regarded as decisive or fundamental. The Turkish economy had been growing since the 1970s, and quite impressively in some years. Yet, the average growth rate in per capita terms was slower than that of Israel. Israel had become a high-income economy in the late 1990s and completed full currency convertibility in 2003. At present, Turkey remains a middle-income country.

Chile, Nicaragua, and Peru: hyperinflation in unsettled societies

Hyperinflation in the three Latin American countries (Chile, Peru, and Nicaragua) and in two African countries (Zaire and Angola) had something in common: they all occurred against a backdrop of a domestic society and political conditions that were in tatters, or under a government that was engaging in external conflicts. There were certain failures in economic policy, but dysfunctional politics or foreign policy were the main causes of the hyperinflation. Hyperinflation in these countries had little to do with the "Age of Inflation" in the 1970s and 1980s.

Chile in 1973: hyperinflation in a coup

In Latin America, Chile had the first hyperinflation in the last three decades of the twentieth century. CPI inflation climbed to 353 percent in 1973 and peaked at 505 percent in 1974, as shown in Figure 6.5. In monthly terms, CPI inflation started to soar in August 1972, when it increased by double digits, culminating at 87.7 percent in October 1973.[50] Monthly CPI inflation decelerated from its peak level in the last two months of 1973 and throughout 1974, but in annual terms, the 1974 inflation rate in Chile was higher than that of 1973.

Between 1971 and September 1973, Chile was run by the presidency of Salvador Allende, a pro-Soviet socialist politician who won a general election in 1970. His administration was unprecedented in Latin America. He adopted a series of radical reform programs, including land redistribution and the nationalization of large industries (mainly copper mines owned by American firms). The Chilean economy was relatively healthy in 1971, but it sank into a recession in 1972 amid a trade embargo imposed by the United States against the Allende regime. When his domestic political coalition weakened, Allende was in need of fiscal expansion to consolidate his power. Possible foreign aid from countries like the Soviet Union was too small when it arrived. Inflation accelerated in mid-1972, steadily increasing with a few brief pauses at the turn of the year. When Allende was overthrown in a bloody coup in September 1973, inflation spiraled out of control. Chile was then ruled by a military dictatorship until 1990.

The process of disinflation in the first five years of the new regime was slow, with CPI inflation standing at 40 percent in 1978. It took another five years for

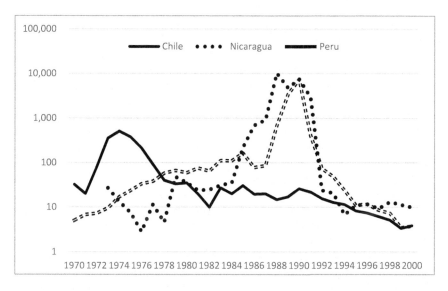

Figure 6.5 CPI inflation rate, percentage, log scale, Chile, Nicaragua, and Peru, 1970–2000[51]

inflation to fall to single digits of 9.9 percent in 1982 (Figure 6.5). A currency reform took place in 1975, with a new *peso* replacing the old *escudo* at a rate 1 to 1,000. The military regime followed policy recommendations from the so-called "Chicago Boys," American-educated Chilean economists under great intellectual influence of the Chicago School of Economics, to conduct privatization and liberalization, and to some extent, to exercise self-restraint in budget planning. The slowness of the disinflation was partly caused by the widespread practice of indexation in the Chilean economy.

Nicaragua in the late 1980s: hyperinflation with a falling administration

Nicaragua in Central America had been ruled by a hereditary dictatorship since the 1920s, until 1979 when a revolution broke out and the populist Sandinista regime was established in the country. As with Chile under Allende, the Sandinista pro-Soviet socialist regime pursued certain radical social and economic reform programs, promoting collectivism and land redistribution in rural areas and conducting nationalization in several sectors of the economy – banking, foreign trade, large-scale mining, forestry, and fishing. The public sector share of GDP rose from 15 percent to 40 percent in the early 1980s.[52]

Despite some setbacks, Nicaragua managed to have a growing economy until the mid-1980s, with domestic inflation kept in single digits, which was healthier than many other Central American countries in the same period. But situations – economic as well as political – became increasingly challenging for the Nicaraguan government starting in 1985. From 1981 on, the U.S. Reagan Administration severed trade relations with Nicaragua because of the latter's secret involvement in revolutionary campaigns in neighboring Central American countries. New foreign loans from multilateral sources ceased to be available, and aid from Soviet Russia (and possibly from Cuba as well) was insignificant in size. In 1985, the Reagan Administration further launched a trade embargo and began to support a rebellious force against the Nicaraguan government. The country could no longer earn foreign exchange from exports to her erstwhile largest trading partners, and the growth of government revenue from domestic sources also ran into difficulties. Meanwhile, fighting the U.S.-backed rebels required large increases in government expenditures. Fiscal deficits were less than 10 percent of GDP in the early 1980s, and they rose to 22.5 percent in 1985, with military spending accounting for more than 18 percent of central government expenditures in 1986–88.[53]

Aware of the danger of enlarging budget deficits and inflation, the Nicaraguan government attempted stabilization programs on its own. The most notable were cuts in non-military spending and currency devaluation. The former included reductions in public service, which took the government away from its earlier populist style. The latter had little effect on stimulating export growth, and in fact further heightened devaluation expectations. Wage controls were also attempted, but implementing them became increasingly ineffective.

The year 1985 was the first year in which Nicaragua witnessed CPI inflation rising into triple digits of 163 percent. After two years of deceleration, CPI inflation skyrocketed to 10,205 percent in 1988 (Figure 6.5), a level matched in Latin America only by Bolivia. Once again, the Sandinista government had to resort to emergency pricing and wage ceilings, further tightening controls on an economy that was in ruins. GDP fell 10.9 percent in 1988 and further dipped to 2.9 percent in 1989.[54]

The Sandinistas were defeated in the general election of 1990, and the new government immediately began a stabilization program. A rapprochement with the United States made international credit accessible again.[55] At home, following the Sandinistas' currency reform of February 1988 – which had replaced the first *córdoba* with the second *córdoba* at a rate of 1,000 to 1, the new government introduced the third *córdoba*, which replaced the second *córdoba* at a rate of 1 to 5,000,000 in April 1991.

Peru at the turn of the 1990s: hyperinflation in an uneasy society

A World Bank country study published in April 1989 warned of the risks of hyperinflation in Peru, which became real by the end of that year.[56] CPI inflation was 667 percent in 1988 and galloped to 3,399 percent in 1989. The year 1990 was an election and power transition year, when CPI inflation reached 7,482 percent (Figure 6.5). GDP growth was already negative at −9.4 percent in 1988, and it further plummeted to −13.4 percent in 1989.

The Peruvian hyperinflation was rooted in the country's wobbly political traditions of past decades, which reflected the historical divisions that had long plagued Peruvian society. The president who came into power in 1980 tried to undo radical programs that had been adopted by an earlier president, and another president taking office in 1985 attempted another policy reverse of a similar nature. As social discontent grew, rebellion resurfaced in several regions, though at a scale smaller than what happened in Nicaragua.

As occurred in many Latin American countries, Peru's government pursued a policy of supporting and promoting public sector development during the second half of the 1980s, largely at the expense of government-controlled resources. Exchange rates were highly regulated in order to prevent the costs of importing materials for use in the public sector enterprises from rising. This was an implicit subsidy to the public sector that resulted in currency overvaluation because of ongoing domestic inflation. Export growth slowed and eventually declined in 1986–88. Peru's current account had a surplus in 1985 but shifted to a deficit in 1986, amounting to 5.4 percent of GDP by 1988. In 1986 and 1987, the government was able to continue lending support to public sector development by increasing the money supply, because CPI inflation at that time was below 100 percent and there were considerable foreign exchange reserves available for use. However, when inflation accelerated, the growth of government revenues began to decelerate and even decline in real terms. The central government's revenue as a percentage of GDP was 14 percent in 1985, falling to 11.9 percent in 1986 and 8.7 percent in 1987.[57] As enlarging current account deficits nearly exhausted foreign exchange reserves, the Peruvian government could not rely on conventional fiscal policy to sustain the economy.

An emergency price freezing was adopted in March 1988, and when it ended three months later as scheduled, prices soared at an uncheckable pace. Black markets in the foreign exchange mushroomed in the country, and the economy rapidly fell into recession. Peruvian society was once again in chaos.

Alberto Fujimori was elected president and came into office in July 1990. He immediately took measures to quell hyperinflation. He ended subsidies to public sector enterprises, and liberalized foreign exchange markets and foreign trade. Price controls in the private sector were relaxed, and minimum wages were raised. He also undertook a currency reform. In 1991, the old currency, the *inti* – a new currency since 1985 – was replaced by *nuevo sol* at a rate of 1 million to 1. Loans from the International Monetary Fund were arranged for Peru in 1991.

CPI inflation steadily decelerated in Peru after Fujimori's stabilization and reform programs. From 409 percent in 1991, it fell to 11.1 percent in 1995, when the Peruvian economy was on a recovery and growth path. Somewhat ironically, the success of Peruvian stabilization did not benefit Fujimori enough to protect him from misfortune in the highly charged Peruvian political scene in later years, again suggesting that old societal wounds had not entirely healed.

Zaïre (Congo) and Angola: hyperinflations in failing states

Many African states resembled Latin American countries in their pursuit of post-colonial development starting in the 1960s. Soon after independence, most African countries either were ruled by a dictatorial regime that replaced the earlier colonial civil government, or various factions or tribes in the country fell into endless internal conflicts. Zaïre (Congo) exemplifies the former and Angola the latter. Both countries experienced hyperinflation in the 1990s.

Zaïre (Congo) in the 1990s: hyperinflations amidst power struggle

Zaïre (Congo) had three episodes of hyperinflation in terms of conventional criteria: the first occurred from October 1991 to September 1992, when monthly CPI inflation reached 114 percent in November 1991; the second occurred from November 1993 to September 1994, with monthly CPI inflation of 250 percent in November 1993; and the third occurred in August 1998, with monthly CPI inflation of 82.4 percent in that month – by this time (1998), the country's name had been changed to the Democratic Republic of Congo.[58] In annual terms, 1994 was the year with the highest inflation: 23,773 percent (Figure 6.6).

Zaïre between 1965 and 1996 was ruled by the autocracy of Mobutu Sésé Seko, who had politically sided with the West during the Cold War period and received considerable financial aid from Bretton-Woods institutions. Extremely rich in natural resources, the country became a kleptocracy under Mobutu's rule and had no stable economic activity other than mineral exports. Copper was a staple export for Zaïre, but its price fluctuated wildly in the world market. However, Zaïre's government "treated the peaks as if they were permanent and the troughs as temporary aberrations."[59] Mobutu's regime constantly ran budget deficits that could be assuaged only by sudden price surges in the international mineral markets.

By the later 1980s, the International Monetary Fund deemed Zaïre ineligible for any new credit, and the country ceased to have access to international finance. As

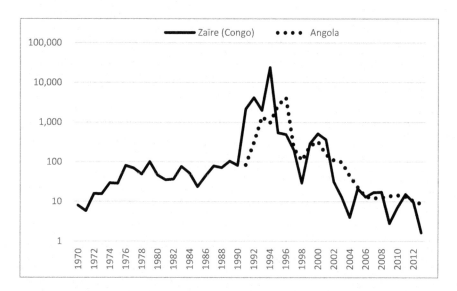

Figure 6.6 CPI inflation rate, percentage, log scale, Zaïre (Congo) and Angola, 1970–2000[60]

the Cold War approached an end, the political significance of an alliance with the West had diminished. Domestic insurgence emerged and gathered force against Mobutu, who found himself increasingly short of resources to suppress rebellions. Between 1991 and 1993, exports from Zaïre were halved in volume, and it is likely that revenue to the government fell by a similar proportion, if not more.

Even during the 1970s and 1980s, when Zaïre had access to international finance, Zaïre's government habitually printed money to finance budget deficits, as there was no securities market at all in the country. As the domestic political situation worsened starting in the early 1990s, the use of inflationary policy became virtually the only means left to the government to finance its operations. As a result, hyperinflation was inevitable.

In 1993, Zaïre's government introduced a new currency, the new *zaïre*, to replace the old *zaïre*, which was in use from 1967, at a rate of 1 to 3 million. Tight controls were imposed on all foreign exchange transactions in order to support the official exchange rate of 3 new *zaïre* to a dollar. By the end of 1994, the official rate had been devalued to more than 1,000 new *zaïre* to a dollar, while the parallel-market (a euphemism for the black market) rate was at more than 3,000 new *zaïre* to the dollar.[61]

The new regime that replaced Mobutu's in 1997 faced a devastated economy and a deeply divided society, and it was soon caught up in another major conflict – a civil war as much as an external war – which was the so-called "the Second Congo War" or "Africa's World War." A few months after yet another new currency, the *Congolese franc*, replaced the new *zaïre* at a rate of 1 to 100,000, the *Congolese franc* itself became a rapidly devaluing currency. As shown in Figure 6.6, CPI inflation once again began to escalate starting in 1998, reaching 514 percent in 2000. High inflation and devaluation were halted in the early 2000s when peace was restored in the Democratic Republic of Congo with help from the international community. Compared to the catastrophic loss of millions of lives during the Second Congo War,[62] hyperinflation in the Democratic Republic of Congo seems a minor tragedy.

Angola in the 1990s: hyperinflations in civil wars after the end of the Cold War

Largely as Zaïre (Congo)'s southern neighbor,[63] Angola gained independence from Portugal in 1975. From the beginning, the country was engulfed in civil war, with each of several Angolan political factions receiving aid from the world's major powers. All of them issued currency notes in separately controlled areas, which were all called *kwanza*. A nominal unification arrived toward the end of the 1980s, when Angola became the 152nd member state of the International Monetary Fund. Although rich in oil and other mineral reserves, the Angolan economy had never been well-structured, and the government's revenue base had faltered from time to time.

As in some Latin American countries, a politically weak coalition government tried various gimmicks in terms of currency reform. A *novo kwanza* was issued in 1990 to replace the earlier *kwanza*, for which the majority of old *kwanza* notes had to be exchanged for government bonds, although the conversion rate between the new and old *kwanza* was 1 to 1. In 1995, another new currency was introduced, known as the *kwanza reajustado* (readjusted *kwanza*), which replaced the previous *kwanza* at a rate of 1 to 1,000. A year later, CPI inflation peaked in the country, reaching 4,145 percent annually or 84.1 percent monthly in May. In 1999, the name of the currency was changed back to *kwanza*, which replaced the *kwanza reajustado* at a rate of 1 to 1,000,000.

The first episode of hyperinflation occurred in Angola after the end of the Cold War from the late 1980s. CPI inflation was 83.6 percent in 1991, more or less a "moderate" one in Sub-Saharan Africa. It climbed to 299 percent in 1992 and further escalated to 1,379 percent in 1993. The country's first multiparty elections were held in 1992, and they were declared "free and fair" by United Nations observers.[64] But this could not stop the country from sliding into a full-blown armed conflict between two major rivalry parties, at a scale far larger than their earlier fights during the Cold War period. Superpower support had elapsed, and revenue from oil production and export was either disrupted by domestic conflicts or dimmed due to falling prices in international oil markets. Running on currency issues appeared to be the most manageable way to finance Angola's government budget, which was heavily spent on military items. An estimate shows that during the second half of the 1990s, defense accounted for more than one-third of the country's GDP on average.[65]

A temporal cooling down in domestic conflicts that was largely prompted by efforts made in the international community helped ease the momentum of inflation. CPI inflation decelerated to 949 percent in 1994. When political tensions resumed and intensified in the following two years, inflation once again jumped. It culminated at 4,145 percent in 1996, when the government believed it was under threats of renewed fighting. The pattern was repeated in the following years until 2002 when the leader of the rivalry force was killed and his party agreed to cease-fire and start of political reconciliation. CPI inflation was 325 percent in 2000, a triple of 1998's 107 percent, but down to 153 percent in 2001 and 109 percent in 2002. From 2003 on, CPI inflation in Angola decelerated into double digits, and was not above 20 percent since 2006.

Angolan stabilization from the early 2000s also benefited enormously from rising oil prices in international markets. Before the end of the 1990s, petroleum oil already became the country's most important sector in the economy. By 1999, the oil sector had accounted for 41 percent of Angola's GDP and contributed over 80 percent of revenue to the Angolan government.[66] In fact, about 90 percent of total exports from Angola were crude oil, and the level remained basically unchanged for decades since the late 1970s. Large foreign firms, including ones from China since the early 2000s, came to Angola and helped make her become an important oil exporter in world market.

Yet, overreliance on the oil sector had also complicated the issue of stabilization. It is because not only would oil prices never be stable in international markets, but more importantly the non-oil sector of the Angolan economy has lagged behind considerably, which could eventually become a drain on government finance. For this reason, an IMF research report held that the stabilization in post-2000 Angola was "fragile."[67]

In wrapping up, one may find an interesting geographic pattern of the episodes of hyperinflation highlighted in this chapter: six in Latin America, two in Africa, and two in Asia. The Latin American and African ones all satisfied the most rigorous criterion of hyperinflation, but the two Asian countries – Israel and Turkey in the 1980s or 1990s – did not actually meet the definition strictly. The pattern can apply further in a broader perspective. A research paper published in 1998 surveyed the worldwide incidence of high inflation in 1960–94 and had a list of 31 countries: 14 in Latin America, nine in Africa, four in Asia (with Bangladesh and Indonesia included), and four in Europe (Iceland, Poland, Romania, and Yugoslavia, obviously not counting the successor countries of the Soviet Union).[68] The picture of geography is clear: Latin America and Africa were where hyperinflation or high inflation most frequently occurred, mainly in the period from the 1970s to the first half of the 1990s.

In retrospect, two things had significantly distinguished Latin America and Africa from others: dollarization and the shadow economy. In a sense, dollarization and the shadow economy were everywhere in the world. But they were most conspicuous in many Latin American and African countries in the 1980s and 1990s, if not earlier. Dollarization, measured in the proportion of deposits in foreign currencies in the total domestic money supply, had been as high as over one-half in several Latin American countries in the 1990s.[69] An estimate shows, on average, the size of the shadow economy as a share of GDP was 41.1 percent in Latin America and 41.4 percent in Africa, in the period from 1999–2007. Meanwhile, it was 30 percent in Asia and 17.7 percent in OECD countries – mainly industrial economies.[70]

Dollarization and the shadow economy can be both cause of and effect of hyperinflation or high inflation. Their increased presence in an economy would make the government less able to collect revenue and therefore more prepared to resort to inflationary means of finance, regardless of political circumstances. On the other hand, a rising inflation or hyperinflation would prompt people into dollarization and the shadow economy in order to avoid exploitation attempted by the government. Dollarization and the shadow economy were also significant factors in the tidal wave of hyperinflation in transitional economies in the early 1990s and in the very few countries that fell into hyperinflation in the early twenty-first century.

Notes

1 Cited by Dornbusch, Sturzenegger, and Wolf (1990, p. 18).
2 Capie (1986, p. 156).
3 Fischer, Sahay, and Végh, p. 837.
4 Fischer, Sahay, and Végh, Table 3B, p. 843.
5 Maddison (1982, Table 6.1, p. 126).
6 Maddison (2001, Table 3.1a, p. 116).

7 A survey of inflation-adjusted crude oil prices since 1974 shows that there have been frequent fluctuations and cyclical patterns during those 40 years: a rise in the 1970s; a fall in the 1980s; a large and short rise with fallbacks in the early 1990s, followed by a large decline in the late 1990s; an almost chronic rise from the turn of the twenty-first century, occasionally interrupted by recessions and financial crises, most notably in 2008–09 and 2014–15. In real terms, oil prices in March 2015 stood virtually same as they were in January 1974. Baumeister and Kilian, Figure 1, p. 141.
8 Friedman (1974, p. 17).
9 Friedman (1974, p. 19).
10 Hanke and Krus, Table 30.1, pp. 372–3.
11 Yergin and Stanislaw, p. 231.
12 All the figures are from the International Monetary Fund, *World Economic Outlook Database*, which is available at www.imf.org/external/pubs/ft/weo/2016/02/weodata/index.aspx. Same thereafter unless otherwise stated.
13 Paarlberg, Tables 2.17 and 2.19, p. 98 and p. 101. The raw data of the CPI has a base in 1975 (1975 = 1), and in the figure presented here, it is renumbered as of December 1981 = 10.
14 Paarlberg, p. 99.
15 Sachs, p. 279.
16 Reinhart and Rogoff, Table 7.4, pp. 90–1. Argentina and Mexico did the same in the same year, and Peru in 1985.
17 Paarlberg, p. 100.
18 Sachs (1987, p. 280).
19 Sachs (1987, p. 281).
20 This is a point that has been emphasized in Sachs (1987).
21 Kaufmann, Mastruzzi, and Zavaleta.
22 In fact, from the World Bank's online database of the World Development Indicators (http://data.worldbank.org/indicator), we see that Brazil's GNI per capita ($4,080) was higher than Portugal's (3,230) in 1982 – the earliest year in which the data is available, and Argentina's $2,070 was much higher than Spain's $1,310 in 1971.
23 Yergin and Stanislaw, p. 242.
24 Hanke and Krus, Table 30.1, p. 372–3.
25 World Bank, *World Development Indicator Database*, available at http://data.world bank.org/ (FP.CPI.TOTL.ZG). The earliest year for Argentina is 1980.
26 Brazil started the practice of indexation in 1964, and since then many nominal values – wages, interest rates, rents, insurance, and exchange rates, etc. – had been quantitatively linked to price inflation, which was often called "monetary correction" by the government. In the eyes of economists, the practice is nothing but a way "to institutionalize a rising price level" (Paarlberg, pp. 103, 109).
27 An estimate by IMF staff indicated that "the operational fiscal deficit" – that excludes debt service – was about 5 percent of Brazil's GDP in 1987, and it was necessary for it to be brought down to 2 percent in 1988 for the sake of stabilization (Boughton, 2001, p. 460).
28 Paarlberg, pp. 111–12.
29 Kigue, p. 972.
30 Paarlberg, p. 117.
31 Boughton (2001, pp. 520–4).
32 Boughton (2001, pp. 522–3).
33 Larraín and Selowsky (1991, pp. 7–8).
34 Sachs and Williamson, Table 4, p. 533.
35 Sachs and Williamson, pp. 525–6.
36 Bresser-Pereira, p. 1035.
37 Cardoso, p. 176.
38 Cardoso, p. 180.
39 Kaminsky, Mati, and Choueiri.

40 World Bank, *World Development Indicator Database*, available at http://data.worldbank. org/ (FP.CPI.TOTL.ZG). The earliest year for Argentina is 1980.
41 Blejer and Liviatan.
42 Raw data from the International Monetary Fund, *World Economic Outlook Database*, available at www.imf.org/external/pubs/ft/weo/2016/02/weodata/index.aspx.
43 The budget deficits as a proportion of GNP in Israel were estimated at 14.1 percent in the period from the second quarter of 1979 to the first quarter of 1983, and rose to 17 percent in the period from March 1983 – February 1985 (Fischer, 1987, Table 1, p. 276). As reported by *The Washington Post*, a high-level Israeli delegation visited the United States seeking economic aid in September 1984, but the White House would not grant the requests unless Israeli government finance was restructured properly (Rowen).
44 Garber (p. 96) notes that the war in Lebanon cost Israel $3.5 billion, 5.6 percent of GDP, and "it yielded few benefits."
45 Halevi.
46 Rowen.
47 Fischer (1987, p. 277).
48 Bruno (1989, Table 3, p. 37).
49 Easterly, p. 219. Nevertheless, the U.S. aid is believed one of vital factors to the success of Israeli stabilization (Garber, pp. 96–8).
50 Monthly data of CPI in Chile are available at www.inflation.eu/inflation-rates/chile/ historic-inflation/cpi-inflation-chile-1974.aspx (accessed on January 28, 2017).
51 World Bank, *World Development Indicator Database*, available at http://data.world-bank.org/ (FP.CPI.TOTL.ZG).
52 Ocampo, p. 336.
53 Ocampo, Table 10.8, p. 338.
54 Ocampo, Table 10.1, p. 335.
55 The IMF provided financial assistance under the category of "Enhanced Structural Adjustment Facility" (ESAF) and debt relief under the Highly Indebted Poor Countries Initiative from 1990 (Boughton, 2012, p. 232).
56 The World Bank (1989).
57 The World Bank, p. ix, (1989).
58 Hanke and Krus, Table 30.1, pp. 372–3. For monthly data before 1997, see also Beaugrand.
59 Boughton (2001, p. 805).
60 World Bank, *World Development Indicator Database*, available at http://data.worldbank. org/ (FP.CPI.TOTL.ZG). The Republic of Zaïre was renamed as the Democratic Republic of Congo in 1998.
61 Beaugrand, Table 1, p. 32.
62 As estimate gives a figure of death toll at 3.5 million in the war, of which 90 percent were due to "collateral effects" of the war (Prunier, p. 278 and the source cited there).
63 Angola has an exclave province north to Zaïre.
64 SAIIA (2001, p. 24).
65 SAIIA (2001, Table 2, p. 31). The highest figure is 41 percent in 1999, and lowest 27.2 percent in 1998.
66 Gasha and Pastor (2004, Table 1, p. 25).
67 Gasha and Pastor (2004).
68 Bruno and Easterly, Table 7, pp. 22–4.
69 Cohen, Table 5.12, p. 112.
70 Schneider and Enste, Table 4.4, p. 45.

7   A wave of hyperinflation
in transition economies

"General Secretary Gorbachev, if you seek peace, if you seek prosperity for the
Soviet Union and Eastern Europe, if you seek liberalization, come here to this
gate. Mr. Gorbachev, open this gate. Mr. Gorbachev, tear down this Wall!"
Excerpt from U.S. President Ronald Reagan's speech at
the Brandenburg Gate, Berlin, 12 June 1987

"The destruction – or collapse – of a world system is bound to be cataclysmic,
and the collapse of the world socialist system which is playing itself out at present
across twenty eight countries is no exception. . . . That this collapse has occurred
without a major war has tended to obscure what is happening: the political, social,
and economic relations which governed these societies are all being simultaneously changed in a fundamental way."
Jacek Rostowski, *Macroeconomic Instability in
Post-communist Countries*, 1998

After the dissolution of the Austro-Hungarian Empire in 1918, two successor
states remained – Austria and Hungary. These two states endured brief and
"moderate" hyperinflation in the early 1920s. Seventy years later, in nearby
regions, the demise of the Union of Socialist Soviet Republics (USSR) at the end
of 1991 and of the Socialist Federal Republic of Yugoslavia in the same year was
immediately followed by hyperinflation in all 15 successor states in the former,
and at least four major successor states in the latter. In the case of Yugoslavia,
the level of hyperinflation was astonishing: 313,000,000 percent in January 1994
(which is 64.6 percent per day in that month). Hyperinflation of this magnitude
can be compared only to that endured by Hungary in the 1940s or Zimbabwe in
the 2000s.[1] In the case of the former USSR states, several newly independent
nations withstood periods of hyperinflation that lasted more than three years, and
one country experienced cumulative inflation of 3,050,546.8-fold in ten years (see
Table 7.1 below). The vast number of countries struggling with hyperinflation
in the 1990s, and the length of time that hyperinflation lasted in some of these
countries, was unprecedented to that point in history.

At about the same time, hyperinflation also occurred in several other Eastern
European countries: Poland, Bulgaria, and Romania. These nations once belonged

to the Socialist Bloc, and they were beginning a political and economic transition to a market-based economic system. The collapse of the Soviet Union and Federal Yugoslavia demonstrated how a sudden, unexpected political, economic, and monetary disintegration could instigate inflation. Relatedly, the experience of Poland, Bulgaria, and Romania suggested that the root cause of hyperinflation was to be found in the unsound economic structure (a centrally planned system) of these countries; it also made clear that sound policy decisions and institution building were critical to establishing macroeconomic stability during a transition period. Even if a socialist state strived to conduct reforms by means of a so-called "gradual approach," the road to stable transition and growth would never be easy, as highlighted by Chinese and Vietnamese undertakings in East Asia from the early 1980s.

Repressed inflation in planned economies

Following the Soviet model, many countries in Eastern Europe and East Asia established centralized planning systems in the early 1950s. The socialist economic system adopted in these countries went beyond the Latin American model of import substitution industrialization; indeed, socialism in Eastern European and East Asian countries exerted a virtually all-inclusive command and control over the economy. Such a socialist economic system would necessarily include the following five elements:

- State ownership was dominant in all industries, or collective ownership in the case of Yugoslavia in the 1970s
- Central planning agencies had supreme power to dictate production and distribution of all "important" materials
- The top priority of industrial development was defense-related products and agendas
- Domestic commerce and foreign trade were under tight controls, with prices and highly regulated foreign exchange rates
- The basic well-being of factory workers and urban residents was largely preserved by the public supply of goods and services at fairly low rates, with implicit subsidies from the government.

Because this kind of system could mobilize tremendously large amounts of resources, many socialist countries were able to achieve high levels of industrial growth, especially in heavy industry. Yet, socialist industrialization was fundamentally biased, and even distorted, in that it devoted enormous amounts of resources to military-related purposes; therefore, it became largely disconnected from the needs and demands of the people. Despite the industrial capacity that these countries built, the industrial products of many socialist countries were not competitive on the international market. Industrial products were not the main exports of these countries; instead, they mostly exported agricultural goods or primary mineral raw materials.

Apart from the issue of incentive – a problem that was largely a result of the fact that decision-making of production and distribution was not primarily based on price signals, one of the most serious and persistent problems with the central planning system was the widespread shortage of certain consumer goods. The supply of popular consumer goods constantly lagged behind the demand for them. These shortages may have been caused by a flawed pricing policy that did not yield enough profits for factories that produced the goods, or it may have been an issue of the limited and/or inflexible supply of intermediate inputs, which occurred when planning agencies directed such inputs for alternative usage. By and large, the needs and demands of the people were left unattended or were supplied by inferior substitute products.

The situation was first summarized and theorized by the Hungarian economist János Kornai in his essay, *Economics of Shortage*, published in 1980. He drew his observations mainly from Eastern European countries, and his thoughts are widely believed to also be applicable to the Soviet Union and other socialist economies like China throughout the 1970s and early 1980s.

A macroeconomic implication of "the shortage economy" was the emergence of chronic inflation: aggregate demand for normal goods persistently exceeding aggregate supply of normal goods. Yet, in the heyday of the socialist planning system, the problem of inflation was not so conspicuous because of the stringent price controls and ration schemes that were in place. Rather, it was a problem of "disguised inflation": a general price level such as a retail price index or consumer price index would remain flat over time, giving the impression of zero inflation, while pent-up demand for consumer goods and related products accumulated in the economy.

Meanwhile, concentrated development in heavy industry did not generate sufficient revenue for the government, partly because the sector lacked international competitiveness and was unable to adequately support domestic production of consumer goods. Yet, heavy industry continued to require disproportionally large resource inputs and thus became a considerable strain on government finances. Many state-owned enterprises sustained a "soft budget constraint syndrome" as they became accustomed to the paternalistic role of the state.[2] To overcome budgetary difficulties, socialist governments increasingly resorted to monetary means, in addition to depending on their "orthodox" methods of planned pricing and resource distribution.

It is ironic that money was what socialist governments aimed to eliminate, according to their initial philosophies; yet these governments actually expanded their use of money in the later stages of pursuing economic stability. When prices were kept unchanged, increases in money (the issuance of currency) resulted in an increase in the purchase of goods and services by the issuer of the money (the government).

Researchers of transition economies have found considerable evidence of "repressed inflation" in the 1980s, as measured by various economic methodologies. Repressed inflation in annual percentage terms for the later years of the 1980s was 25.7 percent in Soviet Union, 12 percent in Yugoslavia, 13.6 percent in Poland, 16.8 percent in Romania, and 18 percent in Bulgaria.[3] The essence of repressed inflation is the growth of the money supply exceeding output growth and price inflation during a given period in which prices are under the government's deliberate control for fiscal purposes. Technically, this pattern of money growth may be interpreted as an increase in the balance of real money or a slowdown in the velocity of money circulation. However, its deeper meaning in the case of a socialist economic system was the increased use of monetary means to support the economy and a shift in resources to the government. Scholars regard this situation as "monetary overhang."[4] In a way, "shortages," "excess demand," "monetary overhang," and "repressed inflation" all share common elements.[5]

In Yugoslavia between 1957 and 1965, the growth of money as measured in cash in circulation plus demand deposits, averaged 18.9 percent per year. During the same period, output growth – as measured by means of the "net material product" – was 7.3 percent per year, and price inflation was 7.3 percent (of an unweighted average of wholesale prices and retail prices).[6] The product of the latter two items was 15.1 percent per year, which means that 3.8 percent of the monetary growth of each year could not be explained by output growth or price inflation. It is likely that this increase in the money stock was a result of the Yugoslav government's use of monetary means for fiscal purposes.

One significant danger of repressed inflation is that when price controls are repelled or become ineffective, inflation will soon surface and people's inflation expectations are easily intensified, especially when there have been shortages in the economy.

Peoples in various socialist economic systems became increasingly dissatisfied with the state of affairs as they came to learn about economic progress in the West. With the beginning of the *détente* in the 1970s, several Eastern European countries – notably Yugoslavia and Poland – started to develop economic relations with industrial countries. They began to borrow from abroad, bilaterally and multilaterally. Like many developing countries, they did not expect the international financial markets to become volatile after the collapse of the Bretton-Woods System. They also were not fully aware that their economies would be unlikely to sustain the rising costs of external financing due to effects of interest rate hikes by the Federal Reserve of the United States in the early 1980s.

The Soviet Union was fortunate to develop an oil industry in the 1970s, from which she profited enormously from surges in international oil prices before the mid-1980s. Yegor Gaidar, a Russian economist and briefly prime minister under President Boris Yeltsin in the early 1990s, remarked in retrospect:

> the hard currency from oil exports stopped the growing food supply crisis, increased the import of equipment and consumer goods, ensured a financial base for the arms race and the achievement of nuclear parity with the United States, and permitted the realization of such risky foreign-policy actions as the war in Afghanistan.[7]

Soviet authorities, like many other third world politicians, "were counting on oil prices to remain high. The Soviet leadership clearly did not think about what would happen if prices fell."[8] In the later 1980s, world oil prices dropped to new lows, and the war in Afghanistan consumed tremendous amounts of Soviet resources. By the end of the 1980s, the Soviet Union's economy had fallen into significant distress.

With the fall of the Berlin Wall at the end of 1989, the forces that used to support the cohesion of the Soviet Union began to crumble from the inside. Political unrest started to shake the foundations of traditional price controls, and inflation became increasingly difficult to repress. The progression from the unmasking of inflation to the onset of hyperinflation would play out over the course of the disintegration of the Soviet Union from 1990 to 1992.

Hyperinflations in Russia and other USSR successor states

Data about CPI inflation in all 15 successor republics after the dissolution of the Soviet Union is summarized in Table 7.1. This data cannot be found in a single source, partly reflecting the difficulty of collecting and compiling statistical information on a regular and consistent basis for these countries during this period.

What is astonishing is that all 15 successor republics endured hyperinflation after the end of the USSR, with no exception. The demise of the Soviet Union was "officially" confirmed in December 1991, and hyperinflation spread over every successor republic in January 1992. Table 7.1 shows different months for several of the republics, but these are the highest rates of monthly inflation, demonstrating that these republics had an even higher level of inflation than their own ones in January 1992.

After January 1992, hyperinflation started to diverge among individual states with regard to the highest levels they reached and the timing by which the peaks arrived. All successor states experienced a common shock in January 1992, but the later evolution of inflation in these states was largely shaped by national political and economic events. Notably, as shown in Table 7.1, three states – Ukraine in the west, and Armenia and Georgia in the Caucasus – had annual inflation of more than 10,000 percent in 1993 or 1994, and Turkmenistan in Central Asia had an accumulative inflation of 3,050,546.8-fold between 1989 and 1998. Meanwhile, three small states in the Baltic – Estonia, Latvia, and Lithuania – had the most moderate hyperinflation among the fifteen republics. Their hyperinflation also did not last as long.

Russia was the sometimes contentious leader of the newly formed and loosely structured Commonwealth of Independent States (CIS, which included all former USSR states except the Baltics), and needless to say the largest economy among all of them. Russia's policies exerted a great impact on the other states, especially in the ruble zone – a currency union that was initially attempted alongside the CIS and ultimately failed in chaos. Stabilization and reform in the 15 states was imprinted with each state's distinctive national features.

Eruption of inflation in the Baltic States

Lenin has been quoted by Soviet communists to support their argument that it is possible for proletariat revolution "to break the front of imperialism at its weakest

Table 7.1 CPI inflation in Russia and other USSR successor republics

		Monthly inflation[1]		Annual inflation[2]		Accumulative inflation to 1998 (1989 = 1)[3]
		Highest rate (%)	Month	Highest rate (%)	Year	
The Western	Russia	245	Jan. 1992	2,506	1992	11,050
	Ukraine	285	Jan. 1992	10,155	1993	205,676.5
	Belarus	159	Jan. 1992	1,996	1993	319,052
	Moldova	240	Jan. 1992	2,198	1992	2,267.6
The Baltic	Estonia	87.2	Jan. 1992	953.5	1992	179.7
	Latvia	64.4	Jan. 1992	958.6	1992	110.9
	Lithuania	54	Jan. 1992	1,161	1992	433.9
Caucasus	Armenia	438	Nov. 1993	10,896	1993	73,086.4
	Azerbaijan	118	Jan. 1992	1,788	1994	17,489.7
	Georgia	211	Sep. 1994	7,488	1993	328,443.3
Central Asian	Kazakhstan	141	Jan. 1992	2,984	1992	50,784.8
	Kyrgyzstan	157	Jan. 1992	1,363	1993	2,620.6
	Tajikistan	65	Nov. 1995	7,344	1993	297,937.2
	Turkmenistan	439	Nov. 1993	9,750	1993	3,050,546.8
	Uzbekistan	118	Jan. 1992	1,281	1994	28,448.8

Notes of data sources:

[1] Monthly data from Hanke and Krus, Table 30.1, p. 372–3;

[2] Åslund, 2002, Table 6.1, p. 201;

[3] Ivan Katchanovski, Divergence in Growth in Post-Communist Countries, *Journal of Public Policy*, Vol. 20, Issue 01, April 2000, pp. 55–81.

point."[9] In no way is it appropriate to equate hyperinflation with revolution, but the two do share a common trend in mass movements that come from the bottom of a society. If Lenin's words have a grain of truth, it is applicable in the case of the resurgence of hyperinflation in aftermath of the Soviet Union some 70 years later.

The rise of inflation in a dissolving Soviet Union first occurred in three Baltic Republics – Estonia, Latvia, and Lithuania – beginning in 1989. They were the smallest successor states but not necessarily the weakest. In fact, they were the strongest and earliest in their declaration of independence from the Soviet Union after the fall of the Berlin Wall. *De facto* independence was achieved in these three states at the end of 1990 and early 1991, one year ahead of the other successor states.

An immediate economic consequence of the independence movement was that price controls inherited from the Soviet Union increasingly weakened and became ineffective or irrelevant. At times, the peoples of the three Baltic States clashed with Moscow, which tried at one point to impose a trade boycott on them. This caused inflation to surface in the three states.

As shown in Table 7.2, the average inflation rate in the Baltic Three was 4.3 percent in 1989, much higher than that of 0.7 percent in the other 12 republics. In that year, the inflation rate was 2.2 percent in Russia, and 0 percent in seven other states – Moldova, Armenia, Azerbaijan, Georgia, Kazakhstan, Kyrgyzstan, and Tajikistan. In the years from 1990 to 1992, inflation in both the Baltic Three and all other republics accelerated, with the level of inflation in the former being higher than that in the latter. The difference in inflation levels between these two groups had been narrowing in these three years, indicating that the latter group was actually "catching up" with the former in the process of rising inflation.

When the individual former Soviet republics gained political sovereignty at the end of 1991, a currency union remained in effect among them. Within a common currency area, when prices rise in a region, this will have the demand-switch effect of driving up prices in other, neighboring regions, and it will also have the effect of creating payment deficits in regions where prices are higher than others. A key factor in how inflation behaves in a common currency area is how money supply is controlled by the center, which was Moscow in the immediate aftermath of the demise of the Soviet Union. Apparently, "regional" centers of erstwhile central

Table 7.2 Annual CPI inflation in the Baltic Three and the rest of the USSR successor republics, percentage, 1989–93[10]

	1989	1990	1991	1992	1993
Estonia	6.1	23.1	210.6	1,069	89
Latvia	4.7	10.5	124.4	951.2	109
Lithuania	2.1	8.4	224.7	1,020.3	390.2
Average of the three states	4.3	14.0	186.6	1,013.5	196.1
Average of all other 12 states	0.7	4.5	91.8	990.4	2,008.2
Memo: Russia	2.2	5.6	92.7	1,353	896

banking in individual USSR republics tried hard to act on their own in expanding the money supply and thus generated enormous complications in monetary control in the ruble zone during the process of political and monetary disintegration. Another important factor is how payment-deficit regions are able to meet their liabilities, and whether they have any additional financial resources available.

Moscow had actually substantially relaxed its money supply policy at the time the Soviet Union disbanded, not as a response to demands and requests from other republics, but rather as an accommodation of its own economic problems. Also, considerable foreign resources had flowed into the Baltics as they left the USSR, enabling them to bypass the problem of payment deficits. Together with other developments, the combined forces of inflation accelerated its increase, and a kind of domino effect overwhelmed the entire ruble zone in 1992.

The three Baltic States began the process of stabilization and reform in 1992, with varying degrees of success, but the other successor states – including Russia – were caught up in the trap of hyperinflation or were having difficulty sustaining stabilization and reform. Therefore, the pattern of inflation between the two groups was reversed in that year, as shown in Table 7.2.

Russia's economic woes and a surge of hyperinflation

Mikhail Gorbachev became the Soviet Union's top leader in 1985 and soon started a reform program known as *Perestroika*, which was aimed at reviving the Soviet economy by allowing enterprises some flexibility in arranging and adjusting their production and marketing plans to better meet demands. Enterprises were required to assume more responsibility over their finances, an effort that was meant to reduce their receipt of direct subsidies from the state if they were suffering financial losses. Meanwhile, the state retained the power to determine basic material flows and investment projects, with price controls and credit flows remaining in the hands of the Gosplan (Soviet planning agencies) and the Gosbank (the Soviet state bank, which had an extensive regional network and several affiliated special credit-providing agencies.)

Several sectors, mostly those involved in services and small-goods manufacturing, were tentatively opened to private business. Foreign trade controls were relaxed somewhat, and the establishment of Soviet joint ventures with sources of foreign equity became legally possible. As noted, *Perestroika*

> made some inroads in decentralization, but . . . left intact most of the fundamental elements of the Stalinist system – price controls, inconvertibility of the ruble, exclusion of private property ownership, and the government monopoly over most means of production.[11]

The Soviet economy did not emerge from stagnation in the second half of the 1980s, owing in part to falling oil prices in the world market and resource exhaustion due to the Soviet-Afghan war. Gorbachev's fight against widespread alcoholism in the country had some unintended consequences: alcohol production and consumption went into the shadow economy (also called "second economy") and government revenue from the production and sale of alcohol fell remarkably. Meanwhile, government subsidies to both state enterprises and consumers could not be reduced and even had to be increased rapidly as state enterprises suffered losses and consumers demanded compensation for low wages. As a result, Russia's budget deteriorated throughout the second half of the 1980s.

Gorbachev's Soviet Union was also marked by growing foreign debt. As revealed by a German official in his remembrance of German reunification, Soviet delegations insisted on a large sum of D-mark loans from Bonn as a "catalyst" for their consent to the process during intensive bilateral negotiations between the two sides in 1990.[12] By the end of 1991, the newly formed Russian Federation had inherited $66 billion in foreign debt, with just a few billion dollars in gold and foreign exchange reserves left in hand.[13]

Beginning in 1990, an implicit "war" on revenue and resources emerged between the republics as more cracks in the Soviet Union were perceived. Many republics began to withhold tax revenues or delay payments to Moscow. As documented in Gaidar's reflection in 2007,

> by the first half of 1991, before the August putsch, Russia got from the other republics only 22 percent of the planned deliveries of sugar, 30 percent of tea, 19 percent of cereals, and 22 percent of soap. All the republics, except Russia, introduced customs checks on their borders in order to limit the export of goods to neighbors, especially Russia. The customs restrictions worked only one way: bringing things into Russia was not allowed, bringing things in *from* Russia was.[14]

In his view, the expansion of the money supply in Russia was a natural result of its loss of revenue:

> the very modest capabilities of the Union to collect taxes fell to zero in the fall of 1991. The government got a small amount of money from some of the republics. But now they were closer to gifts than to taxes. And the amounts were incompatible with the needs of the Union budget. Financing of state expenditures came almost completely from Gosbank credits.[15]

Moreover, he believed that: "in monetary policy, the Union lost its monopoly, could not stop the republics' central banks from creating currency, and became one of many competitors offering a supply of money."[16]

It should be noted that Moscow did not lose its control over its monetary policy, or more precisely, over the supply of ruble notes, *until* June 1992 with respect to the Baltic Three, or *until* various later dates with respect to many other USSR successor states. In other words, the rise of inflation in Russia and elsewhere in the Union – except the Baltic Three – in 1991 was largely the result of policies made by decision makers in Moscow.

A Big Bang on ruble notes was conducted in January 1991, known as the "Pavlov Reform," which decreed the withdrawal of 50- and 100-ruble notes of certain issues from circulation. Those holding these notes were given three days, under certain limits, to spend or exchange in order to prevent loss. The publicly-stated purpose of this move was to mitigate the effect of large inflows of ruble notes from abroad on domestic inflation. The true intent of the decision remains mysterious as it was, and one may guess upon reflection that what had happened then is possibly that there were foreigners who bought large sums of ruble notes from Moscow by foreign exchange and were supposedly helping some of the "dissenting" republics, like the Baltic Three.

Also, from the beginning of 1991, Soviet authorities announced price hikes for many consumer goods several times a year. If large amounts of ruble notes had indeed flowed out of the Union in various ways in earlier years, price hikes would have a contrary effect: a higher price level in Russia would compel Russian ruble-holders to spend rubles in places where prices were lower or inflation was slower, meaning that more rubles would flow out of Russia and the demand for locally-produced goods would shrink. In any case, the "confiscation" of large-denomination ruble notes and the price hikes were contradicting policies to a certain extent. Whether the withdrawal of the ruble notes was an anti-inflation move could not be properly judged on its own.

Russia relaxed its monetary policy stance in 1991. As shown in Table 7.2, CPI inflation in Russia was 5.6 percent in 1990, higher than that in all of the other remaining USSR republics and only lower than that in the Baltic Three. The rate of 5.6 percent is a moderate level of inflation. Had Russia maintained a constrained money policy in 1991, inflation likely would not have increased. However, price inflation in Russia soared to 92.7 percent in 1991, which is again higher than the average of 91.8 percent for all remaining 12 republics including Russia, though below the level in the Baltic Three. In 1992, when the political entity of the Soviet Union had dissolved and only a faltering currency union remained, price inflation in Russia rose to a new height of 1,353 percent, once again higher than the average of 990.4 percent for the 12 republics including Russia.[17] The rising inflation and hyperinflation in Russia in 1991 and 1992 were undoubtedly accompanied by an expansionary money supply policy, which was complicated by the machinations in the ruble zone.

The dismantling of the ruble zone: a currency war in a currency zone?

The Baltic Three – and to some extent Ukraine as well – appeared to have decided to leave the ruble zone at the time that they departed politically from the Soviet Union in 1991. They wanted to sever all ties with the Soviet Union. The introduction of a new currency that replaced the Soviet ruble did not occur until May 1992 at the earliest in the Baltic Three; this timing was largely a technical matter that occurred in the process of their preparation for a "currency divorce."

Belarus, on the other hand, was among the earliest to introduce a new currency – this was actually a coupon scheme that was meant to work in parallel with existing Soviet rubles and began in May 1992. As a Russia-affiliated member of the Commonwealth of Independent States, Belarus's motivation for the currency change was based primarily on economics: to have, and to increase, the power to expand the money supply in addition to utilizing the existing Soviet ruble circulation and accessing a monetary supply from Russia. As indicated in Table 7.3, such policy moves in "currency reform" in Belarus did not deter hyperinflation at all.

There were a few other small or moderate-sized republics that introduced a new currency to replace Soviet rubles before Russia did so: Moldova, Azerbaijan, Georgia, and Kyrgyzstan. Unlike the Baltic Three, these were members of the CIS and had remained closely tied – of course with varying degrees of cooperation – to Russia in monetary affairs. They might be regarded as "elusive" or "peripheral" members of the ruble zone until the currency umbrella burnt out almost completely in later 1993.

Table 7.3 Timeline of introduction of new currency in USSR successor republics

	Date	Name of new, national currency	Observation on change in inflation following the currency change
Latvia	May 1992 Mar 1993	Latvian ruble Lats	Continued hyperinflation after the Latvian ruble; Disinflation after the lats.
Lithuania	May 1992 Jun 1993	Talonas Litas	Continued hyperinflation after the talonas; Disinflation after the litas.
Belarus	May 1992 Sep 1993	Belarussian ruble Belarussian ruble	Rising hyperinflation after the Belarussian ruble; Continued hyperinflation after the second.
Estonia	Jun 1992	Kroon	Disinflation after the kroon.
Moldova	Jun 1992 Jul 1993	Moldovan coupon; Leu	Disinflation after the Moldovan coupon; Further disinflation after the leu.
Azerbaijan	Aug 1992	Manat	Rising hyperinflation after the manat.
Ukraine	Nov 1992 Sep 1996	Karbovanets; Hryvnia	Rising hyperinflation after the Karbovanets; Disinflation after the Hryvnia.
Georgia	Apr 1993	Lari	Rising hyperinflation after the lari.
Kyrgyzstan	May 1993	Som	Disinflation after the som.
Russia	Jul 1993	Russian ruble	Moderate disinflation after the Russian ruble.
Armenia	Nov 1993	Dram	Rising hyperinflation after the dram.
Kazakhstan	Nov 1993	Tenge	Rising hyperinflation after the tenge.
Turkmenistan	Nov 1993	Manat	Continued hyperinflation after the manat.
Uzbekistan	Nov 1993 Jul 1994	Sum coupon; Sum	Continued hyperinflation after the sum coupon; Disinflation after the sum.
Tajikistan	May 1995	Tajik ruble	Continued hyperinflation after the Tajik ruble.

Note: The information about the dates of the introduction of national currencies is from Odling-Smee and Pastor, Table 7.1, p. 10, with a certain rearrangement of the sequence to reflect the timing of the first changes made in currencies; the observation is based on annual changes in CPI rates in the next year following the currency change, with raw data from Denizer (the same as for Table 7.2) for the years until 1995 and the IMF, *World Economic Outlook Database*, for the years from 1996.

Monetary authorities in all of these states – including Russia – sharply expanded credit in rubles during the first half of 1992. A kind of race in the credit expansion in rubles occurred, which has been identified as a "free rider" problem in the ruble zone: faster growth in credit in rubles would benefit the local economy without causing the usual suffering generated by an external deficit, as the deficit itself was essentially a ruble liability that might be covered by further increases in ruble liabilities. Russia made certain changes to an earlier inter-republic payments system in July 1992, but it remained supportive of the system until all of the other republics had exited from the ruble zone.[18]

With four significant Central Asian republics – Kazakhstan, Turkmenistan, Uzbekistan, and Tajikistan and one in the Caucasus – Armenia – remaining in the ruble zone, Russia conducted a unilateral currency reform in July 1993 that retired all Soviet rubles with short notice. Ruble-note holders in these republics were badly hurt, as they stood little chance of redeeming their notes in full. Decisions were quickly made in all of the republics to issue their own national currencies and outlaw all Soviet/Russian ruble notes in November 1993. Tajikistan's move was delayed by civil wars in the country; it was pushed through in 1995 and thereby symbolized the final end of the ruble zone. Notably, as indicated in Table 7.3, in each of the last five ruble-using republics outside of Russia, none of the emerging currency reforms was followed by disinflation. This clearly suggests that the currency reforms in these states were more of a declaration of currency independence than part of a stabilization program.

When the Soviet Union dissolved and the Commonwealth of Independent States formed at the turn of 1992, specialists from the International Monetary Fund travelled to many of the CIS states to offer policy advice, despite the fact that none of these states were yet members of the IMF.[19] IMF specialists showed the pros and cons of a monetary union, and in particular highlighted the economic benefits of remaining in a currency union when a state had a concentrated trade relations with other members of the same union. The latter point was relevant for the CIS states, because their trade with Russia and other CIS states accounted for as much as 90 percent of their total foreign trade.[20] Also, for a new currency system to work, it usually required certain conditions that need time to nurture. The IMF position seemed to be supportive of CIS states remaining in the ruble zone. The European Union, an influential outsider in the matter of monetary integration, had also voiced a sympathetic view toward the ruble zone as a way of maintaining a single currency.[21] The IMF's position had been blamed for delaying the departure of several CIS states from the ruble zone, which took place belatedly and was apparently at a cost.[22]

The importance of the IMF view was partly reflective of its role as a credit provider to almost every CIS state during the crucial years of transition. Russia was the first and largest recipient of IMF loans starting in August 1992, followed by the others, with Tajikistan the last to receive loans, in May 1996.[23] IMF aid to Turkmenistan occurred later than for the other CIS states, because the Turkmen economy was highly unstable, and her authorities were not prepared for any significant stabilization program. At this time, it was generally assumed that a country would listen seriously to policy suggestions from the IMF when receiving loans from it.

A more important issue concerning the feasibility of the ruble zone was how an interstate monetary arrangement should be made and implemented, with member states sharing rights commensurate with their obligations in a coherent and transparent way. The flow of events at that time proved that the necessary conditions were not met for the ruble zone.

Right from the start, the Russian Federation formed her own Central Bank in December 1990, taking over all regional branches of the Soviet Gosbank in Russian territory. "The Russian central bank did not respect the Gosbank recommendations and decisions in relation to credit emission, interest rate policy, reserve requirements, etc. It started to finance the republican budget deficit and Russian enterprises through fully autonomous credit emission."[24] Thus, we find the exact and principal reason for the large rise in inflation in Russia in 1991. Monetary conduct in the Russian Federation was a poor example from the start.

Before its liquidation in December 1991, the Gosbank retained monopolistic power to supply Soviet ruble notes to all republics and continued to provide them at least some partial credit. Regardless of how much Russian-bias it might have had, the Gosbank was a factor in the rise of inflation in the non-Russian republics in 1991.

In 1992 and the first half of 1993, the ruble zone was in operation, although it covered a decreasing number of the republics. This is a period in which the traditional, authoritarian regime had gone and a new, rule-based and cooperative-minded institutional arrangement was called upon. Only Russia could have played a pivotal role in making the ruble zone successful, based on her economic capacity and the credibility of her policies and institutions. Unfortunately, with a failed stabilization program and certain narrow-minded policy moves, Russia was unable to keep the handful of remaining partners in the ruble zone by July 1993. For this reason, the ruble zone lacked a stable anchor during its short life (from early 1992 through mid-1993), and hyperinflation raged through the entire ruble zone for most of its existence.

Stabilization and reform: divergent routes and results

Russia was the first USSR republic to embark on a radical stabilization and reform program. As early as October 1991, two months before the official collapse of the Soviet regime and two months after the August 1991 coup (putsch) against the Gorbachev regime, Russian president Yeltsin was supported by a group of young reformists including Yegor Gaidar in launching a "shock therapy." The Yeltsin Economic Program was very comprehensive and penetrating. On the stabilization side, it called for sharp reductions in government spending, cutting outlays for public investment projects and subsidies to producers and consumers. The program aimed at reducing the government budget deficit from its 1991 level of 20 percent of GDP to 9 percent of GDP by the second half of 1992, and further to 3 percent by 1993. New taxes were imposed, and tax collection was to be upgraded to increase state revenues. In early 1992, price controls on 90 percent of consumer goods and 80 percent of intermediate goods were lifted in Russia, with prices on energy and food staples such as bread, sugar, vodka, and dairy products raised and placed under government control. In the monetary sphere, Russia's Central Bank was required to cut subsidized credits to enterprises and to restrict money supply growth. The program called for lowering inflation from 12 percent per month in 1991 to 3 percent per month in mid-1993.[25]

On the restructuring side, the most notable changes were privatization and liberalization. Commerce and trade were opened to domestic private businesses and foreign firms. A voucher privatization system was implemented for every Russian citizen to hold and transact in a share of the equity of state-owned enterprises, mostly those that were not defense-related. Taxation schemes were reorganized.

The program was ambitious and truly intentional toward a market economy, but it was also short of adequate support in many dimensions. At home, political consensus was weak, as Yeltsin was frequently challenged by factions in Russia's parliament. Opponents nearly succeeded in having Yeltsin impeached in mid-1993. He called up tanks to shell the Russian White House, Russia's parliament building, in October 1993, and managed to survive a major constitutional crisis. However, as Yeltsin confessed in 1994, "not a single reform effort in Russia has ever been completed."[26]

Externally, cooperation from other USSR successor states was scarce and diminishing, but this should not entirely be attributed to them. It is obvious that Russia did not consult with them for the reform and stabilization program properly. Moreover, financial aid to Russia from outside sources arrived too late or was too small in size. A Russia expert estimated that for the January program to have had a chance of success, a supporting fund of $5 billion would have been necessary.[27] The first loan from the IMF – SDR 300 million or $438 million – came in June 1992, when the procedure for Russia to become a new member of the IMF had been finalized.[28] The "informational and conceptual chaos" of the old Soviet economic and budgetary system apparently played a role in delaying the membership process.[29] A G-7 meeting in April 1992 promised to support Russia with a financial package of $24 billion; this figure was largely made for headlines and had no real workable schedule for implementation.[30]

To make up for a lack of domestic political backing, Yeltsin had to grant considerable power to Russia's subnational governments – 21 "republics," many of which could make economic policy decisions on their own and were often in conflict with each other. Fundamentally, Russia lacked economic sectors that could quickly benefit from stabilization and reform and become a pillar for economic recovery and government revenue. Even large devaluations in the ruble did not help stimulate Russian exports then.

At the end of 1992, Russia's government budget deficit stood at 20 percent of GDP, which (GDP) had fallen considerably in real terms. Promises of money and credit controls could not be honored. Facing mountainous enterprise debts, including in the defense industry, the Russian government conceded by providing them new credits and subsidies. The year 1992 was thus a year of hyperinflation, and the next year saw only a moderate decrease in high inflation.[31]

In contrast, stabilization and reform in the Baltic Three was much less tenuous than in Russia in general. A stronger domestic political consensus, more inflows of foreign resources, a shorter distance to get goods to the European market, and fewer large state-owned enterprises all helped the Baltic Three pursue stabilization and restructuring programs more successfully than Russia. This does not mean that the three states adopted identical approaches and did not have any setbacks. Estonia adopted a "shock therapy," while Latvia and Lithuania favored a gradual approach. Cuts in government spending and the pursuit of privatization encountered greater difficulties in the latter two states than in Estonia. But, they were all firm in breaking currency linkages with the Soviet/Russian rubles starting in 1992, and they made great efforts in redirecting trade relations from Russia and toward Europe, though they remained significantly dependent on Russia for imports of energy and certain other inputs. Estonia was the first of all of the USSR successor states to have economic growth and macroeconomic stability at the same time, as early as 1993, followed by Latvia and Lithuania.

A review based on statistical data from the mid-1990s showed that the Baltic Three plus Armenia were "successful" in macroeconomic stabilization; Georgia, the Kyrgyz Republic, and Moldova were "uncertain"; and Azerbaijan, Belarus, Kazakhstan, Russia, Tajikistan, Turkmenistan, Ukraine, and Uzbekistan were "unsuccessful."[32] A survey on transition economies by a World Bank researcher in 1997 grouped the Baltic Three as "high intermediate reformers"; Russia, Kyrgyz Republic, Moldova, and Kazakhstan as "low intermediate reformers"; Uzbekistan, Belarus, Ukraine, and Turkmenistan as "slow reformers"; and Armenia, Georgia, Azerbaijan, and Tajikistan as states affected by wars.[33]

Of the latter two groups, Ukraine had the largest economy. Ukraine conducted a Big Bang-style program in the fall of 1994 and received a loan from the International Monetary Fund in October of the same year. The country aimed to cut government subsidies, privatize state-owned enterprises, and improve the legal environment for business. However, budget reorganization and privatization were gravely compromised by the *nomenklatura*'s privileges and widespread corruption in the country. Strong resistance from many large state-owned enterprises in mostly Russian-speaking eastern Ukraine compelled the Ukrainian government to concede on fiscal austerity and relax control on credit. As a result, both stabilization and restructuring achieved only mixed success. Worse even than Russia's, the Ukrainian economy was never truly stabilized during the 1990s, even after a second currency reform in 1996. Chronic high inflation, rapid devaluation, and irregular taxation submerged the entire country into a second economy, the size of which was even higher than in Russia. One estimate indicates that unofficial GDP as a percentage of total GDP rose steadily, from 16.3 percent in 1990 to 48.9 percent in 1995, while that in Russia rose from 14.7 percent to 41.6 percent.[34] The level of aggregate output (GDP) fell by 54 percent in the 1990s, more than Russia's decline of 40 percent.[35] Rarely has a peacetime economy suffered such a loss.

Kazakhstan, the largest country in Central Asia, once struggled between different policy recommendations from the International Monetary Fund versus those offered by a German-led European team. The latter criticized elements of the IMF's plan for insufficient consideration of national particularities, typical of the IMF's universal approach to stabilization. Kazakhstan had a large oil and gas sector, which helped attract vast inflows of foreign direct investment during the 1990s. Measured in per capita terms, the Kazak level of income – together with Azerbaijan, another oil-rich state – was the highest among all CIS states. But the introduction of a new currency in November 1993, prompted by Russia's sudden move in demonetarizing her old ruble notes in August, had no effect on slowing down inflation. Instead, inflation jumped to new heights a few months later. The monthly WPI rate was nearly 130 percent in April 1994, triple earlier levels.[36] Ultimately, new funds from the IMF and the World Bank among others supported a revised fiscal restructuring program that emphasized taxation reform, helping to improve the budget balance and decelerate WPI and CPI rates to single digits by early 1995.

"Better a hundred friends than a hundred rubles": some long-standing effects

"Better a hundred friends than a hundred rubles" was a popular parable in the Soviet era, indicating the great importance of informal social networks on people's welfare. Ironically, the transition to a market system did not end the popularity of the parable and even revived its circulation after some years. Indeed, hyperinflation has had some long-standing effects in Russia and other CIS countries, in that it partially destroyed the normal functioning of money.

To the surprise of the entire international financial community, the Russian government declared a moratorium on its repayment of foreign debt in mid-August 1998, suspending all of its repayments to government bonds-holders and effectively devaluing the ruble. The European financial and investment industry immediately fell into a panic. A large American investment fund, Long-term Capital Management, suffered such losses from the Russian debt default that it had to be rescued by an international consortium convened by the Federal Reserve, after which it survived only a few more months. LTCM had invested heavily on short-term Russian government bonds, betting that a sovereign default could never occur in the country. If the U.S. Federal Reserve had not helped to bail out LTCM, Wall Street would have plummeted and the Global Financial Crisis might have happened ten years earlier.

How did Russia fall so far after a seemingly successful stabilization program in 1994? The answer lies in the country's fractured revenue base and heavy dependence on the oil sector, which were also the outcome of hyperinflation and a stabilization program that led the Russian economy considerably into a barter system. Unfortunately for Russia, international oil prices fell during the second half of the 1990s, inexorably smashing the country's hopes of fiscal improvement.

A book contributed to by leading international scholars on this subject finds considerable evidence of the growth of barter in the Russian economy during the 1990s.[37] As they noted, "an increasing proportion of economic transactions during the 1990s, especially those between large firms, have taken a complex non-monetary form."[38] Many Russian factories were reported to have paid wages and salaries to their workers in kind, such as with commodities such as women's bras, paper cartons, shot glasses, and so on.[39] Some scholars call this type of trade and transaction a "virtual economy."[40]

Widespread barter transactions and tax avoidance resulted in the rise of a shadow economy in Russia and other CIS countries during the 1990s. As shown in an international table listing the size of the shadow economy of 151 countries, the size of Russia's was among the highest 21 countries by the end of the 1990s: 45.1 percent of GDP was estimated to come from the shadow sector.[41] A few other CIS countries – Georgia, Azerbaijan, Ukraine, and Belarus – had levels that were even higher. The size of the shadow economy in Russia continued to grow in the 2000s.

Hyperinflation in 1992 and 1993 increased the prevalence of barter trade and the shadow economy, and the resultant high interest rate of the stabilization program in 1995 and 1996 was another contributing factor. In order to finance its budget deficits with short-term securities – the very securities on which it defaulted in August 1998 – the Russian government raised interest rates on treasury bills to catch up with inflation: 172 percent in 1994 and 162 percent in 1994, as compared to CPI inflation of 311 percent and 198 percent, respectively. When CPI inflation decelerated to 48 percent in 1995 and 15 percent in 1996, the interest rate on the treasury bills was 86 percent in 1995 and 25 percent in 1996 – thus, it was becoming much higher in real terms. The interest rate on lending from Russia's Central Bank was even higher: 110 percent in 1995 and 32 percent in 1996.[42] Russian firms were palpably hit by the high cost of credit, and they tended to react by switching to interfirm financing, which often involved transactions in kind.

Despite significant improvement in Russia's macroeconomic stability starting in 1994, government revenues did not show better performance. Revenue as a percentage of GDP was 31.3 percent in 1995 and 31.8 percent in 1996, much lower than the level of 36.5 percent in 1993 or 36 percent in 1994, and even lower than the 33.1 percent of 1992, which was a year of macroeconomic chaos in Russia. The situation had improved a little in 1997, with the ratio rising to 33.3 percent, but it deteriorated again in 1998, and the ratio fell to 32.1 percent.[43] Budget deficits remained significant in 1997 and 1998 at 7.4 percent of GDP, which was higher than the 5.7 percent of 1995. International oil prices continued to fall, and given the repercussions of this in Russian public finance, even a willing friend like the International Monetary Fund could not stop Russia from tumbling again in the summer of 1998.

Hyperinflation and its aftermath had certain social effects as well, although perhaps in a way that was the opposite of the barter/shadow economy. A study by World Bank researchers carried out in the Kyrgyz Republic in 1999 found a trend of social polarization that resulted partly from the changing role of money in society.[44] As the study observed, the Kyrgyz Republic had become drastically impoverished since her independence. As of 1997, more than half the population lived below the poverty line, and the gap between rich and poor was second only to that in Russia among the post-socialist countries. The poor had increasingly disengaged from society as "the size of networks and frequency of social encounters have significantly decreased among the poor, leading to greater economic, geographic, and social isolation."[45] Unlike in the era of the Soviet Union, money had become central to maintaining informal social networks in the post-transition period, which meant that it was more difficult for the poor to remain part of these networks. While the poor used what little cash they had for survival, those with cash (or access to cash or credit) used it as a tool for mobility. The growing gaps in terms of money and financing between the poor and the non-poor had increased the reluctance of the latter to provide support to their poorer relatives.

The changing role of money has had a social and cultural effect. As noted by the two researchers,

> although the Kyrgyz have had a shorter history with Islam than have many Central Asian groups, it is nevertheless important to add that they have also been influenced by Islam's emphasis on the importance of family solidarity and mutual assistance.[46]

This is another evidence that "nature abhors a vacuum" in mankind's world.

Twice the hyperinflation in Yugoslavia

There were two Yugoslavias at the turn of the 1990s, and each had an episode of hyperinflation that occurred in a short interval. In addition, other successor states and regions suffered hyperinflation immediately after the breakup of the Socialist Federal Republic of Yugoslavia. Compared to what happened during the dissolution of the Soviet Union, hyperinflation in the "*Yugosphere*"[47] appeared to be more virulent because of the quandary of massive ethnic conflict in the region.

Hyperinflation in the socialist Federal Republic of Yugoslavia

Hyperinflation took hold in the last four months of 1989 in Yugoslavia, with CPI rising 59.7 percent monthly in December and 1,356 percent annually in that year. Yugoslavia managed to maintain the political continuity inherited from Josip Tito's authoritarian reign after his death in 1980. Though Tito had promoted a model of "market socialism," and Yugoslavia had a better record of economic growth than many other Eastern European socialist countries in the 1960s and 1970s, the Yugoslav economy endured a series of setbacks and fluctuations in the 1980s. One of its economic problems was creeping inflation.

CPI rose 18.8 percent per year in 1971–80 and 75.2 percent per year in 1981–88. In the latter period, the annual rate of CPI increase accelerated steadily from 30 percent to 199 percent.[48] Apart from factors such as investment from autonomous republics that gained increased power by such economic pursuit, a very Yugoslav system – the so-called "workers' self-management" that later evolved into employee ownership – played a distinctive and self-sustaining role in the process of creeping inflation. Under this system, enterprises were incentivized to link wage adjustment with output price change, which effectively was implicit indexation. Once government weakened its direct control over prices and wages, a price-wage spiral would soon arise.

In 1987, a change in Yugoslav accounting rules was made to allow firms to treat losses due to currency devaluation as production costs.[49] As the currency, the *dinar*, had in fact devalued considerably at the time, the shock could not stop loss-suffering firms from continuing their wage-bills payments, which fed a new round of rising inflation. Together with several other pro-inflation policies and some inconsistent and failed attempts at stabilization in 1988 and the first half of 1989, rising inflation finally culminated in hyperinflation later that year.

The last prime minister of the Socialist Federal Republic of Yugoslavia came into office in March 1989 and launched a major stabilization and liberalization program at the beginning of 1990. It imposed a six-month freezing of wages, prices, and exchange rates. A new *dinar* replaced the old at a rate of 1 to 10,000, and its exchange rate with the Deutsche mark was fixed at 7 to 1 – a large devaluation in effect. Controls over the state banks' money supply and credit provision were tightened, together with budget planning and implementation. Foreign trade was liberalized, and the new *dinar* was made convertible to foreign exchange. State-owned or collectively-owned enterprises were allowed to declare bankruptcy, and foreign direct investment was welcomed into Yugoslavia. In addition, loans from the International Monetary Fund were obtained, although these were only partially realized due to political uncertainties that arose in late 1990.

Inflation quickly decelerated in January 1990 and had fallen to single digits in March, with a further small deflation in June. Exports grew steadily, and foreign exchange reserves increased considerably. In mid-1990, Yugoslavia was expected to restructure foreign debts with the arrival of new foreign financial assistance. Because of its austere nature and some of its short-run effects, the stabilization program had resulted in a decline of industrial output in certain sectors and a rise in unemployment. Yet, the overall outlook for the Yugoslav economy was promising.

A Serbian politician, Slobodan Milošević, who later became the leader of the Federal Republic of Yugoslavia, secretly secured a large sum of loans from state banks to expand government outlays in Serbia in order to win the general election in December 1990.[50] This action was more than sabotage of the stabilization program, and it further destroyed mutual trust between Yugoslav republics, which was already extremely thin. Inflation was reignited in Yugoslavia, and it went on to set new world records.

Much higher hyperinflation in the Federal Republic of Yugoslavia

Three of the six republics of the former Socialist Federal Republic of Yugoslavia – Slovenia, Croatia, and Macedonia – declared independence over the period from June to September 1991, and a fourth – Bosnia and Herzegovina – followed suit in March 1992, after a controversial referendum. The remaining two – Serbia and Montenegro – formed the Federal Republic of Yugoslavia in April 1992, which nominally succeeded the Socialist Federal Republic of Yugoslavia. This second federal republic was also known as "Rump-Yugoslavia" (small/smaller Yugoslavia).

Immediately after the formation of the Federal Republic of Yugoslavia, hyperinflation rolled over the country. It lasted 24 months to January 1994, when the CPI rose 313,000,000 percent (3.138 percent) monthly. Similar to the level of Zimbabwe's hyperinflation of 2008, hyperinflation in the Federal Republic of Yugoslavia was second only to that experienced by Hungary in 1946. The length of time that it lasted was shorter than Russia's in the 1920s by only two months.

All of the Yugoslav successor states suffered the collapse of interregional trade after the political split, and many were afflicted by ethnic conflicts – internally or externally (against Milošević's Serbian forces), and occasionally also with other factions. Declines in output and considerable loss of revenue were obvious reasons for the surge of hyperinflation in almost every successor state (Table 7.4). Fresh memory may also have played a part: the peoples of the Yugosphere had all recently experienced hyperinflation in 1989, and they likely quickly sensed the changes in government financial policies and the potential implications on money and prices, and they therefore responded rapidly.

For the Federal Republic of Yugoslavia, mainly Serbia and Serbia-related regions in Bosnia and Herzegovina, there were a few additional factors. First, a United Nations sanction was imposed in 1992, which involved a trade embargo on all goods except for humanitarian aid. Given this, no significant foreign financial

Table 7.4 CPI inflation in former Yugoslav states since 1991

	Monthly inflation[1]		Annual inflation		Accumulative inflation by 1998 (1989 = 1)[5]
	Highest rate (%)	Month	Highest rate (%)	Year	
Bosnia and Herzegovina	322	Jun. 1993	780[3]	1994	35,845,264
Croatia			1,516[4]	1993	1,215.1
Macedonia			1,925.2[4]	1992	856.9
Slovenia	22.4[2]	Oct. 1991	201[2]	1991	28.1
FR Yugoslavia (Serbia and Montenegro)	3.13[8]	Jan. 1994	116.5[10][3]	1993	44,976.3

Notes of data sources:
[1] Hanke and Krus, Table 30.1, p. 372–3;
[2] www.inflation.eu/ inflation-rates/historic-cpi-inflation.aspx;
[3] Bideleux and Jeffries, Table 35.1(b), p. 563;
[4] Denizer, Stabilization, adjustment and growth prospects in transition economies, *World Bank Working Paper*, Table 7.2, p. 21;
[5] Ivan Katchanovski, Divergence in Growth in Post-Communist Countries, *Journal of Public Policy*, Vol. 20, Issue 01, April 2000, pp. 55–81.

help could be accessed. As is known, Serbia's long-time friend, Russia, was in great economic difficulty at the time. Second, within Serbia, a loose central banking system was in place. In addition to the Central Bank of the Federal Republic of Yugoslavia, there were four regional banks: the Central Bank of Serbia, the Central Bank of Montenegro, and the Provincial Central Banks of Vojvodina and Kosovo. They all conducted credit provisions and issued *dinar* notes, some of which were done illegally.[51] Third, outside the borders of the Federal Republic of Yugoslavia, there were two Serb-dominated "republics" that had each issued a currency pegged to the Yugoslav *dinar*: these republics were the "Republika Srpska" in Bosnia and Herzegovina, and the "Republic of Serbian Krajina" in Croatia. The timing of hyperinflation in these republics was exactly the same as in the Federal Republic of Yugoslavia: 24 months from April 1992, and the magnitude was almost the same: 297,000,000 percent (2.978 percent) monthly in January 1994.[52] It is possible, as in the case of the ruble zone, that note-issuing authorities were in a kind of competition to increase money supply in order to catch up with price inflation and avoid potential losses due to slower growth in the money supply.

Yet, all these factors seem to explain a level of hyperinflation in the hundreds, thousands, or even tens of thousands of monthly percentage points, not a rate of three hundred million percent. As is known, Hungary's astronomical hyperinflation in 1946 was largely the result of a policy on interest rates that were indexed to price inflation, which was not repeated in the case of the Federal Republic of Yugoslavia in 1992–94. The latter's more or less equally impressive level of hyperinflation must have had a distinctive cause.

From anecdotal observations, we know that dollarization took place on a considerable scale in the country during the hyperinflationary period. Professor Steve H. Hanke from an American university was an economic adviser to the vice president of Yugoslavia in 1990–91, and he observed subsequent movements in the country. As he perceived,

> "during the 24-month hyperinflation period, per capita income plunged by more than 50%. Ordinary people were forced to deplete their hard-currency savings. . . . For long periods, all of Belgrade's gas stations were closed, with the exception of one station that catered to foreigners and embassy personnel. People also spent an inordinate amount of time at the foreign-exchange black markets, where they traded huge piles of near-worthless dinars for a single German mark or US dollar note."[53]

What is implied in this observation is that people's demand for foreign currencies was apparently not for savings; rather, it was to pay for their daily expenses. In other words, Deutsch marks and U.S. dollars were the media of payment, and were perhaps also a unit of accounting for many commodities and services during the period. This was categorically a *de facto* dollarization.

Three Yugoslav economists have noted that when the CPI monthly rate was reported by authorities to have reached 313 million percent in January 1994, the *dinar* depreciated only 58 million percent in the black markets in the same month; these estimates were said to be "based on more reliable data" than government estimates. These economists suspect that the official figure of inflation was possibly overestimated.[54] Leaving aside whether or how much the inflation figure had been overestimated, the reference to the reliability of data about the exchange rates in the black markets suggests that the foreign exchange black market in the Federal Republic of Yugoslavia at the time was pervasive and even sophisticated enough to produce "reliable data." Again, this is evidence that foreign currencies were being used for functions beyond being a store of value in the hyperinflationary Federal Republic of Yugoslavia.

The vast availability of foreign exchange in Yugoslavia during this period should not be a surprise. As mentioned earlier, a stabilization program in 1990 helped export growth remarkably when the trade sector was liberalized. Foreign tourists flowed into the country in large numbers. Moreover, overseas Yugoslavs remitted huge quantities of foreign currencies back to the motherland.[55]

The availability of foreign currencies made it possible for locals to have ready access to the foreign exchange market, although mostly through the black markets. Knowing that the value of the domestic currency was falling, and the value of foreign currency was stable or even appreciating, locals would try to exchange any unused amount of domestic currency for foreign currencies and change this back into domestic currency when they needed to spend. This way, they might minimize losses that occurred in the value of the domestic money. When this happened, the velocity of the exchange of domestic money was enhanced and price inflation accelerated. Appreciation in foreign exchange in the daily black markets can thus play a role, such as when interest rates were linked to price inflation in Hungary in 1946. As a result, the value of the *dinar* fell more rapidly in the presence of a parallel foreign currency than it might have otherwise. With foreign currencies being used for local daily transactions, the Federal Republic of Yugoslavia's domestic economy became effectively a parallel currency regime.[56]

One difference with the Hungarian case is that indexing interest rates to an inflation indicator may have provided better certainty, or at least caused less uncertainty, for ordinary people than a situation in which the exchange rates of the black markets were used as a reference point to calculate changes in the relative value of foreign exchange "deposits" – amounts of foreign currency holdings recently obtained by locals via transactions in the black markets.

Accelerated declines in the value of the *dinar*, as reflected in accelerated increases in domestic prices, should have prompted the government to speed up money supply in order to minimize seigniorage losses in real terms. In short, a *de facto* dollarization became a catalyst in the vicious circle of an inflationary spiral.

Tax revenues amounted to 34 percent of GDP in 1991, which fell to 20 percent in 1992 and 13 or 11 percent in 1993. Meanwhile, the fiscal deficit as a percentage of GDP rose from 13 percent in 1991 to 21 percent in 1992 and 34 percent or 28 percent in 1993.[57] Hyperinflation was one of factors that caused the fiscal situation of the Federal Republic of Yugoslavia to rapidly deteriorate in this period.

Entering the winter of 1993, shortages of food, fuels, and even electricity occurred. The unemployment rate rose over 30 percent. To prevent hunger, government agencies began to barter with farmers for food. A general workers' strike in one district demanded payment each day with the real Deutsch mark value of their wages.[58] Departments and schools pondered if they should shut down because of shortfalls in facilities. Yugoslavs tried to use checks whenever possible as payment in order to take advantage of the swiftly rising inflation.

From early 1993, the government attempted many countermeasures to stop hyperinflation. The *dinar* was re-denominated several times, and its official rates versus the Deutsch mark were devalued heavily. Department stores and other retailers were required to file with authorities every time they made a price change. The government tried to freeze wages at certain times. None of these measures slowed the hyperinflation.

The last major attempt occurred in January 1994, when the country's Central Bank announced it would stop printing old *dinars* and the supply of new *dinars* would never exceed a limit equal to US$200 million, which was the total amount of foreign exchange reserves amassed by the Central Bank. Banks could no longer offer to extend credit in old *dinars*, and their lending in new *dinars* had to be backed by their foreign exchange reserves. Also in that month, the Deutsch mark became a legal tender in the country, paralleling the *dinar*. This practice immediately resulted in biased dual pricing against the local currency, the *dinar*, in business exchanges. The *dinar* price label for the same merchandise in the same department store was several times its DM price when compared to prevailing exchange rates on the street.[59] The practice was motivated by firms' desire for hard currency (the DM) over local currency, which apparently also increased inflation in terms of the local currency. This may have been another factor in the final month of the hyperinflation – January 1994 – when prices rose faster than *dinar* devaluation, as noted by the three Yugoslav economists cited above. Another possible relevant factor might be that the supply of hard currencies in the country had substantially increased, due to the earlier devaluations in the *dinar* in both nominal and real terms.

After January 1994, hyperinflation retreated to double-digit levels in annual terms, which persisted in the country for years. Montenegro eventually began to pursue an economic and monetary policy that was increasingly different from Serbia's, unilaterally adopting the Deutsch mark (later the euro) as her currency and leaving the dinar zone in the late 1990s. With Montenegro finally declaring independence in 2006, "Rump-Yugoslavia" and Milošević's "Greater Serbia" were no more.

Inflation and hyperinflation in Eastern European countries

The years 1989 and 1990 were an eventful and turbulent time for many socialist countries in transition toward a market economy. Outside of the Soviet Union and Yugoslavia, many Eastern European countries managed a rather quick and peaceful power changeover, with less ethnic conflict or clashes of other kinds.

Inflation in these countries was, however, vastly divergent. As displayed in Figure 7.1, four countries – Poland, Bulgaria, Romania, and Albania – had each endured triple-digit inflation in the early 1990s, as well as some of them in the later years of the decade as well, while others – notably the German Democratic Republic (which was soon to be reunited with the Federal Republic of Germany), Czechoslovakia (which was soon to be separated into the Czech Republic and the Slovak Republic) and Hungary – only had double-digit inflation at that time. In East Germany (the eastern part of the Federal Germany from 1990), Czechoslovakia, and Hungary, a rise in inflation occurred soon after their political transition, but the magnitude was smaller and the length of time was shorter, than other Eastern European countries. The experiences of these countries should be noted as well.

In 1989, the German Democratic Republic (GDR or East Germany) had a population of 16 million and GDP of $160 billion in terms of 1989's current prices; this was smaller than the Federal Republic of Germany's population of 62 million and GDP of $945 billion at the time.[60] When reunification took place in late 1990, the GDR's currency (*ostmark*) was made fully convertible to the Deutsch mark at par, and the latter soon became the sole legal tender in all of Germany. To facilitate integration, Germany's federal government poured huge amounts of fiscal resources into the eastern Länder, thus expanded its expenditures and budget deficits; this was compounded by a steadily rising public debt.[61] Despite aid, the East German economy rapidly deteriorated, partly because of the *ostmark*'s overvaluation and partly because of de-industrialization due to the opening of markets and inherited inefficiency problems. Had there been no effective countermeasures, inflation would have surged not only in the eastern Länder but

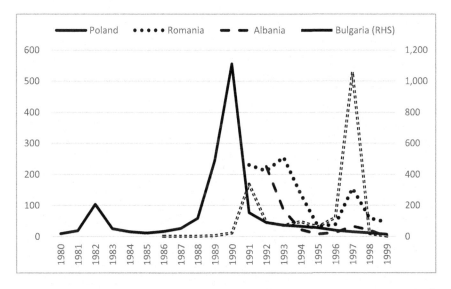

Figure 7.1 CPI Inflation in Poland, Bulgaria, Romania, and Albania, percentage, 1980–99[62]

also possibly in entire Germany. The Bundesbank – Federal Germany's Central Bank – anticipated these fiscal movements and began a conservative monetary policy, including continuous interest rate hikes starting in November 1990.[63] These measures prevented the country from threats of rising inflation. No year in the 1990s saw CPI inflation above 5 percent in Germany. Germany's success in keeping inflation down in a time of increasing inflationary danger should be attributed primarily to the independence of the central bank and prudent monetary policy in the country.

The Velvet Revolution at the end of 1989 resulted in a new, majority-elected government in Czechoslovakia, ushering in the post-communist era. Three years later, a "Velvet Divorce" took place, with the Czech Republic and the Slovak Republic peacefully separating in early 1993. The three years from 1990–92 were, however, a difficult time for these two entities. The GDP declined, and unemployment was rising. Liberalization and privatization had already begun, meaning that traditional, Soviet-style price controls had been abolished. It is not a surprise to see large rises in inflation: 57 percent in the Czech Republic and 61 percent in Slovakia in 1991, and both had an inflation rate of about 10 percent earlier in 1990. If the government had adopted an accommodative fiscal and monetary policy, inflation would have increased at some later point. Apparently, the Czechoslovakian government was willing to bear certain costs of the economic restructuring it was attempting by firmly committing to conservative fiscal and monetary policies. Budget deficits were scaled down via cuts in subsidies to businesses and consumers, and new increases in government expenditures were largely financed by credits obtained from abroad. Conservatism in financial policy was largely inherited in both successor states in 1993. Society had suffered somewhat as a result of certain political shifts in the two countries in subsequent years, but neither country resumed an expansionary financial policy. As output started to recover in the two countries in 1994 – among the earliest for countries with transitional economies – they went on to establish a steady long-term growth path, and each was eventually upgraded into the world's high income group in the 2000s. Slovakia has joined the Eurozone since 2009 and the Czech Republic remains in her currency up to 2017.

Hungary faced a great economic challenge after its political transition in mid-1990. A new, elected government was firm on austerity right from the beginning, perhaps in a memory of two bouts with hyperinflation in the country's past. Large cuts in subsidies to enterprises and consumers were implemented, and privatization was charged – people who wanted to hold equity in state-owned enterprises needed to pay for it. Another policy priority was the reorientation of Hungary's foreign trade. Before 1990, nearly two-thirds of her trade was with other members of the COMECON – an interstate economic and trade organization created and led by the Soviet Union during the Cold War period that consisted mainly of Eastern European socialist countries. Exports were partly boosted by devaluations in the currency, the *forint*, which had negative effects on domestic inflation. This was one reason that inflation remained in double digits when the Hungarian economy began to grow considerably, supported by rapid export expansion staring in the mid-1990s; double-digit inflation lasted till the end of the decade (both Czech's and Slovakia's inflation had previously been in single digits).

Compared to the above-mentioned three or four transitional economies, other Eastern European countries had policies and institutions that were quite different and impinged on the movement of inflation in the period. As shown in Figure 7.1, Poland already had high inflation (104 percent) in 1982, which was the highest among all socialist countries at that time, including Yugoslavia. This was not an accident. Like other Eastern European countries, Poland had a very large industrial sector; industry employed 30 percent of its total labor force at the beginning of the 1980s, which is a level higher than that of countries like Spain and Portugal.[64] Unlike other countries, however, trade union movements in Polish industrial sectors coalesced much earlier, mainly lobbying for economic rights initially and later developing into a strong political force – leaders of the main Solidarity group became heads of government in 1990. Polish workers' demands for wage increases were first provoked by price hikes in agricultural goods, which were part of the government's plan to realign the economy. When concessions were made to workers' demands, an inflationary spiral among sectors of the economy burst out. The government repeatedly and frequently intensified price and wage controls. The Polish economy in the 1980s never really stabilized. Deficiencies in its central planning system and the low efficiency of Polish industry were the basic reasons.

With a worsening economy and tense politics, inflation in Poland soared to 245 percent in 1989 and finally culminated in January 1990 with a monthly CPI rising 77.3 percent, which rendered annual CPI up by 555 percent in 1990. The four months from October 1989 to January 1990 were the hyperinflationary period; this was also a time of political transition. Why did the government allow inflation to reach that high level at the time? Various answers have been proposed: to make time for shock therapy, which did indeed take place later; to let real income fall in order to allow for an easier rebound; to eliminate excess liquidity in the economy, among others.[65]

In the late years of the 1980s, many Polish households kept nearly half of their bank deposits in hard currencies, mostly the U.S. dollar.[66] This was a *de facto* dollarization or currency substitution, and it had significant effects on domestic inflation. Economists believe there was "a wage-price-exchange rate spiral" in the Polish economy.[67] In March 1989, foreign exchange markets became "white," as people could freely conduct transactions in hard currencies. April saw a formal wage indexation that allowed wages to rise in proportion – no less than 80 percent – with CPI increases in the remaining part of the year. In August, food subsidies and retail price controls were suspended. The currency, the *zloty*, sharply devalued at that time. It is possible that because of the vast dollarization in the economy, Polish hyperinflation could have slipped into something similar to the second Yugoslav hyperinflation. The fact that it did not should be credited to the brevity of the hyperinflationary period and the quick implementation of a successful stabilization program.

The Polish stabilization and reform program was comprehensive, typical of a Big Bang or Shock Therapy model. Macroeconomic measures included at least these elements: further cuts in government subsidies and budget deficits; restructuring government debts with foreign creditors, helped by the International Monetary Fund; a restrictive monetary policy by the Central Bank which relinquished its old, almost-free credit provision; retaining price controls on certain key products – energy and transport services among others; temporarily freezing wages; dismantling monopolies and promoting competition in industry, which was largely realized through privatization; and devaluation of the currency that set exchange rates below the market levels at times. In short, the Polish program was a combination of "carrot and stick."[68]

Largely thanks to privatization, liberalization, and economic diversification, resistance from trade unions to the stabilization program was considerably weakened. Monetary and credit tightening measures also helped reduce linkages between exchange rate devaluation and domestic inflation. Consequently, Poland achieved a quick stabilization. CPI inflation decelerated to 76.7 percent in 1991, and a steady disinflation continued thereafter. GDP returned to growth in Poland in 1992, the earliest of all Eastern European transitional economies. One cost of the stabilization and reform program was a persistent increase in unemployment, which was likely a result of industrial restructuring and could be alleviated primarily through social programs that relied on economic growth.

The three Balkan countries – Bulgaria, Romania, and Albania – had a similar political transition after the fall of the Iron Curtain in 1990, with Albania's occurring slightly later, in 1991. Like the other states in the Eastern Bloc, their economies had been stagnant during the second half of the 1980s. Immediately after political transition, inflation surged, with CPI jumping to triple-digit levels from a single-digit level; this occurred in Bulgaria from 1989 to 1991, in Romania from 1990 to 1991, and in Albania from 1990 to 1992 (Figure 7.1). Assisted by the International Monetary Fund and several European Union institutions, they conducted stabilization and reform programs in a similar manner as other transitional economies had. In Romania, the process of stabilization and reform proved more difficult, with triple-digit inflation peaking in 1993 (256 percent) and resurging in 1997 (155 percent). Root causes of the resurgence of inflation are believed to be habitual reliance on credit for investment and state control of the banking industry.[69] Among other things, a less developed and more unstable financial system in the three Balkan countries than in other transitional economies was a conspicuous factor in how their stabilization efforts progressed or were set back.

In Bulgaria, signs of a banking crisis emerged in 1996, and the government responded by expanding budget outlays, which prompted hyperinflation in February 1997, when monthly CPI rose 242 percent, double the level it was five years before, in February 1991 (123 percent). Overall in 1997, CPI rose 1,058 percent. A pro-reform Bulgarian government negotiated with the International Monetary Fund and overhauled the country's monetary and financial system. A currency board regime was adopted in Spring 1997, which fixed the exchange rate of the currency, the *lev*, with the Deutsch mark (later the euro), and allowed monetary growth to be completely based on foreign exchange reserves that the Central Bank held. Bank credit was subjected to tight reserve requirements and regulations. Inflation decelerated to single digits in 1999, with GDP growth resuming starting in 1998.

CPI inflation jumped to 226 percent in Albania in 1992, immediately after the start of transition. It gradually decelerated into a single-digit level in 1995 (7.8 percent), with GDP growth reached above or close to 9 percent each year in 1993–95. Underneath the impressive achievement in macroeconomics was however an immature financial market and poor governance structure in the country that had ultimately resulted in a pyramid-scheme mania in later 1996 and its collapse in March 1997. At the zenith of the mania in 1996, nearly two million Albanians, out of 3.5 million, invested in high interest rate-bearing schemes some of which offered a monthly yield as high as 10 percent. The total liabilities of these schemes amounted to almost half of the country's GDP in the year.[70] In March 1997, several major schemes went bust, and the entire nation fell into chaos. Inflation rose 33.2 percent in 1997, and the GDP plummeted by 10.9 percent. Albania was rescued by the international community and major new reforms had to be undertaken.

The fact that Albania performed generally well in macroeconomics following a liberal approach to economic restructuring since her transition and suddenly plunged into a financial disarray in 1997 has led some to ponder upon so-called "Albanian Paradox," a disproportionally widespread penetration of Ponzi schemes into a young market-based economy without effective hindrance prior to their collapse.[71] Main reasons were obviously the under-education of the populace in market and finance and incompetence of the government in reigning in complexity in an increasingly sophisticated economy. Warnings of dangers of the pyramid schemes were given to the Albanian government by the IMF and World Bank as early as 1994, and "they were not heeded."[72] Admittedly, when alarm bells were raised again 1996, they "may have been too late to do much good in any case."[73]

The experiences of Eastern European countries show that inflation was a common phenomenon in the initial stages of transition, but hyperinflation was not. The fact that hyperinflation occurred in every Soviet Union successor state reflects the stronger legacy of the central planning system and less comfort with the process of political transition, together with the displeasing role played by transitional Russia in the ruble zone in particular and in the Russian sphere in general. On the other hand, stabilization programs followed different routes and created divergent outcomes from country to country. With regard to the last point, East Asian transitional economies appear to present an equally interesting example.

Fighting high inflations: China and Vietnam in East Asia

High inflation was not uncommon in East Asian transitional economies during the 1980s and 1990s. China saw four surges in CPI inflation: 1980 (7.5 percent), 1985 (9.3), 1988 (18.8 percent) and 1993 (24.1 percent). Vietnam had triple-digit inflation in 1986–88 and remained in double-digit inflation for many years until 1996. Inflation jumped to the triple-digit level in Mongolia immediately after

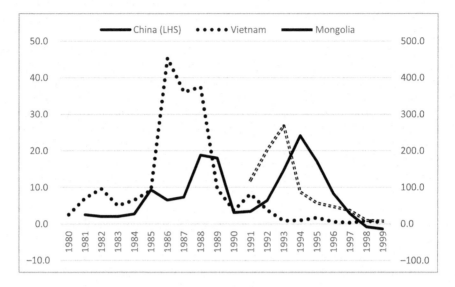

Figure 7.2 CPI Inflation in China, Vietnam, and Mongolia, percentage, 1980–99[74]

a political transition in 1990. Overall, inflation levels in East Asian transitional economies appeared to be significantly lower than that in many of Eastern European and former Soviet Union countries during the 1980s and 1990s.

In particular, the Chinese levels of inflation appear to be extremely "moderate," but this impression may not be right after all. Price controls were never really lifted in China during much of her transition period since the early 1980s. Agricultural goods were the first being put into price hikes and price liberalization, but the government managed to maintain price controls for a number of important grain and meat products until the late 1990s. Price controls of industrial consumer goods were gradually lifted up from the mid-1980s, but at times of rising inflation the government had stepped back from the earlier price liberalization by reintroducing price controls in the field, such as in 1985, 1988, and 1993. Since the first half of the 1980s, so-called "dual-track pricing" – allowing state-owned enterprises to sell a proportion of their products at market prices which were usually considerably higher than the ones thereby they sold to government-designated buyers – had spread in the economy, but presumably the statistics of prices and inflation were largely based on regulated prices rather than transactions in marketplace. Therefore, it is inevitable that official figures of inflation in transitional China were underestimated significantly.

Likewise, Vietnam adopted the two-track system from the mid-1980s. It is found that the difference between official and free market prices for most important consumer and producer goods could be as high as tenfold, and the gap between the official and black market exchange rate – the dollar value of the Vietnamese đồng – fivefold.[75] Many Vietnamese in cities had to work on "unofficial second jobs" to make ends meet,[76] a situation that would be familiar to many urban Chinese in the 1980s and the first half of the 1990s.

China did not have rigorously-compiled data of the money supply – cash in circulation plus public deposits at banks – before the 1990s. Figures of cash in circulation outside of the banking system are available for the earlier period, however. As it is known, the amount of the cash held by the public rose 29.3 percent in 1980, 49.5 percent in 1984, 46.7 percent in 1988, and 36.4 percent in 1992. These are years when inflation had accelerated from the previous year. A commonplace in economics is that when inflation is rising, the velocity of the money (significantly the cash in Chinese society during the 1980s and 1990s) would accelerate, which tends to lead to a faster rise in prices than in the money supply. From this point of view, true inflation levels in these highlighted years should be at least double the published official figures.

Before the mid-1990s, the average income of Chinese urban households was extremely low – much lower than in Eastern Europe or the Soviet Union. China had no significant trade union movements that could demand wage increases in line with inflation; wages in the public sector had been tightly controlled by the government. A "moderate" rise in inflation thus could have a huge impact on people's daily lives, and this is part of why rising inflation in 1988 was one of the underlying movements that led to major political turmoil in 1989.

In many aspects, Vietnam shared an economic and political system with China, but the high inflation in Vietnam in 1986–88 occurred against the backdrop of a country that had just begun to initiate liberal-styled reforms and to relax controls on prices and wages – these factors together resulted in a kind of price-wage spiral.

As in other socialist countries, persistent budget deficits, uncompetitive state-owned industry, and frequent government-led investment pursuits were the common causes of rising inflation. In particular, the older taxation system was established on distorted pricing schemes, such as the depressed pricing of agricultural products installed so that there was little need to tax peasants. Once price controls in the sector were relaxed, the costs of industrial production tended to rise, but revenue to the government may actually have fallen.[77] Thus, inflation would quickly surface.

In official publication, the Chinese government shifted into a pattern of persistent fiscal deficit from 1979, with only one year in the two decades of 1980–99 in which it had a budget surplus. The government decided in that year to borrow from abroad, mainly in the form of concessional loans or development finance, which did not adequately cover budget deficit. From 1981, the government also resumed bond issues, but the marketing of government bonds encountered serious setbacks during the second half of the 1980s. Only 40 percent of planned new bond issues were subscribed in 1988.[78] Fiscal deficits in the late 1980s and early 1990s were largely financed by overdrafts made on the People's Bank of China, the once sole banking institution in post-1949 China that was about to become a modern-styled central bank in the country from the mid-1990s. The practice of direct overdraft made by (or "autonomous advances" made to) the Ministry of Finance on the People's Bank of China halted in 1994, and in the following year the Bank also stopped direct lending to the Ministry.[79] Institutionally, it is the development of financial markets in China from the early 1990s that has made it possible and rather easily manageable for the government to finance its budget deficit primarily by government bond issues. In retrospect, direct bank financing of government budget deficit was the main culprit of surges of inflation in transitional China.

The earliest episode of inflation in post-reform China in 1980 was a result of agricultural price hikes initiated by the government in 1979 as part of its drive for liberalization in rural areas. To minimize the welfare-reducing impact on urban consumers, the Chinese government decided to offer subsidies to city residents, which nevertheless caused a rise in inflation. In 1988, a more ambitious price liberalization program was attempted in order to eliminate price distortions and also dual-track pricing that prevailed in the economy, and the result was a surge in inflation which ultimately turned out to be a political "disaster" in 1989.

Each time it faced a significant rise in inflation, the government had to retreat by cutting its investment projects and tightening price and wage controls, in addition to curtailing credit expansion. China twice implemented an indexed interest rate policy on time deposits – in 1988 and 1993 – in order to stabilize deposit flows in the banking system and woo consumers away from the goods market and the foreign exchange. Vietnam conducted gold sales in 1988 to call back excessive liquidity, which was made possible only by higher gold prices in the Vietnamese domestic market than those on the world gold market, as well as a government monopoly over foreign trade.

Despite huge labor resources and low labor costs, vast state-owned industries in China and Vietnam lacked international competitiveness for a long period. Recurrent devaluations and consequent domestic inflations could not improve Chinese and Vietnamese external balances, as they frequently encountered considerable trade deficits and current account deficits. A new consensus was formed from the second half of 1980s in China, i.e., to follow the example of the Asian Tigers – Hong Kong, Singapore, South Korea, and Taiwan, and to some extent, their pioneer, Japan – by promoting an export-led industrialization strategy. For this purpose, a trade policy of supporting export growth and a policy of attracting foreign direct investment were adopted. Macroeconomic policy priority was given to exchange rate stabilization, which provided a stable anchor in domestic monetary policy conduct and also boosted the price competitiveness of domestic-made products in international markets.

China undertook a major stabilization and reform program in 1994, devaluing the currency, abolishing multiple exchange rates, and increasing currency convertibility. Restructuring of state-owned enterprises was launched a few years later, and private businesses rapidly expanded in the economy. When China joined the World Trade Organization in 2001, her advantages in labor resources began to appear and overwhelm the world economy. The exchange rate policy – a peg to the U.S. dollar, sometimes rigorously kept and other times used with certain flexibility – played an important role in sustaining China's external surpluses and massive accumulation of foreign exchange reserves until recently. This policy was also an implicit guide for domestic monetary policy conduct that could respond to business cycles in the manner of "leaning against the wind."

Vietnam became a member of ASEAN in 1995 and a member of the World Trade Organization in 2007. From the later 1990s, considerable efforts were made there to improve her exchange rate stabilization and inflation control, while economic liberalization was underway. From the mid-2000s, foreign direct investment flowed into the country on a large scale. The Vietnamese economy successfully transformed from a large dependence on rice exports in the 1980s to a one that is witnessing the fastest growth in the export of manufactured goods in the world. Vietnam's export growth overtook China's in the early 2010s.

An economic explanation for transition economies like China and Vietnam that achieved rapid growth without significant inflation is that they successfully reoriented their labor force into outward-looking industrialization, made possible by the age of globalization. As long as foreign demand from countries in North America and Western Europe for made-in-China or made-in-Vietnam items keeps growing, the shift of employment from agriculture to industry and the increase in industrial supply will not be accompanied by a rise in inflation in these emerging market economies.[80] In essence, globalization has helped domestic economic restructuring in these countries follow a smooth macroeconomic process.

However, globalization does not work in a universal way. Since her political transition in early the 1990s, Mongolia has made little and slow progress in economic diversification and sophistication, and she continues to rely heavily on foreign financial aid. The sheer size of mineral production in Mongolia is like that of the oil sector in Russia; when international mineral prices soared, the economy boomed, and vice versa. Yet, the Mongolian government's budget has remained in a deficit situation throughout the decades, frequently amounting to over 5 percent of GDP, and sometimes rising to 10 percent or higher. Price movements in the country are thus vulnerable to external shocks, and inflation has occasionally risen into double digit, even as recently as the 2000s. The fight against inflation remained unfinished in Mongolia.

Among all transitional countries China and Russia appear to stand as somehow contrasting examples. China managed to avoid hyperinflation or output decline and achieve an impressive economic growth since the early 1980s, and Russia suffered hyperinflation and output declines when moving into transition. In the meantime, the style of reform in China matched in many ways the so-called "gradualist model" of transition, characterized by dual-track pricing, partial ownership restructuring, weak property right protection, and slow movement in political reform, among others. There were several "mini-Big Bangs" in price reform, but some of them were withdrawn soon after launch. On the other hand, the transition in Russia began with a Big Bang in early 1992, comprising price liberalization and privatization, not to mention the rapid political change that was a prelude to the economic program. For this reason, Russia has been considered by many a sample of the shock therapy model.

"Which model is better?" had been a subject under debate for many years since the early 1990s, which involves a great deal of complexity that is much beyond the scope of this book. One must think of some fundamental differences between the two countries before arriving at a conclusion. As emphasized by two dedicated scholars of transitional economies, economic structures that Russia and China had before their transition were sharply different, and that had profound implications for their latter macroeconomic performance in the transition period. Output declines that occurred in Russia immediately after the start of transition were bound to aggravate inflation, which, when coupled with policy mistakes, would inevitably degenerate into hyperinflation. On the other hand, China managed to avoid output decline by a combination of policy and non-policy factors, including a surplus labor force that was incrementally shifting to the industry and the export sector, which greatly helped prevent her from falling into traps of inflationary spiral.[81] In view of all political and economic complications in reality, it seems fair to say that in neither country had policy choices been made always or even for a significant span of the time in a way that conformed to the idea of "optimal." Macroeconomic stabilization in both countries had considerable costs.

Notes

1   Hanke and Krus, Table 30.1, pp. 372–3.
2   Kornai (1980, Vol. A, p. 27; Vol. B, p. 196); Kornai (1998); Lipton and Sachs, p. 86.
3   De Melo, Denizer, Gelb, and Tenev, Table 2, p. 43; and Katchanovski, Table 1, p. 58.
4   Cottarelli and Bléjer.
5   A formal discussion of the relation between these concepts is given in Lipton and Sachs, pp. 90–9.
6   Mitchell, Europe, Tables G4, H1, H2, and J1.
7   Gaidar (2007, p. 102).
8   Gaidar (2007, pp. 102–3).
9   Commission of The Central Committee of the CPSU (B), p. 168.
10 Raw data source is Denizer, Table 2, p. 21.
11 Curtis, section of The Economy-Historical Background.
12 Teltschik, pp. 155–7 and elsewhere.
13 The Soviet Union's official holdings of gold at the end of 1991 were reported at 290 tons (then worth approximately $3.2 billion), and a substantial portion of this stock was already pledged as collateral for various foreign obligations. As of the end of March 1992, Russia informed the IMF of net international reserves of $2.25 billion (Boughton, 2012, Footnote 3, p. 288).
14 Gaidar (2007, p. 228).
15 Gaidar (2007, p. 228).
16 Gaidar (2007, p. 228).
17 The figure used here for Russia in 1992 is different from that in Table 7.1, as it is from the same source as that used for the other republics (see the data source of Table 7.2).
18 Dąbrowski, pp. 17–18.
19 The Soviet Union was not among the founding states of the International Monetary Fund in the 1940s but made informal inquiries about membership in the 1980s (Boughton, 2001, pp. 963, 967).
20 The share of exports to other former USSR republics was more than 90 percent in the Baltics in 1990 and declined to around 50 percent in 1994. That figure in Russia fell from 64.4 percent to 24.3. Other CIS states changes similar to that of Russia (Åslund, 2002, Table 5.5, p. 180).
21 Åslund (2002, p. 205).
22 Pomfret (2002) and Granville (2002).

23 Odling-Smee and Pastor, Figure 1, p. 4. By early 1995, Russia's borrowing from the IMF had amounted to $10.5 billion (SDR 7.2 billion), more than any other country but Mexico (Boughton, 2012, p. 308).
24 Dąbrowski, p. 15.
25 Curtis, section of Economic Reform in the 1990s.
26 Quoted in Boughton (2012, p. 287).
27 Rostowski (1998, p. 158).
28 Boughton (2012, Figure 7.1, p. 309).
29 Rostowski (1998, pp. 158–9).
30 Boughton (2012, p. 292).
31 A diagnostic explanation of Russia's failure in macroeconomic stabilization and liberalization in the early 1990s is that the people in the ruling group were "neither democratic nor genuinely reformist," instead, they were "market Bolsheviks" who "never possessed a coherent, detailed economic program or rigorous economic strategy" (Reddaway and Glinski, p. 236).
32 Rostowski (1998, Table 1, p. 3).
33 Denier, Table 2, p. 21.
34 Åslund, Table 4.4, p. 123. The highest level was in the Caucasus states, over 60 percent.
35 Åslund, p. 118.
36 Hoffmann et al. (2001, Figure 2, p. 19).
37 Seabright (2000).
38 Seabright, p. 1.
39 Blustein, p. 245.
40 Blustein, p. 244; original sources are quoted therewith.
41 Schneider and Enste, Table 4.2, pp. 37–40.
42 Seabright, Table 1.1, p. 22.
43 The figures before 1998 are from Seabright, Table 1.1, p. 22, and that of 1998 from the International Monetary Fund, *World Economic Outlook Database*, updated in October 2016.
44 Kuehnast and Dudwick (2004).
45 Kuehnast and Dudwick, p. 3.
46 Kuehnast and Dudwick, p. 2.
47 "Yugosphere" is a term coined by *The Economist* in its article, "Former Yugoslavia patches itself together: Entering the Yugosphere" (*The Economist*, 20 August 2009).
48 Kolodko, Gotz-Kozierkiewicz, and Skrzeszewska-Paczek, Figure 1 and Table 1, pp. 40–1.
49 Kolodko, Gotz-Kozierkiewicz, and Skrzeszewska-Paczek, p. 45.
50 Bideleux and Jeffries, p. 522.
51 Petrović, Bogetić, and Vujošević, footnote 6, p. 340.
52 Hanke and Krus, Table 30.1, p. 371.
53 Hanke (2007).
54 Petrović, Bogetić, and Vujošević, footnote 3, p. 338.
55 It was estimated that the average Yugoslav family held "hard currency" (the Deutsch mark or the like) between DM 10,000 and DM 40,000 in the early 1990s (Lyon, footnote 2, p. 294).
56 In the paper by the three Yugoslav economists, this process is called "exchange rate-based pricing," which means that domestic money expansion affected inflation "via currency depreciation" (Petrović, Bogetić, and Vujošević).
57 Petrović, Bogetić, and Vujošević, Table 1, p. 339.
58 Lyon, p. 313.
59 Lyon, p. 323.
60 CIA *World Factbook* 1990 (retrieved from www.theodora.com/wfb/1990/index.html on February 11, 2017). The GDP figure for the GDR was based on official exchange rates, which may exaggerate the true level.

61 Federal Germany's fiscal deficit as a percentage of GDP rose from 3.2 percent in 1991 to 9.4 percent in 1995, and gross debt as a percentage of GDP rose from 38.9 percent in 1991 to 60 percent in 1999 – which was the maximum set forth by all countries that were entering the Eurozone that year. The figures are from the IMF, *World Economic Outlook* database.

62 Data source: The World Bank, World Development Indicator Database (FP.CPI. TOTL.ZG).

63 Baltensperger, p. 481.

64 Lipton and Sachs, Table 1, p. 81.

65 Kolodko, Gotz-Kozierkiewicz, and Skrzeszewska-Paczek, p. 77.

66 Kolodko, Gotz-Kozierkiewicz, and Skrzeszewska-Paczek, p. 83.

67 Lipton and Sachs, p. 109.

68 de Menil (2003, p. 284).

69 De Menil (2003, pp. 286–93).

70 Jarvis (1999).

71 Bezemer (2001).

72 Jarvis (1999, p. 13).

73 Jarvis (1999, p. 13).

74 International Monetary Fund, *World Economic Outlook Database*. The China figure for 1980 is missing here, but it is known from Chinese sources that CPI rose 7.5 percent in the year, up from 1.9 percent in 1979. Elsewhere, Vietnamese official sources indicate that in 1986 retail prices rose 587.2 percent, and CPI 487 percent; these values are both higher than that of 453.5 percent shown in Figure 7.2 here (Kolodko, Gotz-Kozierkiewicz, and Skrzeszewska-Paczek, Table 12 and Figure 23, p. 117). Mongolia figures from before 1991 are not available.

75 Wood, p. 564.

76 Wood, p. 565.

77 Naughton (1991).

78 Wang, p. 456.

79 The People's Bank of China, pp. 243–4.

80 A formal analysis is given in Copeland (2014), Case Study 5.1, pp. 162–4.

81 Sachs and Woo (1994) and Woo (2001).

8 World trend outliers

Zimbabwe and Venezuela in the twenty-first century

"Chavismo is not Latin America's future – if anything, it is its past. . . . The irrationality of Chavistanomics will not be felt until oil prices fall."

Francis Fukuyama's reply to Hugo Chávez in
The Washington Post, Sunday, August 6, 2006

"The End of History" is a phrase popularized by Francis Fukuyama, who published a book with this title in 1992 that succinctly and prophetically generalized megatrends of world development from the later decades of the twentieth century. In essence, "the end of history" means more than the end of the Cold War; it refers to the phenomenon in which a majority of contemporary nations begin to share common values and adopt similar policies toward fundamental social and development issues. Fukuyama argues that violent conflicts, internal and external, tend to diminish over time.

If there is a phrase in economics akin to the political science concept of the end of history, it might be the idea of "Great Moderation": inflation falls worldwide, with less volatility in business cycles and more stability in macroeconomic movements. Widespread disinflation since the mid-1990s occurred against the backdrop of economic globalization; economies across the world became more and more open and liberalized and cross-border trade and capital flows accelerated.

When distortions in economic institutions and policies lessened, people naturally expected that the likelihood of hyperinflation would be minimal. Indeed, hyperinflation has become a rare incidence in the twenty-first century. It has occurred only in the few countries that did not participate in global economic trends.

The world trend: a "Great Moderation" in the twenty-first century

In its biannual report on global macroeconomic movements, issued in April 2006, research staff at the International Monetary Fund noted that globalization – increasing openness of individual national economies and rapid growth in international trade and investment flows – had contributed to steady declines in inflation worldwide since the mid-1990s.[1] Inflation had fallen everywhere: in industrial countries, emerging-market economies, and transitional economies. Only a hand-ful of countries had an inflation rate in the double digits in the 2000s and 2010s.

However, the current age of globalization does not mean that every nation has been free of economic troubles. In fact, many countries – both emerging market and industrialized countries – had been fret with financial crises since the 1990s. Mexico's peso crisis in 1994 was probably the first of its kind in the post-Cold War period. A few years later, several East Asian economies – notably Thailand, Indonesia, and South Korea – were caught up in a major financial turmoil shortly after enjoying spectacular growth. In the shadow this East Asian financial crisis, Russia and Brazil – and to an extent Argentina as well – fell into a foreign debt crisis in 1998, only a few years after stabilization in the mid-1990s.

Each of these financial crises was characterized by rapid currency devalua-tion and an increase in inflation, with the banking system wavering and fiscal resources being exhausted. As each crisis unfolded, there was every reason to believe that these crisis-hit economies would slip into hyperinflation and depres-sion if they were not helped by outside forces.

Forces of globalization played a major role in stabilization in many economies on a scale unprecedented in past economic history. Countries from Mexico to Argentina and Indonesia to Russia were assisted by the international community, and the International Monetary Fund provided pooled financial resources and a package of policy guidelines for crisis containment. No country was left alone to deal with her economic problems in the age of globalization, even when she had sunk into a major financial crisis.

Financial crises hit industrial countries as well. When asset bubbles burst in the early 1990s, Japan's economy became stagnant. As a major banking-system crisis emerged and the economy was further depressed in the later 1990s, Japan's Central Bank responded by adopting a zero interest rate policy in 1999, which has lasted until recently. The year 2000 was a year of recession, and Japan's budget deficit – exclusive of interest payments – rose to 6.6 percent of GDP, increasing to 9.9 percent in 2009. Japan's gross government debt as a proportion of GDP exceeded 100 percent in 1996, 200 percent in 2009 and 250 percent in 2016 – these rates were the highest in the world at the time. Yet, inflation has remained low in the country throughout recent decades.

In the United States, a wave of defaults in the subprime mortgage market ultimately escalated into an overwhelming financial crisis in 2008. The Federal Reserve Board had to undertake an extremely expansionary monetary policy, the so-called QE (Quantitative Easing), starting at the end of 2008. Meanwhile, the U.S. federal government's budget deficit soared to 11.2 percent of GDP in 2009, with its gross debt approaching 100 percent of GDP in 2011. In Britain, a major banking crisis in 2007 and 2008 led the government to sharply increase spending and borrowing in order to bail out troubled financial institutions, which resulted in a large increase in its budget deficit to 9.1 percent of GDP in 2009; gross debt rose to 75.7 percent of GDP in 2010 – double the level it had been in 2004.

Large budget deficits and high public debt are believed to be important factors that lead to high inflation and hyperinflation. The reason these factors did not trigger inflation in the United States, Japan, and the United Kingdom in recent years is fundamentally institutional: the governments of these countries operate their monetary and fiscal policies under institutional constraints, and "checks and balances" have been applied to their macroeconomic policy decision-making as well. Consider the United States with regard to fiscal constraints: the federal government has certain discretion in its fiscal policy, but it has no power to borrow beyond the ceiling set by Congress. If (for example) a Democratic-led administration approached borrowing limits and a Republican-controlled Congress did not agree to raise the debt level, a fiscal crisis necessarily would occur and would be followed by a federal government shutdown. The suspension of federal government functions did indeed happen several times in recent decades: October 2013, November 1995, and from December 1995 to January 1996. Though these events were largely the result of intense partisan politics in the United States, they underscore the reason that fiscal powers are separated in a broad governmental system, reducing the capacity of a single authority to arbitrarily expand budget spending and borrowing.

The Eurozone monetary system – built on the postwar German model – provides another example in which monetary policy decision-making was separated from member states' fiscal processes. Greece endured a major sovereign debt crisis in 2011, during which her budget deficit exceeded 10 percent of GDP, while the original Eurozone criteria was 3 percent. The economic ramifications were huge, and the Greek economy plummeted into a deep recession in 2011–12 and revenues to the government shrank. Had the Greek government been able to conduct its own monetary policy, it is likely that inflation in Greece would have soared and the currency – the one she would have had outside of the Eurozone – would have rapidly been devalued. Hyperinflation would have been very likely, had Greece not been rescued in a timely manner. As it happened, the power to implement monetary policy in EU countries rested (and still rests) with the European Central Bank in Frankfurt, which safeguarded Greece from falling into hyperinflation in the midst of this sovereign debt crisis.

The world in the age of globalization has seen many changes in social institutions, economic policies, and international relations. Still, in a handful of countries there has been a lack of progress in modern institution building, ineffective or even harmful economic policies have been followed, and self-isolating foreign policies have been continued. It is therefore no surprise to see hyperinflation occurring in certain countries in the twenty-first century.

Zimbabwe: a hyperinflation that ends its own currency

The world in 2008 was besieged by the shocking news of financial turmoil in the United States and the United Kingdom, and few people took notice of seemingly disastrous movements in a remote southern African country: hyperinflation in Zimbabwe.[2]

The Zimbabwean hyperinflation started in March 2007 and ended in mid-November 2008, lasting about 21 months. In a measure, the level of monthly inflation reached 7.96×10^{10} percent in mid-2008, higher than Yugoslavia's 3.13×10^8 percent in January 1994, and second only to Hungary's 4.19×10^{16} percent in July 1946.[3] Unlike many other countries, Zimbabwe ended the hyper-inflation by abandoning her currency and legalizing the use of foreign currencies in her domestic economy. Many years have passed since this crisis, yet the Zimbabwean people still today live in fear of hyperinflation.

Events leading to hyperinflation

Zimbabwe gained independence in 1980 after a years-long fight between a pre-dominately white regime and a group of black nationalists. Despite being a land-locked country, Zimbabwe has rich mineral reserves and was an attractive place for international tourism. With a GNP per capita of $630 in 1980, the country was considered a middle-income nation at that time. Since independence, the population in Zimbabwe experienced accelerated growth of 3.3 percent per annum during the 1980s, which exceeded GDP growth of 2.7 percent, resulting in zero growth in output or income in per capita terms.

Robert Mugabe emerged as a new national leader during the 1980s, and he was able to consolidate power after several major campaigns against opponents and dissidents. Under his leadership, Zimbabwe increasingly moved toward an authoritarian regime of one-party rule in the 1990s. The economy became virtu-ally stagnant in the second half of the decade. Before that time, slow growth had allowed Zimbabwe to fall into the status of a low-income nation.

Mugabe decided to join the Second Congo War in 1998 on the side of an anti-establishment force by dispatching tens of thousands of Zimbabwean soldiers into Zaïre (Democratic Republic of Congo), a country with which Zimbabwe does not share borders.[4] Though the rebels won a four-year fight, the cost of this war to Zimbabwe was largely borne by her people, and the government had not budgeted for this cost, nor was it supported by national savings.[5] The Zimbabwean govern-ment apparently began an inflationary budget deficit-financing policy at this time.

Zimbabwe's covert involvement in the Congo War provoked international criti-cism, and the country's relations with the international community have deterio-rated since then. At home, Mugabe was determined to pursue land reform as a blatant challenge to the British government's decision to discontinue its financial support for a Zimbabwean land reform program that had been negotiated in 1980. According to this earlier agreement, white owners of land were to be compensated when land was transferred to a willing black buyer; a joint effort by the British and Zimbabwean governments was to provide a fund to support this. In 2000, a so-called "Fast-Track Land Reform Program" was initiated by Mugabe's govern-ment, effectively promoting a nationwide campaign of land redistribution without proper compensation to white landowners who sold property. In addition to this development, in some cases, skilled farmers were replaced by inexperienced agri-cultural workers who often found themselves unable to acquire credit and capi-tal from market sources to invest in agriculture. Considerable farmland was left uncultivated after the resultant land redistribution. Together with the impact of severe droughts, agricultural production and exports have declined significantly in Zimbabwe in the years since Mugabe came to power. Food shortages occurred, as did food riots in city streets.

Severe violations of human rights in Zimbabwe, as well as conduct during the Second Congo War that was universally condemned by the international community, prompted a spate of international sanctions against the Zimbabwean government in the late 1990s. The World Bank and International Monetary Fund both withdrew financial support for aid programs in Zimbabwe in 1999. The United States froze the assets of top Zimbabwean officials and denied Zimbabwean access to international credit in 2000. Spurred by a British initiative, Zimbabwe's membership in the Commonwealth of Nations was suspended in 2002. Zimbabwe was adrift in the international arena.

There had been no single year since independence that the Zimbabwean government had a balanced budget, let alone a surplus. In the 1980s, the annual budget deficit was less than 10 percent of GDP, and it occasionally rose above this level in the late 1990s. The ratio of budget deficit/GDP jumped to 24 percent in 2000,[6] reflecting a rapidly worsening economy and demonstrating the detrimental effects of rising inflation on revenues. Zimbabwe relied on international financing to make up for budget deficits in the 1980s and much of the 1990s, but this was no longer possible in the 2000s when international sanctions were in place.

An unusual practice in Zimbabwe was that the Central Bank (the Reserve Bank of Zimbabwe) started to provide loans directly to new farmers for their purchases of inputs and the costs they incurred to run their operations. This was hailed in Zimbabwe as an approach to economic development that was superior to Western-styled conventional methodology.[7] The move was apparently motivated by multiple considerations: to facilitate the "Fast-Track Land Reform Program"; to avoid a literal increase in government budget expenditures; and to support agricultural production. As it has been noted, the RBZ's staff increased 120 percent to 1,360 in 2007 from 2001, the largest rate among all central banks in the world during this period.[8]

Zimbabwe at the time had already a substantial banking industry that provided usual credit and other banking services to businesses in standard commercial terms. Bypassing commercial banking, the RBZ's direct lending to farmers was in effect a supply of cheap credit or even free money. As agricultural output stopped growing for various reasons, increases in credit to farmers did nothing more than fuel inflation. Even for the entire banking industry in Zimbabwe, the real interest rate – the lending rate charged by commercial banks on loans that are adjusted for inflation – had become negative on a yearly basis since 2001.[9]

Zimbabwe's CPI rose 56.9 percent in 1999 and 112 percent in 2001. Two years later, the level reached 598.7 percent. After a dip in 2004 (133 percent), it jumped to 586 percent in 2005 and 1,033 percent in 2006. Meanwhile, the government's managed exchange rate of the currency, in terms of Zimbabwean dollar to U.S. dollar, devalued from 38 in 1999 to 30,000 in 2006.[10] Overall, CPI rose 19,533 times between 1999 and 2006, while the Zimbabwean dollar was devalued by a factor of 789.5 in official exchange rates. It is evident that Zimbabwe's currency was overvalued in official ratings, which rendered exports shipped through "official" channels unprofitable. This in turn meant that exports would decrease and the economy would be driven underground into a parallel, or second/shadow economy, as the government tightened controls over its foreign exchange.

Hyperinflation and the end of a national currency

Monthly CPI inflation in Zimbabwe first reached the threshold of 50 percent in March 2007 (50.5 percent), with certain dips during the three months from July to September 2007, and followed an escalating path thereafter. Between October 2007 and June 2008, the pace of inflation was in the triple digits, exploding into quadruple, quintuple, and many higher levels. As shown in Figure 8.1, in mid-November 2008, monthly inflation was 7.96×10^{10} percent, and the annual level was 8.97×10^{20} percent.

Zimbabwean authorities – including the Reserve Bank of Zimbabwe – stopped publication of monthly CPI inflation levels on a regular basis in March 2008, and the latest available figure released by the Reserve Bank (belatedly) was 2,600.2 percent for July of 2008. The figures for August to mid-November of that year were derived by scholars based on exchange rates and purchasing power parity.[11]

A large multinational insurance and investment corporation – Old Mutual – had its stocks dual-listed in London and Harare, and these were quoted in the British pound sterling and the Zimbabwean dollar, respectively. At the time of high inflation, official exchange rates made little sense for normal businesses, and even the black markets had certain exchange limits. People were in need of a

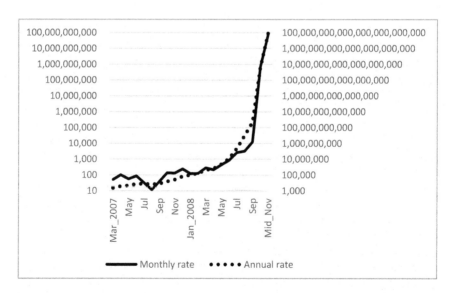

Figure 8.1 Monthly and annual inflation, percentage, log scale, Zimbabwe, March 2007–mid-November 2008[12]

more reliable indicator of exchange rates that could be readily recognized and be updated with fairly regular frequency. Daily information about the share prices of Old Mutual in London and Harare provided exchange rates between the sterling and the Zimbabwean dollar, which – via sterling/U.S. dollar exchange rates in the international currency market – could be translated into exchange rates between the Zimbabwean dollar and the U.S. dollar. The latter had been called OMIR – Old Mutual Implied Rate – which was made readily known to the business community in Zimbabwe during the time of hyperinflation.

In mid-November 2008, trading in the Zimbabwe Stock Exchange was suspended, and therefore the OMIR ceased to be available. Zimbabwean authorities legalized the use of foreign currencies in domestic retail transactions in December 2008, and when the Zimbabwe Stock Exchange reopened in February 2008, all quotations were made in U.S. dollars.

Alternative estimates based on exchange rates in Zimbabwean parallel markets suggest that in later 2008, the level of hyperinflation was even higher than what is shown in Figure 8.1.[13] At the time of rising inflation, several types of foreign exchange markets were in operation in addition to the official one: cash-based transactions in the business community, cash value-based transactions through the bank payments system (Real Time Gross Settlement, RTGS), and daily retail transactions on the streets.[14] The RTGS was suspended in October 2008, and before that, there was close interaction between transactions in these different markets and the official markets, which involved illegal dealings and corruption.

As it is known from the case of the second Yugoslav hyperinflation, *de facto* dollarization could become a powerful catalyst of an inflationary spiral. In the case of Zimbabwe, especially in the last few months toward the end of 2008, the level of inflation was determined in lockstep with the devaluation of the currency. A plausible reason for the higher level of hyperinflation in Zimbabwe than in the second Yugoslav episode is the possible higher scarcity of foreign currency supply in Zimbabwe: per capita income in Zimbabwe was considerably lower than in Yugoslavia, and per capita income in Zimbabwe's neighboring countries was also substantially lower than that of Yugoslavia's neighbors.

Shortages in foreign currency supply in hyperinflationary Zimbabwe were evident and demonstrated by the fact that many foreign currencies were simultaneously in circulation, which is contrasts with the situation in Yugoslavia, where mainly the Deutsch mark and the American dollar were used by the local people. Zimbabwe is encircled by four countries – South Africa, Botswana, Zambia, and Mozambique – and the currencies of these neighboring countries were all accepted by the Zimbabweans, mostly in individual bordering regions.[15] When Zimbabwean authorities formally allowed the use of foreign currencies in the domestic economy – a move from *de facto* dollarization to *de jure* dollarization – in December 2008, the currencies of Zimbabwe's four neighbors were listed as accepted, in addition to the U.S. dollar, the British pound sterling, and the euro.

Zimbabwean authorities were aware of the dangers of imminent hyperinflation, and they undertook several steps to check the pace of rising inflation. These measures were in vain, and some of them actually fueled inflation. A price freeze was launched in 2007, and a number of business people were arrested for violation of price regulations. Bearer's checks – with face values from the smallest unit to the multimillions – were issued by the Reserve Bank of Zimbabwe in 2006, with the aim of facilitating regular transactions and forfeiting foreign ownership of Zimbabwean currency notes. Interest rates on loans from the Central Bank were raised several times, except for those given to small farmers. The Zimbabwean dollar was also devalued considerably, though it still lagged behind market rates.

Beginning in 2004, the Reserve Bank of Zimbabwe introduced an auction scheme for foreign exchange allocation that allowed the Central Bank to sell foreign exchange to the highest bidders. This move effectively placed Zimbabwe into a pure floating system, and helped aggravate devaluation expectations in the market. Given the exchange rate differentials in several tiers of foreign exchange transactions, there would be enormous opportunities for arbitrage in Zimbabwe's currency market. Moreover, people with access to cheap credit from the Central Bank could participate in the foreign exchange auction scheme and incessantly drive up devaluations of the Zimbabwean dollar. The auction scheme was thus likely a most lethal factor in Zimbabwe's super hyperinflation.

Redenomination of the currency appeared to be the Zimbabwean authorities' last attempt to save the country from hyperinflation. This first occurred in August 2006, when the second Zimbabwean dollar was set at 1,000 (10^3) of the first Zimbabwean dollar, and the second redenomination occurred in August 2008, with the third Zimbabwean dollar being set equal to 10 billion (10^{10}) of the second Zimbabwean dollar; at this time, monthly inflation had already reached 3,190 percent. After the start of *de jure* dollarization, the third attempt at redenomination was made in February 2009, with the fourth Zimbabwean dollar being set equal to 1 trillion (10^{12}) of the third Zimbabwean dollar. All in all, the fourth Zimbabwean dollar was equal to 10^{25} of the first Zimbabwean dollar. The last attempt made no sense in real terms, as the Zimbabwean government finally decided in March 2009 that the national currency would no longer be the legal tender of the country. Since that time, taxes have been levied in foreign currency, and wages and salaries in the public sector are also paid in foreign currency.

De jure dollarization and its impacts

Before Zimbabwe, there were only a handful of small Caribbean island states or Balkan countries that had unilaterally adopted dollarization. Unlike countries that used a single foreign currency as legal tender in their domestic economies, the de jure dollarization in Zimbabwe has been a multicurrency regime.[16] At the end of 2008, 60 percent of the Zimbabwean labor force was out of formal employment.[17] Economic collapse and natural diasters had been so catastrophic that more than 4 million Zimbabweans, out of some 12 to 13 million total, left the country during the 2000s.[18] When Mugabe was recognized once again as president late in 2008, the Zimbabwean government seemed to see that retaining the domestic currency would not help it fight hyperinflation at all, and it decided on a switch to *de jure* dollarization.

As suggested by a well-known currency expert, Steve H. Hanke, Zimbabwe in mid-2008 had three options for ending hyperinflation: dollarization, currency board, and free banking.[19] Of the three choices, free banking meant the government would be completely hands-off in terms of the banking industry, and Mugabe apparently would not like to approve of this. A currency board system would require a thorough transformation of Zimbabwe's Central Bank and would rely on the credibility of the Zimbabwean government, which again was not favored by Mugabe. In addition, both options would require utterly dismantling the Reserve Bank of Zimbabwe or at least a thoroughly restructuring such that it could be kept away at arm's length from Mugabe. Dollarization was thus left as the only feasible option. With *de jure* dollarization, the role of the Reserve Bank of Zimbabwe would have to be minimized; the bank would become primarily a cashier and treasury manager for the Ministry of Finance. Yet, it may have been Mugube's hope that one day he would restore the Central Bank's full functions.

The benefits and costs of *de jure* dollarization in Zimbabwe were mixed. On the positive side, price stability returned to the economy, and businesses resumed transparency and regularity. Certain long-term investments and contracts became possible, and short-term speculation ebbed away. As a result, in 2009, CPI in dollar terms rose 6.2 percent as a yearly average and fell 7.7 percent by the year end. In the year, GDP in real terms grew 7.5 percent after having declined for more than a decade. Exports of goods surged in 2010 (59 percent) and 2011 (21.3 percent); these had also been declining for the eight years prior to 2009.

The Zimbabwean government lost seigniorage due to the *de jure* dollarization, but was able to steadily increase revenues starting in 2009 thanks to economic growth. Government revenue as a proportion to GDP rose from 2.2 percent in 2008 to 12 percent in 2009 and 23.3 percent in 2010. With certain fiscal adjustments, budget deficits were also minimized.

A multicurrency dollarization caused many practical inconveniences in Zimbabweans' daily lives. Mulitple price listings aside, retailers and their customers both suffered from shortages of cash or had to unwillingly submit to mismatched currency exchanges. Automation in modern banking sustained substantially larger costs than in a single currency environment.

Loss of monetary policy autonomy may have been the largest negative result of the dollarization of the country. However, compared to risks of a recurring hyperinflation, it appears to be a smaller concern. The Zimbabwean government had pronounced several times since early 2009 that dollarization was a temporary measure, and it would restore the national currency when conditions permitted. Indeed, such attempts have been made recently. The Reseve Bank of Zimbabwe was reported in November 2016 to be planning for an issue of US$10 million worth of "Bond Notes" in small denominations. These bond notes would be at par with the U.S. dollar and be fully convertible. Apparently, the Zimbabwean government has intended to make the "Bond Notes" a legal tender in the future and increase its discretion in monetary policy. However, whether conditions for such a move have been met or not remains a question. As a Zimbabwean think-tank report reiterates, conditions for a successful shift to a new currency regime will require "policy consistency, political commitment and leadership, socio-economic convergences, institutional reforms and the adoption of prudent monetary and fiscal policies."[20] Anything on the list that is believed to be short of recognition by the Zimbabwean people would affect the timing and method of Zimbabwe's return to her own national currency system in the future.

Venezuela: heading to hyperinflation and crisis

Comparing inflation movements in Venezuela with those in other Latin American and the Caribbean countries since 1980, as shown in Figure 8.2, we may note several conspicuous changes. First, between 1980 and 1995, inflation in Venezuela was considerably lower than that in Latin American and the Caribbean countries, which reflects a better macroeconomic performance in that country during that period, although Venezuela did occasionally endure episodes of foreign debt crisis. Second, from 1995 onward, while inflation in most Latin American and Caribbean countries had subsided, generally because of successful stabilization programs in countries like Brazil and Argentina, inflation in Venezuela rose and remained above the group's average level.

Looking closely at the data in Figure 8.2, one can see a significant event that occurred in 2003: Venezuela's inflation (31 percent) rose to triple the group's average level (9.3 percent), and the difference has gradually enlarged since. Since 2013, inflation in Venezuela has escalated, reaching as high as 475.8 percent by the end of 2016. It is projected that CPI inflation in Venezuela will further increase to over 1,000 percent in 2017.[21]

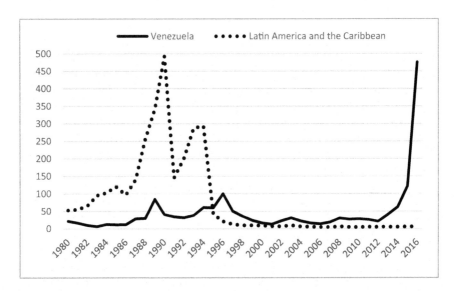

Figure 8.2 Change in annual average CPI in Venezuela and Latin America and the Caribbean countries, percentage, 1980–2016[22]

In fact, by using a method of purchasing power parity and the data of market exchange rates in Venezuela, observers have been able to derive estimates of latest inflation movements in the country and to arrive at the conclusion that Venezuela in November, 2016, has become the world's 57th country principally in the monthly criterion required to qualify as a hyperinflation: in that month, Venezuela's inflation as measured in the change in exchange rate rose 221 percent over the previous month.[23] The method used in the estimation is the same as that in the case of Zimbabwe as shown in Figure 8.1. A simple reason for making the estimates is that official data of price movement are no longer available in the two countries. As it happened, the *Economist* stopped updating Venezuela's monthly inflation in its weekly international macroeconomic table from January 2016.

Unlike in all other countries in the "World Hyperinflation Table,"[24] the hyperinflation in Venezuela is an ongoing process, and there is no clue as of 2017 when and how its end would come.

The current monetary and economic crisis in Venezuela has had a cause that can be traced back to events in the early 2000s. In particular, it is the policy on capital controls – government controls on foreign exchange transactions in Venezuela – that helped deteriorate the economy and finance in the country and led the country to eventually fall into crisis.

The year 2003 was a year in which foreign exchange controls were introduced in the country, allegedly to prevent capital flight. At the time, Venezuela had a sizable current account surplus, about 14 percent of her GDP. Also, she expected a promising export growth to arrive, as international oil prices were rising – oil accounted for more than 90 percent of Venezuelan exports in 2003.[25] Venezuela should not have had any problems with foreign exchange had she pursued a prudent economic policy.

Hugo Chávez became Venezuela's president in 1999, and he led the country into what has been dubbed "Chavismo," a set of anti-liberal economic and social policies marked by radical nationalization of industry, disproportionate promotion of public-sector development, and heavy subsidization of social welfare programs. Certain elements of Chavismo may have been positive, as the program was aimed at correcting past policy biases and reducing social inequality – typical problems in many Latin American countries. Some progress was indeed achieved in Venezuela during the late 1990s and early 2000s: poverty declined from 50 percent in 1998 to approximately 30 percent in 2013, according to official figures. The Gini Index, an indicator of inequality, decreased from 0.49 in 1998 to 0.40 in 2012 – the lowest in Latin America in that year.[26]

However, tensions with the private sector brought about by Chavismo caused increased macroeconomic instability in Venezuela. The foreign exchange controls of 2003 were likely part of Chávez's attempt to establish a state monopoly over the economy by rendering private-sector businesses subordinate. As revenue from the state-controlled oil sector was the main source of foreign exchange supply, and was required to sell to the Central Bank at designated exchange rates, the main demand for foreign exchange in Venezuela came from the private sector, which was "characterized by demanding more foreign currency for imports than those generated by its export activities."[27] In other words, Venezuelan authorities could play a decisive role in allocating foreign exchange to the private sector.

Before the introduction of capital controls and fixed exchange rate, Venezuela had adopted a crawling band system in 1996–2001, a scheme that allows currency depreciation over time within a predetermined range, as the one implemented by Argentina and other Latin American countries in the past. In 2002, Venezuela briefly moved into a free floating system, allowing exchange rates to be determined in the market with little government intervention. A large-scale workers' strike in December 2002 – "the disruption of oil activity" as it is called formally[28] – prompted the government to shift to the new foreign exchange system.

In order to implement foreign exchange allocation to the private sector by the will of the government, a special administrative agency was established in early 2003: *Comisión de Administración de Divisas* (CADIVI). It had power to decide who should get how much at what time in foreign exchange. By regulation, the PDVSA, Venezuela's state oil enterprise and probably the sole supplier of foreign exchange for most of the time, must sell its foreign exchange revenue to the Central Bank of Venezuela (BCV), whose sales of foreign exchange was largely determined by the CADIVI, rather than by itself, as established under Venezuelan law.

With the introduction of foreign exchange controls, a multiplier exchange rate regime was adopted in the country. Three levels of exchange rates – all official – were applied to three categories of imports, with the most preferential rate given to imports of food and pharmaceutical goods. Individual Venezuelans could buy a limited, regulated amount of foreign exchange goods.

An immediate effect of the exchange controls was the reemergence of black markets in foreign exchange, which eventually became a market signal of public expectations about currency devaluation and domestic inflation. The Venezuelan government banned any publication of information about exchange rates in the black markets, apparently for the sake of stopping the spread of devaluation and inflation expectations.

At one point in early 2015, as documented by an observer, there were four exchange rates in Venezuela: the most preferential rate for "an elite few," 6.3 *bolívars* a dollar; the second rate for permitted credit card holders who would spend the money when travelling abroad, up to a maximum, 12 *bolívars* a dollar; the auction rate for permitted business owners who participated in the CADIVI-run process of foreign exchange sales where the quantity offered was determined on auction basis, 50 *bolívars* a dollar; last, the black market rate free for everybody, 150 *bolívars* a dollar.[29] With these vast disparities in exchange rate, trading in foreign exchange had become a profession that attracted numerous Venezuelans "to abandon their careers altogether to trade dollars illegally."[30]

Initially, the Venezuelan government proclaimed in early 2003 that capital controls were for a six-month emergency only. What happened later is, however, the government found itself increasingly unable to terminate the policy as its financial position was weakening along with rising inflation. The fact the Venezuelan government kept maintaining its official exchange rates whilst relaxing its control on monetary expansion, willingly or unwillingly, had resulted in resulted in the overvaluation of the currency, the *bolívar*. Running an average annual inflation of 21 percent in the first decade of the twenty-first century, with occasional devaluations, made the currency chronically overvalued and caused persistent devaluation expectations. A currency reform in 2008 that replaced the *bolívar* with the *bolívar fuerte* at a rate 1,000 to 1 could not save the country from the plight of foreign exchange shortages and rising devaluation expectations.

When Nicolás Maduro succeeded Chávez in 2013, the Venezuelan government had run a budget deficit for seven years in a row, which was 10.9 percent of the GDP excluding annual interest payments and 14.3 percent including annual interest payments. The period from 2012 to the first half of 2014 was a window of opportunity for Venezuela's economic realignment, as international oil prices were high and Venezuela had the opportunity to collect revenue windfalls from oil exports. Unfortunately, Venezuelan exports stopped growing that year, and the country's current account surplus continued to diminish, from 4.9 percent of GDP in 2011 to 1.7 percent in 2014. From 2015, Venezuela's current account turned to deficit, which amounted to 7.8 percent of the GDP in the year. A preliminary estimate is that the current account deficit would be 3.4 percent of GDP in 2016.[31]

It is ironic that Venezuela witnessed significant shortages of food and pharmaceutical goods in 2015, as their imports had been categorically supported under the government's complex exchange rate regime. Mismanagement, fraud, and corruption on a considerable scale must have occurred for such shortages to have afflicted the country at this time. In a period of devaluation expectations, Venezuelans would have sought to obtain foreign exchange allocations through all possible channels. When they did, any allocated foreign exchange would likely not have been used for imports of food or pharmaceutical goods, at least not to the level desired by government authorities. It is also possible that the more severe the devaluation expectations, the more likely the occurrence of food and pharmaceutical goods shortages.

In February 2016, Maduro's administration simplified exchange controls into a two-tier scheme accompanied by a large devaluation: the first category remained imports of food and pharmaceutical goods, for which the exchange rate of the *bolívar fuerte* to the U.S. dollar dropped from 6.3 to 10, and the second category was set for all other imports, for which the allocation of foreign exchange would be based on the government's import priorities, and applicable exchange rates would be a managed float.[32] Apparently, this move did not address the issue of the misuse of foreign exchange allocation through the most preferential channel. Rather, it signaled to the market that the government was prepared to let the currency continue to devalue.

Despite intensified price controls in Venezuela, which were largely inherited from Chávez's Bolivarian practice, inflation surged to triple digits in 2015. It is estimated that in that year, the fiscal deficit rose to 20 percent of GDP, and two-thirds of this had to be financed by monetary expansion.[33] Unsuppressed by government prohibition, an app known as "Dollar Today" began to disseminate daily news about the exchange rates of the *bolívar fuerte* versus the U.S. dollar, which were based on transactions in a border town in neighboring Colombia. Guided by this information, an increasing number of Venezuelans began to practice price arbitrage and currency speculation. For example, many Venezuelans bought gasoline at very cheap prices, as it was subsidized in the Venezuelan domestic market, and sold it in bordering Colombian towns at prices closer to market for a hefty profit.[34]

The macroeconomic situation in Venezuela in 2016 was much worse than in 2015. Because of over-dependence on oil exports, which relied on the import of intermediate inputs, devaluation and shortage of foreign exchange in Venezuela posed great threats to industry. Venezuela was on the verge of defaulting on her foreign debts, and her relations with major international financial institutions had been tenuous in recent years.

Had default occurred, hyperinflation or higher hyperinflation would have become inevitable. CPI inflation of 475.8 percent in 2016 was already the world's highest for the year. In the midst of surges in unemployment and irregularities in business, Venezuela's GDP declined 10 percent in 2016. Without a major policy change, 2017 will be an even more difficult time for Venezuela. As remarked by an author on the sad story of Venezuela in the recent decade,

> Venezuela's reality is a tale of how hubris, oil dependence, spendthrift ways, and economic ignorance can drive a country to ruin. Venezuela can teach us all an important lesson: too much money poorly managed can be worse than not having any money at all.[35]

North Korea: "Unrepressed" hyperinflation in a Hermit Kingdom

An international reporter has written a book about the Venezuelan economy – "the world's craziest economy" in his words – in the shadow of Chávez's Bolivarian Revolution; this work is largely based on his investigative work, about which he admits: "in Venezuela, speaking about the economy can get people into legal trouble. And many Venezuelans are forced to engage in illegal activities to survive or go ahead."[36] This caution applies as well to North Korea (DPRK) perhaps more than anywhere else in today's world. A news report claims that when the country applied to Beijing in early 2015 for membership in the China-initiated Asian Infrastructure Investment Bank – a new, large multilateral financial institution – the request was turned down because there was no access to data about North Korea's economy or finances.[37]

In a closed-door meeting with IMF representatives in 1997, North Korean officials provided some data that indicated "that output had fallen by half in the preceding four years and that the condition of the economy was dire."[38] Due to political complications, North Korea's request to join the IMF has never been realized.

As the North Korean government has had no practice of publishing statistics on regular basis, much of the information presented here about the North Korean economy has been based on third-party estimates, and it is not always possible to update this information timely.[39]

Two economists believe that if a country follows any one of five specific policy lines, it should be regarded as a closed economy with a closed trade policy: (1) non-tariff barriers that cover 40 percent or more of trade; (2) average tariff rates of 40 percent or more; (3) a black market exchange rate that is depreciated by 20 percent or more relative to the official exchange rate, on average; (4) a state monopoly on major exports; (5) a central planning economic system.[40] Among all nations in the world today, perhaps only North Korea fits all five criteria.

How may hyperinflation occur in an economy in which almost everything – from prices of commodities to domestic commerce and foreign trade – is controlled by the state, and there is no CPI or RPI information? Indeed, ordinary urban North Koreans are allocated basic supplies of simple food, housing, medical care, and schooling, virtually free of charge, although in limited quantities. If there were inflation or high inflation in North Korea, it could happen only in certain unallocated areas.

From the late 1990s, after a period of economic stagnation and natural disasters which caused famine and starvation, North Korea relaxed state controls by allowing private business on a small scale, while continuing to pursue a Stalinist-styled economic system. A number of joint ventures with foreign businesses – from South Korea and other countries – have been established in the country in recent years. Foreign tourism has become an important source of earning foreign exchange. As a result, a shadow economy has been evolving in the country. Research based on interviews with refugees from North Korea concludes that "practically the entire population is involved with the shadow economy in some way, as producers, sellers or, at the very least, consumers."[41]

One estimate says that in 2000, North Korean households held approximately US$964 million in total foreign currency, for an average of $186 per family, of which 60 percent was in U.S. dollars, with the rest being mainly in Chinese *renminbi*.[42] Foreign exchange holdings enable North Koreans to buy luxury imports or save money that has a stable value. There are shops in North Korea in which merchandise may be bought only with foreign currencies, such as the U.S. dollar, the Japanese yen, and the Chinese *renminbi*. Exchange rates on the black market have been noted to differ considerably from official rates.[43]

It is known that the North Korean government conducted a public bond issue in 2003, for an unspecified amount. The bonds were of 10-year maturity with no fixed interest rate. Reward to bond holders was a lottery-based cash prize.[44] Since 2003, there has been no similar bond issue, nor does the government show any intent to develop a securities market.

As long as a country's household sector holds a significant amount of money, it is in principle possible for a government to maneuver monetary policy or currency to secure financial gains. This is in effect what has been happening in North Korea's relatively short history of currency.

Like South Korea, North Korea has had a currency system from the second half of the 1940s. Since then, there have been at least four major "currency reforms" in the country: 1959, 1979, 1992, and 2009. Each time, old notes were withdrawn within a short window of time, and new notes of larger denominations were put into circulation. The two reforms in 1959 and 2009 involved redenomination, with old notes being replaced by new ones at a rate of 100 to 1. These events suggest that the North Korean government not only forced the invalidation of "excessive" currency holdings by its residents, but also almost constantly pursued an expansionary monetary policy. The money stock in North Korea must have been growing at a rapid pace that was faster than that of repressed inflation.

The currency reform in 2009 was particularly a harsh one. In December, North Koreans were given two weeks to exchange their existing currency notes for new, re-denominated, ones at a rate of 1 new note to 100 old notes; there were maximum limits set for each family in the exchange. Upper limits extended to households' bank deposits. This is nothing more than a "wealth tax program."[45] Wealthy North Koreans or anyone with savings of more than the maximum that was permitted to be exchanged were obviously in danger of seeing their savings be effectively wiped out.

The North Korean government did not conduct public announcements about the currency reform in 2009. Instead, apparently in order to make the matter purely "internal," news about the currency conversion was broadcast only by cable radio and loud speakers in local communities. It was claimed that the objectives of the reform were to deter inflation, curb the black markets, and realign the economic structure. The reaction of North Koreans was panic and chaos. Those who had earlier heard of the move rushed to rural areas to buy rice and corn, or flooded into the black markets to buy foreign currencies. People with foreign currencies queued at the doors of shops that sold commodities in foreign exchange.

It was reported that the government had to postpone the currency conversion for a day from the start, and that it also had to close all shops and department stores for three days in mid-December.[46] Armed police forces were dispatched to the streets to maintain security and order in cities. Two months later in February 2010, Pyongyang decided to ease the restrictions in order to avoid more protest and resistance from the public.[47] More than a year later, several Chinese websites cited South Korean reports that a high-ranking North Korean official in charge of the implementation of the currency reform was executed for its disastrous result without any public explanation.

In a matter of one or two months, prices of rice and corn soared in North Korea's rural markets. As can be seen from Figure 8.3, rice prices doubled to 44 won in one week in mid-December 2009, and the won's exchange rate with the dollar soared to 134 at the end of December, from late November's rate of 38.5. Overall, between December 2009 and March 2010, rice prices rose 28.5-fold, and the dollar rate versus the new currency rose 58.7-fold. In February 2010, both quotations rose by 100 percent or more.

Of course, the inflation rates are derived from the prices of rice and the exchange rates that prevailed in black currency markets, which are not comparable to usual indicators such as CPI or RPI. Nevertheless, these figures reflect that even in a highly state-controlled economy, hyperinflation can still erupt in unregulated areas.

Inflation in North Korea was not stopped by the government's efforts of March 2010, and it has continued in the country since then. Black market exchange

Figure 8.3 Weekly or bi-weekly exchange rates and rice prices in Pyongyang markets, new won, North Korea, August 2009–December 2015[48]

rates remain remarkably higher than official rates. With trade flows increasingly restricted by the United Nations' resolutions on North Korea's nuclear program, the country's economy has been unprecedentedly isolated, and foreign exchange scarcity has become even more severe for the regime. To overcome budget difficulties that have arisen from a stagnant economy and the worsening international opinion of the country, North Korea's government may have to rely more on monetary means to sustain its budget and its people's needs; i.e., it may need to embark on an inflationary policy on a greater scale. The fate of North Korea's economy is difficult to predict.

What is certain is that dollarization has gained a firm foothold in the economy. If hyperinflation were to occur, its magnitude likely would be much more severe than anything North Korea has endured to date.

A perhaps most enlightening point to the student of contemporary international finance is that all three countries that had fallen into hyperinflation or monetary disorder – Zimbabwe, Venezuela, and North Korea – shared a distinctive policy approach: capital controls or foreign exchange controls either before or during the crisis. To some, capital controls are regarded as a most powerful instrument to prevent an economy from sliding into a financial crisis. Yet, the experiences of the three countries in the twenty-first century have unambiguously demonstrated the contrary: capital controls can never make an economy immune from what the government least expects to occur in the financial and monetary world. If capital controls had roles at play, their most significant one would necessarily have been a disguise of fundamental problems in economic structure and/or policy making.

Appendix note: did China help?

Diplomatic disputes that Zimbabwe, Venezuela, and North Korea have had with the United States and other Western countries have resulted in stalemates in their external economic relations. Their access to international financial assistance and private financial markets has been largely deadlocked. With an ideological affinity and a degree of common interest in geopolitics, China appeared to be a potential source of economic aid to these three countries when they were suffering through hyperinflation and economic collapse.

Indeed, China's economic relations with these three countries have been either rapidly growing in the recent years, or already became well developed years ago. China has been Zimbabwe's largest trading partner for a number of years, accounting for 27.8 percent of Zimbabwe's exports in 2015, an amount that is far greater than that of the Democratic Republic of Congo's 14 percent, Botswana's 12.5 percent, and South Africa's 7.6 percent.[49] In the case of Venezuela, the United States has remained the largest export destination (26.6 percent) in 2015, followed by India (13.7 percent), China (11.7 percent), and Cuba (6.4 percent). For North Korea, China alone accounted for 75.8 percent of the country's exports in 2015.

After many years of rapid economic growth, China seems able to provide financial assistance to "friends in need" in recent years and to play a significant role in international finance. China's GDP in current prices and exchange rates reached $5.1 trillion in 2009, exceeding Japan's and becoming the world's second largest economy after the United States. Based on purchasing power parity, an IMF estimate indicates that China's GDP was $18.2 trillion in 2014, more than the United States' $17.4 trillion. The turnover of China's total exports has exceeded the United States and Germany since the mid-2000s, and the sum of China's total exports and imports has been the world's largest since the early 2010s. Moreover, decades-long currency account surpluses have enabled China to accumulate enormous foreign exchange reserves, which peaked at $3.98 trillion in mid-2014, accounting for nearly 30 percent of global foreign exchange reserves.

As an emerging power on the world stage, China seems willing to play a self-affirmative and increasingly important role in international financial relations. In the field of offering financial aid to developing countries, China undertook her first move in a large debt relief program to African countries in 2000, which amounted to RMB 10 billion yuan – equivalent to $1.3 billion U.S. dollars. Another major initiative of debt relief to 50 highly-indebted developing countries and least-developed countries was announced in 2010. In 2015, the Chinese government committed to take steps to relinquish financial claims to funds given to less-developed countries in an amount that may be the equivalent of billions of U.S. dollars.

Against this backdrop, a question that has been asked is whether China helped these three countries at the time when they were struggling with hyperinflation. Clues may be sought by looking at movements in the bilateral trade and investment relations between China and these countries around the time of their crises.

In this regard, three sets of data are available: China's imports and exports, direct investments, and various construction projects undertaken by the Chinese.[50] Usually, Chinese undertaking of construction projects is either part of Chinese aid programs abroad or a result of bilateral economic cooperation programs.

In the case of Zimbabwe, Chinese merchandise exports to the country had been steadily growing prior to 2008 when Zimbabwe's monetary crisis occurred. In that year, Chinese exports to Zimbabwe fell to $133 million from 2007's level of $202 million, and Chinese imports from Zimbabwe remained basically unchanged – 2007's $143 million versus 2008's $148 million. Chinese direct investment in Zimbabwe amounted to $12.6 million in 2007, but there was actually a divestment of $0.7 million in 2008, with 2009 returning to an investment level of $11 million. The dollar amount of Chinese undertaking of construction projects in Zimbabwe increased considerably during this period, to $149 million in 2008 from 2007's $87 million, but it was cut by more than half to $65 million in 2009. It is clear that during the crisis year of 2008 and part of 2009, Chinese trade with Zimbabwe and direct investment in the country took a large downturn, with construction projects suffering immediately afterwards. These figures do not suggest that Chinese economic relations with Zimbabwe were "unusual" around the time of the crisis. In other words, China was not initiating any effort to increase her economic involvement with Zimbabwe in a programmatic effort to help the country through her economic problems.

The year 2009 was the year in which North Korea underwent drastic changes in currency and finance. Chinese exports to the country fell to $1,887 million in 2009 from 2008's $2,032 million, and further plummeted to $228 million in 2010. Chinese imports from North Korea increased moderately at 4.2 percent to $793 million in 2009, and further increased a significant 51 percent to $1,195 million in 2010. However, Chinese direct investment flow was down to $5.9 million in 2009 from 2008's $41 million, and her construction projects dropped from 2008's $33.5 million to 2009's $18 million. As in the case of Zimbabwe, Chinese exports, investment flow, and construction projects all took a large dip. The fact that Chinese imports had grown during the crisis year should be interpreted as Chinese importers taking advantage of the falling values of the North Korean local currency in real terms, and not the result of any *ad hoc* Chinese policy moves taken purposely by the government to help North Korea stabilize her economy.

The monetary and economic crisis in Venezuela is still evolving and has not yet approached its end at the time of the writing of this book. Preliminary evidence has, however, shown that Chinese economic behavior is not much different with respect to Venezuela from what it had been in the case of Zimbabwe and North Korea. Chinese exports to Venezuela slowed to $5,316 million in 2015 from 2014's $5,657 million, and Chinese imports from the country fell from 2014's $11,320 million to 2015's $6,778 million – a result largely of falling oil prices. Meanwhile, Chinese direct investment in Venezuela has declined since 2013, having peaked at $1,542 million in 2012, bottomed out at $116 million in 2014 and then recovered to $288 million in 2015. Chinese undertaking of construction projects amounted to $5,967 million in 2013, and it then steadily declined to $4,942 million in 2015.

Again, all of these figures suggest that Chinese bilateral economic relations with Venezuela have not been on the upswing in the past two or three years.

Chinese initiation of or participation in stabilization programs in foreign countries in a bilateral manner is obviously unprecedented and has yet to occur. It is clear that China did not provide any specific financial assistance to any of the three countries discussed above for purposes of stabilization that may be compared with other episodes that we have seen repeatedly in this book. Perhaps we can also say that the inaction is not because China is politically unwilling or financially unable to offer a helping hand to countries in need. Rather, it is because China's foreign policy approach to countries in economic crisis has not been clearly defined, and China has not made intellectual preparation adequate to address issues related to the principles of a stabilization program. China has cherished a foreign-policy tradition of "non-interventionism," which would likely conflict with conducting a bilateral stabilization program that necessarily requires conditionality on the part of recipient governments in order to achieve desirable results and avoid moral hazard – an issue that a recipient government may have incentive to behave unexpectedly which would therefore jeopardize the interest of the aid-giving country. In a sense, the question "did China help" presents a philosophical dilemma that has no immediate answer. It may be more accurate to note that China "did not help," because she could not help by means of a conventional bilateral stabilization program.

Further, from a global perspective, it is most likely that in the foreseeable future, Bretton-Woods institutions such as the International Monetary Fund will remain the primary source of international help for stabilization programs that help countries deal with hyperinflation or financial emergencies of other types.

Notes

1 The IMF: *World Economic Outlook: Globalization and Inflation*, Chapter III – How Has Globalization Affected Inflation? April 2006.
2 A probable only exception is Professor Steve H. Hanke's publication that appeared in a Cato Institute journal in June 2008, which attested the situation of hyperinflation in the country and assessed policy options for Zimbabwe to walk out the demise (Hanke, 2008).
3 Hanke and Krus, Table 30.1, pp. 372–3.
4 An explanation of Mugabe's decision to intervene in Congo is his pursuit of economic and financial gain in the conflict and his geopolitical consideration pinpointed to the role of South Africa in the region (Prunier, pp. 190–2).
5 Noko, p. 341.
6 Kararach and Otieno, Tables 1.1–1.3, pp. 9, 12 and 13. The figures cited in the original source come directly from the Zimbabwean government, and may have been under-reported for the later years.
7 Noko, pp. 343–4.
8 Hanke (2008, p. 4).
9 Hanke (2008, Table 1, p. 3).
10 Kararach and Otieno, Table 1.3, p. 13.
11 Hanke and Kwok.
12 Hanke and Kwok, Table 1, p. 355. Figures of the last four months from August 2008 are derived from the OMIR (see the text), and the annual rates are the change of the indicator in a month over past twelve months.

13 McIndoe, Table 2 on p. 19, Figure 4 on p. 23, and Table A3 on p. 43.
14 McIndoe, pp. 18–9, and Noko, pp. 356–7.
15 Noko, p. 353.
16 As an IMF staff report documents, five foreign currencies have been recognized since 2009 for settling taxation and other public liabilities in Zimbabwe (Kramarenko *et al*, Footnote 3, p. 3).
17 Noko, p. 347.
18 Noko, p. 341, Footnote 3.
19 Hanke (2008).
20 Kararach, Kadenge and Guvheya, p. 37.
21 An IMF project of CPI inflation in Venezuela, made in October 2016, was 720 percent in 2017 and 2,028 percent in 2018 as a yearly average, and 1,133 percent in 2017 and 2,529 percent in 2018 as a year end change (IMF, *World Economic Outlook Database*, updated in October 2016).
22 The International Monetary Fund, *World Economic Outlook Database*, updated in October 2016, with figures for 2016 projected.
23 Hanke and Bushnell (2016), "The Hanke-Krus World Hyperinflation Table," pp. 4–6.
24 Hanke and Krus, pp. 372–4; Hanke and Bushnell, pp. 4–6.
25 Figures of Venezuela's current account balance from 1980 can be found in the IMF, *World Economic Outlook Database*, and that of Venezuelan oil in the World Bank, *Country Overview: Venezuela*, available www.worldbank.org/en/country/venezuela/overview, updated in September, 2016.
26 The World Bank, *Country Overview: Venezuela*, available at www.worldbank.org/en/country/venezuela/overview, updated in September, 2016.
27 Giner and Mendoza, p. 292.
28 Giner and Mendoza, p. 292.
29 Gallegos, pp. 11–2.
30 Gallegos, pp. 15.
31 All the figures in this paragraph are from the IMF, *World Economic Outlook Database*, updated in October 2016.
32 The Central Intelligence Agency, *The World Fact Book: Venezuela – Economy*, 2016, available at www.cia.gov/library/publications/resources/the-world-factbook/geos/ve.html.
33 Walter Molano's email-distributed newsletter of *The Emerging Market Adviser*, August 24, 2015.
34 Walter Molano's email-distributed newsletter of *The Emerging Market Adviser*, August 24, 2015.
35 Gallegos, p. 7.
36 Gallegos, Author's Note, p. xv.
37 Tencent Finance and Economy News Report, "China rejects DPRK's application for joining the AIIB", March 31, 2015 (http://finance.qq.com/a/20150331/051295.htm). (In Chinese).
38 Boughton (2012, p. 75).
39 A website run out of Seoul provides daily information about the North Korean currency exchange rates with the dollar and prices of rice from 2009, based on observations in black markets in three North Korean cities (www.dailynk.com/english/market.php). As reported by the *Economist*, February 11, 2017, South Korean scholars have begun to use satellite images to analyze the economic situation in North Korea with reference to a one-time census conducted in the country, which cannot be frequently updated.
40 Sachs and Warner, p. 22.
41 Joo (2010, p. 134). A paper published in 2016 envisages that "[t]o this day, the shadow economy and the official sphere continue to coexist warily" in DPRK (Dukalskis, 2016, p. 496).
42 Worden, p. 160.

43 During the 1990s and 2000s, the North Korean government devalued its currency several times, but black market dollar rates remained ten times the official rates (Worden, p. 162).

44 Worden, pp. 162–3.

45 Hanke (2013).

46 Hanke (2013).

47 The Central Intelligence Agency, *The World Fact Book: North Korea – Economy*, 2016, available at www.cia.gov/library/publications/resources/the-world-factbook/geos/kn.html.

48 The data source is an online daily-updated watchdog based in Seoul, South Korea: www.dailynk.com/ english/market.php, accessed on March 30, 2017. Prices of rice are per kilogram. Raw data shows quotations for three cities including Pyongyang. All quotations prior to December 2009 have been converted into the new won at a rate 100 to 1. There is a missing figure in the exchange rate for the week of December 9–15, 2009.

49 All figures regarding trade for these three countries are from the CIA's *The World Fact Book* unless otherwise noted.

50 All data about bilateral trade and direct investment flows and construction projects can be found on the website of China's State Statistical Bureau (www.stats.gov.cn/).

9 Conclusion

Mankind knows a lot about diseases and how they spread. It still has a lot to learn.
The Economist, Feb 13th 2016, p. 77

This journey through the world's hyperinflation history over the past 2,000 years or so tells us a number of important truths about the nature and causes of hyperinflation, which can be summarized as follows.

First, hyperinflation or high inflation occurred long before the advent of paper currency. In ancient China and the Roman Empire, when rulers were technologically able to debase metal coins and had any reason to do so, high inflation ensued. It is government monopoly of money – be it metal coinage or paper currency – that makes possible inflationary monetary policy and its inflationary effects. In the late medieval period, when debasement became widespread in Europe and elsewhere, inflation was a common phenomenon. A probable reason why inflation in many places did not evolve into hyperinflation is that the use of money in the society or the development of commerce was not as great as in modern times.

Second, almost every early adoption of non-convertible paper currency was soon followed by a sharp rise in inflation, as we have seen with such episodes in the Sung, Ming, and Ching (Qing) dynasties in China as well as in France and America, all before the twentieth century. They are indeed cases where a paper currency system helped increase the government's ability to implement an expansionary monetary policy when it was under pressure to finance its budget deficit through unconventional means. Often, it was either domestic or international tensions that caused abnormal budget deficit problems. Yet, given the fact that a monetary system norm – the customary use of commodity money such as gold or silver – was well established in the past, stabilization measures in the early episodes of paper currency-based hyperinflation or high inflation were invariably a return to a metal specie standard.

Third, it is during the twentieth century that the world experienced the highest incidence of hyperinflation, which affected a great number of countries, with various economic and social systems, at different times. At the turn of the century, monetary and financial developments across the world displayed a new trend wherein all market-oriented economies gradually moved beyond the money supply boundaries set by traditional gold standards. Bank deposits and debt securities had become the primary source or method of financing for both the private and public sectors. As a result, the inflation process was increasingly affected by interaction between government policy and people's reactions. Not only did more governments occasionally resort to inflationary policy than before, they also encountered greater difficulty in controlling inflation or could make use of inflation when people's inflation expectations worsened.

In addition, during the twentieth century, the world was searching for a new political and economic order on a global scale, but the pursuit was troubled by clashes and confrontations between rival powers and competing regimes. In the first half of the century, a wave of hyperinflation occurred in several European countries soon after the end of the First World War, and another occurred in many more countries during and immediately after the Second World War. All of the hyperinflation-inflicted countries had undergone abrupt changes in social, economic, and political conditions. Common to these countries were disorganization in domestic economics and politics, reckless policy decision-making, and international isolation. The many misfortunes in the countries that experienced hyperinflation and the relatively low inflation in other belligerencies or war – affected countries during the period suggest that the hyperinflations were caused by more than budget deficits alone, however large those had been.

The second half of the twentieth century was marked by the rise and fall of the Cold War, and the incidence of hyperinflation actually sharply increased as the end of the Cold War approached. Many Latin American countries encountered hyperinflation in the aftermath of the collapse of the Bretton-Woods System, partly reflecting disturbing impacts of external shocks. Nonetheless, it was deep-rooted problems in domestic economic structure and the inability of governments to address macroeconomic instability in a decisive manner that caused chronic inflation to culminate in hyperinflation in the later stages of economic and monetary crisis. In these cases, hyperinflation looked like the raised tail of a long inflationary process. The wave of hyperinflation mostly in Latin America and a spate of high inflation in many African countries during the 1980s and 1990s reveals the importance of economics – not that of politics – in the dynamic process of hyperinflation: it was deficiencies in economic structure and failures in earlier stabilization attempts that caused inflation to run out of control. By and large, hyperinflation was essentially an unintended consequence of incompetency in domestic policy design and institutional management.

The cluster of hyperinflation in all successor states of the Soviet Union and several other transition countries in the 1990s shows how fragile a once-almighty political and economic system was at the start of a new social configuration. Deep-rooted inflexibility and market disconnectedness in industry, coupled with the unfortunate outburst of inflationary pressures that had been "liberalized" by price de-controls, were fundamental factors in the economic distress that occurred during the transition process. In particular, within the sphere of the foregone socialist empire, hyperinflation appeared to be a contagious disease at one time, which demonstrates how ill-equipped a new leading role played by Russia was to handle nascent international economic and political relations.

Fourth, three isolated instances of hyperinflation in the early twenty-first century – in Zimbabwe, Venezuela, and North Korea – highlight how much worse it could be for a country to pursue a distinctive approach while refusing to conform to international norms in the age of globalization. Zimbabwe and Venezuela both had rich natural resources – envied by probably many developing economies – and impressive economic growth not long before heading into economic and monetary disasters. It was their policy swings that ignited the flames of hyperinflation. Most notable is their perplexing treatment of foreign exchange: an auction scheme that drove up shortages of foreign exchange and devaluation expectations (and therefore inflation expectations); and a retreat to capital controls that distorted the domestic economy and finance (and therefore worsened monetary order). In North Korea, the prolonged totalitarian regime reckoned it had the ability to keep a tight rein on a mostly closed economy whilst attempting a deceptive currency program. Nonetheless, the regime found itself trapped by the menace of hyperinflation, which, if not checked, could have shaken the foundations of its tyrannous rule.

Fifth, China, as a populous country with long traditions in politics and money, stands out in the world history of hyperinflation. Wang Mang was probably the first statesman in the world who systematically manipulated coinage for political gain. The Sung promulgated a national paper currency to facilitate prospering commerce, but the system eventually degenerated into the world's first nationwide paper-currency hyperinflation amid defeats in battle against the Mongols. At intervals of decades or centuries, fears of hyperinflation prompted the Ming and Ching to abort paper currency systems and leave monetary affairs largely unregulated, which was one of latent factors that caused Nationalist China to rush into the *fabi* system. In the crossfire of internal and external conflicts, China endured currents of hyperinflation throughout the 1940s, a lengthy tragedy unmatched by many other countries either at the time or since.

The history of hyperinflation in the world also sheds light on three issues that interest a general reader: "How high can hyperinflation be?" "How long can hyperinflation last?" And, "How disastrous can hyperinflation become?"

"How high can hyperinflation be?"

Hungary created the world record of hyperinflation in July 1946, when her monthly increase in CPI reached 4.19×10^{16} percent. Following Hungary are Zimbabwe in mid-November 2008, with her implied exchange rate rising 7.96×10^{10} percent, and Yugoslavia in January 1994, when her CPI rose 3.13×10^8 percent. Other episodes with monthly rates in quadruple digits or more are Germany's 29,500 percent in WPI in October 1923, Greece's 13,800 percent in exchange rate in October 1944, and China's 5,070 percent in WPI in mid-May 1949. These are actual levels that have been documented, not possible levels that hyperinflation could have reached if the process of inflation had not been stopped by contemporaneous events. In essence, there is no upper limit of hyperinflation: The level of inflation is primarily dependent on how rapidly people respond to expected changes in prices and money supply, which in turn are greatly affected by the presence of alternative currencies – foreign exchange or domestic commodity money. Availability of alternative currencies in a domestic economy has the effect of automatically increasing the money supply, which therefore sets no limit for price inflation. A policy that indexes interest on demand deposits to price indicators can also act as a means of automatic money creation, as exemplified in the case of Hungary in 1946. With such an automatic money creation mechanism in effect, the level of hyperinflation is largely a matter of how long the process of inflation can keep going.

"How long can hyperinflation last?"

Many episodes of hyperinflation narrated in this book lasted between several months and a few years. In certain cases, such as China in the 1940s and Turkey from the 1970s to the 1990s, when inflation was below the usual level of hyperinflation or high inflation intermittently fell to lower levels, the process of near-hyperinflation can last a decade or more. As we have repeatedly seen in many cases of successful stabilization programs, whose positive outcomes were principally the results of policy making and the government's regaining of resources, the duration of hyperinflation can be said to depend on three factors: political tolerance of high inflation; the domestic political process; and the economic consequences of hyperinflation. With regard to the second factor, it is known that in some countries, hyperinflation ended simply because one political and currency regime was replaced by another in the midst of civil or international war, such as in the cases of the Philippines in January 1944, Greece in October 1944, and China in August 1945. In several Latin American countries, mainly during the 1980s, drastic policy changes on hyperinflation often occurred after a presidential election.

"How disastrous can hyperinflation become?"

Hyperinflation creates a great deal of new uncertainty in an economy, which affects people's decision-making on saving, consumption, and investment. The functions of money and the performance of financial markets and institutions become enormously distorted during periods of hyperinflation. Output growth and employment are likely to suffer as the already-high inflation rises further. But the economic impacts of hyperinflation can vary from country to country and from time to time, depending on the underlying economic and social structures. Strong labor unions can help reduce the effects of hyperinflation on workers' real wages, but cannot stop the economy shifting toward barter or unofficial markets. The practice of indexation may superficially relieve the pains of hyperinflation for certain members of a society, but it also possibly elongates the healing process.

Not only can hyperinflation lead to economic collapse, when it has not been effectively checked and its impacts on a country's financial and fiscal systems have spread, it can also cause social unrest and political disorder that derail a nation's development path. Unlike some other financial and economic crises, hyperinflation tends to persist in the memories of members of the society, which affects the process of social development in subsequent decades. Political and social developments in Germany in the 1920s and China in the late 1940s all bore the imprints of hyperinflation.

Thanks to globalization and the emerging convergent trend in the world's political and economic development, the incidence of hyperinflation declined considerably from the 1990s and further reduced to just a few isolated episodes in the early twenty-first century. Hyperinflation appears to be no longer a major threat to the development path of any nation. The fact that the Global Financial Crisis in 2008 and the subsequent great monetary and fiscal expansion in virtually all major economies in 2009–10 did not provoke any significant inflation, not to mention hyperinflation, should be largely attributed to achievements in institution building, policy decision-making, and international cooperation that many leading nations purposely endeavored to bring about. Without sound foundations in institutions, policy making and international cooperation, the world would likely have fallen into a new wave of hyperinflation by the late 2010s.

In a sense, hyperinflation is like a virus which can change its form or become dormant for a period of time as long as its environment – a monetary climate in which financial institutions and governments continue to operate an expansionary and inflationary policy – remains in existence. Since the 1990s, many mature economies and emerging market economies have witnessed bouts of "asset bubble" growth, a phenomenon wherein prices of property and securities rise excessively relative to their underlying, long-term values. Whether asset bubbles are instances of inflation in disguise – a latent virus that could lead to an incidence of high inflation or a financial crash – is apparently a new economic issue under debate. By and large, the world today cannot be said to be free of the disease of inflation.

References

Abelshauser, Werer. 1998. "Germany: Guns, Butter, and Economic Miracles." As Chapter 4 of *The Economics of World War II: Six Great Powers in International Comparison*, ed. Mark Harrison. Cambridge: Cambridge University Press, pp. 122–176.

Akira, Hara. 1998. "Japan: Guns before Rice." As Chapter 6 of *The Economics of World War II: Six Great Powers in International Comparison*, ed. Mark Harrison. Cambridge: Cambridge University Press, pp. 224–267.

Åslund, Anders. 2002. *Building Capitalism: The Transformation of the Former Soviet Bloc*. Cambridge: Cambridge University Press.

Baltensperger, Ernst. 1999. "Monetary Policy under Conditions of Increasing Integration (1979–96)." As Chapter 9 of *Fifty Years of the Deutsche Bank: Central Bank and the Currency in Germany since 1948*, ed. The Deutsche Bundesbank. Oxford: Oxford University Press, pp. 439–523.

Bank of International Settlements. 2005. *Foreign Exchange Market Intervention in Emerging Markets: Motives, Techniques and Implications*. Basel: BIS Papers No 24, May.

Baumeister, Christiane, and Lutz Kilian. 2016. "Forty Years of Oil Price Fluctuations: Why the Price of Oil May Still Surprise Us?" *Journal of Economic Perspectives* 30(1): 139–160.

Beaugrand, Phillipe. 1997. "Zaire's Hyperinflation, 1990–96." *International Monetary Fund Working Paper WP/97/50*. International Monetary Fund, Washington, DC.

Beller, Steven. 2007. *A Concise History of Austria*. New York and Cambridge: Cambridge University Press.

Bernholz, Peter. 1989. "Currency Competition, Inflation, Gresham's Law and Exchange Rate." *Journal of Institutional and Theoretical Economics* 145(3): 465–488; reprinted in Siklos. 1995. pp. 97–123.

———. 1996. "Currency Substitution during Hyperinflation in the Soviet Union, 1922–1924." *Journal of European Economic History* 25(2): 297–323.

———. 2003. *Monetary Regimes and Inflation: History, Economic and Political Relationships*. Brookfield, VT: Edward Elgar Publishing.

Bezemer, Dirk J. 2001. "Post-Socialist Financial Fragility: The Case of Albania." *Cambridge Journal of Economics* 25(1): 1–23.

Bideleux, Robert, and Ian Jeffries. 2007. *A History of Eastern Europe*. 2nd edition. London: Routledge.

Bielenstein, Hans. 1967. "Restoration of the Han and Later Han." As Chapter 3 of *The Cambridge History of China: Volume 1, The Ch'in and Han Empires, 221 B.C.–A.D. 220*, eds. Denis Twitchett and John K. Fairbank. Cambridge and New York: Cambridge University Press, pp. 223–290.

Blackburn, Keith, and Michael Christensen. 1989. "Monetary Policy and Policy Credibility: Theories and Evidence." *Journal of Economic Literature* 27(March): 1–45.

Blanchard, Charles. 2003. *Macroeconomics*. 3rd edition. New Jersey: Prentice Hall.

Blejer, Mario I., and Nissan Liviatan. 1987. "Fighting Hyperinflation: Stabilization Strategies in Argentina and Israel, 1985–86." *International Monetary Fund Staff Papers* 34(September): 409–438.

Blustein, Paul. 2001. *The Chastening: Inside the Crisis That Rocked the Global Financial System and Humbled the IMF.* New York: Public Affairs.

Boatswain, Timothy, and Colin Nicolson. 2003. *A Traveller's History of Greece.* London: Interlink Pub Group Inc.

Bomberger, William A., and Gail E. Makinen. 1980. "Indexation, Inflationary Finance, and Hyperinflation: The 1945–1946 Hungarian Experience." *Journal of Political Economy* 88(June): 550–560.

———. 1983. "The Hungarian Hyperinflation and Stabilization of 1945–1946." *Journal of Political Economy* 91(October): 801–824.

Bordo, Michael D., and Eugene N. White. 1991. "A Tale of Two Currencies: British and French Finance During the Napoleonic Wars." *Journal of Economic History* 51(June): 303–316.

Boross, Elizabeth A. 1984. "The Role of the State Issuing Bank in the Course of Inflation in Hungary between 1918 and 1924." In *The Experience of Inflation: International and Comparative Studies*, eds. Gerald D. Feldman, Carl-Ludwig Holtfrerich, Gerhard A. Ritter, and Peter-Christian Witt. New York: Walter de Gruyter, pp. 188–227.

Boughton, James M. 2001. *Silent Revolution: The International Monetary Fund 1979–1989.* Washington, DC: International Monetary Fund.

———. 2012. *Tearing Down Walls: The International Monetary Fund 1990–1999.* Washington, DC: International Monetary Fund.

Brandt, Loren, and Thomas J. Sargent. 1989. "Interpreting New Evidence about China and U.S. Silver Purchases." *Journal of Monetary Economics* 23: 31–51.

Braudel, Fernand, and Frank Spooner. 1967. "Prices in Europe from 1450 to 1750." As Chapter 7 of *The Cambridge Economic History of Europe: Volume 4, The Economy of Expanding Europe in the Sixteen and Seventeen Centuries*, eds. E. E. Rich and C. H. Wilson. Cambridge and New York: Cambridge University Press, pp. 374–486.

Bresciani-Turroni, Constantino. 1937. *The Economics of Inflation: A Study of Currency Depreciation in Post-War Germany.* Northampton: John Dickens & Co ltd. (3rd edition, 1968).

Bresser-Pereira, Luiz Carlos. 1987. "Inertial Inflation and the Cruzado Plan." *World Development* 15(8): 1035–1044.

Brezis, Elise S., and François H. Crouzet. 1995. "The Role of the Assignats during the French Revolution: An Evil or a Rescuer?" *Journal of European Economic History* 24: 7–40.

Bruno, Michael. 1989. "Israel, Crisis and Economic Reform: A Historical Perspective." *NBER Working Paper 3075.* National Bureau of Economic Research, Cambridge, MA. August.

———. 1993. *Crisis, Stabilization and Economic Reform: Therapy by Consensus.* Oxford: Clarendon Press.

Bruno, Michael, and William Easterly. 1998. "Inflation Crisis and Long-Run Growth." *Journal of Monetary Economics* 41(February): 3–26.

Buchheim, Christoph. 1999. "The Establishment of the Bank Deutscher Länder and the West German Currency Reform." As Chapter 2 of *Fifty Years of the Deutsche Mark: Central Bank and the Currency in Germany since 1948*, ed. Deutsche Bundesbank. Oxford and New York: Oxford University Press, pp. 55–100.

Burdekin, Richard C. K., and Fang Wang. 1999. "A Novel End to the Big Inflation in China in 1950." *Economics of Planning* 32(3): 211–229.

Cáardenas, Enrique, and Carlos Manns. 1987. "Inflation and Monetary Stabilization in Mexico during the Revolution." *Journal of Development Economics* 27: 375–394. North-Holland.

Cagan, Phillip. 1956. "The Monetary Dynamics of Hyperinflation." In *Studies in the Quantity Theory of Money*, ed. Milton Friedman. Chicago: University of Chicago Press, pp. 25–117.

———. 1987. "Hyperinflation: Theory." In *The New Palgrave Dictionary of Money and Finance*, Vol. 2, eds. Peter Newman, Murray Milgate, and John Eatwell. London and New York: Macmillan, pp. 323–325.

Campbell, Colin D., and Gorden C. Tullock. 1954. "Hyperinflation in China, 1937–49." *Journal of Political Economy* 62(June): 236–245.

Capie, Forrest. 1986. "Conditions in Which Very Rapid Inflation Has Appeared." *Carnegie-Rochester Conference Series on Public Policy* 24: 115–168. North-Holland.

Cardoso, Fernando Henrique. 2006. *The Accidental President of Brazil: A Memoire*. New York: PublicAffairs.

Carr, Edward Hallett. 1984. *International Relations between the Two World Wars, 1919–1939*. London: Palgrave Macmillan. (Reprint).

Carter, Susan B., Scott S. Gartner, Michael R. Haines, Alan L. Olmstead, Richard Sutch, and Gavin Wright, eds. 2006. *The Historical Statistics of the United States, Colonial Times to the Present*, Millennial edition, 5 vols. New York and Cambridge: Cambridge University Press.

Castronuovo, Valerio. 2000. *La stroia economica – Storia d'Italia, and dall'unità ad oggi*. Torino: Einaudi. (Chinese translation by Commercial Press, Beijing).

Challi, Christopher Edgar. 1978. *The Tudor Coinage*. Manchester: Manchester University Press.

Chang, Kia-ngau. 1958. *The Inflationary Spiral: The Experience in China, 1939–1950*. New York: The Technology Press of Massachusetts Institute of Technology and John Wiley & Sons, Inc.; London: Chapman & Hall.

Chen, Cheng. 2009. *Memoir of Chen Cheng: Anti-Japanese War*. Beijing: Dongfang Press. (In Chinese).

Chou, Shun-hsin. 1963. *The Chinese Inflation, 1937–1949*. New York: Columbia University Press.

Choun, John F. 1994. *A History of Money from AD 800*. London: Routledge and the Institute of Economic Affairs.

Cippolla, Carlo M., ed. 1976. *The Fontana Economic History of Europe: The Twentieth Century*, Part Two. Glasgow: William Collins Sons & Co.

Cohen, Benjamin J. 1998. *The Geography of Money*. Ithaca and London: Cornell University Press.

Combs, Matthew T. 2015. "Chungking in 1943." As Chapter 8 of *1943: China at the Crossroads*, eds. Joseph W. Esherick and Matthew T. Combs. Ithaca: Cornell University East Asia Program.

Commission of the Central Committee of the CPSU (B), ed. 1939. *History of the All-Union Communist Party (Bolsheviks): Short Course, Authorized by the Central Committee of the CPSU (B)*. Moscow: International Publishing Co. Inc.

Copeland, Lawrence. 2014. *Exchange Rates and International Finance*. 6th edition. Harrow, England: Pearson Education.

Cottarelli, Carlo, and Mario I. Bléjer. 1991. "Forced Savings and Repressed Inflation in the Soviet Union: Some Empirical Results." *International Monetary Fund Working Paper 91/55*. International Monetary Fund, Washington, DC. June.

Cukierman, Alex, Sebatian Edwards, and Guido Tabellini. 1989. "Seignorage and Political Instability." *NBER Working Paper 3199*. National Bureau of Economic Research, Cambridge, MA. December.

Dąbrowski, Marek. 1995. *The Reasons for the Collapse of the Ruble Zone*. Warsaw: Case Research Foundation.

Dai, Xianglong, ed. 1998. *50 Years of the People's Bank of China, 1948–1998*. Beijing: China Finance Press. (In Chinese).

Davies, Glyn. 2002. *A History of Money: From Ancient Times to the Present Day*. 3rd edition. Cardiff: University of Wales Press.

Davies, R. W. 1989. "Soviet Union's Economic and Social Policy, 1917–1941." As Chapter 14 of *The Cambridge Economic History of Europe*, Vol. 8, eds. Peter Mathias and Sidney Pollard. New York and Cambridge: Cambridge University Press, pp. 983–1047.

de Bordes, J. van Walras. 1924. *The Austrian Crown: Its Depreciation and Stabilization*. London: P. S. King & Son.

De Melo, Martha, Cevdet Denizer, Alan Gelb, and Stoyan Tenev. 1997. "Circumstance and Choice: The Role of Initial Conditions and Policies in Transition Economies." *World Bank Working Paper 1866*. Washington, DC: World Bank.

de Melo, Martha, and Alan Gelb. 1996. "A Comparative Analysis of Twenty-Eight Transition Economies in Europe and Asia." *Eurasian Geography and Economics* 37(5): 265–285.

de Menil, Georges. 2003. "History, Policy, and Performance in Two Transition Economies: Poland and Romania." As Chapter 10 of *In Search of Prosperity: Analytic Narratives of Economic Growth*, ed. Dani Rodrik. Princeton, NJ: Princeton University Press, pp. 271–295.

Denizer, Cevdet. 1997. "Stabilization, Adjustment and Growth Prospects in Transition Economies." *World Bank Working Paper 1855*. World Bank, Washington, DC.

De Vries, Margaret G., and John Keith Horsefield. 1969. *The International Monetary Fund 1945–1965: Twenty Years of International Monetary Cooperation*. Washington, DC: International Monetary Fund.

Dornbusch, Rudiger. 1992. "Monetary Problems of Post-Communism: Lessons from the End of the Austro-Hungarian Empire." *Weltwirtschaftliches Archiv* (Review of World Economics) 128(3): 391–424. (also as *NBER Reprint No. 1765*, December 1992).

Dornbusch, Rudiger, and Alberto Giovannini. 1986. "Monetary Policy in Open Economy." As Chapter 23 of *The Handbook of Monetary Economics*, Vol. 2, eds. Benjamin M. Friedman and Frank H. Hahn. Amsterdam and New York: North Holland, pp. 1232–1303.

Dornbusch, Rudiger, Federico Sturzenegger, and Holger Wolf. 1990. "Extreme Inflation: Dynamics and Stabilization." *Brookings Papers on Economic Activity* 1990(2): 1–84.

Drabek, Zdenek. 1985. "Foreign Trade Performance and Policy." As Chapter 7 of *The Economic History of Eastern Europe, 1919–1975*, Vol. 1, eds. Michael C. Kaser and E. A. Radice. Oxford: Clarendon Press, pp. 379–531.

Dukalskis, Alexander. 2016. "North Korea's Shadow Economy: A Force for Authoritarian Resilience or Corrosion?" *Europe-Asia Studies* 68(3): 487–507.

Eagleton, Catherine, and Jonathan Williams. 2007. *Money: A History*. 2nd edition. London: British Museum Press.

Easterly, William. 2007. *The Elusive Quest for Growth*. Boston: MIT Press.

Economic Research Institute of the Academy of China, and Economic Research Institute of Shanghai Academy of Social Sciences, eds. 1958. *Collection of Price Information in Shanghai before and after the Liberation 1921–1957*. Shanghai: Shanghai People's Press. (In Chinese).

The Economist. 2012. "The Price of Cooking the Books: Argentina's Inflation Problem." February 25: 43–44.

———. 2017. "North Korean Data: Best Guesses." February 11: 62.

Eichengreen, Barry. 1992. *Golden Fetters: The Gold Standard and the Great Depression, 1919–1939*. New York and Oxford: Oxford University Press.

Fairbank, John King. 1982. *Chinabound: A Fifty-Year Memoir*. New York: Harper and Row.

Farber, Howard. 1978. "A Price and Wage Study for Northern Babylonia during the Old Babylonian Period." *Journal of the Economic and Social History of the Orient* 21: 1–51.

Feldman, Gerald D. 1997. *The Great Disorder: Politics, Economics, and Society in the German Inflation 1914–1924*. New York and Oxford: Oxford University Press.

Ferguson, Naill. 1995. *Paper and Iron: Hamburg Business and German Policies in the Era of Inflation, 1897–1927*. Cambridge: Cambridge University Press.

Ferguson, Niall, and Brigitte Granville. 2000. "'Weimar on the Volga': Causes and Consequences of Inflation in 1990s Russia Compared with 1920s Germany." *The Journal of Economic History* 60(4): 1061–1087.

Fergusson, Adam. 2010. *When Money Dies: The Nightmare of Deficit Spending, Devaluation, and Hyperinflation in Weimar Germany*. New York: PublicAffairs.

Fetter, Frank Whitson. 1977. "Lenin, Keynes and Inflation." *Economica* 44(173): 77–80.

Fischer, Stanley. 1987. "The Israeli Stabilization Program, 1985–86." *American Economic Review* 77(May): 275–278.

Fischer, Stanley, Ratna Sahay, and Carlos A. Végh. 2002. "Modern Hyper- and High Inflations." *Journal of Economic Literature* 40(September): 837–880.

Fischer, Wolfgang Chr. 2010. *German Hyperinflation*. Germany: Josef EUL Verlag, Lohmar.

Fratianni, Michele, and Franco Spinelli. 1997. *A Monetary History of Italy*. New York and Cambridge: Cambridge University Press.

Frederick, Taylor. 2015. *The Downfall of Money: Germany's Hyperinflation and the Destruction of the Middle Class*. London: Bloomsbury Press.

Friedman, Irving S. 1974. "Inflation: A Worldwide Disaster." In *Britannica Book of the Year 1974*, eds. Daphne Daume and J.E. Davis. Chicago: Encyclopedia Britannica, Inc., pp. 17–24.

Friedman, Milton. 1992. "FDR, Silver, and China." As Chapter 7 of his *Money Mischief: Episodes in Monetary History*. San Diego and New York: Harcourt Brace & Company, pp. 157–187.

———. 1992. "Bimetallism Revisited." As Chapter 6 of his *Money Mischief: Episodes in Monetary History*. San Diego and New York: Harcourt Brace & Company, pp. 126–156.

Friedman, Milton, and Rose D. Friedman. 1979. *Free to Choose: A Personal Statement*. San Diego and New York: Harcourt, Inc.

Friedman, Milton, and Anna J. Schwartz. 1963. *A Monetary History of the United States, 1867–1960*. Princeton, NJ: Princeton University Press.

Gaidar, Yegor. 1999. *Days of Defeat and Victory*. Jackson School Publications in International Studies. Seattle and London: University of Washington Press.

———. 2007. *Collapse of an Empire: Lessons for Modern Russia*. Washington, DC: Brookings Institution Press.

Galbraith, John Kenneth. 2001. *Money: Where It Came, Where It Went*. New York: Houghton Mifflin.

Gallegos, Raúl. 2016. *Crude Nation: How Oil Riches Ruined Venezuela*. Lincoln: Potomac Books. (University of Nebraska Press).

Garber, Peter M. 1988. "Comment on Israeli Inflation and Stabilization." In *Inflation Stabilization: The Experience of Israel, Argentina, Brazil, Bolivia, and Mexico*, eds. Michael Bruno, Guido Di Tella, Rudiger Dornbusch, and Stanley Fischer. Cambridge, MA: MIT Press, pp. 95–98.

Gasha, Jose Giancarlo, and Gonzalo Pastor. 2004. "Angola's Fragile Stabilization." *International Monetary Fund Working Paper WP/04/83*. International Monetary Fund, Washington, DC.

Giner, Iván, and Omar Mendoza. 2005. "Foreign Exchange Intervention in Venezuela." In *Foreign Exchange Market Intervention in Emerging Markets: Motives, Techniques and Implications*, edited by BIS Monetary and Economic Department. Basel, Switzerland: Bank of International Settlements, BIS Paper No. 24, May, pp. 292–300.

Gould, John Dennis. 1970. *The Great Debasement: Currency and the Economy in Mid-Tudor England*. Oxford: Oxford University Press.

Graham, Frank D. 1930. *Exchange, Prices, and Production in Hyperinflation Germany, 1920–1923*. New York: Russell and Russell.

Granville, Brigitte. 2002. "The IMF and the Ruble Zone: Response to Odling-Smee and Pastor." *Comparative Economic Studies* 44(4): 59–80.

Grossman, Peter, and János Horváth. 2000. "The Dynamics of the Hungarian Hyperinflation, 1945–6: A New Perspective." *Journal of European Economic History* 29(2–3) (Fall–Winter): 405–427.

Halevi, Nadav. 2008. "A Brief Economic History of Modern Israel." In *EH.Net Encyclopedia*, ed. Robert Whaples, March 16. Available at http://eh.net/encyclopedia/a-brief-economic-history-of-modern-israel/.

Hamilton, Earl J. 1936. "Prices and Wages at Paris under John Law's System." *Quarterly Journal of Economics* 51(November): 47–70.

———. 1977. "The Role of War in Modern Inflation." *Journal of Economic History* 37(March): 13–19.

Hanke, Steve H. 1998. "The Case for a Russian Currency Board System." *Cato Institute Foreign Policy Briefing* (49) (October 14): 1–11.

———. 2007. "The World's Greatest Unreported Hyperinflation." Available at www.cato.org/publications/commentary/worlds-greatest-unreported-hyperinflation.

———. 2008. "Zimbabwe: From Hyperinflation to Growth." *Development Policy Analysis No. 6*. Cato Institute, Washington, DC. June 25.

———. 2013. "North Korea: From Hyperinflation to Dollarization?" Available on http://www.cato.org/publications/commentary/north-korea-hyperinflation-dollarization.

Hanke, Steve H., and Chares Bushnell. 2016. *Venezuela Enters the Record Book: The 57th Entry in the Hanke-Krus World Hyperinflation Table*. Baltimore: Johns Hopkins Institute for Applied Economics SAE/No.69, December.

Hanke, Steve H., and Nicholas Krus. 2013. "World Hyperinflations." As Chapter 30 of *Routledge Handbook of Major Events in Economic History*, eds. Randall E. Parker and Robert Whaples. London and New York: Routledge. (Taylor & Francis Group), pp. 367–377.

Hanke, Steve H., and Alex K. F. Kwok. 2009. "On the Measurement of Zimbabwe's Hyperinflation." *Cato Journal* 29(Spring/Summer): 353–364.

Hanson, Philip. 2003. *The Rise and Fall of the Soviet Economy: An Economic History of the USSR from 1945*. Boston and New York: Longman/Pearson Education.

Hardach, Karl. 1980. *The Political Economy of Germany in the Twentieth Century*. Berkeley: University of California Press.

Harris, Seymour E. 1930. *The Assignats*. Boston: Harvard University Press.

Harrison, Mark. 1998. "The Economics of World War II: An Overview." As Chapter 1 of *The Economics of World War II: Six Great Powers in International Comparison*, ed. Mark Harrison. Cambridge: Cambridge University Press, pp. 1–42.

Hausmann, Ricardo. 2003. "Venezuela's Growth Implosion: A Neoclassical Story?" As Chapter 9 of *In Search of Prosperity: Analytic Narratives of Economic Growth*, ed. Dani Rodrik. Princeton, NJ: Princeton University Press, pp. 244–269.

Heichelheim, F. M. 1935. "New Light on Currency and Inflation in Hellenistic-Roman Times, from Inscriptions and Papyri." *Economic History Supplement to the Economic Journal* 10(February): 1–11.

Hitchcock, William I. 2008. *The Bitter Road to Freedom: A New History of the Liberation of Europe*. New York: Free Press.

Hoffmann, Lutz, Peter Bofinger, Heiner Flassbeck, and Alfred Steinherr. 2001. *Kazakstan 1993–2000: Independent Advisers and the IMF*. New York: Physica-Verlag Heidelberg.

Holtfrerich, Carl-Ludwig. 1986. *The German Inflation 1914–1923: Causes and Effects in International Perspective*. New York: De Gruyter.

Homer, Sidney, and Richard Sylla. 2005. *A History of Interest Rates*. 4th edition. New Jersey: Rutgers University Press.

Hong, Jiaguan. 2008. "The Republic Period 1927–1949." As Volume 4 of *A General History of Finance in China*, eds. Li Fei, Zhao Haikuan, Xu Shuxin, and Hong Jiaguan. Beijing: China Financial Press. (In Chinese), pp. 1–576.

Hoover, Herbert. 2007. *The Memoirs of Herbert Hoover: Years of Adventure 1874–1920*. Whitefish, MT: Kessinger Publishing, LLC. (Kessinger Legacy Reprints).

James, Harold. 1999. "The Reichsbank 1876–1945." As Chapter 1 of *Fifty Years of the Deutsche Mark: Central Bank and the Currency in Germany since 1948*, ed. Deutsche Bundesbank. Oxford and New York: Oxford University Press, pp. 3–53.

Jarvis, Christopher. 1999. "The Rise and Fall of the Pyramid Schemes in Albania." *International Monetary Fund Working Paper 99/98*. International Monetary Fund, Washington, DC. (A shorter version in *Finance and Development* (A quarterly magazine of the IMF) Vol. 37, No.1, March 2000).

Jones, F. C., Hugh Borton, and B. R. Pearn. 1955. *The Far East, 1942–1946* (Survey of International Affairs, 1939–1946, ed. The Royal Institute of International Affairs). London: Oxford University Press.

Joo, Hyung-min. 2010. "Visualizing the Invisible Hands: The Shadow Economy in North Korea." *Economy and Society* 39(1): 110–145.

Kaminsky, Graciela, Amine Mati, and Nada Choueiri. 2009. "Thirty Years of Currency Crises in Argentina: External Shocks or Domestic Fragility?" *Economía* 10(Fall): 81–123.

Kararach, George, Phineas Kadenge, and Gibson Guvheya. 2010. *Currency Reforms in Zimbabwe: An Analysis of Possible Currency Regimes*. Harare: The African Capacity Building Foundation Occasional Paper 10.

Kararach, George, and Raphael O. Otieno, eds. 2016. *Economic Management in a Hyperinflationary Environment: The Political Economy of Zimbabwe, 1980–2008*. Oxford: Oxford University Press.

Karatzas, George. 1988. "The Greek Hyperinflation and Stabilization of 1943–1946: A Comment on Makinen." *Journal of Economic History* 48(3): 139.

Katchanovski, Ivan. 2000. "Divergence in Growth in Post-Communist Countries." *Journal of Public Policy* 20(1): 55–81.

Kaufmann, Daniel, Massimo Mastruzzi, and Diego Zavaleta. 2003. "Sustained Macroeconomic Reforms, Tepid Growth: A Governance Puzzle in Bolivia?" As Chapter 12 of *In Search of Prosperity: Analytic Narratives of Economic Growth*, ed. Dani Rodrik. Princeton, NJ: Princeton University Press, pp. 334–397.

Kemmerer, Edward. 1940. *Inflation and Revolution, Mexico's Experience of 1912–1917*. Princeton: Princeton University Press.

Keynes, John Maynard. 1919 [2009]. *Essays in Persuasion*. New York: Classic House Books.

Kiguel, Miguel A. 1991. "Inflation in Argentina: Stop and Go since the Austral Plan." *World Development* 19(August): 969–986.

Kindleberger, Charles P. 1984. *A Financial History of Western Europe*. London: George Allen and Unwin.

Klein, John J. 1956. "German Money and Prices, 1932–1944." As Chapter 3 of *Studies in the Quantity Theory of Money*. 1st edition, ed. Milton Friedman. Chicago: University of Chicago Press, pp. 121–159.

Kolodko, Grzegorz W., Danuta Gotz-Kozierkiewicz, and Elzbieta Skrzeszewska-Paczek. 1992. *Hyperinflation and Stabilization in Postsocialist Economies*. New York: Springer Science+Business Media.

Kornai, János. 1980. *Economics of Shortage*. Amsterdam: North Holland Press.

———. 1998. "The Place of the Soft Budget Constraint Syndrome in Economic Theory." *Journal of Comparative Economics* 26: 11–17.

Kramarenko, Vitaliy, Lars Engstrom, Genevieve Verdier, Gilda Fernandez, S. Erik Oppers, Richard Hughes, Jimmy McHugh, and Warren Coats. 2010. *Zimbabwe: Challenges and Policy Options after Hyperinflation*. Washington, DC: International Monetary Fund, June.

Krugman, Paul. 2013. "The Conscience of a Liberal. It's Always 1923." *The New York Times*, February 12, The Opinion Pages.

Kuehnast, Kathleen, and Nora Dudwick. 2004. "Better a Hundred Friends Than a Hundred Rubles? Social Networks in Transition: The Kyrgyz Republic." *World Bank Working Paper No. 39*. World Bank, Washington, DC.

Larraín, Felipe, and Marcelo Selowsky, eds. 1991. *The Public Sector and the Latin American Crisis*. San Francisco: ICS Press.

Laursen, Karsten, and Jørgen Pedersen. 1964. *The German Inflation 1918–1923*. Amsterdam: North Holland.

Lerner, Eugene. 1956. "Inflation in the Confederacy, 1861–65." In *Studies in the Quantity Theory of Money*, ed. Milton Friedman. Chicago: University of Chicago Press, pp. 163–175.

Lipton, David, and Jeffrey Sachs. 1990. "Creating a Market Economy in Eastern Europe: The Case of Poland." *Brookings Papers on Economic Activity* 1990(1): 75–147.

Lyon, James. 1996. "Yugoslavia's Hyperinflation, 1993–1994: A Social History." *East European Politics and Societies* 10(Spring): 293–327.

MacGregor, Neil. 2014. *Germany: Memories of a Nation*. London: The British Museum and Allen Line.

Maddison, Angus. 1982. *Phases of Capitalist Development*. Oxford and New York: Oxford University Press.

———. 2001. *The World Economy: A Millennial Perspective*. Paris: Organization of Economic Cooperation and Development.

———. 2003. *The World Economy: Historical Statistics*. Paris: Organization for Economic Cooperation and Development.

Mair, John. 1956. "Four-Power Control in Austria, 1945–1946." As Part 2 of *Four-Power Control in Germany and Austria, 1945–1946 by Michael Balfour and John Mair (Survey of International Affairs, 1939–1946),* ed. The Royal Institute of International Affairs. London: Oxford University Press, pp. 267–376.

Makinen, Gail E. 1984. "The Greek Stabilization of 1944–46." *American Economic Review* 74(December): 1067–1074.

———. 1986. "The Greek Hyperinflation and Stabilization of 1943–1946." *Journal of Economic History* 46(3): 795–805.

———. 1987. "Hyperinflation: Experience." In *The New Palgrave Dictionary of Money and Finance,* Vol. 2, eds. Peter Newman, Murray Milgate, and John Eatwell. London and New York: Macmillan, pp. 326–328.

———. 1988. "The Greek Hyperinflation and Stabilization of 1943–1946: A Reply." *Journal of Economic History* 48(1): 140–142.

———. 2014. *Studies in Hyperinflation and Stabilization.* New York: Center for Financial Stability.

Makinen, Gail E., and G. Thomas Woodward. 1989. "The Taiwanese Hyperinflation and Stabilization of 1945–1952." *Journal of Money, Credit and Banking* 21(February): 90–105.

Markham, Jerry W. 2002. *A Financial History of the United States, Volume I: From Christopher Columbus to the Robber Barons (1492–1900).* New York and London: M.E. Sharpe.

Marsh, David. 1992. *The Bundesbank: The Bank That Rules Europe.* London: Heinemann.

Mazower, Mark. 1995. *Inside Hitler's Greece: The Experience of Occupation, 1941–44.* New Heaven: Yale University Press.

McIndoe, Tara. 2009. "Hyperinflation in Zimbabwe: Money Demand, Seigniorage and Aid Shocks." *Trinity College Dublin Institute for International Integration Studies Discussion Paper No.293.* July.

Meiselman, David, ed. 1970. *Varieties of Monetary Experience.* Chicago: University of Chicago Press.

Michell, H. 1947. "The Edict of Diocletian: A study of Price Fixing in the Roman Empire." *Canadian Journal of Economics and Political Science* 13(February): 1–12.

Mishkin, Frederic S. 2012. *The Economics of Money, Banking and Financial Markets.* 10th edition. Upper Saddle River, New Jersey: Prentice Hall.

Mises, von Ludwig. 2009. *Memoirs.* Alabama: The Ludwig von Mises Institute. (English translation by Arlene Oost-Zinner, Auburn).

Mitchell, Brian R. 1998. *International Historical Statistics, Europe: 1750–1993.* 4th edition. London: Macmillan.

———. 1998. *International Historical Statistics, Africa, Asia and Oceania 1750–1993.* 3rd edition. London: Macmillan.

Mohr, Joan McGuire. 2012. *The Czech and Slovak Legion in Siberia 1917–1922.* Jefferson, North Carolina and London: McFarland & Company.

Molnár, Miklós. 2001. *A Concise History of Hungary.* Cambridge: Cambridge University Press.

Mundell, Robert. 1998. "Uses and Abuses of Gresham's Law in the History of Money." *Zagreb Journal of Economics* 2(2): 3–38.

Naughton, Barry. 1991. "Why Has Economic Reform Led to Inflation?" *American Economic Review* 81(May): 207–211.

Nenovsky, Nikolay. 2006. "Lenin and the Currency Competition Reflections on the NEP Experience." *Working Paper 22.* International Centre for Economic Research, Italy.

Neumann, Manfred J. M. 1999. "Monetary Stability: Threat and Proven Response." As Chapter 6 of *Fifty Years of the Deutsche Mark: Central Bank and the Currency in*

Germany since 1948, ed. The Deutsche Bundesbank. Oxford and New York: Oxford University Press, pp. 269–306.

Ocampo, José Antonio. 1991. "Collapse and (Incomplete) Stabilization of the Nicaraguan Economy." As Chapter 10 of *The Macroeconomics of Populism in Latin America*, eds. Rudiger Dornbusch and Sebastian Edwards. Chicago: University of Chicago Press, pp. 331–368.

Odling-Smee, John, and Gonzalo Pastor. 2001. "The IMF and the Ruble Area, 1991–93." *International Monetary Fund Working Paper WP/01/101*. International Monetary Fund, Washington, DC.

Ouithwaite, R. B. 1966. "The Trials of Foreign Borrowing: The English Crown and the Antwerp Money Market in the Mid-Sixteenth Century." *Economic History Review* 19(2): 289–305.

Paarlberg, Don. 1993. *An Analysis and History of Inflation*. Westport, Connecticut: Praeger.

Palairet, Michael. 2000. *The Four Ends of the Greek Hyperinflation of 1941–1946*. Studies in 20th & 21st Century European History. Copenhagen: Museum Tusculanum Press, University of Copenhagen.

Peng, Kaixiang. 2006. *Grain Prices since the Ching Dynasty*. Shanghai: Shanghai People's Press. (In Chinese).

Peng, Xinwei. 2007. *Monetary History of China*. Shanghai: Shanghai People's Press. (1st revised edition in 1965). (In Chinese).

People's Bank of China. 2012. *Short History of Financial Development under the Leadership of the Chinese Communist Party*. Beijing: China Finance Press. (In Chinese).

Pepper, Suzanne. 2008. "The KMT-CCP Conflict 1945–1949." As Chapter 13 of *The Cambridge History of China*, Vol. 13, Part 2, eds. John K. Fairbank and Albert Feuerwerker. Cambridge: Cambridge University Press, pp. 723–788.

Petrov, Vladimir. 1967. *Money and Conquest: Allied Occupation Currencies in World War II*. Baltimore: Johns Hopkins Press.

Petrović, Pavle, Željko Bogetić, and Zorica Vujošević. 1999. "The Yugoslav Hyperinflation of 1992–1994: Causes, Dynamics, and Money Supply Process." *Journal of Comparative Economics* 27: 335–353.

Pomfret, Richard. 2002. "The IMF and the Ruble Zone." *Comparative Economic Studies* 44(4): 37–47.

Prunier, Gérard. 2009. *Africa's World War: Congo, the Rwandan Genocide, and the Making of a Continental Catastrophe*. Oxford and New York: Oxford University Press.

Qian, Jiaju, and Guo Yangan. 2014. *Evolutionary History of Money in China*. Shanghai: Shanghai People's Press. (In Chinese).

Radford, R. A. 1945. "The Economic Organisation of a P.O.W Camp." *Economica* 48(November): 189–201.

Rawski, Thomas G. 1989. *Economic Growth in Prewar China*. Berkeley: University of California Press.

Reddaway, Peter, and Dmitri Glinski. 2001. *The Tragedy of Russia's Reforms: Market Bolshevism against Democracy*. Washington, DC: U.S. Institute of Peace Press.

Reinhart, Carmen M., and Miguel A. Savastano. 2003. "The Realities of Modern Hyperinflation." *Finance and Development* 40(June): 20–23.

Rockoff, Hugh. 2000. "Banking and Finance 1789–1914." As Chapter 14 of *The Cambridge Economic History of the United States, Vol. II: The Long Nineteenth Century*, eds. Stanley L. Engerman and Robert Gallman. Cambridge and New York: Cambridge University Press, pp. 643–684.

Rostowski, Jacek. 1998. *Macroeconomic Instability in Post-Communist Countries*. Oxford: Oxford University Press.

Rowen, Hobart. 1984. "Israel's Hyperinflation." *The Washington Post*, October 14. Available at www.washingtonpost.com/archive/business/1984/10/14/israels-hyperinflation/25c854c9-cb4e-4e34-83b6-4cdcec0377b6/?utm_term=.f178a80261d7. Accessed on 20 January, 2017.

Sachs, Jeffrey D. 1987. "The Bolivian Hyperinflation and Stabilization." *American Economic Review*, May: 279–283.

Sachs, Jeffrey D., and Felipe B. Larrain. 1993. *Macroeconomics in the Global Economy*. New York and London: Harvester Wheatsheaf.

Sachs, Jeffrey D., and Andrew Warner. 1995. "Economic Reform and the Process of Global Integration." *Brookings Paper on Economic Activity* 1: 1–117.

Sachs, Jeffrey D., and John Williamson. 1985. "External Debt and Macroeconomic Performance in Latin America and East Asia." *Brookings Papers on Economic Activity* 1985(2): 523–573.

Sachs, Jeffrey D., and Wing Thye Woo. 1994. "Structural Factors in the Economic Reforms of China, Eastern Europe, and the Former Soviet Union." *Economic Policy* 9(18): 101–114.

SAIIA (South African Institute of International Affairs). 2001. *Angola: War without End?* Johannesburg: SAIIA Country Report No.2.

Sargent, Thomas J. 2013. *Rational Expectations and Inflation*. 3rd edition. Princeton: Princeton University.

———. 2013 [1982]. "The Ends of Four Big Inflations." As Chapter 3 of his *Rational Expectations and Inflation*. 3rd edition. Princeton: Princeton University, pp. 38–110. (originally as Chapter 2 of *Inflation: Causes and Effects*, ed. by Robert Hall. Chicago: University of Chicago Press for National Bureau of Economic Research, 1982, pp. 41–97).

Sargent, Thomlas J., and Francois R. Velde. 1995. "Macroeconomic Features of the French Revolution." *Journal of Political Economy* 103: 474–518. Also as Chapter 9 of Sargent 2013.

Savage, James D. 2002. "The Origins of Budgetary Preferences: The Dodge Line and the Balanced Budget Norm in Japan." *Administration & Society* 34(July): 261–284.

Schneider, Friedrich, and Dominik H. Enste. 2013. *The Shadow Economy: An International Survey*. 2nd edition. Cambridge and New York: Cambridge University Press.

Schuettinger, Robert L., and Eamon F. Butler. 1979. *Forty Centuries of Wage and Price Controls: How Not to Fight Inflation*. Washington, DC: Heritage Foundation.

Schumpeter, Joseph A. 1994. *Capitalism, Socialism and Democracy*. London: Routledge. (1st edition in 1942).

———. 2006. *History of Economic Analysis*. Routledge: Taylor & Francis. (1st in 1954 by Allen & Unwin).

Seabright, Paul, ed. 2000. *The Vanishing Ruble: Barter Networks and Non-Monetary Transactions in Post-Soviet Societies*. Cambridge: Cambridge University Press.

Sebestyen, Victor. 2014. *1946: The Making of the Modern World*. London: Macmillan.

Shang, Ming, ed. 1989. *Financial Pursuit in Contemporary China*. Beijing: China Social Science Press. (In Chinese).

Shen, Zhihua, 2001. "Basic Situations of Soviet Union's Economic Aid to New China during the Early Years: Findings from Chinese and Russian Archives, Part I." *Journal of Russia Study* (1), pp. 53–66. (In Chinese).

Shirer, William L. 2011. *The Rise and Fall of the Third Reich: A History of Nazi Germany*. 50th anniversary edition. New York and London: Simon & Schuster; Reissue edition.

Sicat, Gerardo P. 2003. *The Philippine Economy during the Japanese Occupation, 1941–1945*. Manila: University of the Philippines School of Economics Discussion Papers 0307, November.

Siklos, Pierre L. 1989. "The End of the Hungarian Hyperinflation of 1945–1946." *Journal of Money, Credit and Banking* 21(2): 135–147.

———. 1991. *War Finance, Reconstruction, Hyperinflation and Stabilization in Hungary, 1938–48*. New York: St. Martins Press.

———, ed. 1995. *Great Inflations of the 20th Century: Theories, Policies, and Evidence.* Brookfield, VT: Edward Elgar.

Smith, Lawrence. 1936. "The Zloty, 1924–1935." *Journal of Political Economy* 44(2): 145–183.

Sommariva, Andrea, and Giuseppe Tullio. 1987. *German Macroeconomic History, 1880–1979: A Study of the Effects of Economic Policy on Inflation, Currency Depreciation and Growth.* London: Macmillan Press.

Spang, Rebecca L. 2015. *Stuff and Money in the Time of the French Revolution.* London and Cambridge, MA: Harvard University Press.

Stuart, John Leighton. 2010. *Fifty Years in China: The Memoirs of John Leighton Stuart Missionary and Ambassador.* Chinese translation by Hainan Press in Haikou, Hainan. (1st English edition by Random House in New York in 1954).

Su, Ning, ed. 2006. *China Finance Statistics 1949–2005.* Beijing: China Finance Press. (In Chinese).

Sullivan, Barry. 1999. "More Than Meets the Eye: The Ethiopian War and the Origins of the Second World War." As Chapter 10 of *The Origins of the Second World War Reconsidered: The A. J. P. Taylor Debate after Twenty Five Years*, ed. Gordon Martel. London: Routledge, pp. 178–202.

Sun, Huairen, ed. 1990. *A Short History of Socialist Economic Construction and Development in Shanghai, 1949–1985.* Shanghai: Shanghai People's Press. (In Chinese).

Sylla, Richard. 2000. "Experimental Federalism: Economics of American Government, 1789–1914." As Chapter 12 of *The Cambridge Economic History of the United States, Vol. II: The Long Nineteenth Century*, eds. Stanley L. Engerman and Robert Gallman. Cambridge and New York: Cambridge University Press, pp. 483–541.

Tan, Wenxi. 1994. *History of Prices in China.* Wuhan: Hubei People's Press. (In Chinese).

Tang, Tsou. 1963. *America's Failure in China 1941–50.* Chicago: University of Chicago Press.

Taylor, Jay. 2011. *The Generalissimo: Chiang Kai-shek and the Struggle for Modern China.* 2nd edition. Boston: Belknap Press. (Harvard University Press).

Teichova, Alice. 1989. "Central and Eastern Europe and Southeastern Europe: 1919–1939." As Chapter 13 of *The Cambridge Economic History of Europe*, Vol. 8, eds. Peter Mathias and Sidney Pollard. New York and Cambridge: Cambridge University Press, pp. 887–983.

Teltschik, Horst. 1991. *329 Tage: Innenansichten der Einigung.* München: Siedler Verlag. (Chinese translation by Social Science Document Press in Beijing, 2016).

Temin, Peter. 2002. "Price Behavior in Ancient Babylon." *Explorations in Economic History* 39: 46–60.

Toniolo, Gianni. 2005. *Central Bank Cooperation at the Bank for International Settlements, 1930–1973.* New York and Cambridge: Cambridge University Press.

Toshiyuki, Mizoguchi. 1972. "Consumer Prices and Real Wages in Taiwan and Korea under Japanese Rule." *Hitotsubashi Journal of Economics* 13(1): 40–56.

Toynbee, Arnold, and Veronica Toynbee, eds. 1955. *The Realignment of Europe.* London: Oxford University Press.

The United States Bureau of the Census. 1976. *The Statistical History of the United States: From the Colonial Time to the Present.* New York: Basic Books.

Wang, Bingqiang. 2009. *60 Years of China Finance: Retrospect and Reflection.* Beijing: China Finance and Economy Press. (In Chinese).

Weatherford, Jack. 1997. *The History of Money*. New York: Crown Publishers, Inc.

Webb, Steven B. 1984. "The Supply of Money and Reichsbank Financing of Government and Corporate Debt in Germany, 1919–1923." *Journal of Economic History* 44(June): 499–507.

———. 1989. *Hyperinflation and Stabilization in Weimar Germany*. New York and Oxford: Oxford University Press.

White, Andrew Dickson. 1896. "Fiat Money Inflation in France: How It Came, What It Bought, and How It Ended." *Reprint: Cato Institute, Paper No. 11, 1980*.

White, Michael V., and Kurt Schuler. 2009. "Who Said 'Debauch the Currency': Keynes or Lenin?" *Journal of Economic Perspectives* 23(Spring): 213–222.

Wilkinson, Toby. 2010. *The Rise and Fall of Ancient Egypt: The History of a Civilization from 3000BC to Cleopatra*. London and New York: Bloomsbury.

Wolf, Nikolaus. 2005. "Path Dependent Border Effects: The Case of Poland's Reunification (1918–1939)." *Explorations in Economic History* 42: 414–438.

Woo, Wing Thye. 2001. "Recent Claims of China's Economic Exceptionalism Reflections Inspired by WTO Accession." *China Economic Review* 12: 107–136.

Wood, Adrian. 1989. "Deceleration of Inflation with Acceleration of Price Reform: Vietnam's Remarkable Recent Experience." *Cambridge Journal of Economics* 13(4): 563–571.

Worden, Robert L., ed. 2008. *North Korea: A Country Study*. Washington, D.C.: U.S. Congress.

World Bank. 1978. *World Development Report 1978*. Washington, D.C.: World Bank. Available at https://openknowledge.worldbank.org/handle/10986/5961

———. 1989. *Peru: Policies to Stop Hyperinflation and Initiate Economic Recovery*. Washington, DC: World Bank.

———. 2003. *World Development Report 2003: Sustainable Development in a Dynamic World – Transforming Institutions, Growth, and Quality of Life*. Washington, DC: World Bank. Available at https://openknowledge.worldbank.org/handle/10986/5985 License: CC BY 3.0 IGO.

Yang, Lien-sheng. 1971. *Money and Credit in China: A Short History*. Harvard-Yenching Institute Monographs 12. Cambridge: Cambridge University Press.

Yang, Xitian, ed. 2002. "The People's Republic Period 1949–1996." As Volume 6 of *A General History of Finance in China*, eds. Li Fei, Zhao Haikuan, Xu Shuxin, and Hong Jiaguan. Beijing: China Financial Press. (In Chinese), pp. 1–496.

Ye, Shichang. 2002. *General History of Finance in China, Volume I: From the Time Prior to Ch'in to the Opium War*. Beijing: China Finance Press. (In Chinese).

Yergin, Daniel, and Joseph Stanislaw. 1998. *The Commanding Heights: The Battle for the World Economy*. New York: Free Press.

Yoshio, Zuzuki. 1987. *Financial System in Japan* (Chinese translation). Beijing: China Finance Press.

Young, Arthur N. 1963. *China and the Helping Hand, 1937–1945*. Cambridge, MA: Harvard University Press.

———. 1965. *China's Wartime Finance and Inflation, 1937–1945*. Harvard East Asian Series 20. Cambridge, MA: Harvard University Press.

———. 1971. *China's Nation-Building Effort, 1927–1937: The Financial and Economic Record*. Stanford: Hoover Institute Press, Stanford University.

Yuji, Kikuchi. 2002. *Internationalization of the Japanese Yen: Process and Outlook* (Chinese translation). Beijing: China Renmin University Press.

Yule, Henry. 2000 [1914]. *Cathay and the Way Thither, Being a Collection of Medieval Notices of China*, Vol. 1–2. Cambridge: Cambridge University Press. (First edition by Hakluyt Society, London, 1914).

Yusuf, Shahid. 2008. *Development Economics through the Decades: A Critical Look at Thirty Years of the World Development Report*. Washington, D.C.: World Bank.

Zamagni, Vera. 1998. "Italy: How to Lose the War and Win the Peace." As Chapter 5 of *The Economics of World War II: Six Great Powers in International Comparison*, ed. Mark Harrison. Cambridge: Cambridge University Press, pp. 177–223.

Zamoyski, Adam. 2012. *Poland: A History*. New York: Hippocrene Books.

Zhang, Chengquan. 2005. *Wan Mao-in and Hsien-feng's Currency Reform*. Hefei: Huang-shan Press. (In Chinese).

Zhang, Guohui. 2003. *General History of Finance in China, Volume II: From the Opium War to Later Ching*. Beijing: China Finance Press. (In Chinese).

Index

Africa 193, 254; *see also specific country*
Africa's World War 191
Age of Inflation (1980s and 1990s): advent of 168–71; Angola in 189, *190*, 191–3; Argentina in 168, *176*, 177–82; Bolivia in 171–4, *172*; Brazil in 168, 174–82, *176*; Bretton-Woods System collapse and 168–71; Chile in 186–7, *187*; effects of 170–1; hyperinflation in 167–8; interest rates and 170; Israel in 168, 182–5, *182*, *183*; Nicaragua in 187–8, *187*; overview 167–8; Peru in *187*, 188–9; Turkey in 168, 182–6, *182*, *183*; Zaïre in 189–91, *190*
Albania 222–3
Albanian Paradox 223
Allende, Salvador 186–7
Allied Control Council 121
Allied States' Reparation Commission 81, 87
American-British War (1812–14) 43
American Civil War 33, 42–7
American Revolution 33–6
Anglo Greek Financial Agreement 98, 100–1
Angola 189, *190*, 191–3
Antoninianus 21
Argentina 168, *176*, 177–82, 232
Aristotle 1
Armenia 200, 210
ASEAN 228
asset substitution 4
assignats 9, 38–40, 44, 72
Augustus Octavian 20
Aurelian 21
aureus 20
austerity policies 11, 72, 87–8, 112, 174, 177, 210, 220
austral 181
Austral Plan 177
Austria: austerity policy in 87; bank industry in 124; consumer price index in 63, **63**; currency devaluation in 56–7, *56*, 78–81; currency reform in 81; depreciation-driven inflation in 78–83, *80*; domestic borrowing and 62; exchange rates in 80, *80*; gold standard in 61; Marshall Plan and 125; 1920s hyperinflation in 52, **52**, 53, *53*, 55–6, *55*, *56*, 78–81, *80*, 196; 1940s hyperinflation in 124–5; price levels in 80, *80*; stabilization programs in 87–8; state-owned assets in 87; Treaty of Saint-Germain and 79, 81
Azerbaijan 210

Bacon, Francis 51
Balkan countries 222–3; *see also specific country*
Baltic Three: consumer price index in **201**, 202, **202**; inflation in 200, **201**, 202–3, **202**; ruble zone and 205–8; Russia's monetary policy and 204–5; stabilization programs in 203, 210–11
banking industries: Austria 124; Germany 57–8, *58*, 60, 72, 121–2, 124; Greece 99; Hungary 110; Nationalist China 136–40, *139*, 148–52, 160; 1920s hyperinflation and 51, 60–3; post-reform China 225–6; Russia/USSR 77–8; state-owned 61, 145; United States 43; *see also* central banks
Bank of Israel 185
barter 13–14, 16, 156, 212
Belarus 205–6, 210
Berlin Wall, fall of 200
Big Bangs 17–18, 152–3, 173, 204–5, 210, 227
black markets 3, 108, 224, 242, 246–7
bolívar 242–3
bolivar fuerte 243
Bolivia 168, 171–4, *172*
boliviano 173
Bolsheviks 66, 73–5, 78
Bond Notes 239

bonds and bond financing 43–4, 46, 132–5, 147, 154
borrowing, government 6–7, 62–3; *see also* bonds and bond financing; foreign debt
Bosnia 215
Brazil 168, 174–82, *176*, 232
Bresciani-Turroni, Costantino 89
Bretton-Woods System 169
Bretton-Woods System collapse 168–71, 199, 254
Britain *see* England
Brüning, Heinrich 90
budget deficit, government: in Argentina 178–9; in Brazil 178–9; in Greece 110; in Hungary 110; hyperinflation and 5–6; inflation and 6; in Japan 114; post-reform China 225–6; in Russia/USSR 209–10; in Zaïre 190; *see also* foreign debt
Bulgaria 222–3
Bundesbank 220

Cagan, Phillip 2
capital controls 247
Cardoso, Fernando Henrique 180–1
Carr, E. H. 64
Cavallo, Domingo Felipe 181
central banks: in Argentina 181; in Brazil 180; in Eastern European countries 220; governments and 6; independence of, establishing 11; in Italy 103; in Japan 232; in Nationalist China 133, 148–50, 154, 156; in Poland 222; in Russia/USSR 208–9; in Taiwan 160; in Venezuela 242; in Yugoslavia 216, 218; in Zimbabwe 235–6, 238–9; *see also* banking industries
Central Bank of Venezuela (BCV) 242
Chang Kia-ngau 156
Ch'ao 26–7
Chase, Salmon 43–4
Chávez, Hugo 241, 243
Chavismo 231, 241
chervonets 76–7
Chiang Kai-shek 141, 147, 149–50, 153–4, 161
"Chicago Boys" 187
Chicago School of Economics 187
Chile 186–7, *187*
China Aid Act (1948) 152
China, early: credit markets in 32; debasement in 16–17; deflation in 30; hyperinflation in 30, 253, 255; interest rates in 32; Jurchen regime in 24–5; Ming Dynasty in 30–1; monetary policy in 16–19, 22–7, 30–3; Mongol rule

25–6, 32; paper currency in 22–7; Qing (Ching) Dynasty in 31–3; Sung regime in 23–4, 255; Wang Mang and 16–19, 255; Yuan Dynasty in 25–6, 32; *see also* Nationalist China; post-reform China
Choun, John F. 13
Chu Yuan-chang 30
Cicero 13
Code of Hammurabi 14–15
coinage: early 15–16; grading system in 17–18; monopolization 17; private, outlawing of 17, 19; silver 29; Wang Mang and 16–19; *see also* debasement; gold standard
Coin Houses 31
Cold War 124, 191, 231, 254
Colombia 52
COMECON 220
Comisión de Administración de Divisas (CADIVI) 242
Commonwealth of Independent States (CIS) 200, 207, 212, 254–5; *see also* Russia/USSR; *specific state*
Commonwealth of Nations 235
Confederacy 45–7
Congo *see* Zaïre
Congolese franc 191
Constantine I 22
consumer price index (CPI): in Albania 223; during American Civil War 44; in Angola *190*, 192; in Argentina *176*, 178, 181; in Austria 63, **63**; in Baltic Three **201**, 202, **202**; in Bolivia 168, 171, *172*; in Brazil 175–6, *176*, 180–2; in Bulgaria 222; in Chile 186, *187*; defining 2–3; in Eastern European countries 219, *219*; in England 63, **63**; in France 63, **63**; in Germany 63, **63**; in Greece 100; in Israel 182–3, *182*, *183*, 185; in Italy 103–4, *104*, *105*; in Japan 118, *119*; in Nicaragua *187*, 188; 1920s hyperinflation and 63, **63**; in Peru *187*, 188–9; in Poland 221; in post-reform China 223–4, *224*; in Romania 222; in Russia/USSR 200, **201**, **202**, 212; in South Korea 118, *119*; in Turkey 182, *182*, *183*, 185; in Venezuela 240, *240*; in Yugoslavia 213, 215–17, **215**; in Zaïre 190, *190*; in Zimbabwe 235–6, *236*, 239
Continental bills 44–5
Continental Congress 34–6
Convertibility Plan 181
córdoba 188
cost of living index (CLI) 3, 136, 143
credit 3, 8, 51

crown/krone 79
Cruzado Plan 176–7
cruzeiro real 181
currency *see specific type*
currency board 239
currency depreciation *see* currency devaluation
currency devaluation: in Austria 56–7, *56*, 78–81; in Germany 56–7, *56*; in Hungary 56–7, *56*, 81–3, *82*, 108; in Italy 107; during Napoleonic wars 40; in Poland 83–5, *84*, 222
currency reform: in Angola 191–2; in Austria 81; in Bolivia 173; in Brazil 176–7; in Germany 72, 91, 120, 123; in Hungary 112–13; in Nationalist China 152–5, 158, 255; in Nicaragua 188; in North Korea 245–6; in Peru 189; in Poland 84; in Russia/USSR 76–7, 206, **206**; in stabilization programs 11; in Zaïre 191; in Zimbabwe 239–40
currency substitution 4, 221
Czechoslovakia 85–6, 220

Danzig 52
Dawes Plan 72
debasement: in China, early 16–17; in England, Renaissance 27–30; Great Debasement 27–30; in Greece 16; in Roman Empire 19–22; Russia/USSR 61
debauching currency 64, 66
debt-for-debt swap program 36
de facto dollarization 5, 216–17, 221, 237
de-facto gold standard 41
deficit-financing policy 6–7
de jure dollarization 5, 12, 237–40
denarii 20–1
depreciation, currency 40, 56–7
Deutsche Bundersbank 124
Deutsche mark (D-mark or DM) 123, 214, 216, 218–19, 237
devaluation *see* currency devaluation
dinar 214, 216–18
Diocletian 21–2
Dionysius of Syracuse 16
Dodge, Joseph M. 116
Dodge Line 116–17
dollarization: in Africa 193; *de facto* 5, 216–17, 221, 237; defining 4–5; *de jure* 5, 12, 237–40; in Latin America 193; multicurrency 239; in North Korea 247; partial 5; in stabilization programs 239; in Yugoslavia 216
drachma 16, 97, *98*, 99–100

dual-track pricing 224–5
Duke of Orleans 37

East Asia *see specific country*
East Asian financial crisis 232
Eastern European countries: central banks in 220; consumer price index in 219, *219*; hyperinflation in 218–23, *219*; inflation in 218–23, *219*; *see also specific country*
Economic and Financial Organization (EFO) 87–8
Economic and Financial Section/ Department 87–8
Edict of Prices 21–2
Elizabeth I 29–30
Engels, Friedrich 73
England: American-British War (1812–14) and 43; consumer price index in 63, *63*; debasement in Renaissance 27–30; First World War debt 67; gold standard and 60; hyperinflation in, escape from 232–3; interest rates in 29–30, 41–2; Napoleonic wars and, financing 40–2; South Sea Bubble and 41; unionization of 37; wholesale price index in 41
Erhard, Ludwig 123
eseudo 187
Eshnunna, law codes of 14
Estonia 200, 210; *see also* Baltic Three
Ethiopian War 102–3
Europe *see specific country*
European Recovery Program (ERP) 107, 124
European Union 207; *see also specific country*
Eurozone monetary system 233
exchange rates: in Austria 80, *80*; in Bolivia 174; in Bulgaria 222–3; depreciation of 56–7, *56*; floating 170; in Germany 56, *56*; in Hungary 56, *56*; hyperinflation and 3; in Israel 184–5; in Italy 106–7; in Nationalist China 145–6; 1920s hyperinflation and 56–7, *56*; in North Korea 245, *247*; in Poland 56, *56*; stabilizing 11; in Venezuela 241–2; in Vietnam 224–5, 227; in Yugoslavia 214, 217

fabi 130–2, 134, 138–40, 143–5, 147, 149, 152, 255
Fairbank, John King 141
Federal Republic of Germany 124; *see also* Germany
Federal Republic of Yugoslavia *see* Yugoslavia
Fetter, Frank Whitson 64

First World War 62–3, 67, 78, 96, 254
fiscal austerity policies 11, 72, 87–8, 112, 174, 177, 210, 220
Flying Money 22
foreign aid: Bolivia and 173–4; as common element of stabilization programs 11; Hungary and 83; Israel and 183, 185; Nationalist China and 134–5, 147–8, 152–3; Russia/USSR and 209; Turkey and 183; Zaïre and 190
foreign debt: Argentina and 174, 178–80, 232; in Bolivia 173–4; Brazil and 174, 177–8, 232; as cause of hyperinflation 5; in Russia/USSR 204, 211, 232; in Venezuela 240, 244; in Yugoslavia 214
foreign exchange: black markets for 3, 246–7; hyperinflation and 3, 8; in North Korea 246–7; *see also* exchange rates
forint 112, 220
France: assignats and 9, 38–40, 44, 72; consumer price index in 63, **63**; First World War debt 67; foreign aid to United States and 35–6; French Revolution 36–42; hyperinflation in (1790s) 36–42; interest rates in 40–1; mandats and 39–40; Mississippi Bubble and 41; Napoleonic wars, financing 40–2
Franklin, Benjamin 34–5
French Revolution 36–42
Friedman, Milton 6, 40, 162–3, 167
Fujimori, Alberto 189
Fukuyama, Francis 231

G-7 meeting (1992) 209
Gaidar, Yegor 199, 204, 208
Galbraith, John Kenneth 33, 96
Gallienus 21
Georgia (country) 200, 210
German Democratic Republic (GDR) 219
Germany: austerity policy in 72; banking industry in 57–8, *58*, 60, 72, 121–2, 124; consumer price index in 63, **63**; countertrade in 122; currency devaluation in 56–7, *56*; currency reform in 72, 91, 120, 123; Dawes Plan and 72; domestic borrowing and 62–3; "economic miracle" in 124; exchange controls in 124; exchange rates in 56, *56*; Four De-s in 121; gold standard in 60–3, 72; hyperinflation records in 255; interest rates in 69, 220; Land Central Banks in 123; League of Nations and 88; Marshall Plan and 124; money stock in 120; Nazi regime and 89–91, 120; new nation building

and 121; 1920s hyperinflation in 52, **52**, 53, *53*, 54–6, *55*, *56*, 59–60, *59*, 63, **63**, 68–72; 1940s hyperinflation, escape from 119–24; Passive Resistance movement in 70–1; Potsdam Agreement and 121; price liberalization in 123; recession of 1923 in 71; reconstruction of 121; reparations and 67–72, 121; Second World War and 119; stabilization programs in 72, 90; Treaty of Brest-Litovsk and 73; Treaty of Rapallo and 73; wholesale prices in 67, *68*
Global Financial Crisis (2008) 211, 257
globalization 51, 227, 231–3, 254, 257
Glorious Revolution (1688) 41
Golddiskontbank 72
"Golden Age" of world economy 168–9, 175
Gold Savings Deposit Program (Taiwan) 161
gold standard: in Austria 61; *de facto* 41; demonetization and 17; early use 15–6; England and 60; in Germany 60–3, 72; in Hungary 61; international trade and 61; nationalization 17; 1920s hyperinflation and 60–3; in Roman Empire 22; true, first 60; U.S. dollar and 170
Gold Yuan program 152–5
Gorbachev, Mikhail 203–4, 208
Gosbank 77, 203, 208
Gosplan 203
Greece: Anglo-Greek Financial Agreement and 98, 100–1; banking industry in 99; budget deficits in 110; coinage in, early 15–16; consumer price index in 100; debasement in ancient 16; debt crisis (2011) in 233; hyperinflation records in 255; 1940s hyperinflation 96–102, *98*, *100*, *101*; poverty in, hyperinflation-induced 99; price levels in 97, *98*, 101, *101*; stabilization program 100–2; wages in 99, *100*
greenbacks 44
Gresham, Sir Thomas 9
Gresham's Law 9–10, 21, 29
gunpyō 117, 130

Hamilton, Alexander 43
Hanke, Steve H. 216, 239
Henry VIII 27–30
Herodotus 15
Herzegovina 215
historical perspective of monetary policy: American Civil War 33, 42–7; American Revolution 33–6; ancient world 13–16; China, early 22–5; England, Renaissance 27–30; French Revolution 36–42; Ming

Dynasty 30–3; Mongol Empire 25–6, 32; Napoleonic wars 40–2; overview 13, 253–5; questions raised by 255–7; Roman Empire 19–22; Wang Mang 169; *see also specific country and time period*
Hitler, Adolf 89–91
Hobsbawm, Eric 51
Homestead Act (1862) 42–3
Hsien-feng 31–3
Hui-zi (Hui-tzu) 23–4
Hungary: austerity plan in 112; austerity policy in 88, 112, 220; bank industry in 110; black market prices in 108; budget deficits in 110; cost of living index in 108, *108*; currency devaluation in 56–7, *56*, 81–3, 108; currency reform in 112–13; domestic borrowing and 62; economic isolation of 110; exchange rates in 56, *56*; foreign aid and 83; gold standard in 61; government budget in 111–12, *112*; hyperinflation records in 2, 107, 255–6; indexation in 217; inflation-led depreciation in 81–3, *82*; interest rates in 217; 1920s hyperinflation in 52, **52**, 53, *53*, 55–6, *55*, *56*, 81–3, *82*, 88, 196; 1940s hyperinflation in 96, 107–13, *108*, *112*, 196, 216; 1980s and 1990s hyperinflation in 220–1; price levels in 81–2, *82*; reparations and 109; reparations in 81; Second World War and 109; stabilization programs in 111–12; state-owned enterprises in 110, 220; Tax Pengö and 110–11; Three-Year Reconstruction Plan 113; time-changing index and 111; valorization accounts in 117
hyperinflation: in Age of Inflation 167–8; anticipated 8; asset bubble growth and 257; budget deficit and, government 5–6; causes of 1, 5–8; in civil wars *190*, 191–3; contrasting experiences of 182–6, *182*, *183*, 227–8; in coup 186–7, *187*; credit costs and 8; currency termination and 233–40; curve of seignorage and 10; defining 1–5; domestic credit and 3; exchange rates and 3; in failing administration 187–8, *187*; in failing states 189–93, *190*; foreign exchange and 3, 8; globalization and 257; government strategies and 7–8; Gresham's Law and 9–10; heading toward 240–4, *240*, 249–50; impacts of 1, 8–10, 256–7; incidence of 1; inflation measurement and 2–4; institutional deficiencies and 7–8; interest rates and 3, 8; Keynes and 63–7;

length of 256; Lenin and 63–7; monthly definition of 1–2; nationalities and 11; Olivera-Tanzi effect and 10; ordinary inflation and 8–9; paper currency, first 22–7; parallel experiences of 174–82, *176*; peacetime experience of 171–4, *172*; in power struggle 190–1, *191*; price jumps and 8; price levels and 1–2, 8; qualitative definition of 4–5; quantitative definition of 1–2; records 255–6; stabilizing 10–2; state ownership/control and 245; Thiers' Law and 9–10; truths about 253–7; as twentieth-century phenomenon 13; in twenty-first century 255; in uneasy society *187*, **188**–9; unrepressed 244–7, *247*; as virus 257; *see also specific country and time period*

indexation 111, 155–6, 159–60, 217; *see also specific index*
Indonesia 232
Industrial Revolution 51
infant industry argument 179–80
inflation: American Civil War and 33, 42–7; American Revolution and 35; in ancient world 13–6; anticipated 8; in Baltic Three 200, **201**, 202–3, **202**; budget deficit and, government 6; causes of 5; Confederacy and 45–7; deficit-financing policy and 6–7; defining 1, 15; depreciation-driven 78–83, *80*; in Eastern European countries 218–23, *219*; in England, Renaissance 41; hyperinflation and ordinary 8–9; measurement and hyperinflation 2–4; merits of 66; modern periods of 5; money creation and 7; money and price 6; price 6, 14–15, 27; repressed, in planned economies 197–200; in twenty-first century 231–2; ubiquity of 1; unanticipated 8; *see also* Age of Inflation; hyperinflation
interest rates: Age of Inflation and 170; during American Civil War 44; during American Revolution 35, 46; backward 57; in Bolivia 172–3; in Brazil 176; in China, early 32; in England 29–30, 41–2; forward rate 57–8; in France 40–1; in Germany 69, 220; Hammurabi Code and 14; hikes in 11, 199, 220; in Hungary 217; hyperinflation and 3, 8; in Japan 232; in Latin America 179; monetary policy and 5–6; in Nationalist China 133–4, 149–51, 153, 159–61; negative real 58; 1920s hyperinflation and 57–8, *58*; nominal 57;

in Poland 84–5; in post-reform China 226; real 11, 57–8, *58*; in Russia/USSR 77, 212; in Zimbabwe 235, 238
international assistance *see* foreign aid; *specific type*
International Bank for Reconstruction and Development 89, 169, 173–4, 188, 212, 215, 235
International Monetary Fund (IMF): Argentina and 177–8; Bolivia and 173–4; Bretton-Woods System and 169–70, 250; Bulgaria and 222–3; Commonwealth of Independent States and 207; function of 87, 89; globalization and 231–2; Italy and 107; Kazakhstan and 211; multilateralism and 89; North Korea and 244; postwar survey by 168; Yugoslavia and 214; Zaïre and 190–1; Zimbabwe and 235
inti 189
Israel 168, 182–5, *182*, *183*
Italy: central bank in 103; consumer price index in 103–4, *104*, *105*; currency devaluation in 107; Ethiopian War and 102–3; exchange rates in 106–7; Fascism in 91; International Monetary Fund and 107; League of Nations and 102; liberalization in 106; Marshall Plan and 107; 1940s hyperinflation 102–7, *104*, *105*; price levels in 103–4, *104*, *105*; real money balance in 104, *105*; Second World War and 99; seigniorage in 104; stabilization programs in 106–7; Treaty of Versailles and 102; wholesale price index in 103, *104*, *105*

Japan: budget deficit in 114; central bank in 232; consumer price index in 118, *119*; *de facto* bimetallic system of gold and silver in 114; Dodge Line and 116–17; gold standard in 113–14; hyperinflation in, escape from 232–3; interest rates in 232; military spending in 114; monetary system in 113–14; money-holding behavior in 114 15, *115*; New Currency Act in 114; 1940s hyperinflation in 113–17, *113*, *115*; price levels in 114, *115*, 117; Second World War and 114; stabilization programs in 116–17; surrender of, after World War II 118–19; U.S. occupation of 116
Japan Reconstruction Finance Bank 116
Jiao-chao 25
Jiao-zi (Chiao-tzu) 23
Jurchen regime 24–5

Kazakhstan 210–11
Keynes, John Maynard 63–7
Khubilai Khan 25–6
Korean War 119
Kornai, János 198
koruna 85
Krugman, Paul 89–90
Kuomintang 149–50
kwanza 191–2
kwanza reajustado 192
Kyrgyz Republic 212–3

Land Reform 157, 161–2, 234–5
Land Tax (Nationalist China) 138
Latin America: development strategies in 178–9, 189; distinction between other country economies and 193; dollarization in 193; foreign borrowing and 179–80; interest rates in 179; 1980s and 1990s hyperinflation in 171, 254; shadow economy in 193; *see also specific country*
Latin Monetary Union 102
Latvia 200, 210; *see also* Baltic Three
Law, John 37–8, 44
League of Nations 79–80, 83, 86–9, 102
Lenin, Vladimir 64–7, 75–7, 200, 202
lev 222
liberalization: in Chile 187; in Czechoslovakia 217, 220; in Italy 106; in Poland 222; in post-war China 226; price 123, 224, 227; in Russia/USSR 75, 209–10, 224, 227; as structural reform 11; in Vietnam 227; in Yugoslavia 214
Liberty Loan 133
Lincoln, Abraham 42–3
lira (Italian) 102, 106–7
lira (Turkish) 185
Lithuania 200, 210; *see also* Baltic Three
livres (notes) 38–9
Locke, John 37
London Schedule 68–9
Long-term Capital Management (LTCM) 211
Louis XIV 37
Louis XVI 38–9
Lydia kingdom 15

MacArthur, Douglas 116–17
Maduro, Nicolás 243
mandats 39–40
marka 84
Marshall, Alfred 1
Marshall, George 147

Marshall Plan 107, 124–5
Marxism 66, 73
Marx, Karl 32, 73
Mary I 29
Massachusetts Bay Colony 34
Mesopotamia 14–15
Mexican financial crisis (1994) 182, 232
Mexico 52, 182, 232
Milošević, Slobodan 214
mina 14
Ming Dynasty 30–1
Mises, Ludwig von 87–8, 110
Mississippi Bubble 41
Mississippi Company 37–8
Mobutu Sésé Seko 190–1
Moldova 210
monetary policy: American Civil War and
    33, 42–7; American Revolution and 33–6;
    in ancient world 13–6; Big Bangs 17–18;
    in China, early 16–19, 22–7, 30–3;
    expansionary 5; interest rates and 5–6;
    in Japan 113–14; reforms 18; in Russia/
    USSR 65–6, 204–5; *see also* historical
    perspective of monetary policy; *specific
    country*
money: in ancient world 13–16; bad 9;
    barter versus 16; biblical references to 14;
    creating 7; good 9, 29; government control
    of 6; imaginary value of 37; legal tender
    and 4; price inflation and 6; quantity
    theory of 6; real balance 6, 46; seigniorage
    and 6, 10; sound 4; as store of value 4;
    supply 44, 55–6, *55*, 225; *see also specific
    currency*
Mongol Empire 25–6, 32
Mongolia 227
Morgenthau, Hans 135
Mugabe, Robert 234, 238
Muhammad ibn-Batuta 26
Mussolini, Benito 102–3

Napoleonic wars, financing 40–2
National Bank of Austria 124
Nationalist China: Banking Control Bureau
    in 149; banking industry in 136–40, *139*,
    148–52, 160; barter in 156; Big Bang in
    152–3; Board of Joint Administration
    of Government Banks and 150; bond
    financing in 132–5, 147, 154; budget
    deficit financing in 132–5, *135*; Central
    Bank in 133, 148–50, 154, 156; checks
    in 150; Communist triumph in 156–7;
    cooling down of inflation in, temporary
143–6; cost of living index and 136, 143;
    credit controls in 159; currency issues
    in 136–40, *137*, *139*; currency reform in
    152–5, 158, 255; currency reunification
    in 144–5; currency war in 130–1;
    dollar-backed securities in 134; early
    1940s inflation in 129–42; exchange rates
    in 145–6; fiscal expenditures in 138,
    139; foreign aid and 134–5, 147–8,
    152–3; Foreign Exchange Stabilization
    Fund Committee in 149; Friedman's
    view on 162–3; Gold Yuan program
    in 152–5; hoarding behavior in 142,
    149–50; hyperinflation periods in
    96; hyperinflation records in 255–6;
    impacts of hyperinflation in, economic
    and political 155–7; indexation in 155–6,
    159–60; in-kind saving deposit program
    in 160; interest rates in 133–4, 149–51,
    153, 159–61; Land Reform in 157;
    Land Tax in 138; late 1940s inflation in
    142–57; Liberty Loan and 133; monetary
    warfare in 130–1; money supply in *139*,
    140, 151–2, *151*; multiple currency areas
    in 129–32, **131**; pegging policy in 131,
    149; People's Bank of China in 157–60;
    postwar overview 129; price ceilings in
    158–9; price controls in 140–2, 148–9;
    price levels in 148; printing money in
    138; ration schemes in 158–9; real money
    balance in 151–2, *151*; rent controls
    in 140; savings accounts in 150–1;
    seigniorage in, declining 136–40; Silver
    Yuan program in 154–5; Sino-British
    Stabilization Fund 134; speculation in
    149–50; stabilization programs 144,
    146–9, 157–60; state ownership/control in
    145; United States and 147–8; voluntary
    labor in 157; wholesale price index in 137,
    137, 143, *146*, 158; *see also* China, early;
    post-reform China
National Socialism 89–91
Navigation Acts (1650s) 33
Neo-Sumerian Empire 14
Nero 20
New Currency Act (1871) 114
New Economic Policy (NEP) 74–8
New Taiwan Dollar (NT$) 161
Nicaragua 187–8, *187*
1920s hyperinflation: alarm bells 63–7;
    Austria 52, **52**, 53, *53*, 55–6, *55*, *56*, 63,
    63, 78–81, *80*, 196; banking industry
    and 51, 60–3; consumer price index and

63, **63**; Czechoslovakia 85–6; deposits and 55–6, *55*; exchange rates 56–7, *56*; facts of, basic 53–60, *53, 54, 55, 56, 58, 59, 63*; Germany 52, **52**, 53, *53*, 54–6, *55, 56*, 59–60, *59*, 63, **63**, 68–72, 89–91; gold standard and 60–3; Hungary 52, **52**, 55–6, *55, 56*, 78, 81–3, *82*, 88, 196; interest rates 57–8, *58*; League of Nations and 86–9; Lenin *vs*. Keynes and 63–7; multilateralism and 86–9; overview 51–2, **52**; periods of 68–72, 253–4; Poland 52, **52**, 56, *56*, 78, 83–5, *84*; political economy of 78–86; price levels and 53, *53*; real money balance and 53–5, *54*; Russia/USSR 52, **52**, 66, 72–8, *74*; Treaty of Versailles and 67–9, *68*; wages and 59–60, *59*

1940s hyperinflation: Austria 124–5; Germany's escape from 119–24; Greece 96–102, *98, 100, 101*; Hungary 96, 107–13, *108, 112*; Italy 102–7, *104, 105*; Japan 113–17, *113, 115*; overview 96–7; Philippines 117–19, *119*; South Korea 117–19, *119*

1980s and 1990s hyperinflation: Albania 222–3; Angola 189–93, *190*, 191–3; Argentina 168, *176*, 177–82; Bolivia 168, 171–4, *172*; Brazil 168, 174–82, *176*; Bulgaria 222–3; Chile 186–7, *187*; Eastern European countries 196–7, 218–23, *219*; factors contributing to 168; Hungary 220–1; Israel 168, 182–5, *182, 183*; Latin America 171, 254; Nicaragua 187–8, *187*; overview 196–7; Peru *187*, 188–9; Poland 221–2; post-reform China 223–8, *224*; Romania 222; Russia/USSR 196, 200, **201**, 202–13, **202**; Turkey 168, 182–3, *182, 183*, 185–6; Vietnam 223–8, *224*; Yugoslavia 196, 213–8, **215**; Zaïre 189–91, *190*

Nixon Administration 170
nomenklatura 210
Northern Sung regime 23
North Korea (DPRK) 244–7, *247*, 249, 255
novo kwanza 191–2
nuevo sol 189

October Revolution 63, 72–3, 78
Oil Shock 170, 184
Olivera-Tanzi effect 10
OMIR (Old Mutual Implied Rate) 237
ostmark 219

Papiermark 72
par value system 85, 102, 107, 169–70, 180–1

Pavlov Reform 204–5
Payne, Thomas 35
pengö 107, 109–12
Perestroika 203
Perón, Juan 167
Persia 26–7
Peru *187*, 188–9
peso 181–2, 187, 232
Philippines 117–18
Plan Primavera 178
Poland: central bank in 222; consumer price index in 221; currency depreciation in 56; currency devaluation in 83–5, *84*, 222; currency reform in 84; détente and 199; exchange rates in 56, *56*; interest rates in 84–5; liberalization in 222; 1920s hyperinflation in 52, **52**, 53, *53*, 56, *56*, 83–5, *84*; 1980s and 1990s hyperinflation in 221–2; price levels in 83, *84*; privatization in 222; stabilization programs in 221–2; state ownership/ control in 61
Polo, Marco 26
Portugal 60
post-reform China: banking industries in 225–6; budget deficits in 225–6; consumer price index in 223–4, *224*; dual-track pricing in 224; economic relations with outliers and 248–50; financial aid to other countries and 248–50; financial system and, international 248–50; gradualist model and 227; income in, average 225; interest rates in 226; liberalization in 226; money supply in 225; 1980s and 1990s hyperinflation in 223–8, *224*, 255; North Korea and 249; price controls in 224; privatization in 226; stabilization programs in 226–7; state-owned enterprises in 61, 226; Venezuela and 249–50; Zimbabwe and 249; *see also* China, early; Nationalist China
Potsdam Agreement 121
Preferential Interest Rate Deposit (PIR) 161
price: ceilings 158–9; controls 11–12, 35, 47, 140–2, 148–9; domestic 56–7, *56*; dual-track pricing 224–5; fixed 15; freeze 237–8; inflation 6, 14–15, 27; information, collecting 3–4; liberalization 123, 224; oil, crude 170, 184; real 181; transparency 9
price levels: in Austria 80, *80*; in Greece 97, *98*, 101, *101*; in Hungary 81–2, *82*; hyperinflation and 1–2, 8; in Italy 104, *105*; in Japan 114, *115*, 117; jumps in 8; in Nationalist China 148; 1920s hyperinflation and 53, *53*; in North Korea

246, *247*; in Poland 83, *84*; in Russia/ USSR 73–4, *74*; *see also* consumer price index (CPI); wholesale price index
privatization: in Argentina 181; in Bolivia 173; in Chile 187; in Czechoslovakia 220; in Poland 222; in Russia/USSR 75–6, 209–10; as structural reform 11; in Taiwan 161–2
producer price index (PPI) 2, 118, *119*

QE (Quantitative Easing) 232
Qing (Ching) Dynasty 31–3

Reagan Administration 188
Reagan, Ronald 196
real money balance: in Confederacy 46; defining 6, 46; in Italy 104, *105*; in Nationalist China 151–2, *151*; 1920s hyperinflation and 53–5, *54*
Real Plan 180
Real Time Gross Settlement (RTGS) 237
Reconstruction Finance Bank 116
Reichsbank 57–8, *58*, 70, 72
reichsmark 56, 90, 122–4
renminbi (RMB) 158, 160, 245
Rentenbank 72
Reparation Commission 81, 87
repressed inflation 197–200
Reserve Bank of Zimbabwe (RBZ) 235–6, 238–9
retail price index (RPI) 3, 41
retenmark 72
Robbins, Lionel 89
Roman Empire 19–22
Romania 222
Roosevelt, Franklin Delano 162
Rostowski, Jacek 196
roubles, paper 76
Royal Bank (formerly Banque Générale) 37
ruble notes 204–5, 207
ruble zone 205–8
Russian Revolution 63, 72–3, 78
Russia/USSR: alcohol and alcoholism in 203–4; banking industry in 77–8; barter in 212; Bolsheviks in 66, 73–5, 78; budget deficit in 209–10; central bank in 208–9; consumer price index in 200, **201**, **202**, 212; currency reform in 76–7, 206, **206**; debasement in 61; demise of Soviet Union and 200, 207; economic problems of 203–5; effects of hyperinflation on, long-standing 211–13; famine of 1921 in 75; foreign aid and 209; foreign debt in 204, 211, 232; free rider problem in 207; Gosbank in 77, 203, 208; Gosplan in 203;

inflation in 1922 and 75; interest rates in 77, 212; liberalization in 75, 209–10, 224, 227; monetary policy of 65–6, 204–5; New Economic Policy in 74–8; 1920s hyperinflation in 52, **52**, 53, *53*, 66, 72–8, *74*; 1980s and 1990s hyperinflation in 196, 200, **201**, 202–13, **202**, 254–5; October Revolution in 63, 72–3, 78; oil industry in 199–200; Pavlov Reform in 204–5; Perestroika in 203; price levels in 73–4, *74*; privatization in 75–6, 209–10; rapid industrialization and 77–8; ruble zone and 205–8; scissors effect in economy of 76; shadow economy in 204, 212; shock therapy and 208, 210, 227; social networks and 211–13; stabilization programs in 208–11; state-owned enterprises in 76, 197–8, 209–10; taxation in 208–9; Treaty of Brest-Litovsk and 73; Treaty of Rapallo and 73; Truman Doctrine and 101; Yeltsin Economic Program in 208

Sachs, Jeffrey 173
Sandista regime 187–8
Sargent, Thomas 85, 162
Schilling 81
Schumpeter, Joseph A. 37, 66, 81
Second Congo War 191, 234
second economy 204, 212
Second Oil Shock (1980) 184
Second World War 96–8, 109, 114, 119, 129, 254
seigniorage: curve of 10; defining 6; government revenue and 6; in Italy 104; money and 6, 10; in Nationalist China, declining 136–40; in Zimbabwe 239
Serbia 215–6
shadow economy 193, 204, 212
shekels 14
Shirer, William L. 90
"shock therapy" 208, 210, 227
Silver Houses 31
silver purchase program 162
Silver Yuan program 154–5
Sino-British Stabilization Fund 134
Slovak Republic 220
Southern Sung regime 23–4
South Korea 118–9, *119*, 232
South Sea Bubble 41
South Seas Development Bank (SSDB) 117
Soviet Union *see* Russia/USSR
sovznak 76
stabilization programs: in Albania 223; in Angola 192–3; in Argentina 177–8, 181–2;

in Austria 87–8; in Baltic Three 203, 210–1; in Bolivia 173–4; in Brazil 176–7, 180–1; Bretton-Woods institutions and 250; in Chile 186–7; common elements of 11–12; currency board and 239; currency reform and 11; in Czechoslovakia 220; dollarization in 239; free banking and 239; in Germany 72, 90; in Greece 100–2; heterodox approach 12; in Hungary 111–12; in Israel 184–5; in Italy 106–7; in Japan 116–17; macroeconomic 210; in Nationalist China 144, 146–9, 157–60; in Nicaragua 188; orthodox approach 12; in Peru 189; in Poland 221–2; in post-reform China 226–7; post-reform China in initiation other countries' 250; in Russia/USSR 208–11; in Taiwan 160–2; in Turkey 184–5; variety of 11–2; in Venezuela 242–4; in Yugoslavia 214; in Zaíre 191; in Zimbabwe 239–40; *see also specific country*
state ownership/control: in Argentina 181–2; in Austria 87; in Hungary 110, 220; hyperinflation and 245; Marxism and 66, 73; in Nationalist China 145; in Poland 61; in post-reform China 226; in Russia/USSR 76, 197–8, 209–10; in Vietnam 226
Stuart, John Leighton 153
Sung regime 23–4, 255

Taiping Rebellion 31
Taiwan 96, 142, 160–2
Tajikistan 210
Tang Dynasty 22
taxation: American Civil War and 45; American Revolution and 36; in Roman Empire 20; in Russia/USSR 208–9
Thailand 232
Thiers' Law 9–10
Thiers, Louis Adolphe 9
Tito, Josip 213
Trajan 21
transition economies and hyperinflation: Eastern European countries 196–7, 218–23, *219*; overview 196–7; planned economies and 197–200; post-reform China 223–8, *224*; Russia/USSR 200, **201**, 202–13, **202**; Vietnam 223–8, *224*; Yugoslavia 213–18, **215**
Treaty of Brest-Litovsk 73
Treaty of Rapallo 73
Treaty of Saint-Germain 79, 81

Treaty of Trianon 81
Treaty of Versailles: Danzig and 52; Italy and 102; Keynes and 63–4; League of Nations and 86; 1920s hyperinflation and 67–9, *68*
Trotsky, Leon 66
Truman Doctrine 101, 116
Truman, Harry S. 116
Turkey 168, 182–3, *182*, *183*, 185–6
Turkmenistan 200, 207, 210

Ukraine 200, 210
Union of Socialist Soviet Republics (USSR) *see* Russia/USSR
United Nations Relief and Rehabilitation Administration (UNRRA) 105, 109, 121, 148
United States: American-British War and 43; American Civil War and 33, 42–7; American Revolution and 33–6; Federal Reserve 199, 211; Federal Reserve in 232; financial crisis (2008) in 232–3; financial markets in 42–7; financial system in early nineteenth century 43; foreign aid to Israel and 185; France's foreign aid and 35–6; hyperinflation in, escape from 232–3; international finance and, influence on 170–1; Japanese occupation by 116; Nationalist China and 147–8; silver purchase program in 162
Ur Dynasty 14
U.S. dollar 60, 169–70, 216, 226, 237, 243
U.S. Economic Cooperation Administration in China (ECA) 152
Uzbekistan 210

valorization accounts 111
Velvet Revolution/Divorce 220
Venezuela 240–4, *240*, 249–50, 254
Vietnam: consumer price index in *224*; dual-track pricing in 224–5; exchange rates in 224–5, 227; 1980s and 1990s hyperinflation in 223–8, *224*; state-owned enterprises in 226

wages: in Greece 99, *100*; 1920s hyperinflation and 59–60, *59*; real 59–60, 99, *100*
Walre De Dordes, J. van 79–80
Wang Mang 16–19, 255
Washington Consensus 181
Washington, George 34–5
Wedemeyer, Albert C. 148

White, Harry D. 132

wholesale price index (WPI): defining 3; in England 41; in Germany 67, *68*; in Italy 103, *104*, *105*; in Kazakhstan 211; in Nationalist China 137, *137*, 143, *146*; in South Korea 118, *119*

Wilson, Woodrow 86

Witte, Sergei 61

World Bank 89, 169, 173–4, 188, 212, 215, 235

World Development Indicators 174–5

World Development Report 174–5

World Trade Organization 226–7

World War I 62–3, 67, 78, 96, 254

World War II 96–8, 109, 114, 119, 129, 254

Yeltsin, Boris 199, 209

Yeltsin Economic Program 208

Yom Kippur War 170, 184

Young, Arthur N. 129, 162–3

Yuan Dynasty 25–6, 32

Yugoslavia: central banks in 216, 218; consumer price index in 213, 215–17, **215**; détente and 199; dollarization in 216; exchange rates in 214, 217; foreign debt in 214; hyperinflation records in 255; independence of republics in 214–15; International Monetary Fund and 214; liberalization in 214; market socialism in 213; money growth in 199; 1980s and 1990s hyperinflation in 196, 213–18, **215**; shortages in 218; stabilization programs in 214; state-owned enterprises in 197; workers' self-management in 213–14

Yung Lo 30

zaïre 191

Zaïre (Congo) 189–91, *190*

Zimbabwe 196, 233–40, *236*, 249, 254

Zimbabwean dollar 237–8

Zimbabwe Stock Exchange 237

zloty 84, 221

Printed in the United States
by Baker & Taylor Publisher Services